Also in the series

BROKE
NOT BROKEN

HOMER MAXEY'S
TEXAS BANK WAR

BROKE NOT BROKEN

HOMER MAXEY'S TEXAS BANK WAR

By Broadus A. Spivey and Jesse Sublett

Foreword by Gordon Morris Bakken

Sketches by Glenna Goodacre

Texas Tech University Press

This book is typeset in Perrywood. The paper used in this book meets the minimum
requirements of ANSI/NISO Z39.48-1992 (R1997). ∞

Designed by Kasey McBeath
Cover designed by Kasey McBeath
Cover photographs courtesy of the Southwest Collections/Special Collections
Library at Texas Tech University.

Library of Congress Cataloging-in-Publication Data
Spivey, Broadus A., author.
    Broke, not broken : Homer Maxey's Texas bank war / by Broadus A. Spivey and
Jesse Sublett ; foreword by Gordon Morris Bakken ; sketches by Glenna Goodacre.
        pages cm — (American liberty and justice)
    Includes bibliographical references and index.
    ISBN 978-0-89672-855-4 (hardback) — ISBN 978-0-89672-856-1 (e-book)
1. Maxey, Homer, 1911-1980—Trials, litigation, etc. 2. Citizens National Bank of
Lubbock--Trials, litigation, etc. 3. Judicial sales—Texas—Lubbock—History—20th
century. 4. Corruption—Texas—Lubbock—History—20th century. I. Sublett, Jesse,
author. II. Goodacre, G. (Glenna), illustrator. III. Title.
    KF228.M316S67 2014
    346.76404'363—dc23   2013050899

14 15 16 17 18 19 20 21 22 / 9 8 7 6 5 4 3 2 1

Texas Tech University Press
Box 41037 | Lubbock, Texas 79409-1037 USA
800.832.4042 | ttup@ttu.edu | www.ttupress.org

The authors wish to extend special acknowledgment to Carla Maxey Elliott (9/13/35–4/06/13), whose contributions and support for this book about her father were essential to producing an important, accurate, and readable account of her father's life.

The law doth punish man or woman
Who steals the goose from off the common,
But lets the greater felon loose
Who steals the common from the goose.

Anonymous eighteenth-century rhyme

CONTENTS

Contents

ILLUSTRATIONS

COMMENTARY

OF SKETCHES

As the book was in the final stages of production, Glenna Good-acre found a sketchbook that she used during the first week of the first jury trial in the Maxey case. In the limited time available to them, the authors were able to identify all of the principle figures she drew, with the exception of the jurors. Some of the figures were easy to identify, and the more difficult identifications were made after consultation with Glenna and some basic detective work. The easy ones were Homer Maxey (page iv), Charlie Jones (page 111), George N. Atkinson (pages 221), and Judge Pat Moore. Glenna says the windmill on page 19 was drawn from memory and does not represent any specific location. Identification of attorney Barney Evans, who represented Citizens National Bank of Lubbock, was made much easier after the authors found a photo of Evans in the Southwest Collection archives online. The attorneys in the full courtroom picture (page 196), were identified after comparison with other individual drawings in the sketchbook. Glenna, along with her sister, Carla Elliott, and her mother, sat in the same place every day of the trial, therefore, her visual perspective of the attorneys seated at their respective tables: plaintiffs were on the left, defense on the right. The sketchbook is dated November 3, 1969. During that time, Homer Maxey was in the witness box as he is depicted in the courtroom scene.

FOREWORD

As books and articles about banking and litigation go, this work is unique and a tribute to the tenacity of Homer Maxey and the Texas judicial system. Justice was served and the limits of law exposed in the appellate process. Yet this was unlike so many other episodes in American history.

Popular movements against debt collection via the judicial system were part of our early national experience. Daniel Shays was the catalyst for a rebellion in 1786 that shut down the Massachusetts court system to prevent the collection of debt both private and public. The rebellion was against debt collection for taxes and private encumbrances such as mortgages and promissory notes. Debtors had inadequate specie to pay taxes and debt. Money supply problems were endemic and government wanted payment in hard money, not worthless paper money. Shays's Rebellion was put down by force.[1]

Debt in American society also was endemic, with every entrepreneur borrowing money to create wealth whether agricultural or mercantile. Bruce Mann's *Republic of Debtors: Bankruptcy in the Age of American Independence* (2009) opens this window to people in debtors' prison, from the wealthiest man in America to a justice of the United States Supreme Court. Without a bankruptcy statute, creditors put people in jail to encourage payment. A stable banking system contributed to a stable currency; Alexander Hamilton, with the US Constitution's authority and President George Washington's blessing, helped create the Bank of the United States. The bank issued "a new paper currency" based on gold, silver, and government bonds on deposit that "would vastly increase the country's supply of money and therefore stimulate its economy."[2] Hamilton was right.

The Second Bank of the United States under Nicholas Biddle strengthened the value of the dollar and "applied strict and consistent standards before accepting local bank note issuance," thereby increasing greatly "interior liquidity." The result was that foreign merchants and creditors "stopped demanding payment in coin."[3] Of equal importance, Biddle "turned his collection procedures to the state of the economy." Biddle "let his notes remain uncollected until conditions eased—effectively expanding the money supply." In speculative times, Biddle reduced "his discounting activity and speed[ed] up on collections."[4] The American economy grew accordingly until President Andrew Jackson vetoed the recharter of the Second Bank of the United States and plunged the nation into a depression with "pet" banks, currency inflation, and the specie circular.[5] The specie circular—requiring specie for public land sales—pushed the flow of gold and silver to Washington, and debtors were without the ability to pay local debt in hard money.

The Republican Party under President Abraham Lincoln returned the country to central banking. Congress passed a bankruptcy act in 1898, and mortgage debt became subject to judicial process or bankruptcy or both. The American West created "a more efficient capital market, although exploitation was still evident in the commission charges of brokers."[6] Mortgages were short-term contracts for three to five years. In California debt secured by real estate did not reach the term of ten years until the 1880s, and creditors secured payment by judicial process.[7] This relationship between debt and judicial foreclosure survived recessions and depressions until the 1930s.

Minnesota responded to the Great Depression with a mortgage-moratorium law, and the United States Supreme Court upheld the act in *Home Building and Loan Association v. Blaisdell*, 290 US 398 (1934). It was "the first Supreme Court decision to uphold a law designed to combat the economic crisis—"recovery legislation" in the language of the day."[8] The high court set a new standard for legislation aimed at averting an economic disaster. Yet in 2008 with the banking crisis and the foreclosure epidemic in the housing sector, "the federal government dipped into mortgage-relief policy, as well, but its programs have been largely ineffectual or only modestly successful."[9] The Great Recession lingers and banking practices again are clearly at fault.

Homer Maxey's Texas bank war was of a different kind. Wrongful foreclosure and the litigation hold-up game stretched his resources but not his tenacious desire for economic justice. This is a story of civil litigation and personal will. It is an outstanding read and a thought-provoking history of the banking industry. Enjoy!

Gordon Morris Bakken
California State University, Fullerton

Notes from
the Authors

ne evening in 1970, my last year in Lubbock before moving my law practice to Austin, I was having dinner at a place called the Depot when Charlie Jones came in and sat down at my table. In addition to being a longtime friend of mine, Charlie was a trial lawyer of legendary reputation and a frequent courtroom adversary.

I couldn't remember ever seeing him looking so depressed. You could hear the resignation in his voice when he ordered his usual drink, vodka straight up.

"Well, I guess I'm finished as a lawyer," he said.

"Why would you say that, Charlie?" I asked.

"The verdict came in on the Maxey case today," he explained. "They awarded Maxey $2.7 million."

He was referring to the multimillion-dollar lawsuit by Lubbock businessman Homer G. Maxey, filed against Citizens National Bank of Lubbock. Charlie had served as cocounsel for the defense. The $2.7 million judgment was the largest in the history of Lubbock County and almost all of West Texas, a record that stood for many years.

About a month later I saw Charlie again, and this time he looked as bright as sunshine, his usual big grin intact again. "How's it going, Charlie?" I said.

"You know, Broadus, I thought I was at the end of my career," he said. "The Maxey verdict hit me like a freight train. But three days later I got a call from a fellow with the TADC (Texas Association of Defense Lawyers). He asked me to go on their speech circuit and lecture other defense lawyers on how to try big cases. Even if you're going to *lose* big."

The Maxey case made a big impression on me. The allegations at issue in the lawsuit had occurred in the early 1960s, when I was living in Lubbock, during my term as assistant county attorney, and later, after I moved into private practice. There were two jury trials and nine appeals. The first trial was the longest ever held in Lubbock County; the final settlement was not until 1980, almost 15 years later. By then Maxey was an old man in declining health, but he never gave up. The legal and ethical issues were complex and fascinating, almost as complex and fascinating as Homer Maxey.

Decades later, in 2002, I was in Russia with a group of lawyers. My wife Ruth Ann and I were sharing a table with Glenna Goodacre, the daughter of Homer Maxey, and C. L. Mike Schmidt, her husband. It was a very eventful trip and a wonderful evening of fine food and drink. At one point, our conversation turned to her father. Aware that he was not only beloved as a father but had been a huge influence on Glenna's own career, I ended up urging her to write a book about him.

"Your father's commitment and his perseverance were legendary," I said. "His struggle to obtain justice and regain his good name, and all the other stories entwined in those cases, that's the stuff they write novels about, but this really happened."

"Broadus, you knew Daddy," Glenna said. "You write as part of your law practice. Why don't you write the book?"

"OK," I said, "I'll do it." My answer was an impulsive but informed one, although it's possible that my confidence was overly influenced by a few too many drinks.

Procrastination of personal goals is a fellow traveler in my life. It's true that writing is a very important part of practicing law. But it's also true that a legal career is a full-time occupation and then some. I also realized, belatedly, that competence in drafting pleadings and briefs does not necessarily translate to a project of this scope.

Several years passed, during which I managed to accomplish some basic research. In one major coup, I succeeded in rescuing the transcript of the first trial just before it was scheduled to be destroyed. I also recorded three interviews with some of the principal figures in the case, along with my own personal memories. But all of that was a long way from a book.

In a friendly sort of way, Glenna taunted me about my lack of progress. "Broadus," she said, "Will I ever live long enough to read this book?"

Her question stung, but it also prompted me to take positive action. While sharing an elevator ride with Craig Barker, an entertainment lawyer par excellence who happens to have his office in our building, I related my problem and asked his advice. A few days later Craig introduced me to his friend and client, Jesse Sublett.

With no further delay I checked Jesse out. He had written several books and was an artist of some standing, both as a musician and an author of crime novels and nonfiction. I was very impressed by his memoir, *Never the Same Again: A Rock n' Roll Gothic*. The book breathlessly weaves adventures with his band, the Skunks, with his battle with throat cancer and the murder of his girlfriend by a serial killer in 1976.

Among other accomplishments, Jesse has been published in the *New York Times*, the *Texas Observer, Texas Monthly*, and the *Austin Chronicle*. He's written for the History Channel, and he wrote the screen adaptation for a play called *In the West*, which was released as a feature film titled *Deep in the Heart*.

After meeting for lunch at Hoover's Home Cooking (a popular soul-food cafe in East Austin), I immediately formed a strong favorable opinion of Jesse. We made a deal, and I'm still so happy that I had the good judgment to ask this man with a gifted pen to do the hard work of completing the research. He talked to almost everyone still living who had any relationship to this case, including the trials and the many appeals of Homer G. Maxey. He also went through piles of papers and scoured microfilm records for just the right bit of information. Then, with his gifted hand, he worked with me to preserve for posterity the memory and history of these extraordinary events and this special individual.

Broadus Spivey, Austin, Texas, May 31, 2013

roadus Spivey's law offices are located in a three-story building on East Avenue in Austin, a hip pocket neighborhood shaded by pecan trees near the north shore of the Colorado River. The street was laid out on a survey map by Edwin Waller in 1839, not long after Mirabeau Lamar, then vice president of the Republic of Texas, fell in love with the area after killing a buffalo on a hill near present-day Eighth and Brazos streets. In the years immediately following the Civil War, the former Confederate state of Texas began flexing some economic muscle by sending herds of braying longhorn cattle north to the railheads in Kansas, and a good many of them traversed Central Texas by heading up a portion of the dusty Chisholm Trail along East Avenue.

Thanks to Henry Ford and the internal combustion engine, the tree-shaded thoroughfare eventually became one of the primary north-south conveyors of millions of honking, ozone-layer-destroying cars and trucks between Mexico and Canada. The next transition for East Avenue came during the 1950s and 60s, as the East Avenue right-of-way was coveted and concreted up by the interstate highway program. Today, the vestigial portion in front of Broadus Spivey's law offices is all that remains of historic East Avenue.

But enough about streets. The point is, once you realize Broadus's passion for history and literature, it seems perfectly fitting to find him on this slightly obscure, historically significant site. Our introduction was a byproduct of a legal matter, a case of copyright infringement, handled brilliantly by attorney Craig Barker. On my second meeting with Craig, he told me "the attorney upstairs would like to meet you."

The attorney's name was Broadus Spivey. Broadus is what I call "a big-time lawyer," not just because he's won so many big cases, because he's been president of the State Bar of Texas and the International Academy of Trial Lawyers, or because so many different professional organizations and honorary societies have given him awards that there's not enough space here to list them all (one of them is called the

Broadus A. Spivey Lifetime Achievement Award). Broadus is greatly admired by not only his peers, and also by just about everyone who knows him.

Broadus will go to bat for a billionaire or a pauper, as long as he believes in their cause. During the time I've worked with him on this book and met so many of his fellow attorneys, I developed a much deeper understanding of their passion for the legal profession. The US Constitution tells us that we're all equal. Lawyers relish the challenge of standing beside you in a courtroom to fight for your rights, and to remind the bad guys that the concept of equality isn't just wishful thinking. They *really, really* like their work.

Broadus has won multimillion-dollar judgments for his clients. Those aren't the ones he talks about most, however. He likes to tell the story of the elderly couple duped by an insurance company. When the husband died, the widow learned that their life insurance policy only covered them against death from childbirth or mad dog bites.

I was immediately won over by Broadus's passion for the Homer Maxey story. Maxey originally sought over $20 million in damages from Citizens National Bank of Lubbock, naming as codefendants his own former attorneys, most of the directors of the bank, the bank president, and several of its vice presidents. The list of codefendants included more than two dozen citizens of Lubbock, many of them being among the town's richest and most influential. Inevitably, Lubbockites had close ties to individuals on both sides of the case. Small wonder it was the talk of the town.

Broadus Spivey, who had a private law practice in Lubbock at the time, greatly admired Homer Maxey and believed him to be a man of integrity. Broadus also had great respect for his friend and colleague, Charlie Jones, cocounsel for the defense. He was deeply shocked by Maxey's allegations of unethical conduct by Jones.

Being a man of intelligence and experience, not to mention all the strange human behavior to which Broadus has been exposed during his legal career, he realized early on during the writing of this book that certain truths would be exposed that were unflattering to people on both sides of this case. This wasn't supposed to be a book that nominated either Homer Maxey or Charlie Jones for sainthood. Broadus wanted the truth, the whole truth. We have done our best to find it and deliver it to the reader.

In the cold light of day, certain allegations in Maxey's petition pertained to actions which, if not strictly illegal, certainly had the appearance of impropriety. One might conclude that, if these allegations were true, then there is a strong possibility that at least some of the darker deeds attributed to the defendants were also probably true. Those allegations, which were harder to prove, required detailed testimony about incredibly complex financial transactions, loan records, and exchanges of property that took place over five to six years. During that time, Homer Maxey often bought and sold property more often than the average Joe takes out the trash.

And yet, in two different trials, twelve of Maxey's peers patiently listened to several weeks' worth of this testimony; in the end, they concluded that he had been wronged by the defendants. As Broadus explained one day over lunch at Hoover's (where, being a wise and seasoned lawyer, he almost always gets the chicken-fried steak), "That tells me a lot, because juries are a pretty good representation of the values of a community. And they believed Maxey." Researching and writing this book required a significant investment of time and effort, and we took it very seriously. We wanted the scholarship to be solid, the presentation objective. Just as in everyday life itself, many aspects of the story remain ambiguous. We learned an awful lot about this case, but not everything. Some secrets will probably go to the grave with the individuals who knew all the answers.

Inevitably, certain people may conclude that their side of the story was represented in an unfair light. We may also have made mistakes here and there, and if so, we apologize in advance. We're human, too.

Jesse Sublett, Austin, Texas, May 31, 2013

BROKE
NOT
HOMER MAXEY'S
TEXAS BANK WAR
BROKEN

Homer Maxey, probably in the early 1980s. The stress of fifteen years of legal battles with Citizens National Bank of Lubbock aged him profoundly, but he was always working on new projects and ideas, Homer was a perpetual motion machine till the end. Courtesy of the Maxey family.

INTRODUCTION

The conflict at the heart of this book is Homer Maxey's fifteen-year battle against Citizens National Bank of Lubbock (which in 1973 merged with Texas Commerce Bancshares to become Texas Commerce Bank of Lubbock). The lawsuit filed in Lubbock County 72nd District Court on July 16, 1966, alleging fraud, conspiracy, and other irregularities arising from a foreclosure action on February 16, 1966, that left him penniless. After two jury trials and nine separate appeals, including two decisions from the Texas Supreme Court, the case was settled on September 22, 1980.

In the conservative, pro-business community of Lubbock, the litigation and the circumstances that precipitated it were the subject of intense controversy. Hard feelings on both sides survive to the present day. The litigation had a powerful impact on the business and legal community in the South Plains, in part because it set new benchmarks for duration, size of monetary damages sought, and amount awarded by the juries in both trials. The case had many unusual twists, and scandalous allegations were made against many prominent local individuals. The case was followed so closely by the media, with such a large number of individuals involved, that practically the entire community became emotionally invested in its outcome.

Innuendo, ambiguity, and myth were integral parts of the case from the beginning. While endeavoring to produce a reliable and readable chronicle of the case and the events surrounding it, the authors also strive to bring clarity where it has been lacking in the past. In some instances, the authors were forced to revise their own previously held notions of the facts.

Maxey's litigation consumed fifteen years of his life. During those years, his normal business activities all but screeched to a halt. Friends and family observed that Maxey thought of little else during that time. But if the defendants made the mistake of equating Maxey's "grand obsession" (a term used by E. W. Williams, Jr., president of Citizens National Bank of Lubbock, and the leading individual defendant in the litigation) with weakness, they soon learned otherwise.

Contained within the voluminous documents, transcripts, and media coverage of the Maxey case is an extremely detailed chronicle of Maxey's life and career and, by extension, life and business in Lubbock and the South Plains. These same records also provide indelible impressions of the man's personality. The transcripts of his testimony bristle with tenacity, combativeness, and sense of pride.

Maxey's simple answers to questions about business transactions give us insight to the character and tenor of daily life during his time. There are discussions of accepted notions of propriety, "gentleman's agreements," handshake deals, and codes of ethics for businessmen as well as attorneys. There is a palpable feeling of discomfort when Maxey, as a witness, describes the circumstances in which the defendants flouted certain ethical codes in their business dealings with him. One can almost see the expressions of disapproval by members of the jury.

The Maxey case broke all previous records on the South Plains for its length and the size of damages. The first trial ended in 1970, with a judgment for Maxey that totaled $2,689,767, or $15,959,816 in 2012 dollars; the second ended in 1976 with a judgment for Maxey totaling $3,730,140.53. Prejudgment interest at six percent over ten years added an additional $2,238,080 for a total of $5,968,220, or the equivalent of $24,147,796 in 2012.[1]

The Maxey case occupies a significant role in the history of jurisprudence of the State of Texas. Several rulings in the appellate cases are still cited today in civil courts. The Appendix discloses a listing of all nine appeals, as well as a detailed summary of the most important rulings. A decision written by Texas Supreme Court Justice James G. Denton, for example, cleared the way for Maxey to obtain a second jury trial in 1976. Previously, a court of appeals ruling had upheld a summary judgment issued by a Lubbock County district judge in favor of the individual defendants in the case. The court of appeals had ruled that the bank could not be sued again by Maxey because all the individual agents of the bank that had been named in the litigation had been exonerated. The Denton decision, however, ruled that a bank (corporation) can be liable for acts and misconduct by its agents, directors, shareholders, or employees, even though those individuals may not be legally liable them-

OCTOBER 1983 $2.00

CAN MAYOR STARKE TAYLOR RUN DALLAS? BY JIM ATKINSON

TexasMonthly

MONEY AND POWER

Banks Have Got Both—But Who's Got the Banks?

Homer Maxey's precedent-setting lawsuit against Citizens National Bank of Lubbock was one of the central background stories in a lengthy investigative article on the banking industry in Texas in the October 1983 issue of *Texas Monthly*. Reprinted with permission from *Texas Monthly*.

selves. This ruling, which has been relied upon by appellate courts, trial judges, and lawyers ever since, is another of the lasting legacies of the Maxey case.

The concepts of corporate responsibility raised by the Maxey case are relevant to ongoing debates regarding the rights and responsibilities of corporations, including the concept of corporate personhood. Such discussions have been heard with more frequency since the 2010 US Supreme Court ruling in the case of *Citizens United v. Federal Election Commission,* including during the 2012 presidential campaign when Mitt Romney said, "Corporations are people, my friend."

The Maxey case was also sensational because of accusations of unethical behavior by the bank's attorneys, some of whom had at one time represented both Maxey and the bank. Allegations of impropriety were also made against one of the district judges who heard the case. Maxey and his attorneys also made a number of allegations (not all of which were part of the trial record) that, while never proven, did contribute to the atmosphere of sensationalism and scandal. There were suggestions of sabotage: one of Maxey's attorneys, J. Michael Liles, claimed that the brake lines on his car had been cut, and a key witness was nearly killed in a mysterious plane crash. Liles, who represented Maxey in the second trial, also believed he was targeted by a spy for the defense. An attractive girl claiming to be a former Maid of Cotton approached and seduced Liles, but she asked so many questions about the Maxey case Liles concluded that she could not have been motivated by mere desire.

Repercussions of the Maxey case were felt throughout the banking and business communities. Average folks worried that it gave the town a bad image; people associated with the bank and law office worried that the lawsuit would result in the eventual demise of both.[2] While the law firm representing Citizens National Bank survived, the bank did not. The Maxey case, and the role it played in forming the toxic public image of the bank, was treated at length in a feature story about the rise of bank holding companies in Texas in the October 1983 issue of *Texas Monthly* magazine.

Builder, businessman, civic leader, and courtroom brawler, Maxey exerted considerable influence on Lubbock and the region. The narrative of his life is sufficiently intriguing that a biography of the man is not only warranted, but long overdue.

The story of Homer Maxey's phenomenal success in his business activities during the boom of the postwar years, as well as his place in local politics, charitable foundations, and his church, is an integral part of the history of Lubbock and the South Plains during that era. Homer's three brothers, Robert, Carl, and Herschel, were also in the building industry. Since the context of this story also includes Homer's father, J. B. Maxey, who was a builder and civic leader in the South Plains in the early 1900s, our narrative covers the evolution of Lubbock from small West Texas outpost to one of the fastest growing communities in the United States after World War II.

Homer Maxey was born March 14, 1911, in Plainview, a town fifty miles north of rival Lubbock. His father had moved to the South Plains in 1906, when Lubbock was still a village. With his many business and community responsibilities in Plainview, J. B. Maxey was invested in the future of that town, but in early 1924, J. B. moved the family to Lubbock. Lubbock had been named as the site of Texas Tech University (originally called Texas Technological College), and the elder Maxey realized, as did most people in the region, that the college was the key to Lubbock's future economic security and vitality. It meant, among other things, that Homer Maxey came of age during the years that Lubbock was also coming into its own as the "Hub City of the Plains."[3]

In 1924, at the age of thirteen, Homer's first summer job in his adopted hometown of Lubbock was as a carpenter's helper in the employ of his father, who had contracted to build the President's Home at the new university. Therefore, in a town that derived a good deal of its identity from Texas Tech, and where a person's relationship or history with Tech also figured into their identity, not to mention their status, Homer Maxey could claim to have roots as deep as almost anyone in Lubbock. He not only helped build Texas Tech, he graduated from Tech in 1931 with a BA in business and would later donate time, money, and influence to the university in countless ways, from serving as president of the Red Raiders Club to providing employment for football players.

Maxey married his high school sweetheart, Melba Mae Tatom, in 1932. Getting his start in business during the Depression years, Maxey worked two jobs and invested in business opportunities on the side.

After the United States entered World War II, Maxey received a commission in the navy. Commanding a flotilla of amphibious craft, he participated in countless combat operations in the Pacific. After the war, Homer returned to Lubbock and became one of the driving forces in the postwar building boom. He developed shopping centers, office buildings, housing subdivisions, and apartment complexes. Maxey was one of ten directors who founded American State Bank, along with various other businesses and construction concerns.

Like many leading members of the business community, Maxey participated in charity drives, community improvement projects, and other opportunities to serve the city. He also served two terms on the city council.

"Homer Maxey was one of the top developers of the postwar years," says Delbert McDougal, a present-day Lubbock developer. "Without any question, he was a major player in the development of Lubbock, Texas, and he was simply one of the great people who caused Lubbock to be, quite honestly, what it is today."[4]

Homer Maxey's accomplishments, social status, and general reputation all contributed to a general sense of disbelief when people learned that Citizens National Bank of Lubbock had foreclosed against him, dissecting and distributing almost every one of Maxey's assets. According to Maxey's appraisals, the foreclosed assets were worth $5.5 million, an amount comparable to approximately $38.5 million in 2012 dollars.[5]

By the end of that day, Maxey was left with nothing. Even more humiliating was the fact that, as he later alleged, the bank had sold the properties for a fraction of their actual value. One of the buyers was a member of the bank's executive board. Another board member was summarily named president of one of Maxey's corporations.

People in Lubbock were shocked to hear that Maxey, a pillar of the community, was broke. A great many were scandalized when they learned details of the bank's actions. A large proportion of Lubbockites agreed with Maxey that he had been cheated.

Another vivid detail of Maxey's allegations was that his troubles with Citizens National Bank began when its president, E. W. Williams, Jr., reneged on a handshake agreement that promised him an unsecured line of credit for up to one million dollars. In a place like Lubbock in the 1960s, a man's handshake was still considered a sacred bond. Going back on a handshake deal was regarded as scandalous behavior.[6]

Within a month, Maxey filed a lawsuit against the bank, seeking a total of more than $20 million in damages.

Thus began Homer Maxey's fifteen-year battle to reclaim his fortune and his reputation. That he would continue to fight on despite what seemed to be insurmountable opposition was consistent with his personality and the place that produced him—Lubbock, Texas. Maxey's long struggle in the courts to regain his fortune and his good name is the story of one individual's dogged determination to fight for what he believed was right.

Homer's daughter, Glenna Goodacre, was a coplaintiff in the litigation and sat with her family in the courtroom every day of both trials. Her description of the ordeal tersely conveys the sense of humiliation and disappointment endured by her family and the rock-solid determination that got them through it.

I have continued to admire the growth and achievements of my hometown and I have always been very proud to be from Lubbock, with one bad exception. In 1966, all of Homer's assets were seized in a suspicious bank foreclosure. Everything. He sat in a chair and wept as the documents were read to him. They had to move out of their beautiful home that Daddy had built and Mother had furnished and decorated. A man of tremendous integrity, Homer was outraged and devastated, but he knew he had been the victim of illegal scheming and he fought back hard. Years of litigation followed and his David-and-Goliath battle with the bank is legendary in Texas legal history. It was a triple whammy for Homer because he had always believed in the banking system, the legal system, and in his fellow citizens of Lubbock. I shared his upset and helplessness, but we all know he was right, and that kept us in the fight.[7]

Glenna's words remind us that civil trials are not just about points of law; they are about real people, social issues, and the values of a community.

Citizens National Bank was one of the biggest banks in Lubbock. Officers of the bank, the board of directors, and the law firms that represented it included a who's who of the richest and most influential people in the South Plains. Despite Homer Maxey's background and reputation, he was the underdog in the fight.

The case was the talk of the town and the normally staid, close-knit community split into opposing camps. Maxey's allegations against the bank, as well as the counterallegations that were made against him, shocked many people. No plaintiff in Lubbock had ever sought such a large monetary award—$20 million—in the first trial.

Maxey's allegations against the bank were complex. They included fraud, conspiracy, and other irregularities that led to foreclosure and seizure of his assets. The case boiled down to the question of fairness. The central arguments always came back to the concept that a lending institution is legally obliged to be fair in its dealings with its clients. By focusing on complicated details of the case, the bank successfully appealed the jury verdicts, but in the end, the higher court rulings agreed that Maxey had not been treated fairly.

In the original lawsuit, Maxey had named as defendants the attorneys who

Homer Maxey and daughter Glenna Goodacre in the 1980s. Acknowledging her power-ful affinity for her father, Glenna says, "I'm an exact replica of Homer." Courtesy of the Maxey family.

had represented him and the bank during the time of the events under liti-gation. Although the judge in the first trial issued a summary judgment in favor of Maxey's attorneys (as well as the other individual defendants), the accusations of unethical behavior on the part of his attorneys, chiefly those against attorney Charlie Jones, were troubling to many Lubbockites. Especial-ly troubled were Jones's colleagues in the legal community, even those who had tried cases against him in court. Broadus Spivey was one of them. He respected Charlie Jones and considered him a personal friend.

Born and raised in the Texas Panhandle area, Broadus attended school at Goodnight, then attended and graduated from high school in Clarendon in 1954. After completing two years at Clarendon College, he attended the Uni-versity of Texas at Austin, where he obtained a bachelor's degree in history and government and a law degree in 1962. After passing the bar exam, he was hired as assistant county attorney in Lubbock. Two years later, Broadus en-tered private practice. In 1970 he moved his practice to Austin, where he lives and practices law today. Broadus has tried over 400 civil and criminal cases to a jury verdict. He has been president of the State Bar of Texas, the Texas Trial Lawyers association, and the International Academy of Trial Lawyers.

The eight years during which Broadus practiced law in Lubbock encompassed the time in which the facts in Maxey's lawsuit occurred. Broadus was acquainted with Maxey and many of the other principals involved, including the attorneys of both sides and both of the judges, as well as Maxey's younger daughter, Glenna Goodacre.

In 1983 Glenna moved to Santa Fe, which has been her home ever since, and in 1995 she married C. L. Mike Schmidt, a Dallas attorney and good friend of Broadus's (Glenna and Bill divorced in 1984). Over the years, Broadus and Glenna discussed the fact that a book about Homer Maxey and his legal battles for his life needed to be written. Broadus finally agreed to write the book in 2002. The groundwork for the project was laid over the next several years. Due to the full-time commitments of his robust law practice, work on the manuscript proceeded slowly but not without some singular achievements, including the act of locating the transcript of the first trial just before it was scheduled to be destroyed. Between 2002 and 2009, Broadus recorded interviews with some of the principal figures in the case and made detailed notes of his own personal recollections.

In the summer of 2009 another attorney introduced Broadus to Jesse Sublett, an Austin author of crime novels and nonfiction. Sublett was born in Fredericksburg, Texas, and raised in Johnson City and the rural Hill Country. As a result, he had many opportunities to observe Lyndon B. Johnson during his terms as Vice President and President. During those years Johnson frequently returned to his ranch on the Pedernales River and attended Trinity Lutheran Church (founded and built by Sublett's German immigrant ancestors) in Stonewall. Momentous historical events were taking shape in the world, including the Civil Rights Act, the foundation of the Great Society, and the war in Southeast Asia, and Johnson was the towering, complex figure at the center of it all.

Johnson City seemed a remote rural outpost to Sublett in his teens, but he would always treasure his connections to LBJ, and he credits his interest in history to growing up in LBJ country. He graduated valedictorian of Lyndon B. Johnson High School in Johnson City in 1972, excelling in English and creative writing, and was awarded scholarships to attend Texas State University (which Johnson also attended) in San Marcos.

In the late 1970s, Sublett gained fame as a musician. He later turned to writing, publishing numerous crime novels, nonfiction books, and articles.

He has been involved in the production of dozens of historical documentaries.

With his background in crime writing, Jesse was immediately drawn to the allegations of fraud and unethical behavior in the Maxey case, activities that also bore strong similarities to those of the lenders and securities professionals in the 2008 mortgage and securities scandals.

Despite extensive media coverage and detailed court records, many aspects of the case remained murky and clouded by rumor. Definitive answers to some questions may never be found. Some of the darkest of Homer Maxey's allegations and suspicions remain unproven, but the evidence indicates that the judges in both jury trials may well have been biased against Maxey.

Among the many individuals the authors interviewed were E. W. Williams, Jr., the banker; Ken Bowlin, the lawyer who tried the first Maxey lawsuit; Mike Liles, the lawyer who handled the second jury trial; and both Maxey daughters (Carla Maxey Elliott and Glenna Goodacre). It required a tremendous effort of coordination and analysis to piece together all the differing opinions, attitudes, and recollections of folks on both sides of the issues.

The Maxey case was covered extensively in the press, including daily coverage of the trials in the *Lubbock Avalanche-Journal* and other Texas newspapers, as well as the October 1983 feature in *Texas Monthly*. Several chapters in Lawrence L. Graves's book *Lubbock: From Town to City*, published in 1986, also mention the great impact of the Maxey case on the Lubbock area. The microfilm collections of the *Lubbock Avalanche-Journal* and the *Fort Worth Star-Telegram* were invaluable.

The Homer Maxey story is an important part of the larger story of the growth and development of Lubbock, Texas, and the people who helped usher it into the modern era.

We hope this book will prove to be of value to researchers as well as readers invested in the history of the region. Even casual readers may find this story as dramatic and intriguing as a complex, high-profile murder trial. It is studded with characters and events as quirky and mysterious as any detective novel or Hollywood film, but as those who lived this story can attest, the characters are real and the events actually happened.

Chapter 1

THE PUZZLE

Sitting high and dry on the southern plains, with its straight-line horizon and a street grid aligned with the compass, Lubbock, Texas, looks quiet and peaceful, a place where radicals and other troublemakers have no room to hide. One of the most culturally and politically conservative areas in the nation, it does not seem like the kind of place where a pillar of the community would carry out a fifteen-year legal battle against one of the town's leading banks and, by proxy, dozens of the wealthiest and most powerful individuals and families in the region.[1] But that is just what Homer Glen Maxey did. It happened over four decades ago, and despite all those years, more than a few of the surviving partisans are still upset about it.

Exceptional in his achievements, Homer Maxey was an everyman in many respects among his peers. He was conservative, stubborn, a tireless worker, churchgoing, and civic-minded. He was also a decorated veteran of the Pacific theater in World War II. He was the kind of businessman and full-time citizen they called a "go-getter." Maxey's shrewd ambition and enormous talent helped Lubbock grow in size and economic vitality in the postwar years, during which time he also became a multimillionaire and wielded considerable influence as a community and civic leader.[2]

Like others of his generation, Homer Maxey held an outlook and attitudes that were shaped to a great degree by the Great Depression. Because he was so often preoccupied with business, he sometimes gave the impression of being distant or even cold in social environments. At other times he was quite

Homer Maxey (middle, wearing hat), on the bridge of the LCM (landing craft, medium) he commanded in the Pacific theater of World War II. Maxey was a commander of a flotilla of twelve amphibious vessels. Courtesy of the Maxey family.

rambunctious, and his sense of humor could be downright earthy. Instead of hailing a colleague with a conventional salutation, he often said, "Well, what do you know, here comes old fuzzy balls."[3]

Maxey had a complexion that was ruddy even at his calmest moments. Anyone who encountered or witnessed him in a red-faced tirade would tell you that Homer Maxey had a temper and that he was a real scrapper.

It was the afternoon of February 16, 1966, that Citizens National Bank of Lubbock foreclosed on Homer Maxey. Many people in Lubbock did not hear about it until the following day, and when they did, there was a general feeling of disbelief—not just because a pillar of the community was suddenly bankrupt, but because the details of the foreclosure sounded rather unusual. The foreclosure proceedings had taken place during a secret meeting in a ninth-floor boardroom, at which the bank president and a small cadre of vice presidents and other officers dissected and disbursed nearly every one of Maxey's assets, a financial empire that, according to Maxey's appraisals, was worth $5.5 million, an amount comparable to approximately $38.5 million in 2012 dollars.[4]

By the end of that day, Maxey was left with nothing. Even more humiliat-

Left to right: Carla Maxey Elliott, Glenna Goodacre, Melba Maxey, and Homer Maxey. The happy family celebrating Glenna's graduation from Colorado College in 1961. Courtesy of the Maxey family.

ing was the fact that, as he later alleged, the bank had sold the properties for a fraction of their actual value.

As more details of the foreclosure leaked out, many Lubbockites agreed with Maxey that he had been defrauded by the bank. One particularly troublesome detail about the foreclosure was that Citizens National Bank had sold Plaza Building Corporation, which Maxey controlled, for a mere $749. The single most valuable component of Maxey's financial empire, the Plaza Building Corporation had been established early in his career, and he was the majority stockholder. The corporation controlled the greater portion of Maxey's various assets, including working ranches and farms, commercial real estate, and residential properties.[5]

Within a month, Maxey filed a lawsuit against the bank, seeking a total of more than $20 million in damages.

Thus began Homer Maxey's long struggle to reclaim his fortune and his reputation. Maxey sued not only the bank but also thirty-three individual

H. G. Maxey & Co., a plumbing, electrical, and home furnishings business founded by Homer Maxey right after the war. With enterprises like these, Maxey helped put the boom in the post-war era. Photo by Winston Reeves. Courtesy of the Southwest Collection/Special Collections Library at Texas Tech University.

defendants employed or otherwise associated with the bank—including his former attorneys—who, he said, had betrayed his trust and acted against his best interests. The petition accused the defendants of fraud, conspiracy, and numerous other misdeeds and irregularities. The Maxey case was the largest and longest civil case in the history of Lubbock County.[6]

The way Maxey told it, losing his money was the least of his concerns. He believed he had been cheated, not only of money, but of his good reputation. It was important for him to prove once and for all that his business judgment was not at fault for the collapse of his fortunes. He wanted his reputation back. He wanted an apology.[7]

Such conflicts often reveal both good and not-so-good traits of the respective parties. In this case, the fight spoke volumes about the individual combatants and also the community in which they lived. It was a major scandal that rocked the town and divided it into rival camps.

Despite being the central hub of a large, economically significant (but sparsely populated) region of the state, Lubbock still had the look and feel of a small town. In a place where local leaders convened weekly round-table meetings, where deals were sealed with a handshake, and where attorneys on opposite sides of court cases often carpooled to out-of-town proceedings, Lubbock was a town that was built on relationships.[8]

In such a place, any major strain in those relationships creates a ripple effect that touches almost everyone. In a small pond, two big fish turning on each other can create a tidal wave for everyone else. Many of the bank directors and officers named in Maxey's lawsuit were his neighbors, and he had been a partner in business with several of the bank's attorneys. The lawsuit and all the peripheral damage it inflicted, including broken relationships, uncomfortable social situations, and gossip, affected a large cross section of the populace.

There are always at least two sides to such stories, and even Maxey's family and best friends would agree that he was not entirely blameless. In the United States, however, every citizen, rich or poor, is supposed to be equal under the law. As Atticus Finch might have said, Homer Maxey deserved his day in court.

Just as Homer Maxey wasn't just any businessman, Citizens National Bank wasn't just any old bank. One of the top four banks in Lubbock, Citizens was founded in 1906, and its board of directors included a good portion of the wealthiest men in West Texas, some of whose families owned the largest ranches in the region. They were also among the most powerful people in the state. By filing a lawsuit against them, Maxey was putting himself in an adversarial relationship with many men he had socialized with or done business with in the past. In some cases, their fathers had similar ties with Maxey's father.

Although Maxey believed he had been the victim of a conspiracy involving many parties affiliated with Citizens, there was no one he blamed more or held in lower esteem than E. W. Williams, Jr., who assumed the position of president of the bank in 1962 and began soliciting Maxey's business. Williams, a native of the town of Post, Texas, was a young and ambitious banker. When he was hired by the bank's new owners, two oilmen from Odessa, he had been charged with taking the bank in a more aggressive direction. According to Maxey, Williams had made certain promises to him before Maxey began doing business with the bank. The promises were agreed to with a handshake, not a contract.[9]

Such "gentleman's agreements" were still common then. Lubbock contractor W. G. McMillan, Jr., has stated that, in his own father's day, many building

Melba Maxey at the home on Vicksburg, before it was seized by the bank. Courtesy of the Maxey family.

projects were initiated this way. "My dad told me he did lots and lots of work by just the man saying, 'Go ahead and build it.' . . . You would do business with just a shake of a hand instead of a contract."[10]

The fact that E. W. Williams had reneged on such a pledge, along with the irregularities connected with the bank's secret sale of his assets on the day of foreclosure, were the foundation of Maxey's grievances against the bank. Also disturbing to Maxey was the fact that two of his attorneys, Charlie Jones and Chauncey Trout, Jr., both of whom also represented Citizens National Bank, appeared to have, at worst, conspired with the bank to deprive him of his property and, at best, ignored the appearance of a conflict of interest between the two clients.[11] Bill Evans, the senior partner of the firm, had been a friend to Maxey and his father, J. B. Maxey. Evans had also been a partner in numerous business ventures with Homer Maxey, dating back to 1937.[12]

When Maxey's relationship with the bank began to sour, he worried that his former friends and business partners at the law firm had a conflict of interest. Indeed, when the case went to trial, Maxey had the discomfiting experience of being questioned on the witness stand by his own former attorneys and ex friends. Jones served as second chair in the first trial and took the lead in the second.

Homer's daughter Glenna Goodacre can still vividly recall the experience and the toll that it took on the entire family.[13] Thinking back on the events from her home in Santa Fe, New Mexico, she can still see her father, red-faced and bald-headed, wiping his face with a handkerchief as he tried to "puzzle it out."

"Sometimes he would put his hands over his face and sit in his chair and sob," she says. "He'd say, 'How could all of this happen?'"

The Puzzle

Chapter 2

MOVERS AND SHAKERS

To appreciate who Homer Maxey was, it helps to know a bit about the town of Lubbock and how it came to be. Lubbock is in the center of the South Plains, part of one of the largest tablelands of the North American continent and one of the flattest places on earth, the Llano Estacado. Covering about 37,500 square miles of West Texas and eastern New Mexico, the region is bordered on the east by the raw, red cliffs of the Caprock Escarpment and on the west by the Mescalero Escarpment and the Pecos River valley. The Canadian River marks its northern boundary, beyond which the Great Plains extend all the way to Canada. To the south, near Big Spring, the southern plains merge into the Edwards Plateau.[1]

It was Spanish conquistador Francisco Vásquez de Coronado who came up with the name Llano Estacado, Spanish for "staked plains," although historians disagree about the precise meaning of the name. Searching for cities of gold and silver in 1541, Coronado complained about the lack of scenery and landmarks, writing: "[T]here was not a stone, nor bit of rising ground, nor a tree, nor a shrub, nor anything to go by."[2]

Native Americans were familiar with the region, having followed the buffalo herds on their migrations, hunting them for food, clothing, and a plethora of other uses, but as late as the 1870s, few other Americans knew or cared much about the South Plains. After Lewis and Clark made their survey of

The Nicolett Hotel, after being moved from its original location at the Old Lubbock settlement to the intersection of two streets later designated Broadway and Avenue H. Courtesy of the City of Lubbock.

the continent between St. Louis and the Pacific in 1804–6, they labeled the surrounding plains "immense and trackless deserts." Thomas Jefferson, who envisioned the young republic growing up to become a "nation of yeoman farmers," must have been quite disappointed. If he were alive today, Jefferson would have to annotate his copy of the map, noting that the South Plains region is the largest contiguous cotton-producing area in the world.[3]

Geographers in the 1820s were even harsher in their comments about the region. Edwin James, a member of the Stephen Long expedition in 1823, complained that the area was "almost wholly unfit for cultivation, and of course, uninhabitable by a people depending upon agriculture for their subsistence."[4]

On his trek through the area in 1852, General Randolph Marcy wrote: "not a tree, shrub, or any other object, either animate or inanimate, relieved the dreary monotony of the prospects; it was a vast illimitable expanse of desert prairie." "[T]he almost total absence of water," the general went on, "causes all animals to shun it: even the Indians do not venture to cross it except at two or three places." It was a land "where no man, either savage or civilized, permanently abides; it spreads into a treeless, desolate waste of uninhabited solitude, which always has been, and must continue, uninhabited forever."[5]

Rainfall and surface water are indeed sparse, but the numerous shallow playa lakes in the Lubbock area were well-known to Native American groups for at least ten thousand years. Such sources of water were also visited by Spanish missionaries and Comancheros, and in the last quarter of the nineteenth century, by white buffalo hunters, who were, with the blessing of the federal government, slaughtering buffalo to visit hardship on the natives and force them onto reservations.[6] Atrocities were committed by both sides and as a consequence, certain landmarks in the area, including Yellow House Canyon, lent their names to some of the last, bloody conflicts with Native Americans in West Texas.

Lubbock County was created by the Texas Legislature in 1876, but years passed before there were any significant efforts at settlement. The name of the county paid tribute to Thomas Saltus Lubbock, the younger brother of Francis R. Lubbock, who was elected governor of Texas in 1861.[7] Both brothers fought for the Confederacy.

The census of 1880 counted twenty-five inhabitants living in the county, and the number of permanent residents did not increase much over the next half decade. George W. Singer's store, established in about 1882 (and possibly earlier) in Yellow House Canyon, served for a time as the federal post office called "Lubbock" and as a gathering place for hunters, sheepherders, cattlemen, and other plainsmen. Although the main commercial activity in the county at the time was cattle ranching, some patrons of Singer's store had already discovered that conditions there were ideal for dryland farming.

Topsoil in the region overlays a clay subsoil and, just three or so feet beneath that lies the Caprock, a hardpan of calcium carbonate better known in Texas as caliche. Beneath the Caprock zone are the beds of water-soaked sand up to three hundred feet deep, which form the vast Ogallala Aquifer. Formed by the rivers that carried eroded mountain debris from Canada, the Ogallala, the Caprock, and those fertile loams are all the result of many millions of years of natural geologic forces that combined to create one of the most prodigious areas for agricultural cultivation on earth.[8]

The first farming town established on the South Plains was Estacado, about twenty-five miles northeast of present-day Lubbock on the eastern boundary between Lubbock and Estacado counties. The town was founded as a Quaker colony by Paris Cox in 1879. After having a well dug on his land and reporting favorably on his agricultural experiments, Cox was able to entice ten families to move there in 1882. The town thrived for a time, and in 1890 the Central Plains Academy was established there, the first college on the Llano Estacado.[9]

Rollie Burns, a pioneer cattle rancher who recorded his observations of West Texas ranching and settlement during the late 1800s and early 1900s, described driving cattle herds through the Estacado a number of times in the years 1884–89. One Sunday morning in December 1888, Burns and his family joined the Estacado congregation for Sunday church services. Afterward they accepted an invitation to dine with a local family. Burns was impressed by the sumptuous meal. The Quakers were successful farmers and "lived well," he said, referring to the bountiful crops their farms produced. But without a railroad connection within a reasonable distance, farming was an unprofitable proposition. As a consequence, the people of Estacado were discouraged and disillusioned.

A short time earlier, Burns had accepted a position as manager of the sprawling IOA Ranch, a vast operation founded in 1884 with a large capital investment by the Western Land and Live Stock Company. The ranch stretched approximately fourteen by thirty miles and took up most of the southern half of Lubbock County.[10] The owners of the company were Iowa businessmen, and the name they chose for the ranch was an expression of home state patriotism: IOA, which they preferred to be pronounced like the state. The operation was plagued from the start by ill-advised business decisions, which were compounded by other factors, including two years of terrible drought followed by severe winter weather and an economic downturn.

By 1888 the owners of the IOA were desperate to find new ways to make a return on their investment, while also trying to find a graceful exit from the cattle ranching business. Stillman Wheelock, the vice president of the company, sent word to Boston for his twenty-four-year-old nephew, Frank E. Wheelock, to come to Lubbock County to lend a hand, and in 1889 he took charge of an experimental farming operation. Wheelock planted sorghum on 250 acres south of Yellow House Canyon. According to Burns, the crop grew well but it was unprofitable. The farming operation on the IOA was discontinued after 1890.

Burns said that he was more interested in the feasibility of growing cotton on the Caprock. In the spring of 1889 he planted three acres of cotton but did not bother to thin the plants or tend to the crop in any way. Burns claimed that, by his estimate, the planting yielded more than a half bale to the acre. "I predicted then that some day the South Plains would be a great cotton country," wrote Burns, "but until a railroad was built cotton farming would not be practical."

If Burns was correct about the above dates, his cotton planting efforts coincided with the beginnings of the first permanent settlement called "Lubbock" in the county.[11] Burns and Wheelock, with the collaboration of other interested parties, were busy establishing a village on the north side of Yellow House Canyon, near the present-day site of the Lubbock Country Club in 1899. The date could have been somewhat earlier, according to *Historic Lubbock County: An Illustrated History*, by Donald R. Abbe and Paul H. Carlson. "North of Yellow House Draw and east of Blackwater Draw" puts a finer point on the geographic location. The site soon boasted a touch of elegance with the construction of the three-story Nicolett Hotel, after the Nicollet Hotel in Wheelock's hometown of Minneapolis. It appears that the original spelling (two Ls, one T) did not survive the transition to West Texas.

Nice accommodations were a plus for a frontier town, but being designated the county seat was a primary goal of town promoters like the Lubbock group. It was also the aim of a group who, sometime in 1890, established a rival town three miles away, just north of the present-day Texas Tech University football stadium. This group was led by W. E. Rayner, a cattle company manager and town promoter with a reputation as a "wheeler-dealer."[12]

The official name of the town was Monterey, but in practice, it was known by several other names, including Ray Town, South Town, and South Lubbock.[13] Two years earlier, Rayner had platted a town called Rayner. He appears to have liked the sound of his own name.

The rivalry between such towns was a serious matter. Conflicts between communities competing to become the county seat had been known to turn violent. The individuals involved here, however, were too pragmatic to allow that to happen. They realized that joining forces offered the best opportunity for success. The two groups began discussing a possible compromise in late

Citizens National Bank of Lubbock in 1906, its first year of operation. E. Y. Lee is the man on horseback and to his right are Frank Wheelock, George Wolfforth, Allie G. Hunt, and Claude A. Burrus. The Masonic Lodge headquarters was on the second floor. Maxey filed his suit against Citizens National Bank in 1966, the sixtieth anniversary of the bank. Courtesy of the Southwest Collection/Special Collections Library at Texas Tech University.

summer 1890 and came to an agreement in early December. "We dickered around for a while and finally came to an understanding," said Burns. "We agreed to purchase a section of land on the south side of the canyon equidistant from our town and Rayner's town. The new town was to be laid out on the same plan as Monterey, but was to have the name of Lubbock."

Some of the buildings were rudimentary enough that they could be dismantled and hauled to the new site. Others presented more of a challenge. Wheelock hired freighters from Carson City to move the Nicollett Hotel. Most of the building was moved intact by mounting it on skids, with much of the furniture remaining in the rooms during the three-mile transit. George

W. Singer's store was the first building in Monterey moved to the new site.

County residents voted to name Lubbock the county seat on March 10, 1891, after which the county was organized on official basis. A drug store occupied the street corner opposite the Nicolett Hotel. The new town also had a barbershop, a blacksmith shop, a livery stable, and a real estate office. The population exceeded 250 in August 1891.

In subsequent years Frank Wheelock continued to play a leading role in the affairs of Lubbock and Lubbock County. In addition to his post as a county commissioner, Wheelock also served as Lubbock's first postmaster and, after the town was incorporated in 1909, its first mayor. Wheelock continued in the cattle ranching, finance, and mercantile businesses.

Once the town was established, growth continued apace as other large-scale landholders in the area followed the example of the IOA Ranch, carving out portions of their estates and offering special inducements to farm owners and tenant farmers. The large landowners in the region at the forefront of moving from the open range to contemporary ranching included George W. Littlefield, a cattleman and banker, and Isaac L. Ellwood, an entrepreneur from DeKalb who bought a one-half interest in Joseph Glidden's patent on a type of two-strand barbed wire, then made millions manufacturing it.[14]

As blocks of rangeland were put on the market, new communities were settled in the areas outside Lubbock. Many would become thriving communities that depended on Lubbock as a center of commerce. Still, even as the large cattle ranches were whittled down, traded, and sometimes consolidated, the owners continued to exert considerable influence in the development of the region. Ellwood's heirs, for example, continued their ranching operations, while also investing in a wide array of business interests in Lubbock, such as banking.[15]

Sorghum cane was by far the leading crop in the early years but, before long, cotton farmers who had been put out of business by the boll weevil elsewhere in the state were arriving in Lubbock, drawn by cheap land, favorable climate, fertile soil, and an absence of boll weevils. Lubbock soon became the agricultural trading center for the region. With an eye ensuring contined growth and prosperity, town leaders worked to obtain a rail line. Historic maps are dotted with the names of long-gone pioneer towns, places that were bypassed by the railroad companies. The fact that the people of Lubbock understood the reality of the situation helps explain why, on September 25, 1909, two thousand citizens from a county numbering only 3,600 turned out to celebrate the arrival of the first train that rolled into town from Plainview.

J. B. Maxey, seated at the office with sons (left to right) Robert, Herschel, Carl, and Homer. Following in their father's footsteps, all four sons entered the building industry in Lubbock and exerted a significant influence on the city. Courtesy of the Maxey family.

Plainview, which was located less than fifty miles north of Lubbock and was the county seat of Hale County, had become a rail connection by 1906. Plainview was founded two years earlier than Lubbock (1888) and for the first two decades of the 1900s, the two towns rivaled each other in growth and development.

The story of the Maxeys and the South Plains begins in Plainview rather than Lubbock. Homer Maxey's father, J. B. Maxey, moved to Plainview from Frisco in 1906, an ambitious twenty-five-year-old building contractor searching for a new lease on life. For the previous two years, while engaged in contract work for the Frisco Railway, he had suffered from malarial fevers and jaundice. Although he stood six foot four, his normal weight of 190 pounds had fallen to a mere 153.

In the high, dry climate of the South Plains, Maxey's health and vigor improved and, with the establishment of the Santa Fe line through Plainview, he found business opportunities as well as chances to help grow the community in other ways.[16] In a scrapbook journal of photographs, newspaper clippings, and assorted ephemera documenting the highlights of his life, Maxey noted that he had to borrow $100 to move from Frisco to Plainview.[17]

Born on a farm near Prosper in Collin County in 1881 and christened James Barney Maxey, the father of Homer Maxey was an energetic and ambitious individual who had taken up the carpentry trade at age seventeen and started his contracting business at age twenty-one.

In 1907, Maxey married his fiancée from Collin County, Effie Glen Nicholson. All the Maxey siblings were born in Plainview. Homer was born in 1911, followed by Robert, Carl, and Herschel. Their first child, James Barney, born in 1908, died at the age of six months.

Between 1907 and 1923, Maxey built churches, homes, schools, courthouses, and other structures in Plainview and numerous other plains communities, including Lubbock. The towns that existed in the region were rough works in progress, as he later chronicled in his scrapbook journal:

> Plainview at the time did not have gas, sewer, telephone, telegraph, railroad, hotels, electric or water service, just a few small stores, residences, only two churches, no paving, sidewalks, or brick buildings. All supplies [were] hauled in by freight wagons from Canyon . . . At times roads were so bad that mail hacks could not make the trip, so many times we did not get mail for more than a week. Most of the homes had water wells with long handle pumps or windmills.
>
> We used coal for fuel, kerosene for lamp lights, which of course was hauled in from Canyon, with all other supplies. During bad weather some folks would run out of coal, then would have to burn cow chips, which was handled in the local markets.
>
> Within three days after our arrival in Plainview, we had plenty of construction work and have been busy most of the time since, doing some of the larger buildings through the South Plains area.[18]

In March 1907, the town of Plainview signed a contract with Maxey to build a calaboose (jail) for the sum of $337.50, including all materials and labor. In 1910, Maxey's contract work included a new building that would serve as home to city hall and the volunteer fire department. In 1911, Maxey constructed Lubbock's first public water system.

Maxey was elected to the Plainview board of aldermen in 1914, beginning a lifetime of involvement in civic affairs, charities, and social clubs. He built the First Methodist Church of Plainview in 1916 and served on the board of stewards until moving to Lubbock in 1924, where he served on the board of stewards at the Methodist church there.

Maxey began his scrapbook with memories of his parents, James Joseph Maxey and Nannie Elizabeth Goodnight. He gave them credit for his work ethic and sense of duty to the community.

> Papa would plow from sunup to sunset, come in and do the chores, get a bite to eat, [then ride] his horse a distance from one to four miles to help with their sick neighbors, night after night. They also took a great interest in helping the poor in times of trouble.

J. B. worked hard, but he also made time for fishing, traveling, and playing dominoes. Every summer the Maxey family embarked on long driving trips across the country. In addition to their four sons, J. B. and Effie also took along young W. B. "Dub" Rushing. The Rushings and the Maxeys had been friends back in Collin County. The Rushings moved to Plainview around the same time that J. B. brought his new bride there in 1907. Both families also moved to Lubbock in 1924. Dub, who was Homer's age, was regarded as "the fifth Maxey brother." Dub and Homer became lifelong friends.

"We called J. B. 'Big Daddy,' and Effie, our grandmother, was 'Mommie,'" says Glenna Goodacre. "I remember sitting at his feet and playing with his boots. He wore those tall lace-up boots, and he died with a hammer in his hand."[19]

The elder Maxey suffered a fatal heart attack while doing home repairs. "He was outside repairing the rose trellis in the back yard alcove when he fell over with a heart attack and died," says DeEtte Maxey Cobb, daughter of Homer's brother Carl. "He was doing what he loved."

The fact that Lubbock was growing in size and sphere of influence did not escape J. B. Maxey's attention. He purchased a couple of residential lots in Lubbock in 1917, but sold them two months later. He also oversaw construction projects in Lubbock.

The Lubbock Chamber of Commerce adopted the slogan "Lubbock, the Hub of the Plains" in 1917.[20] By that time it was indeed the center of transportation and commerce for the region; it was another big prize that helped secure Lubbock's future prosperity: a new state university.

The idea of establishing a state university for West Texas was older than almost every town in the region. Residents had been lobbying the legislature

J. B. Maxey, during the war, with three grandchildren. Homer's first-born, Carla, stands in front, and her sister, christened Glendell, held by his right arm. The infant is probably Robert and Kathleen's daughter, Marcia, born in 1941. After graduating from high school, Glendell was shortened to Glenna. Courtesy of the Maxey family.

for that purpose as far back as the 1880s.[21] Support from Fort Worth newspaper publisher Amon G. Carter, who never overlooked an opportunity to promote West Texas, helped make the dream a reality in 1923. That year Senate Bill 103, which provided for the creation of a new, four-year state university to serve the region, was passed by the legislature and signed into law by Governor Neff.

A panel of education experts, appointed to serve as the Locating Board, was given a list of thirty-seven West Texas communities that had applied to be selected as the location for the school. When population size, geography, economy, infrastructure, and other quantifiable factors were compared, the relative assets many of the towns in the running, such as Lubbock, Plainview, Sweetwater, and Floydada, were not that different. When members of the Locating Board arrived in Lubbock, huge crowds lined the streets, waving signs and voicing support for the university and pride in their community. The residents of Plainview, likewise, rolled out the red carpet, and, according to contemporary newspaper accounts, some of them felt confident that they had won the board's vote.[22]

The Administration Building for Texas Technological College under construction in 1925. Courtesy of the City of Lubbock.

But they were mistaken. On Wednesday, August 8, 1923, it was announced that Lubbock had won approval by unanimous consent of the members of the selection committee.[23] The feelings of pride, vindication, and celebration were vividly expressed by journalists of the day.

That was the message that set Lubbock, the plains, and West Texas on fire. And that is the message that is being carried in every newspaper in the United States, Canada and in many foreign countries today. For the Texas Technological College is no ordinary, one-horse institution. It is a state, a national and an internationally known institution already. It starts with the most brilliant promises and possibilities that have ever accompanied the founding of a like institution in America and the realization of those promises and possibilities are so closely tied and woven into the promise and possibilities of Lubbock that every sane thinking citizen has a right to stop and think upon the inestimable importance of the events of the past 24 hours and wonder how Lubbock is going to measure up to the great future that is hers for the making.

To say the town went mad would be to put the matter too mildly. Old men and women, children and the hound pups of Lubbock, with one accord, went into a series of ecstasies. Horns were tooted, fire trucks thundered up and down the streets, automobiles honked, screeched and scooted around with bells, tin cans and scrap iron dragging. The stores were closed by a proclamation written by a man that was not even a member of the city commission—and the proclamation was observed to the letter.

A dozen bonfires started in a dozen minutes. Placards appeared as if by magic. In thirty minutes the sidewalks had overflowed into the streets and the uproar had spread into the residential sections of the city. In an hour delegations from nearby towns began pouring in to further swell the mass—for Lubbock got the Texas Tech.

Freak stunts were staged. Hat brims were torn off and the crowns worn Happy Hooligan style. A Texas Tech Glee Club was quickly organized with more enthusiasm than harmony. Candidates for "Freshman Class President" appeared and started lecturneering [sic] for election. The Rix Furniture Company changed its "Where Else Could They Put It?" to "There Was Nowhere Else They Could Have Put It."[24]

Messages of congratulations, pride, and good wishes poured in from across West Texas. Senders also pledged "to Lubbock and the Plains their fullest support and cooperation in making the Texas Tech the greatest institution in Texas."[25] The choice of Lubbock meant rejection for thirty-six other West Texas towns; yet, if any feelings of resentment were made public, those expressions appear to have been completely overlooked by the media of the day.

Buoyed by a renewed sense of enthusiasm and optimism, the people of Lubbock embarked on a new era of influence and responsibility. Few of them were more enthusiastic about the challenges and opportunities ahead than Charles A. Guy, the new editor of the *Plains Journal*. Guy, who had moved to town as a twenty-one-year-old at the beginning of 1924, sang the praises of Lubbock far and wide, in print and in person, for over fifty years.[26] His primary soapbox was a folksy column written under the byline "the Plainsman," with a drawing of a grizzled cowpoke with a dangling cigarette standing in as Charlie Guy's alter ego. The image was created for Guy by Tige Formby, a member of the newspaper's advertising staff.[27]

Guy never tired of writing or talking about all the attributes and potential of Lubbock. When he retired the column in 1972, he stated that his job was an easy one because "it was done in a city and an area which have been on the upswing all the way." Above all, Guy believed that the very best thing about the area was the people who lived there. It made him feel blessed, he said, "to live nearly half a century in a country where there are more good people, in ratio to the population, than anywhere else under the sun."[28]

The newspaperman found a kindred spirit in J. B. Maxey, who had moved his family to Lubbock around the same time as Guy. Local leaders tapped Maxey for his expertise as a civic leader. In Lubbock, the elder Maxey would end up serving in most of the same offices and unofficial public roles he had held in Plainview.[29] He was an active member of the chamber of commerce, serving several terms as president, and was instrumental in the establishment of a Board of City Development.

When Maxey was president of the chamber, Charlie Guy often used his column to publicize a particular concern of his by setting it in the form of a letter to Maxey. The newspaperman wasn't shy about letting readers know that he was on a first-name basis with everyone of importance in Lubbock, so it was characteristic of him to address Maxey in his own individual style, beginning each publicized exchange with the salutation, "My Dear Barney . . ."

When contracts were let for the construction of Texas Tech, J. B. Maxey submitted the winning bid for the President's Home. The more important of the two structures erected at that time was the Administration Building. That project was contracted to Ramey Brothers, an El Paso firm that was also building the city hall.

On November 11, 1924, ten days after ground was broken at the new campus, an official celebration was held to commemorate the laying of the cornerstone of the Administration Building. The crowd numbered some twenty thousand.

J. B. Maxey was present at the cornerstone ceremony, not only as one of the contractors, but as chairman of the grounds committee and a member of the university's board of directors. Amon G. Carter was chairman of the board. In the newspaper coverage leading up to the event (which one headline heralded as being possibly the "biggest occasion" in Texas history[30]), Maxey reported that he had "practically perfected all plans for handling the crowds expected on the 11th and that no one need have any fears that he will be unable to see and hear" the day-long proceedings.[31]

Bringing a new state university to Lubbock was one of the most pivotal events in the city's history. The cornerstone laying ceremony was a time of speeches and celebration, with over twenty thousand in attendance. J. B. Maxey chaired the platform committee. Courtesy of the City of Lubbock.

All four Maxey boys were there, including thirteen-year-old Homer, who, in the employ of his father, would work on the construction of the first buildings of the new university and, later, attend classes in them.[32]

Growing up in a town where their father was so well-known and well-connected added an interesting dynamic to the lives of J. B.'s four sons. Although they benefitted from his connections and prestige, they were also expected to make it on their own.

Big Daddy wasn't the only one who made demands on his family. Effie Maxey had her expectations as well. Children, spouses, and grandchildren were drilled in Maxey protocol from an early age.

After church every Sunday, there was family dinner at the Maxey house on Thirteenth Street. Christmas Day was orchestrated with precision. "When you went over there for Christmas morning for all the folderol," says Glenna, "you did what the Maxeys wanted, period. That's just how it was. Big Daddy ruled the roost, but Effie decorated the house with such wonderful things and there were gifts for all the grandchildren. They were wonderful people and I loved them."

"Mrs. Maxey always had gifts for everybody," says Kathleen Maxey Luther, the widow of Homer's brother Robert. "She always had the most delicious

J. B. Maxey won the contract to build the President's Home at the new college. Homer, age fourteen, worked on the project, too. Courtesy of the City of Lubbock.

meals and the loveliest table and decorations. She was known for all that."[33]

"Effie Glen had lunch on Saturdays," recalls Robert and Kathleen's daughter, Marcia Abbott. "Anybody in the family who was working could come over to the house and have lunch at her house. That was the rule; if you weren't working you couldn't go." Marcia became a regular during high school when she had a job working in a bank.[34]

By 1924, at forty-four years of age, J. B. Maxey had built fifty-nine residential homes and lived in seventeen of them. The next house he built was in Lubbock, and he lived there until his death in 1953. Like the desk and typewriter he bought in 1912 and used for the next forty-one years, once Maxey found something that suited him, he stuck with it.

J. B. Maxey died on April 9, 1953, not long after the city dedicated a one-hundred-acre city park in his name. The dedication was only fitting, since J. B. had been instrumental in creating the city park system. Maxey Park has a playa lake in the middle, and is a fine spot for bird watching, children's recreation, or grabbing a moment of solitude. Because of his advocacy on behalf of physically disabled children, J. B. Maxey would be happy to know that the facilities at the park are all handicap accessible.

The park is also the setting of the most unusual photograph in J. B. Maxey's scrapbook. In the photo, the seventy-one-year-old builder is crouching on one knee to feed a squirrel. It's the only picture that shows him with a smile on his face.

J. B. Maxey's obituary in the *Lubbock Avalanche-Journal* paid tribute to his innumerable contributions to the city: "Not only in the construction field but in citizenship, Maxey was known as a leader, and in the 47 years he had lived in this section he had joined hands in the building of his home towns."

J. B. assembled his scrapbook between his discharge from the hospital after a heart attack in mid-1952 and his death in the spring of 1953. He must have

Movers and Shakers

known that he didn't have a lot of time left. One of the many gems it contains is a drawing by Herschel Maxey, his youngest son. It is dated February 5, 1924, just after the Maxeys moved to Lubbock, and it bears the caption: "Herschel's picture of Daddy, 4 years, 10 months old." It's not a bad caricature for a four-year-old artist. Herschel gave his father's face only a minimalist squiggle, but the set jaw of a determined man is unmistakable. Wearing a high, starched collar and a fedora, the figure looms across the frame like a giant, long arms and big hands in motion, legs in mid-stride. He looks as though he's about to march off the edge of the page.[35]

Even as a child, a Maxey boy could tell that Big Daddy was a tough act to follow.

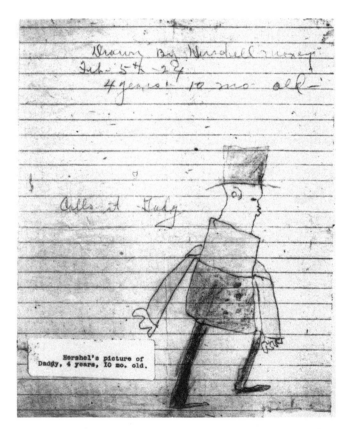

At not quite five years of age, Herschel Maxey was already demonstrating the artistic talent and drafting skills that he would put into architectural design as a young man. He depicts his grandfather, commonly referred to as "Big Daddy," which young Herschel shortened to "Gady." Courtesy of the Maxey family.

Broke, Not Broken

Chapter 3

A Go-Getter

The son of a wealthy man, Homer Maxey took great pride in having worked hard to make his own way in the world. He often mentioned how, at age thirteen, he worked for his father, building the President's Home at Texas Tech, earning $11.85 for his first week's wages, which he claimed was the very first paycheck issued by the university. For a time, he was employed part-time cleaning the president's of

Homer Maxey, diploma in hand, sweetheart at his side, ready to conquer the world in 1931, Depression be damned. Courtesy of the Maxey family.

Hotel Lubbock around 1928, when the additional floors were being added to the structure. Construction was complete in 1929, the same year the stock market crash signaled the beginning of the Great Depression. Photo by Chester Houswerth. Courtesy of the City of Lubbock.

Hotel Lubbock in the 1940s. Photo by Chester Houswerth. Courtesy of the City of Lubbock.

fice, which Maxey would later say made him the school's first janitor. Thus, in a few brief remarks, Maxey signaled his empathy with the common working citizen while also making a sly boast of his long association with Texas Tech, the premier state university of West Texas.[1]

When Maxey graduated from Texas Tech in 1931, the college was only in its sixth year of existence. Maxey was a lifelong booster of Tech, and as an adult always bought season tickets to Texas Tech football games. Glenna Goodacre says that her father was such an avid sports fan that new acquaintances often assumed he played football in high school and college. Some queries were from high school football players who were dating Glenna and Car-

A Go-Getter

This building is believed to be Cash Delivery Grocery, the retail business established by Homer Maxey in 1929, during his first year in college, with partner Cecil Bickley. Bickley is in the doorway, with Homer at his left, with an unknown colleague at far left. Courtesy of the Maxey family.

la when they were teenagers. Glenna says that Maxey had a stock answer for whenever a football player or fan asked if he played in high school or college.

"Hell, yes," Maxey would say. "I played the tuba."[2]

Homer graduated from Lubbock High School in 1927 at the age of sixteen. He worked throughout the summer following graduation and earned a total of $950 to put toward college in the fall. Although his father paid his tuition, Homer was expected to support himself during his four years of college.[3]

Instead of drawing from his savings or getting a part-time job for his portion of the expenses, Homer and a friend named Cecil Bickley formed a business partnership. The two young men built a small grocery store called Cash Delivery Grocery at the corner of Avenue W and Sixteenth Street. Homer used his $950 to stock the store.

For the next four years, Homer was able to live on the profits from the grocery store. He graduated with a BA in business administration, and that summer he sold his share of the business to Bickley for $1,500.[4]

When the stock market crashed on October 29, 1929, Homer was in the middle of the fall semester of his second year at Texas Tech. Even before the crash, however, many farmers in the South Plains had lost everything. Once a farmer became overextended on credit, he was often only one small setback away from ruin. Oftentimes, that last setback came in the form of one of the hellish dust storms that plagued West Texas in the twenties and thirties. The air would turn into sandpaper, blotting out the sky. Dirt sifted through every crack and crevice in every type of residence. If you were unlucky enough to be driving during a dust storm, visibility might be only the distance between the steering wheel and the radiator cap. Vast portions of South Plains real estate were moved from one state to another and left behind in drifts.

The severity of the stock market crash was not immediately felt in West Texas. In fact, the following summer J. B. Maxey still felt confident enough about the economy to take the family (including, as always, Dub Rushing) on a five-week vacation trip with stops in New York City, Quebec, Chicago, and St. Louis. Proceeds from stock sales paid for the trip. But the Maxeys returned to Lubbock to discover that all building projects in town, with the exception of the construction of Lubbock High School, had been halted.[5] That the entire United States was suffering a calamitous economic depression was now official.

On graduating from Tech, Homer Maxey took a job with Waples-Platter Grocery Company, where he worked an eleven-hour shift driving a delivery truck. After a short dinner break at six in the evening, he returned to work as the company bookkeeper, which entailed another three hours of work, adding up to a fourteen-hour workday.

Homer and Melba Mae Tatom were high school sweethearts who stayed together throughout their college years at Tech, with Homer studying business and Melba studying home economics. Over the course of their long marriage, photographs of the couple—Melba slender and attractive and Homer stout and bald-headed—chronicle a relationship between two people who were always delighted to be in each other's presence.

Homer and Melba waited a year after graduating college to get married. The ceremony was held at the First Methodist Church in downtown Lubbock on June 21, 1932. As reported in the Lubbock *Daily Journal*, Homer's brother

Robert served as best man and Dub Rushing's sister, Dorothy, was one of the bridesmaids.[6] The newspaper also noted that Melba's father (since deceased) had been manager of the Higginbotham-Bartlett Lumber Company.

Around the end of 1932, Maxey took a job with the Continental Oil Company (later known as Conoco), again working as a combination truck driver and bookkeeper. In 1933, while working for the oil company, Maxey and two colleagues bought a store called Caprock Dry Goods & Uniform. The store was located on Broadway.[7] The store's previous owner, I. A. Stephens, was anxious to sell it after learning that the manager, a Mr. Profit (the actual name of the manager), had embezzled all the store's funds.[8]

Stephens, a native of San Angelo, Texas, was born in 1901. He moved to Lubbock in 1930 to run Stephens Dry Goods, located next door to Caprock Dry Goods & Uniform, and sometime later that year, he made the acquaintance of Maxey and Rushing. Stephens was almost thirty years old and already an experienced entrepreneur, yet despite such differences, he took a liking to the two nineteen-year-old college students.[9]

Many years later, Stephens wrote a fifteen-page tribute to Maxey and Rushing titled "Two Special Friends," a rambling account of their lives that reads like a cross between a Horatio Alger story and a South Plains rendering of *The Three Musketeers*. "From chance meeting to enduring friendship," wrote Stephens, "our relationship with one another is still strong . . . and is the sort that will endure throughout eternity." During their respective careers, they often formed partnerships to invest in various enterprises, including construction, retail, and oil and gas production.

Around the same time Maxey and his partners bought the dry goods business from Stephens, Dub Rushing borrowed $300 to open the Varsity Bookstore on College Avenue (now University). Not long after that, Stephens opened Stephens Department Store (constructed by J. B. Maxey) on Broadway.

Most often their ventures made money, but sometimes they did not. In his tribute speech, Stephens recounted each one with the gleeful tone of a kid with a brand-new bike. It was clear that they enjoyed their work.[10]

In 1933, Maxey sold his share of the dry goods partnership for a profit. He was also able to upgrade from salesman at Continental Oil to distributor. During Maxey's association with Continental Oil, Homer and Melba moved from Lubbock to Corpus Christi, and later to Laredo and Tahoka.[11]

In 1937, Maxey sold his distributorship for $2,500. The Maxeys moved back to Lubbock and Homer used the funds from the sale of the distributor-

Homer, third from left, with fellow gasoline truck drivers. For most of the 1930s, Homer worked a minimum of two jobs. While driving a truck for Conoco, he worked as a bookkeeper at night. Courtesy of the Maxey family.

ship to establish Maxey Lumber Company in a partnership with his brother, Carl. The business was located at 8th Street and Avenue Q. Homer and Carl built the lumber sheds and office themselves. Eight months later Carl sold his share to Homer and started his own contracting business.[12]

Later that year, Homer Maxey became a real estate developer, a trade at which he enjoyed enormous success and made his greatest contributions to Lubbock's growth. One of his first projects was a two-bedroom house, the first in Lubbock constructed with assistance from President Franklin D. Roosevelt's new Federal Housing Authority program. Maxey Lumber began construction on the home just thirteen days after the FHA program for Lubbock was approved. When the building was ready for viewing, more than four thousand people toured the home. The selling price was $2,100.[13]

In addition to providing communities with a flexible means of financial assistance for clearing out slum areas and providing affordable housing for the less fortunate, the FHA was also one of the many programs under FDR's New Deal that helped provide the economic stimulus that would help America recover from the Depression.

From 1937 through 1941, as the US economy began to revitalize, Homer

A Go-Getter

Maxey started developing housing subdivisions in what was then the southwestern edge of Lubbock. The first development, called the Maxey Place Addition, was built on Twenty-Eighth Street. Maxey bought the property, constructed the homes using materials from his lumber company, and then sold them to home buyers through his real estate business. His second project was a smaller one, Melba Addition, located around Twenty-First Street and Avenue F.[14]

Maxey's next big housing development, Green Acres, represented a cooperative effort between the FHA, the US Army Air Corps, the Lubbock Chamber of Commerce, and various other local interests. The project was deemed a high priority because of the new air base and pilot training school being built at a location just west of Lubbock. During discussions in 1941, months before the Japanese bombed Pearl Harbor, army officials sought assurances from town leaders, such as J. B. Maxey, who was president of the Lubbock Chamber of Commerce at the time, that married pilots stationed at the flying school would have no difficulty finding affordable housing in the community.[15]

William H. Evans, a well-connected Lubbock attorney and longtime friend of the Maxeys, did the legal work for organizing Lubbock Homes Inc., the entity that would work with the FHA to build the homes. Along with J. B. Maxey and others, Bill Evans also served as an officer of the corporation.

A newspaper ad for Green Acres included the following pitch to potential buyers: "A minimum down payment of only $50 cash will buy one of these beautiful homes. These homes are built with best materials . . . FHA specifications . . . and FHA approved."[16]

Homer Maxey turned thirty in March of 1941, and by the end of the year it was safe to say that he had established himself as a successful, independent businessman. Being on secure footing was paramount—he had a growing family to support. The Maxeys' first daughter, Carla, was born in 1935. Glenna arrived next, in 1939, and was christened with the name Glendell.[17]

But then, on December 7, Japan launched a series of coordinated preemptive attacks against Allied military bases in the Pacific and Indian oceans, including the US naval base at Pearl Harbor. The following day, President Roosevelt addressed the nation, announcing that the United States had declared war against Japan (Germany and its allies responded by declaring war on the United States).[18]

Like millions of other American citizens, Homer Maxey volunteered to fight for his country. All his other plans for the future would have to wait.

. . .

The Maxey brothers and their mother, left to right, Homer, Carl, Effie, Robert, and Herschel in 1942. Carl was the only brother who didn't serve in the military, having failed his physical due to injuries from a car wreck. Carl headed numerous construction projects for the Department of Defense, including facilities and dormitories for the Manhattan Project. The other brothers all served in the Navy. Courtesy of the Maxey family.

Homer accepted a commission as lieutenant junior grade in the navy in early 1942.[19] He sold Maxey Lumber for $42,500 and left Lubbock for indoctrination school at Harvard University. After eight weeks, he received additional training at a naval school for amphibious warfare. The navy assigned him to command a flotilla of amphibious ships called LCI (landing craft, infantry).[20] An LCI was a small, armed vessel capable of carrying up to 250 troops or an equivalent amount of cargo, which these vessels did, repeatedly, in support of some of the bloodiest battle campaigns of the war in the Pacific.[21]

Homer's brother Robert also attended the Naval Academy and after graduation entered active duty with the rank of lieutenant. Robert served in the Construction Battalions, or Seabees. The Seabees' official motto, *Construimus, Batuimus,* means "We build, we fight." Better known is their unofficial motto: "Can do!"[22]

Herschel, the youngest sibling, also joined the navy and served as an enlisted man.[23] Injuries from a car wreck contributed to Carl Maxey being designated 4F, which precluded his participation in military service. However, Carl dedicated himself to serving his country by doing what the Maxeys did best: construction. Some of the many defense projects contracted to Carl Maxey's company during the war were located at the atomic bomb research facilities at Los Alamos, New Mexico, and Oak Ridge, Tennessee. The details of some of the projects remained secret.[24]

In the first six months of the war, as Homer completed his training, Japanese forces consolidated their control over countless Pacific island bases between Japan and the western coasts of North and South America. In the first bit of good news for the home front, Allied naval forces, under the overall command of another Texan, Fleet Admiral Chester Nimitz of Fredericksburg, halted the Japanese advance in the Battle of the Coral Sea in May of 1942 and won a strategic victory at Midway in June.[25]

Lt. Homer Maxey's first experiences in a combat zone in the South Pacific occurred sometime during the fall of 1942. Like many veterans of his generation, he did not bother to preserve all of his military records. Fortunately, family members assembled a scrapbook of photos, clippings, notes, letters, and other materials from Homer's military career. Included in the scrapbook is a typewritten list of ports of call for the ship under Maxey's command.

With the Japanese momentum on pause by mid-1942, Allied forces began a counteroffensive at Guadalcanal and the surrounding area in the Solomon Islands archipelago east of Papua New Guinea in the South Pacific. Launched with an amphibious invasion in August 1942 and ending in February 1943, Guadalcanal was one of the bloodiest campaigns of the war. The fighting took place in jungles, on beaches, in the air, on the water, and underwater. When the Allies were at last able to claim victory at Guadalcanal, the tally included 7,100 Allied and 31,000 Japanese soldiers killed. A combined total of more than one hundred ships had been sunk and more than one thousand planes destroyed.

After Guadalcanal, Allied forces began their drive across the Central Pacific, using a strategy referred to as "island hopping." The goal was to conquer strategic enemy island bases and leave others to wither and die by cutting off their lines of resupply.[26]

The massive amphibious operations that landed Allied forces on the beaches of contested islands were more than just battles between fighting forces. They were also giant delivery jobs, in which men and materials had to be brought into zones of violent combat. To serve in a position of command in such complex operations—delivering combat forces, weapons, and the essential materials for setting up forward bases, air strips, and other logistic facilities—was not unlike building a subdivision in a combat zone. The thought must have occurred to Maxey at some point.

Of the various types of amphibious craft used in World War II, the best known is the LCVP (landing craft, vehicle, personnel) or Higgins boat, a boxy, flat-bottomed troop carrier that could run straight up on the beach and disgorge soldiers via the bow ramp. The thirty-six-foot-long vessels were, in essence, shallow-water barges, slow and vulnerable.[27]

The LCIs under Homer's command were a very different type of vessel. The 153-foot-long, shallow-draft vessel was a seaworthy workhorse that could carry up to 250 troops or a combination of men and cargo. Men and smaller supplies were offloaded from narrow ramps that descended on the port and starboard sides of the bow.

Records show that, in addition to combat operations in the Solomons, Maxey also participated in the invasion of Treasury Island, plus operations in the Philippines, the Russell Islands, Guam, Okinawa, and at least a half-dozen others.[28]

Because of the large carrying capacity of the vessels under Homer Maxey's command, unloading was an involved process, and therefore they were not used in the first phase of amphibious landings, when enemy resistance was often the most intense. Even under the best of conditions, however, things could and often did go disastrously wrong.

Less than two weeks after the Allies defeated the Japanese on Guadalcanal, Maxey's squadron took part in Operation Cleanslate, the goal of which was to establish a forward naval base in the Russell Islands. Between February 20 and March 15, 1943, amphibious forces landed 15,500 combat troops and almost fifty thousand tons of supplies. The operations were harassed by constant Japanese air attacks and battered by gigantic Pacific storms. By April, however, the Allies had succeeded in establishing a forward air base on one of the islands.[29]

Years later, I. A. Stephens wrote the following about Homer's role in the November 1943 invasion of Treasury Island:[30]

Many New Zealanders took part in the invasion; one who didn't return from battle was a young captain with whom Homer had shared a friendly visit just hours before. During this heated battle the Allies set fire to the Japs' gun placement while troops landed on the beach and soldiers ran toward the Jap dugouts, throwing hand grenades. This was among the most brutal of all the invasions and Homer was in the thick of it. Under his command his squadron unloaded 225 New Zealand troops and 15 tons of supplies on the beach; at the same time they shot down six Jap planes attacking one of our LCI gunboats. Despite their desperate efforts the gunboat was hit and thirty-three crew members were lost.

Maxey's scrapbook from the war includes photos of the incident showing a veil of smoke rising from the Japanese gunner's position. The captions on the pages containing a series of photographs documenting the incident state that they were taken from LCI 330, the vessel under Maxey's command.

"I found during my first landing that I wasn't scared, or as scared as you think you might be," Maxey told a reporter for the *Lubbock Avalanche-Journal* in 1976. "There were just too many things to do."[31]

After eleven months of combat in the Pacific, Maxey was promoted to lieutenant commander and transferred to the command of a flotilla of seventeen LSMs (landing ships, medium).[32] Larger and heavier than the LCI, the LSM was designed for much heavier cargo. With a length of 203 feet, the LSM could carry tanks, tugboats, and other machinery right up on deck. Its maximum load was five medium or three heavy tanks; six LVTs (landing vehicles, tracked) or nine DUKWs (pronounced "duck," a six-wheeled amphibious truck). Unlike the LCIs, the LSM had a snub-nosed bow that opened and served as a ramp for offloading.[33]

Maxey was home on leave in time for Christmas 1944, a welcome gift for his family. At the time Carla was nine years old and Glenna was five.

Homer also took time to do a little business, purchasing the Caprock Lumber Company from his brother Carl.[34] The business, located at Nineteenth and Avenue Q, had struggled to obtain inventory for local, nongovernment projects during the Depression and war years. In 1943, however, the US economy was picking up steam and Maxey surmised that there would be a big demand for homes after the war.

Carl, who was anxious to start his own contracting business, sold his share of the lumber company to Homer for $20,000. Homer changed the name to Maxey Lumber Company (giving it the same name as the business owned and operated between 1937 and 1942 at Eighth Street and Avenue Q) and recruited Carl's former partner, Harold Blank, to operate it. Blank and Maxey formed a new partnership, assigning 25 percent ownership to Blank and 75 percent to Homer.

This photo was taken January 11, 1945, just before Homer returned to the Pacific front after training on a new type of amphibious vessel, the LCM (landing craft, medium). The strain on the family is evident in photos from this period. Glenna is on the left. Carla on the right. Courtesy of the Maxey family.

Homer, holding Glendell (Glenna), arrived home on leave in 1944 just in time to spend Christmas with the family. Courtesy of the Maxey family.

A Go-Getter

. . .

Maxey's LSM Group II arrived off Okinawa around the end of March 1945.[35] Of all the amphibious operations in the Pacific, Okinawa would be one of the most fiercely contested.[36] In close proximity to Japan, the Japanese saw Okinawa as an extension of their home islands, while the Allies saw it as one of the last stepping stones to Japan's defeat. The fighting lasted eighty-two days. Casualties included the death of more than one hundred thousand Japanese and twelve thousand American soldiers. Many thousands of civilians on the island committed suicide.[37]

During a lull in the fighting in the course of the Okinawa operation, Homer wrote a letter to Melba with good news.[38] His brothers, Robert and Herschel, whose tours were also based in the South Pacific, had come to visit him on his ship. Homer treated them to steak dinners and champagne. He even let them sleep in his stateroom bed for the night. It was the first time in twenty-eight months the brothers had seen each other.

On June 2, 1945, Homer took the time to type a letter to his mother and father describing some of his less felicitous experiences in the Pacific.[39]

Saturday afternoon

June 2, 1945

The required 30 days of censorship regulations have passed and now I may tell you the full details of our experiences, which have been related to you vaguely. We were at Okinawa around the 30th of April at the time the naval forces were receiving heavy damaging blows by the Jap air force. The landings made there were on the western shore of the island and many of the naval vessels were anchored in the harbor off of this side. Our original orders stated that we were to enter this harbor, but on nearing the island our orders were changed and we were sent to a harbor on the eastern shore, Nakagusuku Bay. We interpreted this to mean that the western harbor was not yet secured, which was probably the case.

Entering this harbor we found many of the larger naval units anchored off the shore, shelling the beach. This kept up night and day. Our forces had most of the island except for about eight miles of the southern end. Our front lines stretched across the island, west to east from Yonabaru, which was one of the largest villages. Yonabaru was right on the eastern shore and we could see the village very well from the harbor, although most of the [other] villages had been destroyed. During our stay we watched the forward movements of our lines, which were very slow and difficult. That was where we could see tracer shells firing back and forth and could even see tanks operating, with the aid of field glasses. In daytime the larger naval units got in as close to shore as possible, without danger of going aground on reefs, and then at night [they] anchored further away from shore. In some places in the daytime they would be as close as half a mile but never drawing any fire from the Japs.

The larger ships were anchored in such a way that the landing crafts could throw a smoke screen around them with each air alert. This was very effective and I am sure it kept the Jap pilots from spotting any larger ships in the harbor. We had known of the Japs' fanatical weapons, the suicide planes and boats, and were warned to be on the alert. They had used these weapons in the Philippines and to some extent here.

Having no smoke generator and sitting idly by, the first night watching the air raid, the O.T.C. found a job for us the second night. They had continual patrols at night for these suicide boats, using landing crafts because of the hazardous waters. The next afternoon we were sent a message that we would patrol an area of two and a half miles, which was in part off Jap-held territory and part off our own. We were off shore from a half mile to a mile and crossed a cove in the harbor, which at the time was held by Japs. Our orders were to intercept and destroy these suicide boats. The first night most of us stayed upon the pontoon looking for these boats and about 2:00 A.M. everyone was seeing boats, but they all turned out to be reefs. I was a bit anxious but not too much frightened till I realized how concerned Campbell and the chief bo'sun mate were. They both have been through much action and I began to think I was too ignorant to be afraid.

Anyway we all helped the lookouts till about 2:00 A.M. and then decided to hit the sack and did so and slept peacefully until morning. The next night we went back to the same job and most of us who didn't have any watches turned in around 11:30 P.M. I slept soundly until about 1:00 A.M. when there was the most awful noise and it sounded as if the bottom of the ship were torn off. We had run on a reef and firmly grounded and had to sit there until tide at 8:00 A.M. When I heard the noise I was topside first with nothing on but my shorts.

Then came the night of May 3 and 4. We were patrolling and the Japs launched a planned, concentrated land, sea and air attack. About 10:00 P.M. we received an air raid alert but nothing we could do about it but continue our patrol. We were out of range of the smoke screen and it would only be to the suicide boat's advantage anyway.

About 11:30 we came upon a hornets nest. We sighted four of these boats about 400 yards from our starboard bow. We immediately flashed our search lights on them and opened fire with all guns that could be brought to bear on them. With the light and guns firing, one went to the left and one towards shore and the other two came towards us. One going at our stern and one for the con. They kept coming and we kept firing, even Doc with a carbine. The 40 mm finally disintegrated one and caused it to sort of dissolve in the water about 20 feet from the con. The other exploded about 100 yards off the stern and shook the ship. These boats were all trying to evade us and they were discovered.

About a half hour later we sighted another about 500 yards off our bow and the captain had become quite confident by this time. He kept easing up on it and finally turned the search light on it. It turned and came at us, straight for the bow. The 40 mm was the only gun that could train on it and it fired a few blasts but missed and by this time it was under its range. The 40 can't be trained on the water close to the ship because of the bow ramp. The boat kept coming and we had no guns to bear on it except a Tommy gun manned by the bo'sun on the fo'c'sle. When the boat got about 50 feet from us it sheared off to the right and came alongside our forepart of the ship within 10 feet. As it changed course to the right it came in range of the 50s and they all began pouring lead and it soon was aflame. This boat drifted away from us about 25 yards and exploded with another good shake of the ship. Many of us have wondered what caused the boat to shear from its course and many of us are thankful that God was with us. Perhaps what happened, the bo'sun with the Tommy gun killed the driver. This was a larger boat than the other and probably was a squadron leader. The other boats carried only one or two men. Before this boat exploded we could see two men diving out of it but they didn't get far.

An hour later we set a boat aflame 400 yards ahead of our ship. It didn't explode but went up in flames as our shells ignited the gasoline.

The fifth boat was sighted among the reefs and we had to go for him. He began to get behind us, knowing that our firepower was weakest on our stern. As he made a dash past the ship, about 300 yards away, we turned on the searchlight and began firing, but apparently missing him. He turned to come in at the stern and the captain swung the ship in order to bring guns to bear on him. As we swung he stopped momentarily and during the lull of firing he exploded with the biggest explosion of any of the others. Perhaps one of the incendiary shells set off the charge.

I had the opportunity to examine two of these boats captured by the marines in coves. They are especially built for the purpose, and speedy, around 35 knots and carry a charge of about 500 lbs. of TNT. The irony of it all, they are powered by Chevrolet motors with a few changes gearing them up.

During all the excitement, while we were lighted up like a Christmas tree, there was an air raid going on, although at the time we were unaware of it.

Fifteen boats were destroyed that night. Some by other LSM, LCI, but we got more than anyone else and got a "well-done" from the Admiral. I have never been so glad to see daylight come in my life and going back the next night was anything but pleasant.

We found no boats the next night but ran into suicide swimmers. These were swimmers attempting to swim out to the larger ships with the aid of a float. They carried a large charge on their back and would attach it to the side of the ship. I am sure we sent some of them to join their ancestors of the Rising Sun.

This will give you more details of our experiences and clear all questions as to what our flags mean. It was quite an experience but much too personal for me.

The job of conveying the terrors of such combat experience would challenge even the most gifted of writers. For Maxey to say that it was "much too personal for me" appears to be a creative way of saying that it was frightening beyond description, although it could also be yet another expression of his dry wit. It has been observed that World War II veterans tend to be reticent about intensely personal experiences, but a similar generalization has also been made regarding West Texans. Dan Anthony, Glenna Goodacre's longtime studio manager, had the following comment: "Generally speaking, the Maxeys don't do introspection. It's just the way they are."[40]

Regarding the suicide boats, Maxey remarks that "the irony of it all" was that the vessels were powered by Chevrolet motors, leaving unstated the fact that the diesel engines in the US landing craft were also manufactured by Chevrolet's parent company, General Motors.

The goal at the end of such combat operations in the Pacific was Operation Downfall, the invasion of the home islands of Japan. Neither Americans at home nor the soldiers in the field were aware that Allied casualties in Operation Downfall were expected to run into the hundreds of thousands, perhaps millions. Lt. Cdr. Homer Maxey led his group of ships into innumerable battles without a scratch, but in late July or August 1945 he smashed his knee against the bow of his ship while transferring to another ship on a sea ladder.

The accident required surgery and left him with a lifelong limp and a strong aversion to any medical procedures that involved entering an operating room. Maxey was still recovering in Saipan in August when a startling headline came to his attention.[41]

On Monday, August 6, 1945, a US Army Air Corps B-29 had dropped an atomic bomb over the Japanese city of Hiroshima. A uranium fission bomb code-named Little Boy was detonated above the city, killing an estimated 90,000–166,000 people.[42] Three days later, Fat Man, a plutonium implosion-type fission bomb, was detonated over the Japanese city of Nagasaki, killing an estimated 60,000–80,000 people. Japan surrendered. Operation Downfall would not be necessary.

Emperor Hirohito signed the treaty of capitulation on the deck of the battleship USS *Missouri* on September 2, 1945. The following month, Maxey received his discharge from the US Navy. He came home to Lubbock to his family and friends, honored to have served his country, but also eager to get back to work. As his friend, I. A. Stephens put it in his birthday tribute, "Homer set out to make up for lost time."

While home on leave from the Pacific war in 1944, Homer Maxey made time to complete a deal to found his lumber company, which would keep an army of hammers swinging in West Texas once the hostilities ended. Courtesy of the Maxey family.

Two very special photos in Homer's album of World War II pictures depict the unlikely reunion of the three Maxey brothers on Guam in mid-1945. Left to right, Homer, Carl, and Herschel. No one remembers the dog or where it came from, but it could possibly have been a shipboard companion. Courtesy of the Maxey family.

Chapter 4

THE BOOM
YEARS AND THE
MIDAS TOUCH

omer Maxey was still wearing his navy uniform when
he left Lubbock on a series of business meetings in late
1945.[1] It is possible he had not had time to shop for a
new business suit, but a savvy individual like Maxey must have known that a
military uniform could be an advantage during business negotiations.

One leg of the trip took Maxey to Oregon, where he met with lumber
mill representatives and wholesale suppliers to secure new sources of supply
for Maxey Lumber Company. He returned with large quantities of Oregon
lumber and oak flooring. For storage he used army barracks purchased at government salvage sales.

Maxey Lumber would become profitable enough to make both Homer
and his partner Harold Blank very wealthy men. At a time when people were
feeling energized and optimistic after a decade and a half of economic depression and war, Maxey Lumber was the main supplier of building materials for
a region encompassing at least nineteen counties.[2]

The following year, in 1946, Maxey founded Homer G. Maxey & Co., a
wholesale plumbing and electrical supply business.[3] Again, Maxey enlisted
a very capable associate, Lee Fields, to manage the operation for a 25 percent share. A policy of generous credit terms to contractors, coupled with a

The Veterans Administration Building, located on Nineteenth Street in Lubbock, was one of Maxey's two prestigious construction projects of 1949. Homer partnered with his brother Carl on both projects. Photo by Winston Reeves. Courtesy of the City of Lubbock.

continuing commitment to innovational approaches to display and service, proved to be a winning formula for another successful Maxey enterprise. In 1963, the business reported gross sales of $7.5 million.[4]

Maxey was one of the first developers of suburban retail centers in the South Plains region. He partnered again with Harold Blank in 1946 to build the Plaza Shopping Center at the corner of Twenty-Sixth and Boston, adjacent to the Green Acres subdivision. Suburban retail centers were a relatively new development during the postwar era. Plaza was one of the first of several built by Maxey.[5] Construction of the nine-building corner retail strip was contracted to Homer's brother, Robert. The center was the original location for a new dress shop called Margaret's, which later moved to a much larger space on Broadway where it became a downtown retail and cultural landmark. The owner, Margaret Talkington, and her husband, J. T. Talkington, were next-door neighbors of Homer and Melba and were among the Maxeys' closest friends.[6]

Maxey was also one of the first builders of modern apartment complexes

The Plaza Apartments, built by Maxey and partners in 1948 with FHA assistance, were completely renovated in 2010 and the name changed to the Townhomes at O'Neil Terrace. Photo by Winston Reeves. Courtesy of the Southwest Collection/Special Collections Library at Texas Tech University.

in the region. Plaza Apartments, a complex of townhomes and duplexes located at 2104 Thirty-Fourth Street, was the first of several constructed by Maxey and partners between 1948 and the early 1950s. The Plaza residential project was also significant because it was the first built under the auspices of Plaza Building Corporation, an entity Maxey formed with several other investors in 1948, including his longtime friend and attorney, Bill Evans.[7]

During the same time period, Maxey founded numerous other partnerships and corporations with various configurations of investors. Some of the new construction projects were the Lubbock Apartments, a 52-unit complex on A Street; Modern Manor, a 293-unit complex at 4232 Boston Avenue; and in Amarillo, a 346-unit complex also called Green Acres.

"Homer was one of the first post-World War II real estate developers of that type in Lubbock and Amarillo," says S. Tom Morris, an Amarillo attorney who, at one point, would represent the defense in Maxey's lengthy litigation against Citizens National Bank.[8] "There was a huge demand for housing after the war and there was really no such thing as apartment complexes. Homer

Carl Maxey's office in 1947. Photo by Winston Reeves. Courtesy of the Southwest Collection/Special Collections Library at Texas Tech University.

was a pioneer in that. When he built Green Acres in Amarillo, it was far and away the biggest apartment complex in town at the time. Homer was very successful."

Also in 1948, Homer, his brother Robert, and eight other investors put up equal shares to organize American State Bank.[9] With $250,000 in assets and five employees, the bank opened for business on May 20 of that year. Work was still progressing on the building, however, so for the first three months, customers were served from a tiny, temporary, faux log cabin at 1401 Avenue Q.[10]

In 1949, Homer and several partners, including his brother Carl, built two Veterans Administration buildings, one in downtown Lubbock and another in Houston. The Stanolind Oil Building, located next door to the Veterans Administration building in Lubbock, was yet another of Maxey's construction projects, again with Carl as a member of the partnership.

By 1950, Maxey had succumbed to what some called "oil fever."[11] Maxey and I. A. Stephens bought oil leases in Young, Stephens, Throckmorton, and Palo Pinto counties.[12] Stephens said that, like many Lubbock businessmen who became involved in wildcat drilling ventures, he wasn't searching for oil, but a good tax write-off among the contemporaries he included in that group were Homer and Carl Maxey, Dub Rushing, and Vernon Thompson.

One of their most profitable investments came about when George P. Livermore, president of Great Western Drilling Company, offered Maxey, Stephens, and Rushing a half interest in his oil leases in Borden County. Out of sixteen drilling sites, thirteen became producing wells.

Stephens used his share of the profits from the Borden County wells to purchase the Cobb chain of department stores. According to Stephens, Rushing's share "made him stronger financially than any of his other ventures." Maxey sold his share in the leases in 1952 for $395,000, an amount equivalent to over $3,434,000 in 2012 dollars.[13]

Within five years after Homer Maxey returned to civilian life in Lubbock, he was a very wealthy man. In 1949 and 1950, his share of profits from just three of his construction projects—the Stanolind Oil Building and the two Veterans Administration buildings—ran a total of $331,000. He also earned $60,000 a year from his shares of a drilling company, plus monthly salaries or profit distributions from American State Bank, Maxey Lumber, Homer G. Maxey & Co., and numerous other sources. A rough tally of these sums shows that, by the mid-1950s or thereabouts, Maxey was one of Lubbock's millionaires.[14]

In August 1951, large, boisterous crowds came out to celebrate what was one of the splashiest debuts of Homer Maxey's career: the grand opening of the Plainsman Hotel at 2101 Avenue Q. The buzz in the air was tangible, for the Plainsman was an eye-catching showpiece of ultramodern fifties design. Everything about the place was unique and first class, even the color scheme and the fact that all the rooms had ice-cold drinking water piped in from a large underground storage tank. Commanding the southwest corner of Twenty-First and Avenue Q, the hotel was a mere two stories in height, but it presented a lean, long, streamlined façade to Avenue Q, with a covered lobby entrance that gave a bold cue that it was something modern, new, and classy. West Texas had never seen anything like it.

The restaurant offered everything from sixty-cent lunches to six-course dinners for $1.65 to $2.50. A barbershop in the basement advertised haircuts for a dollar. Room prices began at $4.50.

The event was covered in a special section of the *Lubbock Avalanche*. "As hundreds of Lubbockites and South Plainsmen view the richly-decorated interior of the new building this afternoon and tonight, they will be seeing

One of hundreds of modern ranch style homes built by Homer Maxey in the 1940s and 1950s. Photo by Winston Reeves. Courtesy of the Southwest Collection/Special Collections Library at Texas Tech University.

The interior of this Maxey-built home also showcases Homer's fondness for mid-century modern design. Photo by Winston Reeves. Courtesy of the Southwest Collection/Special Collections Library at Texas Tech University.

The man in the white shirt paying close attention to the product demonstration at H. G. Maxey & Company is Dan Law, the ex-Red Raider who started out at the bottom and worked his way up the ladder to the very top. Photo by Rollin Herald. Courtesy of the Rollin Herald Estate and Southwest Collection/Special Collections Library at Texas Tech University.

This classic shot by photographer Winston Reeves showcases the ultramodern design of the Plainsman Hotel, which opened to great fanfare in the fall of 1951. Photo by Winston Reeves. Courtesy of the Southwest Collection/Special Collections Library at Texas Tech University.

Broke, Not Broken

modern hotel design and decoration carried to its highest peak," said the article.[15]

A photo spread for the article included one particular picture that spoke volumes about not only the import of the occasion, but the dynamics of the political and business world of Lubbock: a group shot of W. G. Alderson, president of the Lubbock Chamber of Commerce and owner of Alderson Cadillac dealership; Coby Briehn; Maxey; Mayor Clarence Whiteside; and Charlie Guy. Maxey's face shows just a trace of a smirk, while Guy looks happy, almost giddy.

Homer's smirk and Guy's smile may have had something to do with the name of the hotel. Hanging behind the front desk was a very special framed piece of art: Tige Formby's signed, original drawing of Charlie Guy's alter ego, The Plainsman. The picture had hung in Guy's office for many years. One day before the formal opening of the hotel, Homer asked Guy about borrowing the artwork so he could get a copy made for the hotel. Guy replied, "I'll go you one better. I'll lend you the picture for hanging in your new hotel for so long as you may wish to have it there." The loan of the artwork was the second favor the newspaperman granted to Maxey in regard to the hotel. According to an article in the *Avalanche-Journal*, Guy owned the trademark on the term "The Plainsman" and had granted permission for its use on three other occasions during the twenty-five years he had been writing his column under that byline. The others included a rail line between Floydada and Oklahoma City, a Sunday school class, and a movie theater.[16]

"Homer and his friends knew how to make things happen," says Roy Middleton, a longtime Lubbock real estate developer.[17] "Part of it was the times. After the war it was easy to borrow money and easy to make it. But these guys, and Homer in particular, they were the big wheeler dealers. It's kind of a lost breed. They don't make them like that anymore."

Another reason men like Maxey were able to "make things happen" was that they were members of a tight-knit club whose members either served as public officials or hand-picked the men who were elected to those positions.[18] Maxey served two terms on the city commission (the present-day city council) from 1956 to 1960. It was the only time he served an elected position in a government body, and yet Maxey exerted his influence on local affairs in numerous other ways.

Like his father, Homer also served as a member or president of various committees and boards that were nongovernmental, the most influential be-

Ground-breaking ceremonies for Lub. Auditorium + Col. March 1955

Breaking ground for the new Lubbock municipal auditorium, March 1955. The auditorium project had been in the planning stage for years, but during Homer Maxey's terms on the city commission, the building of the facility finally got under way. Homer, wearing a dark suit, is on the right side of the row of figures standing just behind the men who are bent over with shovels. Those that attended the groundbreaking include members of the city commission and chamber of commerce, civic leaders, and representatives from the university. Courtesy of the Maxey family.

ing the chamber of commerce, which not only performed public relations functions but also helped shape growth and development. As an indication of the Chamber's influence, Maxey was one of the prominent Lubbockites who posed for a photograph of the ground-breaking ceremony for the Lubbock Municipal Auditorium and Coliseum in 1955, a year before he was elected to the city commission.

Maxey's other nonpolitical activities included roles as president or chairman of several charitable organizations. Like his father, Homer served on the board of First United Methodist Church of Lubbock and was an aggressive fundraiser for the church's building fund. In the early 1950s, Homer and several other church leaders made written appeals to congregation members, challenging them to make generous contributions toward a program for building the new sanctuary. The appeals were in the form of letters from each individual, written on their respective business letterheads, and reproduced in the church bulletin. Homer's letter sets the tone with the very first, typed in all caps: "LET'S BUILD OUR NEW CHURCH NOW!" M. C. Overton's letter ended with a view to posterity: "The influence of this church will help to make Lubbock a better place in which to live for the next one hundred years." The pitch by Cadillac dealer W. G. Alderson showed that at least some empire builders were not shy about reminding people of their past and present leadership roles. "Possibly because I was among the first group connected with the movement to build a new church," Alderson wrote, "Miss Young has asked me to write just how I feel about this movement at the present time. It was my privilege to head the group in the early part of 1945 in buying and raising money to pay for the south half of the block and in raising a portion of the money for the building fund . . ."[19]

In 1961 Homer Maxey served as chairman of the Christmas Seals fund-raising drive for the Lubbock County Tuberculosis Foundation.[20] Melba Maxey, too, was active in local philanthropic and social clubs. She was founding member of the Lubbock Chapter of the Women's League and the Lubbock Garden Club. She also awarded twenty-one scholarships through the Texas Tech College of Home Economics.[21]

Besides his business ventures, church, and family, there was nothing Homer Maxey put more energy into than his support for Texas Tech—in particular, the football team. He maintained close ties with coaches, athletic directors, and many of the players.[22] From 1951 to 1953 Maxey served as president of the Matador Club, a Texas Tech athletics booster organization that dated back to at least 1929. It was a volunteer job, as the club had no paid employees until 1958.[23] During Maxey's term the organization voted to change its name to the Lubbock Chapter of the Red Raiders Club ("Matadors" was a holdover from the former name of the Tech football team, which was changed to Red Raiders in 1937).[24] Annual fund-raising efforts during Maxey's term exceeded $100,000, more than meeting the goal of awarding between 100 and 125 scholarships annually.[25]

The typical agenda at a meeting of the city commission in those days revealed an unglamorous grocery list for taking care of the basic functions of a growing city—things like zoning changes, sewer lines, and paving contracts, voting on approving parades, street banners, and free parking for special occasions, the definition of and restrictions on public dances, and permits for music to be played from outdoor loudspeakers in a shopping center. There is little drama to be found in the minutes of the city commission between 1956 and 1960. However, all the signs of a city experiencing tremendous growth and development are there.[26]

During the same time period, the city commenced construction of the city auditorium and coliseum. Being a joint effort with Texas Tech and located on the college campus added numerous complications and delays since the project originated in 1943. Another important step for a fast-growing metropolis in the postwar era was the approval of plans for expansion of runways and other facilities at the Lubbock airport in order to accommodate jet-powered aircraft.[27]

The commission also approved and appropriated funds for expanding city parks and playgrounds and the addition of a third floor to city hall. New subdivisions were being built and annexed on the outskirts of the city, moving Lubbock's population center further to the southwest. Maxey himself built a good number of the new neighborhoods. Lubbock civic leaders had discussed and laid the groundwork for Loop 289, which would accommodate traffic in an outer belt around the urban area, allowing for faster commutes between the new suburbs and other areas, including downtown, which was still the location of the majority of jobs. The loop had been in discussion for years, but it wasn't until Maxey's first term on the city commission that the route was finalized and the city began purchasing rights-of-way and initiating all the efforts in preparation for road construction.

A map obtained from the City of Lubbock titled "City of Lubbock Annexation History by Decade" illustrates the dramatic growth of the city in the first twenty years after World War II, a period that coincides with the years Homer Maxey was building new subdivisions and also includes his two terms on the city commission.[28] In the years 1940–50 Lubbock was the second fastest growing city in the United States, going from population 31,853 to 71,747, which reflects a rate of 125.2 percent. Between 1950 and 1960, the population grew to 128,068, a rate of 79.4 percent.[29]

Urban renewal was one of the more consequential items on the agenda of the city commission during Maxey's term.[30] Under provisions of the US Housing Act of 1949, various urban areas, including Lubbock, could apply for federal assistance in clearing slum areas and substandard housing. Federal money paid for surveys in several sections of the city where substandard housing existed. Once the survey and plans were approved, residents were given help to find new housing, and then the bulldozers went to work. Although the program was well intended, it came under criticism in later years (not only in Lubbock, but across the country), in part because of its uneven

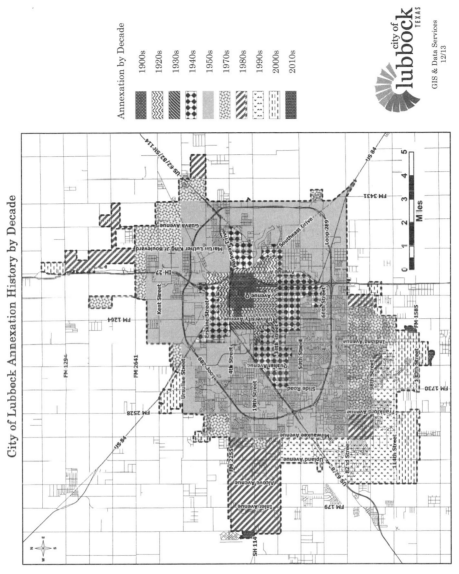

City of Lubbock Annexation History by Decade

Annexation by Decade
1900s 1920s 1930s 1940s 1950s 1970s 1980s 1990s 2000s 2010s

city of lubbock
TEXAS
GIS & Data Services 12/13

This map shows how much the city of Lubbock grew during the 1940s and 1950s, the years when Homer Maxey was most active as a developer. (For a color version of this map, visit the GIS and Data Services Department, City of Lubbock, www.ci.Lubbock. tx.us.) Courtesy of the City of Lubbock.

benefits for the predominantly minority populations it displaced. And even though the program included enticements for redevelopment, it wasn't until the massive recovery effort after the 1970 tornado that the areas were finally rebuilt.[31]

Also in the 1950s, Lubbock, along with the rest of the country, was forced to face the reality of the landmark US Supreme Court unanimous (90) ruling on May 17, 1954, in the case of *Brown v. Board of Education*. The court's ruling stated that the previous doctrine of "separate but equal" school facilities for white and African American students was inherently unequal and unconstitutional. The story of the integration of the public school system in Lubbock is a contentious and complicated one that didn't officially end until 1992, but Maxey played no official role in it. The board of the Lubbock Independent School District was the body charged with responding to federal court orders on integration, and Maxey was never a board member.[32]

On the subject of race, Glenna Goodacre describes her father as "an old Southerner [who] believed in separate races." In the 1950s and 1960s, it was unusual to find a white, middle-aged West Texan who was a progressive on racial issues. Homer Maxey was no exception.[33]

One other rather ambiguous story about political controversy during Maxey's term as a commissioner deserves mention. The story appears to have originated with William Curry Holden, historian, archeologist, and director of the Museum of Texas Tech University. An expert on the indigenous Pueblo Indians of the Southwest, Holden was involved in the construction of the first adobe homes in Lubbock. The first was designed by his wife, Olive Holden, and built in 1929. After her death in 1937, Holden built a second, smaller adobe residence next door.

Holden later claimed that after the adobe homes were built, the city commission passed an ordinance banning the construction of such residences, telling an interviewer that the lumber companies had pushed for the ban because they didn't want adobe construction to cut into their profits. Holden also mentioned the fact that two out of the four city commissioners were in the lumber business.

If the story is true, it would imply corrupt influence on the part of Homer Maxey, owner of Maxey Lumber Company, and S. S. Forrest, Jr., the owner of Forrest Lumber Company. Forrest was elected mayor in 1956, the same year Maxey was elected to place four on the commission. However, an exhaustive search by the staff of the city secretary's office found no such ordinance. A search through the minutes of the city commission from the years 1956 through 1960 also found nothing. Staff members at GIS and Data Services (formerly City of Lubbock Planning Department), who performed extensive research on Holden's adobe homes so that they could be listed on the National Register of Historic Places, found no documentation of a ban on adobe construction in Lubbock.

Dr. Meredith McClain, a Texas Tech language professor who owns and lives in one of the Holden adobes, is well aware of the story. She refers to it as a "legend."[34] Jane Holden Kelly, daughter of William Curry Holden, grew up with the story and regarded it as factual.[35]

Don Bundock, a second-generation builder in Lubbock (his father started H. R. Bundock, Inc., general contractors in commercial construction, in 1936) said, "My recollection on the subject of adobe is that it was spoken of as 'against a city ordinance.'"[36] Berwyn Tisdel, a Lubbock native who worked as a commercial architect for forty-five years, had never heard of a ban on adobe construction. Jackie Cox, who started in the lumber business in Lubbock in 1960 and retired several decades later, never heard of such a thing, either.[37]

Perhaps someday a diligent researcher will turn up concrete evidence of a ban on adobe construction in Lubbock. Or perhaps they will perform an even more exhaustive search and conclude that the story of the adobe ban qualifies as a Lubbock urban myth.

Homer Maxey was a member of an elite circle of powerful Lubbock citizens known variously as the "empire builders" or the "king makers."[38] The group was composed of Lubbock's leading merchants, bankers, attorneys, and other important professionals, such as the head of the chamber of commerce, and Charlie Guy, the editor and publisher of the Lubbock Avalanche-Journal. The men would gather at regular round-table breakfast or lunch meetings to discuss all the major issues facing the town and, after coming to a consensus, decide on plans of action, including the candidates for the next municipal election. The group was, in effect, the town's shadow government.

The arrangement had its beginnings in the 1920s, when J. B. Maxey was an active member of the group. During Homer Maxey's years of involvement with the group, its membership included the aforementioned W. G. Alderson, owner of Alderson Cadillac dealership; Roy Furr, founder and CEO of Furr's supermarkets; Charlie Guy, editor-publisher of the Lubbock Avalanche-Journal; C. E. Maedgen, CEO of Lubbock National Bank; Retha Martin, Dunlap's department stores, board of Citizens National Bank; James Milam, a senior partner at the law firm Crenshaw, Dupree & Milam and a director of First National Bank; Jack Payne, CEO of American State Bank; Walter Posey, CEO of First National Bank; and Parker Prouty, president of the Lubbock Avalanche-Journal.

Although one had to be a member of the group or an invited guest to attend their meetings, there was nothing secret about the existence of the empire builders or the influence they wielded. In fact, election coverage in the *Avalanche-Journal* mentioned which candidates were to be supported by the group and which ones were not. It was a rare thing for one of the group's candidates to lose a race. Until the 1960s, when their power began to dissipate, the empire builders' stamp of approval was, more often than not, a prerequisite for holding municipal office in Lubbock.

To an outside observer, the arrangement could seem incompatible with modern democracy. An authoritative treatment of the subject can be found in the book *Lubbock: From Town to City*, in the chapter by Roger Carl Schaefer (a retired Texas Tech political science professor) titled "Law and Politics in Lubbock 1945 to the Present." According to Schaefer, members of the empire builders held the sincere belief that they were acting in the best interests of Lubbock and the South Plains region.

> Entrance into this group was structured around performance. That is, persons had to earn their way, or "pay their dues," by performing various civic tasks such as serving on city boards or commissions, or working on civic fund-raising committees, or active involvement in the chamber of commerce. Only after demonstrating a commitment to Lubbock by work such as this were individuals regularly invited to attend these candidate slating meetings.[39]

Lubbock was not unique in having a group like the empire builders. Historians have noted that such groups tend to exist in municipalities of a certain size and demographic. In fact, for many years before J. B. Maxey moved the family to Lubbock, he had been fulfilling all the corresponding duties described by Schaefer in Plainview. To a large extent, the dynamic of the group was an extension of the turn-of-the-century frontier ethic. As leaders of the community's business, political, and church life, they made decisions and took actions that helped ensure Lubbock's very survival; in later years, their actions spurred further growth and development.

Whether the individual members of the empire builders club ever realized it or not, they were a vital part of a system in which preservation of the status quo was a major priority. However benevolent and well-intentioned their efforts toward the minority population in Lubbock, the city's at-large system for electing the city commissioners and mayor ensured that the faces of those elected officials remained white for many decades. In 1983 a federal court found the at-large system to be in violation of the amended 1965 Voting Rights Act, and the city adopted a single-member district system for what was by then referred to as the city council.[40]

"These were people who were community driven," said J. C. Chambers,[41] a Lubbock native, civic leader, and businessman. "Everyone said they were an elitist group . . . What I saw was a group of concerned people who said let's pick someone to lead the community."[42]

According to Schaefer, the empire builders' hold on the city dissipated in the early 1960s. After the poor showing of the group's hand-picked candidates in the city election of 1960, members of the group, including Homer Maxey, attempted to create a new citizens' organization that would serve the same function. Despite a well-publicized official launch in 1962, the effort quickly fizzled out.

The irony is that by the 1960s, Lubbock was a town of sprawling suburban neighborhoods with a stagnant, neglected downtown in the center. The empire builders club had always been synonymous with the downtown business interests. As Lubbock grew and its population center shifted, the power of the empire builders faded. They were, in a way, victims of their own success.

Homer Maxey was finished with politics after 1960. He was also determined to get out of urban development. Growth in Lubbock had slowed, and Maxey decided on a new direction for himself. As for state and national politics, it is doubtful that he expended much energy or capital on any campaigns or issues.

Lubbock's conservative, pro-business stance, along with the revved-up economic climate of the postwar years, created an ideal environment for ambitious entrepreneurs, but even Homer Maxey realized there was more to life than making money. According to daughter Glenna Goodacre, her father's primary interests were his family and his church, making money, and Texas Tech—and not necessarily in that order. Although Homer could seem consumed with his business interests to the point of distraction, he was a passionate and very involved father, leaving both daughters with a vivid set of memories.

Just as being the child of Homer Maxey could have both advantages and disadvantages, growing up in an agricultural town hundreds of miles from the nearest big city also had pluses and minuses. The Maxey girls and their contemporaries, however, did have certain bragging rights. Not many American teenagers in the 1950s, for example, could say they had grown up with a rock 'n' roll star.[43]

Back in the fall of 1951, when a good many of the adults in Lubbock were buzzing with excitement over the opening of a swanky new hotel, their school-age children were bopping to the beat of a musical duo named Buddy and Bob, who got their start playing junior high assemblies and local radio shows. Buddy Holly was still spelling his last name "Holley" at the time (the change was adopted when the name was misspelled on the label of his first record). A member of Lubbock High School class of 1956, Buddy had his first hit in 1957 with "That'll Be the Day." The title was inspired by a line spoken repeatedly by John Wayne in the movie *The Searchers*.[44]

Carla, Glenna, and their cousins were among the Lubbock teenagers who enjoyed Buddy Holly's style of rock 'n' roll music long before the rest of the world had ever heard his twanging voice or glimpsed his trademark oversized glasses. "We all thought Buddy was wonderful," says Marcia Abbott. "I think we knew then that he was going to be very, very famous someday."[45]

One of Holly's big breaks was a gig on June 3, 1955, opening for Elvis Presley at Connelly's Pontiac Showroom in Lubbock. It was a free admission show, sponsored by the car dealer to attract customers. Marcia remembers enjoying Holly's performance, but Elvis knocked her socks off. "We were all screaming and carrying on," she says. "He signed my arm, but my mother made me wash it off. Nice girls don't do that, you know."

An airplane crash in an Iowa cornfield on February 3, 1959, claimed the lives of Buddy Holly and fellow performers Ritchie Valens and J. P. "The Big Bopper" Richardson.[46] Holly's legend and his music helped inspire and encourage fellow Lubbockites like Mac Davis, Joe Ely, Butch Hancock, Lloyd Maines, and Terry Allen.

Although they followed in Holly's footsteps, most of these artists would not find their voices until after leaving Lubbock. They credited the town with artistic inspiration, but at the same time felt it was too small and confining for them to realize their full potential as artists. Maxey's daughters, Carla and Glenna, however, had no qualms about growing up in Lubbock. Both daughters recall a happy, loving, and contented home life. No matter how busy Homer was with his business ventures, he always made time for his family.

Glenna and Carla share fond memories of playing at their father's lumberyard as children. "We used to go down to the lumberyard on Saturday," says Glenna, "just to stack nails and screws and be there in the lumberyard. We thought that was really big stuff."[47]

The family spent most of the summer months at a cabin Homer built after the war near Cowles, New Mexico, located on an old dude ranch high in the Sangre de Cristo Mountains. Within a few years, his brother Carl and various friends of the Maxeys, including the Rushings, all had erected cabins in the area.

"In those days," says DeEtte, "Carla was 'Daddy's girl,' and Glenna was closest to her mother. That's because Carla was so much like Melba and Glenna was just like Homer. You get it? Opposites attract."[48]

"Glenna always said I was on one side of the fence with Daddy while she and Mother were on the other," says Carla, "and that's why we got along."

It didn't hurt that Carla loved football. "Homer was the joy of my life," Carla says of her father. "He took me to every football game, in high school and at Tech. He had season tickets on the fifty-yard line for Tech games. In high school we'd take off and drive up to Tulsa, anywhere there was a game I wanted to go to. Even when he was building the Plainsman Hotel, he'd get the managers to drop everything and go with us."[49]

Carla, who married Tommy Elliott upon graduating from high school, attended Tech for two years and juggled the responsibilities of being a mother, homemaker, and college student. She quit school to concentrate on her favorite two of the three. Elliott had received a football scholarship to Tech when he graduated from Lubbock High in 1954, and when he and Carla got married, he felt as though his life was a "Cinderella story."

"I was a hometown boy and Mama and Daddy wanted me to go to Texas Tech," he says. "If you go to Tech you get free tickets for your parents. That's a big deal. So I went to Tech and I did OK."[50]

Elliott's favorite year in football was 1955. That was the year the Red Raiders played the University of Texas Longhorns in Memorial Stadium in Austin. The date, September 17, 1955, is an important one to Longhorns fans, too, because it was the first night game at Memorial Stadium. Elliott relished the occasion because he got to play against a handful of former teammates from Lubbock High. "They kind of belittled me and made fun of me for going to Texas Tech," he says. "I wanted to teach them a lesson, and we sure as hell did." That night, forty-seven thousand spectators, under the brand-new stadium lights, got to watch the Red Raiders beat the Longhorns 20–14.

By about the same time, Glenna was proving she had considerable potential as an artist. Even as she designed the logo and other artwork for the Monterey High School yearbook, Homer realized that his daughter had much loftier goals in mind. In the summer of 1956, the family sailed to Europe on the Cunard ocean liner QE2 for the express purpose of furthering his younger daughter's artistic education.

"It was a fabulous, fabulous experience," remembers Glenna.[51] "I was sixteen years old and it was really something, getting a chance to compare my thinking to, say, Michelangelo's. To go from doing pictures in the high school yearbook and designing the logo for the Plainsman, to the Louvre."

The trip was an intense experience for other reasons as well. "I guess one

Boom Years and Midas Touch

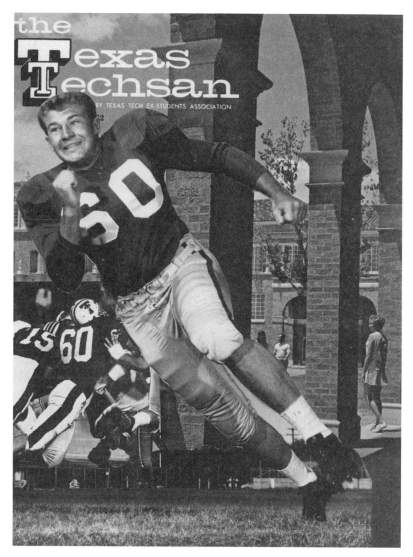

A collage in the Maxey family album featuring Tommy Elliot, who married Homer's daughter Carla during his first year playing football for Texas Tech. Courtesy of the Texas Tech University Alumni Association.

of the main impressions I remember is Daddy's urge to show off his knowledge and his need for everyone to be enamored of what he was doing for us," she says. "He had everything completely planned out to the last detail, every side trip, every museum, everything. Daddy was very, very meticulous."

Glenna's eventual success as an artist, including a sculpture of William Curry Holden on view in the rotunda of the Museum of Texas Tech, a statue of Preston Smith (former Texas governor and Tech alumnus) and the sprawling, interactive Park Place on the Texas Tech campus, can be interpreted as a testament to the work ethic and civic pride she learned at Homer's knee.

During the 1950s, the Maxeys lived in a neighborhood called Tanglewood Estates. The land was part of a tract owned by the Arnett family and was first known as Bobalet Heights, named for the two Arnett siblings, Samuel Cullen "Bobby" Arnett III and Arlett Arnett.

All four of J. B. Maxey's sons built homes in the area. As the neighborhood was developed, the most prominent families in Lubbock could be found there, within a radius of just a few blocks.

Homer and Melba built their first home on 21st Street, right across from J. T. and Margaret Talkington. Carla and Glenna grew up playing at the Talkingtons' house. The Talkingtons had no kids of their own, so they became second parents to the offspring of their closest friends. When interviewed in early 2010, at the age of ninety-five (she died on December 15 of that year), Margaret Talkington's memories of the Maxeys were still vivid. "Homer and Melba were a wonderful couple," she said. "Homer was a wonderful businessman and a very interesting person. He had his lumberyard and other businesses, and he was able to do whatever he wanted to. He had a dry sense of humor, a very, very dry wit."

Talkington recalled that Carla was the quieter of the two Maxey girls. "She was always a sweet girl and well-behaved, but Glenna got the spotlight," she said. "Glenna was the artistic one, always making pictures. Her mother was very artistically talented, too."[52]

On Saturdays the Maxey girls rode their horses through the neighborhood with their boyfriends. On Sundays, they washed and groomed the horses in the front yard.

According to DeEtte Maxey Cobb, her father, Carl, built the first house in Bobalet Heights, at Twenty-Third. "We moved from Green Acres," says DeEtte. "[The house] was made of Austin stone. Robert (Maxey) built his house after that, also on Twenty-Third, but on the other side of Tech Terrace. . . . Our neighbors included the Fultons, Dentons, Keeneys, (E. W.) Williams. . . . Everybody lived around there." Everybody, that is, who was a member of Lubbock's more prosperous clique.[53]

The first home Homer and Melba built in the subdivision is a striking 1950s ranch home that exhibits the best of mid-century design. The architect was Homer's brother Herschel. Judging from his work, Herschel had a great deal of talent and a great eye for design, but he did not enjoy a long and happy life. "Herschel never had a lot of success," says DeEtte, "and then his wife divorced him, and I don't think he ever was happy again. But he was sweet and very funny. He and my dad were the funniest of the Maxey brothers."

Glenna might disagree with that assessment. "Oh, my, he was funny," she says of her father. "I'll never forget standing in line at Shelly Furr's wedding, and Mother said, whispering, 'Homer, your fly is undone.' He said, out loud, 'Oh, well, you know, as Winston Churchill always said, a dead bird can't fall out of its cage.' So that was picked up and repeated by everyone all the way down the line, and people were in hysterics. It was just so funny."[54]

Herschel also designed the house Homer and Melba built in the late 1950s. Located at 2104 Vicksburg Avenue, less than a block from the previous residence, the Vicksburg house is also a showcase of a fifties modern design, but without the ranch home trimmings.

Carla and Glenna grew up as members of what was sometimes referred to as the "Lubbock aristocracy." The term was not always meant as a compliment. Sam Levenson, a former vice president of Citizens National Bank, would use the term sarcastically when commenting about Maxey's litigation against the bank. "The name Maxey was like King Kong in Lubbock," said Levenson.[55]

The irony of those statements is that, when Homer Maxey sued Citizens National Bank, he named as defendants all the members of that bank's board of directors, a group of individuals that included men in Lubbock who possessed far more wealth than he did. Some had parents who, unlike Homer's father, had been born into privilege and influence, moving to West Texas not from a dusty outpost north of Fort Worth but from New England.[56]

One article on Homer Maxey summarized the twenty-year span between the end of the war and 1965 as "[a]n astonishing variety of building projects and business ventures . . . [one after] another, and to it all, Maxey seemed to bring the Midas touch." More to the point, Homer enjoyed a long run of successes in those years because he had good business sense, he worked hard, he knew a lot of people, and he never stopped looking for the next opportunity to—as he liked to put it—"keep moving forward."[57] At the same time, Homer took pride in being able to provide his family, friends, and anyone willing to work hard alongside him with the rewards that come from that level of effort.

Several family members and friends say that Homer Maxey never stopped thinking about business. "If he were sitting here right now," says Kathleen Maxey Luther, "he would have a pad and pencil on his lap and he would be making notes on it, figuring out some new scheme or something." "Daddy had an ability to get people to work for him," says Carla. "He knew how to get people to do things for him."[58]

As Carla Maxey's husband, Tommy Elliott had a front-row seat during the 1950s, the peak years of his father-in-law's professional life, and he worked overtime trying to help salvage Maxey's fortunes in the late sixties. Tommy and Carla's marriage ended in divorce in 1979.

"Mr. Maxey was a visionary," said Elliott. "People who worked with him or who worked for him could see that he was giving them an opportunity to be a part of something. He'd hire these guys who wanted to work hard for him, and he was a taskmaster. They'd work seven days a week for him."[59]

One of those individuals was Dan Law, an ex-college football player who went to work for Homer G. Maxey & Co. in 1959. Law started out at the bottom, driving a delivery truck and pushing a broom. Later, after being promoted to sales, he found his true calling. Law ended up owning the business.[60]

"He had a way of encouraging you in his own way to make you work harder," says Law. "Mr. Maxey was very fair to all his employees, but you needed to make him a hand. You needed to be a good worker and work hard. All the Maxeys had a reputation of being efficient, high-energy, hardworking, successful people, but they wanted you to work right along with them."

Dan Law and his wife, Jean, grew up in Wetumpka, Alabama, the products of working-class families. The Laws first visited Lubbock in 1957 when Dan was being recruited by the Texas Tech football organization.

Tommy and Carla Elliott were assigned to help recruit Dan because Tommy, like Dan, was married. "They brought us to Lubbock for a weekend and that's how we got to know the Maxey family," remembers Law. "They had a big party for us at the Maxey house, and Tommy and Carla were our hosts. They put us up at the Plainsman Hotel, which was absolutely gorgeous and everything was just wonderful. But that was indicative of the Maxeys, because the Maxeys did everything first class. We were very, very impressed. So we moved out here and we're still here. Lubbock is the best place in the world."

Other members of the Maxey clan also made sure that Dan and Jean Law felt at home in Lubbock.

"Carl Maxey gave me a bunch of suits one time," says Law. "These were high-dollar suits from Hemphill-Wells and they had only been slightly worn. Shoot, for a college boy out of the Deep South, I was in tall cotton."

After graduation, Law asked Homer Maxey for a job, armed with personal references from Tommy Elliot and Jimmy Wilson, the business manager for the Texas Tech athletic department. The references may have been unnecessary, however, because Maxey was known for hiring lots of Tech athletes.

"Mr. Maxey provided a lot of opportunity for this old boy and this girl right here," says Law, referring to himself and Jean. "I cannot say enough good things about Homer Maxey, Melba, Glenna, Carla, and all the Maxey family. The Maxeys are certainly one of the most influential families in the development, the growth, and everything that is good about Lubbock. They are one fine family."

In the spring of 1961, ten years after the grand opening of the Plainsman Hotel, Homer Maxey was again at the center of attention as people turned out to see his newest project, the Pioneer Hotel.[61] The eleven-story red brick building, formerly known as the Hotel Lubbock, stood at the corner of Broadway and Avenue K, facing east. Its sunrise orientation was appropriate, because the original hotel was built with that optimistic community spirit that had characterized the town from its beginnings, and, in particular, since the opening of Texas Tech. At a date when some of the local churches were still meeting on Sunday morning in a modified dugout, a community funding effort was organized to build a first-class hotel downtown. One of the first contributions from private citizens came from J. B. Maxey, who demonstrated his civic spirit by purchasing five $100 bonds.[62] The first five floors of the building were completed in 1926, and another six floors were added in 1929, the year of the stock market crash. It was the location of the town's first radio station (KFYO, which began broadcasting in 1932) and also served as a bus terminal for Texas, New Mexico & Oklahoma Coaches until 1947.[63]

For the first two decades of its existence, the Hotel Lubbock was an anchor of political, social, and cultural life in Lubbock. But as the town began expanding toward the southwest, the hotel's fortunes, like downtown itself, began to decline. By 1960, when Maxey bought the property for $460,000 with financing from Great Southern Life Insurance Company, its glory days were long gone.[64] The building and everything in it needed a major overhaul. Maxey announced an ambitious plan of refurbishment and modernization amid a great buzz of publicity and public support. The goal was to make the Pioneer a classy destination for dining, dancing, and social, and business gatherings.

The name change was appropriate, Maxey said, because the Hotel Lubbock had been the pioneer downtown hotel "of the modern era." He followed up that statement with a chuckle, stating that the name change would save him money. "Also, I can buy linen, towels, tableware, etc., with 'P. H' on them because they'll work both at the Pioneer and the Plainsman."[65]

Skimping on expenses, however, wasn't Homer Maxey's style. "Money meant nothing to Daddy," says Carla. "He would just get in there and do whatever he thought needed to be done and to hell with the cost."

Maxey hired his brother Herschel to head the redesign project. Italian marble flooring would go in the lobby.[66] Various spaces would be shuffled around, such as moving the kitchen from one floor to another. There would be three new restaurants, a palatial ballroom, and a new nightclub in the basement. The price tag for all this was $860,000, and that was just for the first phase of the renovation. The grand opening was April 16, 1961, but the refurbishment of the upper floors of the hotel would follow at a later date.

Maxey also swung a deal to have the Lubbock Club moved to the Pioneer from its former home on the mezzanine floor of the nearby Caprock Hotel. The Lubbock Club was an invitation-only organization of local business leaders and professionals whose membership often overlapped with the smaller, more exclusive empire builders group. The new accommodations at the Pioneer would be considerably larger and swankier than those at the Caprock.

Charlie Guy helped drum up excitement for the new hotel in his columns even before Maxey assumed control of the property. "When Homer Maxey takes over the Hotel Lubbock," bubbled the editor, "the fur is going to fly. With his customary go-go-go Homer will begin the first steps to give Lubbock, once again, a downtown, home-owned hotel of the first class."[67]

Thomas Thompson, of the rival *Amarillo Globe-Times*, was not so kind. "The question is, did Maxey get a bargain?" he wrote. "Downtown hotels still have their place, but they have to change with the times. . . . They must provide services that people want." Those services, according to Thompson, should include a parking lot, swimming pool, and additional "motel-like rooms on an adjacent property," which had made a success of older downtown lodgings such as the Lincoln Hotel in Odessa and the Hotel Roosevelt in Los Angeles. At the end of the piece, Thompson admitted that Maxey was "a shrewd businessman" who had "the habit of success."[68]

Boom Years and Midas Touch

Unfortunately for Homer Maxey, the cynical Amarillo newspaper columnist proved to be more prescient than his counterpart in Lubbock. "Homer heard a rumor that a bunch of doctors were going to buy that old hotel and make it into a nursing home," says Tommy Elliott. "I think he was planning to just flip it and sell it to the doctors, but they backed out on him. Nobody else wanted that hotel so he wound up being the owner. He borrowed all that money, spent a fortune upgrading it. Big, big mistake. A loan like that is going to kill you."[69]

In the early 1960s, downtown Lubbock was still a destination for shopping, meeting people, and doing business. Flagship retailers like Hemphill-Wells, Dunlap's, and Margaret's were there but, as the years went by, those places also had satellite stores that were located away from downtown, often in the same retail centers and subdivisions built by Homer Maxey and his partners.

As the decade progressed, suburban drivers would find downtown even easier to avoid, thanks to the completion of Loop 289, which, viewed from above, imposes itself on the neat grid of Lubbock streets like the outline of an eggplant, ballooning out to the southwest suburban developments and venturing no closer than three miles from the county courthouse or the corner of Broadway and Avenue K. As downtown began to wither, Lubbock became one of countless American cities faced with the unintended consequences of encouraging suburban sprawl.

Certain developments in the past decade have brought new energy to the central city, and in a bit of synchronicity, some of them have paid tribute to the Maxey family. In August 2005, in recognition of one of Lubbock's most renowned figures, the name of Eighth Street was changed to Glenna Goodacre Boulevard. The street runs between University Avenue on the eastern border of Texas Tech campus to Avenue Q on the western edge of downtown—the thoroughfare named after the daughter of Homer Maxey geographically connects two vital parts of the city. And in between, the boulevard passes through the residential/commercial neighborhood known as Overton Park. This 325-acre area was once known as the northern portion of the Overton Addition, a historic subdivision that once belonged to the pioneer physician and real estate investor, M. C. Overton. By the 1970s, this northern portion of the Overton Addition was a vivid example of urban blight. Efforts to improve and/or renovate the area came to naught until Delbert McDougal decided to tackle the job, buying almost every one of the nine hundred dwellings—many of which were substandard when constructed and, by 2005, unsafe to live in and unsightly to look at—and putting in their place a new neighborhood that is now one of the jewels of the city. Overton Park is the largest privately funded urban redevelopment project in the United States.[70]

The parallels between Delbert McDougal's ambitious achievements and those of Homer Maxey are too numerous to mention, and that includes the part where some of McDougal's colleagues told him that he was "crazy" to take on such a huge, complex, and expensive project, but he forged ahead anyway.[71]

McDougal, for one, concurs with the notion that Overton Park is just the kind of project in which Homer Maxey would have led the charge, warning all naysayers to roll up their sleeves and pitch in or get out of the way.

During and after the renovations for the Pioneer Hotel, which created a huge drain on Maxey's finances, he was also engaged in a major transformation of his other businesses. By early 1962, Maxey had started shifting his focus to cattle ranching. He began selling his urban assets and disposing of others through various complex trades, all with the purpose of acquiring vast tracts of ranch land, feedlots, and farmland.

Several of the properties Maxey bought were located in Oklahoma. The most promising of the properties was near the Osage County town of Pawhuska, which lay about twenty-one miles northwest of Tulsa. The deal would include 14,800 deeded acres, with another 6,100 acres of leased land. A new dam in the area would create a lake called the Keystone Reservoir. Whenever Maxey visited the ranch and walked the property with the foreman, he could look beyond the scrub and the grazing cattle and see the rising water level in the reservoir. As the level rose, it created lakefront property, which would someday be much more valuable than any cow pasture could ever be. Maxey decided to name the place the Triple M Ranch as a tribute to his wife, Melba Mae Maxey.[72]

Maxey's shopping list also included a ranch near Atoka, Oklahoma, another one near Wilburton, Oklahoma, and a feedlot near Texline in the upper Texas Panhandle. Maxey's foray into ranching was viewed as an unusual move by many of those who were close to him. He had no experience in ranching, for one thing. Or, as Glenna says, "Daddy was a very, very smart home builder, but he didn't know which end of a cow eats."[73]

The property in New Mexico was called the Tucumcari ranch, even though it was west of the town of Tucumcari by a good forty miles. State Highway 104 cut through it, and the western finger of Conchas Lake extended into the northeastern portion. The land was a jumble of high mesas and eroded ravines, and, compared to the Osage County ranch, it wasn't half as valuable for raising cattle, but Maxey wanted it anyway.

In those days, State Highway 104 was one of the best routes across that part of the country if you were heading up into the mountains near Cowles, where the Maxeys' summer cabin was located. Another property in that area, the storied Bell Ranch, would have been well-known to Maxey for various reasons. It was one of the largest and most historic ranches in the Southwest.

Carved from two Spanish land grants in the 1820s, the original Bell Ranch spanned 719,000 acres. In the late 1800s, the peerless Texas cattleman Charles Goodnight used one of the ranch's prominent mesas as a landmark as he drove his herds up the trail to Colorado. The ranch was so big it had its own zip code, 88441.[74]

The Bell Ranch had been split up in the 1940s, the biggest portion being sold to the Keeney family, which included descendants of Isaac Ellwood. Other prominent families in Lubbock, including the Arnetts and the Chapells (both of whom included descendants of the Ellwoods), also owned ranches in the area that were of considerable size. The names Ellwood, Keeney, Arnett, and Chappell were also well represented on the board of directors of Citizens National Bank.[75]

Maxey was well acquainted with these families. Close friendships between the Maxeys and several other families, such as the Arnetts, spanned two generations. Consequently, he was not unfamiliar with the joys and money-making potential of owning large tracts of land.

"He just wanted to do something different," says Carla. "He felt the need to try something new, but it was something he knew absolutely nothing about, plus it was a bad time for ranchers." Glenna believes it was a business decision. "His whole premise," she says, "was that city taxes were eating him up. He thought he was going to go bust."[76]

Of all the ranch properties, the Triple M was the crown jewel of the bunch. To acquire the property from the owners, Mr. and Mrs. Carl Bledsoe, Maxey traded the Plainsman Hotel to the Bledsoes, and then signed a contract to lease the hotel back from Carl Bledsoe for $6,000 a month. Then he used the ranch as collateral to obtain a $550,000 loan from Prudential Insurance Company. It was a complex and unwieldy arrangement, with great potential for additional complications in the future.

Over the next two years, Maxey disposed of Homer G. Maxey & Co., Maxey Lumber, his shares in American State Bank, and various other assets, including lakefront real estate near Austin, a motel in Wichita Falls (referred to by one of his attorneys as "a hot-sheet joint") and the Pioneer Hotel—all in his quest to liquidate his urban holdings and build his cattle ranching business.[77]

The sheer number of transactions and their complexity suggests a whirlwind of wheeling and dealing. At first glance, it would seem that Maxey was frantic to get it all done, but everyone who had ever been close to him knew that Homer Maxey always had a plan for success. This plan appears, however, destined to fail.

Tommy Elliott is under the impression that his father-in-law began trading for ranch land as a way to get out from under the doomed enterprise that the Pioneer Hotel had become.[78] "He started panicking," speculates Elliott, "because he got stuck with that hotel. Here's a guy who grew up in a lumberyard. He doesn't know a bull from a heifer and he's depending on these so called 'experienced cattlemen' who are nothing but a bunch of crooks. They led him down a primrose path and pretty soon he was trading off all his good assets for these ranches."

"Daddy had no patience, and he was very, very stubborn," says Glenna.[79] Some said Maxey was bullheaded, but he had always succeeded in the past, even when the risks were great and the waters untested. "Homer was kind of cut off from people," says Ken Bowlin, a Lubbock attorney who was not well acquainted with Maxey until 1966, when Bowlin began representing Maxey against Citizens National Bank. "It's not that he was unfriendly, but he was just all business most of the time." Bowlin recalls feeling personally snubbed by the businessman in social encounters. Later, however, after spending thousands of hours with the man preparing and trying his case, Bowlin became one of Maxey's biggest admirers.[80]

"Homer was an intense personality all the time," says Marcia Abbott. Abbott remembers picking up on her uncle's preoccupation with business when she was a teenager. She recalls the lunches hosted by Effie Glen for all the job-holders in the family. "We would all be sitting around the table talking about the world and everything, and Homer wouldn't be saying a word. All of a sudden, he would interrupt and say some kind of business thing. He could not carry on a social conversation because he was so intensely focused on his business."[81]

During the period that Maxey was engaged in moving from urban investments to cattle ranching operations, his daughters and sons-in-law found themselves conscripted for various duties, including some in which they had

Bill Goodacre grew up in Red Deer, Alberta, and his skills at playing ice hockey earned him a scholarship to Colorado College, where he met Glenna. The couple were married after graduating from college. Courtesy of Bill Goodacre.

no expertise.

Glenna and Bill Goodacre returned to Lubbock in 1962 after obtaining their degrees at Colorado College in Colorado Springs. "Bill had his college degree and Daddy had him driving a cattle truck," says Glenna, laughing. "I teased Daddy about that. Bill didn't know which end of a cow ate, either."

When Glenna and Bill were expecting their first child, Homer leaned on both sons-in-law for help managing his hotels, apartment complexes, and ranching enterprises. "Daddy said we had to keep all these businesses in the family or we were going to lose them," she says. "But we lost them anyway. It was frustrating because Daddy could not delegate. He thought Tommy and Bill didn't know how to make a living."[82]

"I think he made up a job for me and I was happy to have one," recalls Bill Goodacre. "I mean, he wasn't hiring somebody who had any experience. You don't get any experience in college, you just get book smart. But I was used to working, and working for Homer was a fun type of work."[83]

Despite his father-in-law's stubbornness, Bill Goodacre remembers those times with fondness. Although his favorite task was driving a cattle truck, his first solo trip between Tucumcari and Texline was memorable in all the wrong ways. "I was driving a double-deck trailer with calves on the bottom and the top," he says. "I stopped at Dairy Queen for a milkshake at about ten or eleven in the morning, pulled up right in front of the place, on a slope. I didn't realize it at the time, but these cattle don't ever go to the bathroom until you stop the truck. So I was getting my milkshake and all of a sudden, all this cow piss is pouring out of the truck right in front of the Dairy Queen. I've never been so embarrassed in my life." Another telltale sign of Bill's inexperience in the cattle business was that he was wearing white tennis shoes, which, he notes, did not stay white for very long.

Later on, Maxey hired Bill as manager and maintenance man at Modern Manor apartments, a job for which he was more suited. "Homer's brother Herschel had been in charge of it, but he didn't do a very good job," says Bill. "It was pretty run-down and forty units were vacant. I worked my butt off, had everything fixed and filled everything up in like six months."

Decades later, Bill still has a keen impression of Homer Maxey's gruff, tireless, larger-than-life presence. "When he was doing the transition from all the office buildings, his lumber companies, and hotels and everything, we would go look at all his ranches, all over Oklahoma, Texas, and Missouri, meet the real estate tycoons everywhere. We would work New Year's Day, all the time, seven days a week. We saw more properties than you could ever imagine." "Every night after dinner we'd go to the motel room and go to bed, and Homer would snore like you can't believe," Bill explains. "When six o'clock came around he'd be totally awake and I would just be getting to sleep. He'd say, 'OK, we're ready to roll,' but I was just dead."[84]

While Bill worked for her father, Glenna hustled to get her art career on track. She earned a steady income by teaching zoology, painting portraits, giving art instruction at the Lubbock Garden & Art Center, and buying and selling antiques. She also remembers being frustrated as she encountered the

Boom Years and Midas Touch

old-fashioned expectations of her mother and the very conservative social climate of Lubbock.[85]

"Mother wanted me to join a women's club and all that stuff, and I just wasn't cut out for things like that," she says. "I was always drawing and painting. That's what I always wanted to do."

In Lubbock that was an unusual ambition for a young woman. In Lubbock society, it was much more common for women with artistic yearnings to limit their artistic energies to arts and crafts and the activities promoted by women's clubs.

Glenna's mother, Melba, was one of the founders of the Lubbock chapter of the Junior League and involved in other clubs as well. While she did expect her daughters to be involved in the social and charitable activities of such groups, she also supported Glenna's ambitions to become a professional artist. Glenna also cited her mother's own, more traditional creative outlets—decorating, arts and crafts, and cooking—as an inspiration. Even in the early stages of her artistic career, however, she began to exhibit some of her father's acumen as a businessperson and as a promoter.

"I'm an exact replica of Homer," says Glenna. "I've got his middle name, Glen. I emulated him. For one thing, I love building."[86] In her twenty-seven years in Santa Fe, she counts ten houses and studios among her building projects.

Maxey's combination of stubbornness and impulsiveness had served him well in the past but, during this period of his life, the pace of his activities was so frenetic that some of his contemporaries began to wonder if he knew what he was doing. Dub Rushing had a very different take. "Homer was always [thinking] way ahead of the times. That's the reason he was able to accumulate the wealth he accumulated."[87]

E. W. Williams, Jr., says that he and Homer Maxey were not well acquainted before 1962, but in a place the size of Lubbock, they must have crossed paths from time to time. The Williams residence at 4103 Twenty-First Street was less than a dozen blocks from the Maxey home on Vicksburg Avenue. Today, the concrete abutments of Marsha Sharp Freeway have added physical barriers between the former addresses of the respective combatants.[88]

Williams had been employed at First National Bank from the mid-1950s through 1961. He was a young, ambitious vice president on the loan committee. Maxey had done his banking at First National for many years. He did most of his business with the president, Roy Riddell, but he was also an old friend of many of the directors. Like most old-timers in the area, the owners and directors of the bank had also known Maxey's father.

At the end of 1961, Williams resigned from First National and took over as president of the reorganized Citizens National Bank. The bank's new owners, William Nöel and E. G. Rodman, were oilmen from Odessa, and they liked Williams's style.[89] They wanted an aggressive new president who would improve the bank's position in the market, a man who could go out and bring in big new accounts.

In June of 1962, Maxey and Williams had a meeting at the Pioneer Hotel.[90] Williams wanted Maxey's business. Maxey's former business partner Harold Blank spoke highly of Williams, as did others, and advised Maxey that it would be a smart move. Later, Maxey said his decision was heavily influenced by the recommendation of Bill Evans, his trusted friend, attorney, and business partner. "He felt that I would make a good customer for the bank," Maxey told a reporter for the *Fort Worth Star-Telegram*, "and the bank could do a good job for me."[91]

Williams must have impressed Maxey as a kindred spirit. He had obviously enjoyed the confidence of Roy Riddell. Before Williams left First National, Riddell used to introduce Williams as his right-hand man. "If you trust me," he'd say, "you can trust E. W."[92]

The first time Williams asked Maxey if he would consider bringing his business over to Citizens National Bank, Maxey declined. He explained that he had a great relationship with Riddell, and did not care to move his business at the time. Four months later, Maxey and Williams had another meeting at the Pioneer Hotel. The precarious financial situation of the hotel could not have been far from Maxey's thoughts, but since he had financed the deal through the Great Southern Life Insurance Company, he may not have mentioned that particular situation. The way Maxey described the meeting later, the main topic of discussion was his long-range plan to go full tilt into the beef business. He had already pretty much closed the deal on the Tucumcari ranch, but he needed a short-term loan to buy cattle to stock the ranch.[93]

Like Maxey himself, Williams was ambitious and full of energy. A native of Post, a Caprock community just south of Lubbock, Williams was the son of a rancher and was eager to expand the bank's agricultural department. At the end of the meeting the two shook hands like good West Texas gentlemen who had every reason to believe they were embarking on a mutually beneficial and rewarding new relationship.[94]

Chapter 5

RED IN THE
FACE

I t's hard to pinpoint just when things began to go sour between Homer Maxey and E. W. Williams, Jr. In the beginning, the banker seemed eager to provide all the financing Maxey needed.[1] By early 1964, however, the bank was pressuring Maxey to reduce his debt and collateralize additional assets, while Maxey was complaining about what he considered to be Williams's unnecessary meddling in his business operations. Almost fifty years later, Williams's point of view remains unchanged: He says he was only trying to protect the bank's collateral.[2]

According to Maxey's account of his second meeting with Williams, which occurred in late 1962 at the Pioneer Hotel, he mentioned that he had a line of unsecured credit up to $1 million from Roy Riddell at First National Bank, which meant that whenever Maxey needed financing, he could borrow any amount up to $1 million without pledging collateral. Williams responded to Maxey by stating that he could count on having the same arrangement if he moved his business to Citizens National Bank. Having agreed to terms, the two parties shook hands.

Maxey was the kind of man who prided himself on handshake deals. In Maxey's world, a man's word was his bond and his handshake was an iron-clad contract. Ken Bowlin states that he had a similar relationship with Roy Riddell.[3] "Roy made me a lot of loans," remembers Bowlin. "I'd just go into his office and he would pull out his billfold and make me a loan. If I needed

Homer Maxey, celebrating his fifty-second birthday with friends and family in 1963, was in the midst of a whirlwind of aggressive wheeling and dealing to build his cattle production business. Courtesy of the Maxey family.

three or four thousand dollars, for example, he would pull out his billfold and give me the cash and say, 'Whenever you have time, come by and sign a note.'"

Today, Williams denies there was any handshake deal with Homer Maxey that included an unsecured line of credit up to $1 million. Some customers would warrant that amount, he says, but not Maxey. Williams says he might have guaranteed Maxey a smaller amount, such as $300,000, but no more.

"The problem was, in Homer's mind he probably didn't need to pledge collateral for *any* amount," says Williams.[4]

Williams also denies that Riddell ever gave out any "billfold loans" on a handshake. "I knew Roy Riddell and I worked with him for years," he says. "I can tell you that I know that that didn't happen. It just didn't happen."

Between 1964 and 1966, Maxey was required to sign a series of credit instruments that collateralized almost every asset he owned, including the properties under the umbrella of Plaza Building Corporation. Maxey's indebtedness to Citizens National Bank climbed to $1.366 million.[5]

By that time, there was no love lost between the bank president and the Lubbock millionaire. Realizing that the agreements he had signed placed him in a precarious position, Maxey sought new financial backers and scrambled to put together various deals that would pay off all his debt to Citizens National Bank.[6]

Maxey's relationship with the bank was made even more complex by the fact that attorneys from the law firm who had represented him for many years also represented the bank. The potential for conflict of interest probably did not occur to Maxey until his financial problems began to intensify and the attorneys began pressuring him to follow his bankers' advice. Maxey probably should have sought legal representation from a firm other than Evans, Pharr, Trout & Jones much sooner than he ultimately did. At the time, however, while there were numerous capable law firms headquartered in Lubbock, only a select few attorneys had the necessary expertise for handling Maxey's complex legal business arrangements. Lubbock was not the same as New York City, Los Angeles, Dallas, or even Austin; in some respects, the "hub city of the South Plains" was still a small town in the 1960s.

Maxey's relationship with the firm of Evans, Pharr, Trout & Jones went back over thirty years. Bill Evans and Charlie Jones had both accompanied Maxey on a trip to Washington, DC, in 1956 on FHA business. Evans not only represented Maxey on many of his most important business ventures, but he had a financial interest in a good number of them as well.[7] Evans also served on the State Board of Education and was a respected fixture of the community.

Robert H. Bean, a district judge and former member of Evans's law firm, had also been an investor in some of Maxey's building projects. For a time, he was a co-owner of B&M (Bean & Maxey) Investment Company, a commercial loan company Maxey sold to Bill Dean in 1960.[8]

The firm of Evans, Pharr, Trout & Jones was founded by the pioneer attorneys E. L. Klett and George R. Bean, the father of Robert Bean. These men had known Homer Maxey's father well. They had done business together, and it is conceivable that they may have met and had dealings with each other soon after J. B. Maxey moved to the South Plains as a contractor in 1906. The business relationship between the George R. Bean and E. L. Klett and the founders of Citizens National Bank dated to at least 1906; the law firm had represented the bank's original owners when it was organized and chartered that year. The law firm continued to represent the bank, though not exclusively, for the next seven decades of its existence.[9]

Later, Maxey testified that he began worrying about the conflict-of-interest issue as early as 1964, with the issue becoming obvious to both parties during heated arguments in the bank building in January 1965. By this time, Evans, Pharr, Trout & Jones had moved their offices into the new eleven-story Citizens National Bank Tower at the corner of Fourteenth and Avenue K.

The modern, audacious looking new bank building was part of an expansion program that had been in the planning for well over a decade. Designs for the building had been publicized in the early 1950s, but Citizens National Bank's share of the banking business in Lubbock declined during the fifties.[10] The entire construction program included a new downtown motor bank, the Citizens National Bank Tower, an adjacent structure called Citizens National Bank Center, a high-rise parking garage, and additional office space that could be rented to tenants, such as Evans, Pharr, Trout & Jones, who moved their offices to the ninth floor of the bank tower.

The total price tag was more than $5 million, a number that had a familiar ring to cynical observers when it was learned, just over a year after the building was completed, that Citizens had seized an estimated $5 million in assets from Homer Maxey. That the two figures were roughly the same naturally led to snide accusations that the bank had taken Maxey's money in order to pay their construction bill.[11] And as Maxey's relationship with his lawyers and bankers turned sour, the fact that they were in the same building intensified his suspicions of collusion and conspiracy, not to mention his irritation.

One day in January 1965, for example, a meeting between Maxey and one of his attorneys, Chauncey Trout, Jr., ended in a shouting match. Maxey exited Trout's office on the ninth floor and took the elevator to the first floor, which opened onto the bank lobby. There he ran into Bill Evans. Maxey and Evans argued. Maxey then went in to see Williams, where the two of them likewise conversed in an adversarial manner. The argument came to a chilly end as Evans took his old friend Homer aside and informed him that if there was a lawsuit between Maxey and the bank, Evans would not be able to represent either party.[12]

In early February 1966, Trout and one other partner in Evans's firm,

This architectural rendering of the Citizens National Bank Tower was released for publication in 1955, almost a decade before the bank's new home was actually built. In 1964, the law firm of Evans, Pharr, Trout & Jones moved its offices into new spaces on the ninth floor of the building. This situation caused difficulties for attorney Charlie Jones, who had an acute fear of heights, and also for Homer Maxey, who began to feel that his lawyers and his bank were conspiring against him. Courtesy of the City of Lubbock.

Broke, Not Broken

Charles B. "Charlie" Jones, were named to Citizens National Bank's board of directors. Trout and Jones had joined the law firm in 1955 and began to handle the bulk of Maxey's legal work with the bank—including drafting the many new collateral instruments Maxey claimed he had been pressured to sign.[13]

Maxey testified that on several occasions he had resisted signing such agreements, only to be told by his attorneys that if he refused, the bank would call his note. Typically, the agreements had been drafted by Trout and/or Jones at the behest of Williams, yet, in some cases, Maxey was billed for the work. If Maxey questioned the wisdom of signing the agreements, Trout or Jones would say, "As your attorney, I advise you to sign."

According to Williams, the collateralization of Maxey's assets was a necessary and standard precaution.[14] Williams also maintains that Maxey was given proper notification and sufficient time (including at least six months in extensions) to repair his finances in order to prevent foreclosure proceedings. The way Williams tells it, calling Homer Maxey's note was the last thing he wanted to do.

The way some Lubbockites see it, the story of a prominent citizen suffering financial collapse at the hands of local rivals was nothing new. Sometimes, as one longtime Lubbock resident put it, certain parties would begin coveting what another party owned, after which they "got the man strung out on credit, tied up all his assets, and then dropped the hammer on him."[15]

One specific case cited by many Lubbockites is that of Tom Cobb. About five years before the Maxey foreclosure, Cobb, who operated the chain of Cobb's department stores, found himself in a similar predicament with Citizens National Bank. "After Tom's wife died, the bank called his note and took everything," says Jo Love Nelson.[16] Nelson is one of several individuals who already harbored resentment against the bank before they foreclosed on Maxey. Many Lubbockites who remember the Cobb case regarded the foreclosure as the fruition of a scheme by certain directors of Citizens National Bank to eliminate some retail competition in the area. If nothing else, the Cobb affair did nothing to help allay local sentiment that Maxey's allegations against Citizens National Bank were not only factual but part of a pattern of predatory business practices by area businessmen who were also directors of the bank. "I wouldn't have any problem believing it," says Nelson, when asked about Maxey's version of the foreclosure. "It was common knowledge all over town. People talked about that. People would get overextended and the bank would call their notes."

For Maxey, February 16, 1966, was the day that it all came to a head. At three o'clock that afternoon, a meeting was convened in Williams's office in the Citizens National Bank Tower. The building was just two blocks over from the Pioneer Hotel, a short walk from the town square and the county courthouse.

Whether the meeting was called as part of a nefarious plot or it was a necessary procedure, taken with regret, the actions of that afternoon destroyed Homer G. Maxey's financial existence. A pillar of the community, one of its wealthiest, became one of its brokest. The fortune Maxey had accumulated over thirty-eight years of sweat, toil, and hustle was wiped out in a little over half an hour.[17]

The redistribution of Maxey's assets took place in secret, without the benefit of advance notice for a public auction. For the attorneys, bank officers, and anyone else charged with defending the actions of the bank in its dealings with Homer Maxey, the lack of transparency in which the foreclosure was conducted would always be the most difficult single issue to explain or justify.

The transaction that seemed to shock people most, however, was the "fire sale" price tag assigned to the stock shares of Plaza Building Corporation, which owned most of the ranch land, stock in several of Maxey's businesses, the Maxey family residence on Vicksburg Avenue, and many other assets. The men in Williams's office that afternoon agreed to assign this stock a value of one dollar per share, for a total of $749.[18]

Later, when confronted with allegations and questions about why the stock sale and other transfers of property and assets were handled in such a mysterious manner, Williams said, "It doesn't sound good, but it was legal."[19]

For Maxey's part, he had stepped on a few toes in his day, and many things he had done in his business career would also fail the "sounds good" test. His wife, daughters, sons-in-law, and best friends would admit that he was hotheaded. Homer was a man who had the complexion of a ripe tomato even when he was asleep, dreaming sweet dreams. He could be easygoing and soft-spoken, but he could also chew your ear off in language that would peel the paint from a battleship's hull.

Would Maxey passively accept the bank's actions as "just business" and go home to retire and nurse his wounds? Probably the only surprise was that an entire month went by before Homer's attorneys filed the lawsuit. In addition to Citizens National Bank, the civil suit named as codefendants the Monterey Lubbock Corporation, E. W. Williams, Jr., and two other officers of the bank.

The petition asked for actual damages in the amount of $2,489,705.45 and additional amounts arising from injury to Maxey's credit and reputation, for a grand total of $4,833,705.45.[20]

Those who knew Homer Maxey best always believed that it was the notion of betrayal—not the loss of his fortune—that motivated Maxey's desire for redress in the court system. "Daddy had known Bill Evans for over thirty years," says Carla. "Bill was one of his partners, just like Harold Blank, who ran Maxey Lumber, and Lee Fields, who ran Homer G. Maxey & Co. He included his partners in everything. But some of them, like Bill Evans, they thought the bank was more important than Daddy and they sold him down the river. Daddy was the type of businessman that his word was it; he didn't have to sign anything. But the lawyers kept giving him more papers to sign and they just sold him out, literally."[21]

Bobby Moody, another attorney with Evans, Pharr, Trout & Jones during this period, takes the opposite view. "Bill Evans," says Moody, "would walk a mile barefoot for Homer." In Moody's opinion, Maxey had it in for Bill Evans, Charlie Jones, E. W. Williams, and all the others he sued because he couldn't face the fact that he had been "a very successful businessman . . . and then he wasn't anymore."[22]

"Homer was so trusting, people sometimes took advantage of him," says Glenna.[23] "When they could buy and sell the corporation for $749, that kind of dishonesty was just beyond him. He couldn't believe that people could act in such a corrupt and dishonest manner. He couldn't believe other people would do such things. Some of the bankers and lawyers were just unbelievable, the way they conducted themselves."

"I just always felt that Mr. Maxey had a very, very good relationship with some of these people, and then they turned on him," says Dan Law. "The bank cut his throat, too, and he didn't deserve that."[24]

In Law's opinion, the whole mess could have been averted if the bank had given Maxey a little more leeway. "As a salesman, I always thought if you had a good customer and he kind of got his ox stuck in the ditch a little bit, you help him get it out so he can get back on his feet," he said. "I tell you, there's not too many Homer Maxeys in the world. If he was here today and you gave him the same situation and you gave him a little time, he'd work it out, because he had the know-how to fix it. Because if Homer Maxey couldn't fix it, I don't know who could."

According to Ken Flagg, a longtime Lubbock developer, you didn't even have to love the man to feel that way about it. "People didn't just naturally fall in love with Homer, because he was a grouchy old bastard," says Flagg, "but they took his side because the bank just overhauled him."[25]

In Flagg's view, the damage to the reputation of Citizens National Bank was self-inflicted, for the most part. "I remember how terrible the bank was criticized for the way they treated Homer," says Flagg. "I don't know if it was all justified or not, because Homer definitely had problems, but the way the bank handled it was the worst public relations disaster I've ever seen. Then the bank personnel appeared to have taken over some of his assets themselves, and it just left a horrible impression."

Margaret Talkington said that she knew E. W. Williams quite well. However, she said, "I liked him, but I didn't trust him as much as I trusted other people. I don't mean that in a derogatory way. In the position he was in, it was difficult for him to tell all the sides of the story, including his own involvement in it. I know he got mad at Homer and serious mistakes were made."[26]

According to Williams, the mistakes were all Maxey's, and if there was any chicanery involved, Maxey was the culprit. "Homer was very capable in his business dealings," he says, "but sometimes he was less than totally honest."[27]

In an interview for an in-depth story about the Maxey suit for the *Fort Worth Star-Telegram* in 1979, Williams asserted that the idea that he had solicited Maxey's business, then conspired to take over his assets was "totally and completely a figment of [Maxey's] imagination."[28]

The same article cited an interview with an unnamed "longtime Lubbock attorney" who said that Williams was "a very ambitious young man" when he took over as president at Citizens National Bank and that "Williams was hired at a modest salary by banking standards and told he would receive a percentage of any profits he brought the bank. This, he said, might explain Williams's quest for the Maxey account and his eagerness to foreclose."

Whatever the facts behind the allegations against Williams, it must be said that he is a man who found a profession he loved early in life, pursued it with great passion, and enjoyed substantial success. His reputation was damaged by the Maxey case but, within a few years of the filing of the lawsuit by Maxey, Williams was more prominent in the banking community than ever.[29] Over the years, he founded or cofounded numerous banks and bank holding companies, acquired existing banks in the South Plains and the Hill Country, and served as president of the Amarillo National Bank.

In the 1960s, when Williams was still a youthful, ambitious man, his hair was as dark as his horn-rimmed glasses and, when he smiled, the slight gap between his two front teeth gave him a boyish appearance. Today his hair is gray and thin, and he doesn't get around as well as he used to, but on recent visits to discuss the Maxey case, he was still in possession of a gregarious personality. He's a good talker and he laughs easily. He was guarded in his comments about the Maxey case, and yet he was eager to present his side of the story. He expressed a feeling that his point of view had never been given equal time in the media.

Although Williams grew up in Post, the town founded as a health utopia by the cereal magnate C. W. Post, he attended high school at a military academy in New Mexico. During his college years at Southern Methodist University in Dallas, he was drawn to banking and finance, he said with a wink, because those courses had the least amount of laboratory time and that less lab time meant "more time for drinking beer and playing shuffleboard."[30]

Williams likes to tell a story about how he got his first job. On a Monday morning in 1949, he drove west out of Dallas and stopped at the first bank he saw, which was in the town of Grapevine. Williams says he went inside and asked for a job. "They asked for a resume, but I didn't have one. So I went back to Dallas, made one and turned it in. On Wednesday they called and said, 'When can you start?' I said, 'What's wrong with tomorrow?' That was Thursday, and that was my first job in banking."

On a fall afternoon in 2009, sixty years after his first job in banking, E. W. Williams, Jr., was greeting visitors and catching up on work in his office, which occupies the entire sixteenth floor of the Plaza Two tower of Amarillo National Bank. Here the walls are studded with mementoes from African hunting safaris—stuffed animal heads, horns, guns, hides, and huge photo collages. He has been on more than a dozen hunting safaris in Africa. Among the wild beasts and fowl bagged on those trips, he has killed a total of twenty-seven zebras.

"This is the kind of ethics Homer Maxey had," says Williams. "After the bank foreclosed on his cattle, Homer would have a foreman take a few head of cattle to auction in Tulsa. He'd have Tommy Elliott put them in his name and sell them and keep the money. He took advantage of Tommy."[31]

In the weeks leading up to the foreclosure, there must have been a terrible chill in the air in Tanglewood Estates whenever the Maxeys and the Williamses happened to run into each other on the street, downtown, or perhaps at the

Lubbock Country Club. No small wonder that, after the foreclosure, Homer and Melba packed up and moved—not just from the neighborhood, but away from Lubbock.

The Maxeys first established legal residence in Pawhuska in Osage County, Oklahoma, near the Triple M Ranch (which the bank had taken over by that time). Maxey already had a relationship with a law firm in the area and wasted no time engaging its services to file the lawsuit against the bank. The lawsuit was initially filed in federal court in Tulsa.[32]

Homer and Melba, however, had not left Lubbock merely in order to be near their attorneys or a ranch they no longer legally owned.

"I'm just too embarrassed," he told a reporter. "I just couldn't live [in Lubbock], not being able to pay my own way."[33] "They just wanted to get out of Lubbock," says Carla. "Daddy was just completely and totally humiliated. He didn't feel like he could walk down the street and hold his head up. It was just a complete slap in the face."

Another suit was filed by the Maxeys' attorneys claiming a homestead exemption on their Vicksburg residence, a move they hoped would prevent the bank from being able to take over the property. The court ruled against the Maxeys, however, finding that they did not hold title to the house. When it was built, the Maxeys deeded the title to Plaza Building Corporation and, while living there, they paid $200 a month in rent to the corporation. It was an arrangement that saved them some taxes, but ended up costing them their home.

Although the bank eventually got the house, Maxey made sure that it didn't end up with quite 100 percent of it.

"Before the bank took it over, Daddy went in there and took all the nice fixtures out," says Carla. "He gutted the place before he would let that damn bank have it."[34]

Homer Maxey's attorneys in Tulsa, Bob Kelley and Bruce Gambil, filed the lawsuit in March 1966 in US District Court, Northern District of Oklahoma. A short time later it was transferred to the Northern District of Texas, Lubbock Division. Meanwhile, in Lubbock, attorney Ken Bowlin had been following notices about the lawsuit in the *Avalanche-Journal*, as well as commentary and gossip from colleagues and friends. A few days after the case was transferred to Texas, Bowlin received a phone call from the Tulsa attorneys. They wanted to know if he would be interested in assisting them on the case. Bowlin's involvement was to be minimal; Gambil and Kelley said they would need help with the jury selection if the case ended up going to trial.

Attorney Ken Bowlin was determined to take Homer Maxey's case, despite his law partner's objections. Bowlin's partner, Jim Cade, wanted to refuse the case because a fellow Lubbock attorney, Charlie Jones, was one of the defendants—and Cade wasn't especially fond of Maxey, either. Courtesy of Ken Bowlin.

Bowlin did not immediately say yes. He had reservations about getting involved and wanted to know more about the case before giving an answer. Gambil and Kelley shared few details of the case with him.

"When they first called me," he says, "they said they were going to settle the case with the bank. They didn't really intend on going to trial." An additional hurdle was the fact that Bowlin wanted to be paid, but the Tulsa lawyers told Bowlin that Maxey had no money.[35]

Bowlin conducted some basic research on the case, seeking input from various colleagues. Everyone had an opinion, and some of the comments about Maxey were not complimentary. Bowlin's own impressions were less than favorable. He had always thought of Maxey as "a bully who liked to throw his weight around," and when he heard about the foreclosure, he wasn't terribly broken up about it. At this point in time, the few details he knew about the bank foreclosure left him with the general impression that the fault was all Maxey's. Even worse, one of Bowlin's sources of information insinuated that Maxey might have committed fraud.[36]

Then there was the political aspect. Bowlin was a conservative Republican; Maxey was a New Deal Democrat. Many of Bowlin's assumptions about Maxey, however, including Maxey's political opinions, were based on what his law partner, Jim Cade, had told him. Cade, who was even more conservative than Bowlin, had intense political and philosophical disagreements with Maxey and regarded him as an "obnoxious liberal," but then again Cade had a reputation for being a curmudgeon, although more colorful appellations might have been used to describe Cade's abrasive public persona. Jane Livermore Wofford offered an anecdote in support of this characterization. Shortly after Bowlin and Cade began working together, Bowlin encountered an old friend who expressed surprise that the two of them were getting along. "He's mad all the time," said the friend, to which Bowlin responded, "Well, at least he's even-tempered."[37]

Some clarity can be brought to Bowlin's impression of Maxey by pointing out that in the 1950s, the term "liberal Democrat" did not mean what it means today. Two general issues that could brand a person as a "liberal" in those days were support for FDR's New Deal programs (which were tagged by conservatives with a label that is still used today: "big government") and states' rights, particularly when it came to ownership of the tidelands and public school integration. And in 1952 and 1956, Texas Governor Allan Shivers, a very conservative, segregationist Democrat, labored to convince other conservative Democratic voters in Texas to vote for Republican Presidential candidate Dwight Eisenhower. Loyal Democrats who voted for the Democratic candidate, Adlai Stevenson, were labeled "liberals."

When asked if her father was a liberal or a progressive, Glenna Goodacre could only laugh. "Liberal?" she said. "No, not him. That's a silly adjective for Daddy."[38]

It's possible that Cade considered Maxey a liberal simply because he was a Democratic loyalist, or because he took full advantage of the FHA programs begun under FDR, which helped finance a good many of the houses and apartments built by him in the South Plains region.

A few days after the call from Gambil and Kelley, Bowlin received a call from Homer Maxey himself. Maxey said he could borrow the money to pay Bowlin's fee. Bowlin told him it would be best to charge by the hour, with a thousand dollar retainer up front. Maxey said that would be no problem. Maxey then made an appointment to meet with Bowlin at his office.[39]

The meeting was full of surprises from start to finish. When Maxey, one of the most recognizable men in Lubbock, entered the room, "short and stocky . . . bald-headed and extremely red in the face," remembers Bowlin, he stuck out his hand and said, "We've never met." Suppressing a laugh, Bowlin replied, "but I know who you are, Mr. Maxey."[40]

To Bowlin's surprise, he found Maxey's manner unpretentious and friendly. Bowlin was accustomed to seeing Maxey holding court in public places, such as restaurants and private clubs, where he boomed out greetings to friends and colleagues, or offered his opinion on something in a take-no-prisoners tone of voice. That was the well-known, gregarious, public version of Homer Maxey.

Ken Bowlin was smart, capable, and successful. Some called him brilliant.

Jurors found him easy to like. "He had that charisma," says Tommy Elliott. "In the courtroom he just outshined everybody else. He was really good."[41]

Bowlin grew up in Hermleigh, Texas, a wide spot in the road almost one hundred miles southeast of Lubbock. Forrest Bowers, a Lubbock attorney who hailed from the nearby community of Dunn, has known Bowlin since they were kids.[42]

"Ken and I started competing against each other when we were ten years old. We played softball against one another, tennis, football, basketball, and spelling bees."

Both men came up from hardscrabble beginnings. "I guess our family was about as rich as anybody around there and we didn't have anything," recalls Bowers. "Ken's folks were about the same."

As they entered the practice of law in Lubbock, Bowers and Bowlin resumed their friendly rivalry. Bowers is still comfortable about making light of Bowlin's self-confident air. "He was a pretty good lawyer here in Lubbock," says Bowers. "I tried cases against him here. Ken is classified as a pretty good friend of mine, even though he stretches the truth and he thought everything he did was the only way to do it."

Bowlin served in the marines during World War II and fought in the Pacific. He was stationed on Saipan around the same time Homer Maxey was laid up in a hospital there, recuperating from his knee injury. It was on Saipan that they learned of the A-bomb being dropped on Hiroshima. Two weeks after the second A-bomb was dropped on Nagasaki, Bowlin went ashore with a communications platoon. "We didn't know there was radiation," he says. "The Japanese had just surrendered, but no one was sure it was real or not. A lot of the officers thought we'd be annihilated, but the people were very subservient. We took a lot of candy and cigarettes to give away.

"They dropped the bomb on the Mitsubushi plant there in the harbor, where they made airplanes and all kinds of stuff, and hardly anything was left. There were a few steel beams that had melted. People were horribly wounded and a lot of people had just evaporated. At one point they had moved all of the geisha girls, or the prostitutes, over the hill, out of the city, because they didn't want them there where the families lived. But the harbor side of the hill was where the bomb did the most damage. So when we got there, most of the survivors were prostitutes."

After the war, Bowlin went to law school. He passed the bar in 1950 and began practicing law in an office above the Triple S drugstore, at the corner of Main Street and Texas Avenue. He began as an associate, then as a partner, with an older and well-established attorney, James O. Cade. On the day he began practicing law he remembered the vow he'd made to himself after coming home from the war. His plan was to go to law school, become a successful lawyer, and retire at the age of forty-five. The day Homer came to his office to discuss his lawsuit, Bowlin was just four years away from that goal.[43]

Over the course of his first consultation with Homer Maxey, Bowlin decided, to his surprise, that he liked the man. "He was a bundle of energy and a really likeable guy," says Bowlin. "He had a lot of friends, including some close friends, but he wouldn't just sit down and talk to just anybody. If he didn't have a reason to talk to you, he wouldn't talk to you. I think he had kind of cut himself off from people because he was so involved in his businesses. But I realized that actually, he was a kind of a private person and I'm like that, too. Anyway, I got more interested in his lawsuit because I believed the bank was very guilty in the way they treated him."

Bowlin agreed to join Maxey's legal team. In July 1966, Maxey's lawyers filed a new petition in the 72nd District Court of Lubbock County. As the lawyers continued taking depositions and investigating the state lawsuit, work was discontinued on the suit previously filed in federal court.[44]

Bowlin's role as an assistant to Gambil and Kelley was short-lived. Sometime in August, Maxey came back to see him. He was fed up with his Tulsa attorneys and he wanted Bowlin to take over the case.

"I told him I couldn't do that because Gambil and Kelley brought me into the case; there were legal and ethical standards involved," recalls Bowlin. "A couple of weeks later Homer came in and said, 'Well, they're off the case.' So I called them and they told me, 'That's right, we've been fired.' They weren't too happy about it, either."

"For the next two or three days, Homer was either in my office or on the phone wanting to talk to me," says Bowlin. "I probably talked to him ten or twelve hours over those days, with him telling me about the case at the same time I was trying to practice law. He didn't seem interested in the money. He didn't seem to be interested in that at all. He wanted his reputation back. He was really concerned that the people of Lubbock would think that he defrauded the bank. And I got the impression that he was more hurt about the idea that two of his friends, his lawyers, that is, had defrauded him. He was hurt."

What bothered Bowlin most was the conflict-of-interest issue raised by the same attorneys representing both Homer Maxey and Citizens National Bank.

The more Bowlin learned about the case, the greater his conviction became that both the bank and Maxey's attorneys had acted in bad faith.

Two of those attorneys, Charlie Jones and Bill Evans, were among the most prominent in Lubbock. Their involvement in the case made Bowlin's partner very uneasy. In fact, Cade was angered that Bowlin would even consider taking the case. "Cade's office was next to mine," says Bowlin. "After the second day with Homer, he came into my office and he said, 'OK, what is Maxey's problem? I've seen him hanging around here and using the phone, disrupting the office. We can't run a law office with that.' So I just gave him a summary."

Bowlin told Cade that Williams had made false promises to Maxey in order to get his business and then reneged on them. He told him that on the afternoon of February 16, 1966, Williams and his cohorts, including Charlie Jones, had divided Maxey's assets among their friends and associates. Bowlin said he believed that Jones had not acted in an ethical manner and that he had helped bring about Maxey's downfall.

"Cade said, 'Oh, my God, you aren't going to take that case are you?'" recalls Bowlin. "I told him I'd never taken a case against another lawyer, but that Homer Maxey was not a bully. This guy had been hurt. If his lawyers did what Homer said they did, yes, I was going to stay in the case."

Cade still wasn't happy about it, but he eventually came on board. A third Lubbock attorney, Alton Griffin, would join the plaintiffs' team later.[45] An army veteran, Griffin had served terms as Lubbock's district attorney and also as county attorney. A 1951 graduate of Texas Tech, Griffin put in a few years as a schoolteacher in Anton, Texas, before obtaining his law degree from the University of Texas at Austin in 1956. He joined the partnership of Cade & Bowlin in 1969.[46]

"Homer moved into my office and he stayed in my office two or three years, maybe longer, and he worked every day on this case," says Bowlin. "And of course he took up nearly all my time. Finally, I just talked to my partners and I told them I'd become so involved with the case, I was going to devote all my time to it. Which I did for a couple of years. And then we tried it, and it took a long time to try."[47]

As the Maxey case moved forward with Ken Bowlin at the helm, local interest grew more intense. If a person lived in Lubbock, there was a very good chance that at least one friend or acquaintance was named in the petition, either as plaintiff or defendant. Because they held stock in Plaza Building

Corporation, Tommy and Carla Elliott and Bill and Glenna Goodacre were added on the plaintiff side.

The list of defendants ballooned in size. Bowlin added all the directors of the bank, including the majority owners, Earl George Rodman and William Douglas Nöel of Odessa, plus two other individuals, for a total of thirty-three individual defendants that represented a cross section of the West Texas elite.[48]

The two individuals at the top of the list, Earl George Rodman and William Douglas Nöel of Odessa, had been partners in various business interests in West Texas for a decade and a half before they bought majority shares in Citizens National Bank of Lubbock in the late 1950s. Individually and as partners, the two men invested heavily in ranching and banking after becoming major forces in the oil and gas industry in the 1930s. Rodman began his career as a roughneck in the Kansas oil fields in 1917, moving later into the oil field supply business, bringing his expertise to the Permian Basin in 1935.[49] Nöel graduated from the University of Texas with a BBA in 1935 and got his start in the oil business as a roustabout for Gulf Oil. In 1936 he moved to the Permian Basin, where he was a chemist at Gulf's Wickett refinery. Four years later he formed a drilling company with two partners.[50] Working eighteen hours a day as a tool pusher, pumper, and production supervisor, Nöel was so busy that several years went by before he realized he had made his first million dollars. In 1946, Rodman and Nöel formed a partnership and purchased a refinery. Then, in a series of moves aimed at diversification, they established four major companies with six operating plants. The Odessa petrochemical complex they created was, at one time, the largest inland petrochemical operation in the world. Small wonder the Rodman-Nöel partnership is credited for establishing Odessa's petrochemical complex.

In 1956, about twenty-five years after Rodman briefly worked as a bank teller following World War I, the Rodman-Nöel partnership founded the American Bank of Commerce in Odessa. They also acquired controlling interests in banks located in five other Texas towns, including Citizens National Bank of Lubbock. Rodman's son, E. G. Rodman, Jr., was also appointed to the board of directors and was named in Maxey's lawsuit.

Like many other wealthy West Texas businessmen, Rodman and Nöel owned numerous ranches. Rodman owned a total of seven, both as an individual and in partnership with Nöel. Ranching was one interest that Nöel and Rodman shared with another of the defendants, E. W. Williams, Jr., although it could be said that it would be even more unusual for a well-heeled businessman of West Texas to not be interested in owning and investing in large tracts of agricultural real estate. Today, Williams owns several ranches and cattle feeding operations.

John A. Hughes and John David Hughes constituted another father-son team on the board who were named in the lawsuit. The elder Hughes had served as president of Citizens National Bank from 1954 until 1961. His son, who goes by the name David Hughes, was appointed to the board in 1964. After a brief stint as assistant county attorney (a position that had been recently vacated by Broadus A. Spivey), Hughes went to work as an associate at Evans, Pharr, Trout & Jones. He was also appointed to the board of Citizens National Bank. With his familial and professional ties to the defendants in the case, Hughes had a unique perspective on the unfolding legal drama that followed. He refers to his and his father's experience of being defendants in the Maxey case as "a nightmare . . . a debacle that never should have occurred."[51]

Other Citizens executives on the board were Barclay Ryall, a young vice president and former bank examiner (and assistant to E. W. Williams); George N. Atkinson, a senior vice president; Clyde W. Gordon, vice president in charge of the agricultural department; Sam D. Levenson, a vice president and board member for a short time; and J. W. Smith, a vice president who played a central role in the liquidation of Maxey's ranches.[52]

Bill Evans had been a director of Citizens National Bank for many years, as had many of his predecessors at Evans, Pharr, Trout & Jones. His partners in the firm, Charlie Jones and Chauncey Trout, Jr., also on the bank's board of directors, were also named as defendants.

Other board members sued by Maxey included Dr. D. M. Wiggins, former vice president of Citizens and president of Texas Tech from 1948 to 1952; Harold Hinn, of Abernathy, owner of Harvest Queen Mills and Elevator; Clyde G. Tatum, operator of a feed mill and construction company; S. S. Forrest, Jr., owner of Forrest Lumber Company (also city commissioner 1954–56; mayor 1956–58); Dan Davis, advocate for the South Plains cotton industry; J. L. Irish, of Hale County, operator of a cotton gin and a cottonseed oil mill; T. J. Goad, car dealer; W. D. Hord, owner of West Texas Oxygen Company; Edwin Merriman, CPA; Guy Victory, former general manager of the Fort Worth & Burlington Railroad; Vernice Ford, involved in farm equipment sales; Frank Junell, executive vice president at Citizens National Bank who also had interests in education, radio, and television; and Wesley Blankenship, owner of a theater chain.[53]

Board member Retha Martin was a large stockholder in Citizens National Bank and past chairman of the board. Martin owned the Dunlap's department store chain and many other retail businesses and had a reputation for being aggressive in his dealings.[54] He was also the main instigator behind the hiring of Williams as president of Citizens National Bank. However, judging by his remarks to a reporter from the *Fort Worth Star-Telegram* in 1979, Martin did not feel that Williams had demonstrated good judgment in his handling of the Maxey affair. "It indicates it probably wasn't very good," Martin told the reporter, "or there wouldn't have been any trouble over it."[55]

Two other directors, William Ellwood Keeney and Frank H. Chappell, Jr., were members of the extended Ellwood family. Another director, W. F. Eisenberg, was the executor of the Ellwood estate.[56] The last two directors of the bank named as defendants were R. A. Burford and Herbert Wilcox.

Two defendants, J. E. Birdwell and E. C. Mullendore III, were not members of the board of directors. J. E. Birdwell was, however, related to one of the directors by marriage (his sister, Christine, was married to William Ellwood Keeney). Birdwell hailed from E. W. Williams's hometown (Post), and the two men were longtime friends. During the time of the events at issue in the Maxey case, Birdwell was a close neighbor of Williams and the Maxeys in Tanglewood Estates.[57]

Birdwell was a cattle broker. The only other defendant in the case who was not a member of the board was E. C. Mullendore III, an Oklahoma rancher. Birdwell and Mullendore had been partners in the purchase of Maxey's Triple M Ranch cattle, which were sold after the foreclosure. Maxey had filed an injunction to prevent the sale of the cattle in early 1966, several weeks before he filed the original lawsuit against the bank in federal court. Citizens National Bank's attorneys went to court and successfully argued to have the temporary restraining order lifted, and the sale went through.

Other cattle buyers had offered to buy the herd from Maxey for $230,000. On the day that the restraining order was lifted, Williams telephoned Birdwell and agreed to sell Birdwell and Mullendore the cattle for $173,000. Among other allegations regarding this transaction, Maxey accused the bank of allowing Birdwell and Mullendore free use of the foreclosed ranch properties to fatten the cattle before reselling them, all without crediting Maxey's indebtedness for the use of feed and equipment. The cattle were sold a few months later at a substantial profit.

The defense attorneys for the bank and individual defendants filed a flurry of motions offering reasons their clients should be severed from the case or granted a summary judgment. By the first day of trial in late October 1969, the number of individual defendants whose case would be heard in Lubbock County 72nd District Court had been reduced from thirty-five to fifteen.

Attorneys for nine of the individual defendants who did not reside in the Lubbock area submitted motions for pleas of privilege (for change of venue). These nine asked for summary judgment (a determination made by the court in favor of a party without a full trial). US District Judge William R. Shaver, then presiding judge for the 72nd District Court, granted the pleas of privilege to the nine defendants on June 12, 1968.

The disposition of the cases of Earl G. Rodman, Earl G. Rodman, Jr., and William D. Noel, all of Odessa, was typical of this group. Acting through their attorneys, the three claimed privilege because they resided in Ector County. These defendants asserted that they had little involvement in the day-to-day business of running the bank and no direct involvement in the events at issue in this case. Subsequent to the June 12, 1968, ruling, a district judge in Ector County issued summary judgments in favor of Rodman, Rodman, and Noel.[58]

The remaining defendants in this group were also granted summary judgments in the district courts of their respective counties of residence. The six defendants were Harold Hinn, J. L. Irish, T. J. Goad, Guy Victory, Frank Junell, and Herbert Wilcox.[59]

Summary judgments were granted in favor of twelve other defendants in Lubbock County who maintained that they had little or no knowledge or involvement regarding the foreclosure proceedings on Homer Maxey. The twelve men were all directors of the bank: John A. Hughes, Bill Evans, Dr. D. M. Wiggins, Clyde G. Tatum, W. D. Hord, Dan Davis, S. S. Forrest, Jr., Vernice Ford, Wesley Blankenship, Retha Martin, William Ellwood Keeney, Frank H. Chappell, Jr., W. F. Eisenberg, and R. A. Burford.

By fall 1969, E. C. Mullendore III, who resided in Osage County, Oklahoma, and E. W. Williams, Jr., who had moved to Amarillo to take a position as vice president of Amarillo National Bank, were the only defendants left in the case who lived outside Lubbock County. On October 7, 1969, just three weeks before the start of the trial, District Judge Patricia S. Moore granted Mullendore's plea of privilege. Williams's pleas for severance and a separate trial were denied, but because his residence in Amarillo exceeded the hundred-mile limit of subpoena power, he could not be coerced into attending the trial.

And so, as the Maxey case went to trial in late October 1969, there were nine individual defendants remaining: E. W. Williams, Jr., Clyde Gordon, George Atkinson, Charles Jones, J. W. Smith, David Hughes, Chauncey Trout,

Jr., Barclay Ryall, and J. E. Birdwell. Among the group of nine, Birdwell was the only remaining defendant who was not an officer and/or director of the bank. The list of four corporate defendants remained intact: Citizens National Bank of Lubbock, Monterey Lubbock Corp., Citizens National Bank Corp., and Citizens National Bank Co.[60]

The Maxey case was the first major case tried by Moore after her election. She was the wife of an attorney and the daughter of what is commonly referred to in cotton country as a "ginner," meaning the owner/operator of a cotton gin. Moore had contracted polio as a small child and had to learn to walk with the aid of leg braces and crutches. She also learned to drive, which allowed her to tow a horse trailer for her daughter's riding competitions. After graduating from the Southern Methodist University School of Law in 1949, she entered private practice in Lubbock. In 1953, she was the first female attorney to be elected president of the Lubbock County Bar Association. Four years later she became the first woman elected judge of the Lubbock County Court at Law. She was elected judge of the 72nd District Court in 1968, another first.[61]

"Pat didn't crawl under a bush or anything just because she [was in a wheelchair]," recalls Jack Flygare. "There was a group of women in Lubbock who liked to play poker regularly. You didn't find a lot of women poker players back in those days, but Pat was one of them."[62]

As Judge Moore presided over the last of the pretrial hearings, hearing arguments from the attorneys for both sides of the case, Maxey and his attorneys began to have serious misgivings regarding Moore's impartiality. According to Bowlin, most of the judge's rulings seemed to be in favor of the defendants. Whether Bowlin's assertion is accurate or not, Lubbock County judges weren't the only ones who tended to rule in the defendants' favor. At least twenty-six defendants had been granted pleas of privilege in their respective counties of residence. Each one of them would be found blameless in court.

A number of defendants and former defendants had once been friends and business associates of Homer Maxey, but none of them was ever as close as Bill Evans. The history of their long personal and professional relationship added immense additional strain to what was already a personal crisis for both parties. Evans's being dismissed from the lawsuit had little or no palliative effect. Making matters worse, at the time the case went to trial, Evans was being treated for advanced lung cancer.[63]

The plaintiffs' third amended petition claimed that, at the time of foreclosure, Homer Maxey owned physical assets worth no less than $4,092,669.95

and that the total sum of his liabilities amounted to $1,395,780.72, leaving a net worth of at least $2,696,889.23. The Goodacres and Elliotts also owned stock in several of Maxey's corporations, the most valuable being shares in Plaza Building Corporation valued at $1,535,110.62.

The list of assets valued at $2.8 million owned by Plaza Building Corporation included ranches (three in Oklahoma, two in Missouri, plus the Texline farm), residential homes, commercial real estate, equipment, a Mexican restaurant in Houston (spelled "La Ploma" in the trial transcript), the Pioneer Hotel, life insurance policies, and loans.[64] Separate assets included Maxey's controlling interest in Maxey Lumber Company and a ranch in San Miguel County, New Mexico.

The plaintiff's petition related the story of how Maxey met Williams and was urged to move his business to Citizens National Bank, not only by Williams but also by Jones and Trout, "who had the unqualified confidence of plaintiffs because their law firm had represented Homer G. Maxey for over thirty years, and because of that sacred and valued trust which exists between client and his attorneys of many years, did persuade this plaintiff to transfer all of his banking business to the defendant, Citizens National Bank of Lubbock, Texas."

According to the petition, Maxey was promised and granted an unsecured borrowing capacity, or line of credit, in the amount of $1 million, which meant that only amounts above $1 million would have to be secured by collateral. Sometime in 1964, however, Williams reneged on this promise and pressured Maxey, under threat of foreclosure, to sign numerous mortgages, pledges, collateral notes, and other security instruments. The documents were often presented to Maxey in the offices of Evans, Pharr, Trout & Jones, where one of Maxey's attorneys—most often Trout—urged Maxey to sign them.

Over the following months, the petition further alleged, Maxey was pressured to sign more financial instruments. Before long, almost everything he owned, either personally or through his corporations, had been cross-mortgaged, meaning that if he defaulted on a single debt to the bank, the bank could take everything.

Next, the bank took over the Triple M Ranch and fired all Maxey's employees. The property began to decline due to poor management and the cattle lost value due to neglect. Many more allegations against the bank were detailed in the thirty-page document. One of the most shocking allegations was the one relating to Maxey's 1965 dealings with a financier from Phoenix, Arizona, named William Ed Drumwright. Drumwright subsequently put together a package deal with two other parties that would have extended Maxey a $1.3 million short-term loan, which he would use to pay off his indebtedness to Citizens National Bank and sell his ranches for $4.5 million.[65]

At some point, however, the deal stopped dead in the water, and no one on Maxey's side of it knew why. Almost a year after the foreclosure, Bowlin and Maxey flew to California to meet with Drumwright to discuss the lawsuit. That's when they learned the rest of the story.[66]

"We were sitting in an office on the twentieth floor or something, looking out over the bay," recalls Bowlin. "I asked him why they stopped Homer's loan. He said, 'Homer's lawyer called it off.'"

Maxey and Bowlin looked at each other, stunned. They wanted to know what attorney he was talking about. "Charlie Jones," said Drumwright.

Drumwright explained that, sometime in October of 1965, W. L. Brady, a Kansas City, Missouri, broker who was working on the short-term loan agreement, received a phone call from Maxey's attorney, who informed him that the loan was no longer needed.

Bowlin remembers asking Maxey if he'd ever known anything about such a phone call. Maxey said he had no idea.

"I told Homer that, in essence, this was how they had ruined him," says Bowlin. "That's the guts of the lawsuit."[67]

There were other important components to the petition, including the allegations of damage to Maxey's credit, reputation, and goodwill in the community, plus the recounting of the foreclosure itself, in which Maxey's assets were secretly sold off and divided up for pennies on the dollar. In at least some ways, the Charlie Jones phone call was the most damaging accusation made by the plaintiffs. It spoke not only of fraud, bad faith, and conspiracy, but also a breach of ethical behavior that would undoubtedly be shocking to not just a jury panel, but to all members of the close-knit legal community in Lubbock.

Bowlin knew, however, that this would be a difficult lawsuit to win. He was well aware that the bank, as well as its attorneys, had powerful friends in Lubbock. Before Bowlin filed the case in 72nd District Court, he interviewed various judges to learn if there might be any possible conflict-of-interest issues.

"One of the judges said he resented the fact that I had taken the case," said Bowlin, "and he resented me even coming to talk to him about it. So that eliminated one judge."[68]

The bank had retained Shafer, Gilliland, Davis, Bunton & McCollum of Odessa to join the defense. The twenty-year-old firm, known primarily for defending large corporate clients, was one of the most formidable in the state. W. O. Shafer, the lead attorney trying the case, was a former president of the Texas State Bar. He enjoyed a reputation as an outstanding trial lawyer. Jurors liked him.

Filling out the defense team were Bernard Evans (no relation to Bill Evans) of Key, Carr, Evans & Fouts and Charlie Jones and Chauncey Trout, Jr., of Evans, Pharr, Trout, and Jones. Jones and Trout were well versed in the history of the lawsuit, and Jones was a brilliant attorney. His command of minutiae and case law combined with an outstanding ability to think on his feet would be invaluable to the defense. Jones was popular among the legal community, but brashness did not always endear him to others. "Charlie struck some people as being arrogant," said Forrest Bowers. "Actually, he was super-confident, and that put some people off."[69]

When the case came to trial, Shafer handled most of the examination of witnesses. But no one who knew their way around the Lubbock County Courthouse was surprised when Charlie Jones—the attorney many regarded as "the most self-confident man in West Texas"—came out from behind the defense table, charming the judge, making the witnesses squirm, and astonishing the jury with his number-crunching ability and impressive knowledge in various fields.

Whether performances like that would bring home a verdict for Jones's clients or not, however, remained to be seen. Ken Bowlin was also a formidable trial lawyer.

Red in the Face

Chapter 6

THE FIRST TRIAL: BATTLE LINES DRAWN

The trial began on Monday, October 27, 1969, more than three and a half years after the foreclosure. The case was front-page news and the talk of the town, but Homer Maxey was no longer, as his friend Bobby Day called him, "cock of the walk and King of Lubbock."[1] Maxey was now fifty-eight years old, and instead of retiring and enjoying his wealth and achievements, he was engaged in the fight of his lifetime, trying to recover at least a portion of what he had lost not only in financial assets but his damaged reputation.

All day Monday and part of Tuesday morning were spent on jury selection. By the time the jury of eight men and four women was seated and sworn in, the morning was almost gone. Ken Bowlin rose to give the opening statement, taking the opportunity to read the lengthy plaintiffs' petition to the jury.

The case was complicated, and much of the evidence relied on the presentation of records documenting property trades, evaluations, collateral agreements, and various other financial instruments. In many ways, the case boiled down to an argument about which side was correct in the math. Bowlin, however, made certain to underscore Maxey's allegations of betrayal and unethical behavior, because while the average citizen has little experience in such complex financial dealings, the experience of betrayal by someone they once trusted is universal.

According to Maxey's allegations, his troubles with Citizens National Bank began when the bank reneged on Williams's promise of a $1 million unsecured line of credit. The countless demands for more collateralization of his assets led to counterproductive meddling in his business operations. Each of the developments was alleged to have been part of a conspiracy to defraud Homer Maxey and seize his assets. Finally, after blocking Maxey's attempts to obtain financing elsewhere, the bank called all his loans, leaving him penniless.[2]

The petition sought a total of over $21 million. The rationale behind the computation of this amount was spread out over almost twenty pages of allegations in the petition. The figures included an estimated net worth of $2.7 million for Maxey's assets at the time of foreclosure, plus $1.5 million interest belonging to the Goodacres and Elliots in Plaza Building Corporation, and various amounts ascribed to punitive damages and other losses which the plaintiffs blamed on the bank.[3]

Ken Bowlin, Alton Griffin, and Jim Cade were prepared. No one had worked harder on it than Bowlin. Cade, despite his previous dislike of their client, was convinced that he had been wronged by the defendants, and his expertise as a "book lawyer" (one who is skilled in citing case law and arguing the relevance of same in court) would be of great value in trying the case. The same associates who attested to Cade's well-deserved reputation for being cranky and irascible also regarded him as a formidable trial lawyer.

Maxey must have felt comforted to have so many friends and supporters in the room. Melba was there every day, taking notes, seated alongside Carla and Glenna.[4] All three women, plus Tommy Elliott and Bill Goodacre, had been added as coplaintiffs. However, their physical presence in the courtroom, giving Homer their moral and emotional support, was far more important than their names on the petition.

Glenna had a sketchbook with her every day and everywhere, and the courtroom was no exception. Today Glenna remembers giving some of her courtroom drawings to various jurors during the trial, but the bulk of them could not be located.[5]

Despite all the friendly faces, Maxey also must have felt a strange sense of aloneness in his battle. Big Daddy, J. B. Maxey, had died in 1953, and all three of Homer's brothers had died before the trial began. Carl, the third oldest, passed away in the summer of 1961, at the age of forty-five. That was the same year their mother, Effie Mae, died of cancer. Heart disease had claimed Robert Maxey on Christmas Day 1968, less than a year before the trial began. He was only fifty-six years old. Having just lost her husband, Kathleen Maxey Luther found Homer and Melba's lawsuit too much of an additional burden to bear. "I had just lost Robert and the whole thing upset me too much,"[6] she says. "I saw Homer and Melba during that time, and I was very sympathetic with them, but I couldn't go to the trial. I just didn't want to hear it."

October 1969 also marked three years since Herschel, the youngest sibling, had taken his own life. Family and friends say that Herschel always felt overshadowed by the achievements of his father and brothers. "I just think he was depressed because of that," says Marcia Abbott.[7] "I remember he had been hospitalized for something, some physical ailment, not depression, but after he was discharged from the hospital he killed himself."

W. O. Shafer delivered the opening statement for the defense. Shafer had been retained as lead counsel in the case by E. G. Rodman and William Nöel to represent the bank and its stockholders. Next to Charlie Jones, Shafer presented a sharp contrast in both appearance and style.

"W. O. had a hunchback and a bad leg, but he could swim like a fish," says Jack Tidwell, an Odessa lawyer who was hired in 1950 as the first associate attorney in what was then a two-partner office known as McDonald & Shafer.[8] "When he was young he was a fine bowler. He bowled an average of over 200, and in later years was a decent golfer."

According to Tidwell, Shafer had suffered from a combination of polio and spinal meningitis as a child, which resulted in a severe curvature of the upper spine, the technical term for which is *kyphosis*, a word derived from the Greek word for *hump*. Shafer walked with difficulty and stood a little over five feet tall. He grew up poor. "He didn't have a lot of formal education," says Tidwell. "He went to Cisco or Ranger college, I'm not sure which, then enrolled in law school at Cumberland, Tennessee, which was where poor folks went to law school because you could finish your degree in two years as opposed to three."

Jack Flygare recalls being impressed by Shafer's knack for putting jurors at ease with his physical abnormality.[9] "I remember trying a case with him against Mobil Oil Company in an oil field fire case in Seminole, Texas," says Flygare. "When he started his voir dire to the jury, he said, 'My name is W. O. Shafer and I'm a lawyer in Odessa, Texas. I'm not bragging about it and I'm not apologizing for it. It's just where I live and make a living. Now if any of you have any problem with Odessa, Texas, or think I'm some kind of a big city lawyer from Odessa, Texas, and that gives you some problem, please tell me about it, because I can't handle having you on this jury if you feel that way.'"

When he rose to deliver the opening statement for the defense in the Maxey case, Shafer made a concerted effort to draw a contrast with Bowlin's detailed presentation. He did not want to bore the jurors, he said, with a point-by-point rebuttal of Bowlin's "very long statement."[10] Instead, he said, he thought they might want to know a few salient facts about Homer Maxey and his finances leading up to the foreclosure.

The first point he brought up was that most of the bank's mortgages on Maxey's ranches and other properties were secondary or tertiary liens. In other words, Maxey had already taken out a first mortgage on those properties before mortgaging them again to Citizens National Bank. Then Shafer ran through a list of Maxey's debts and delinquent taxes, letting the jury know when he finished that he had spared them, for the time being, from having to sit through the entire list.

Next Shafer fired off a series of punch lines: "We deny that there has been any conspiracy between or among these defendants or anybody else. We deny as strongly as we know how that Charlie Jones ever made a telephone call to W. L. Brady or anybody else in connection with Mr. Maxey's business." The attorney also contended that there was no such thing as an agreement guaranteeing a million dollars unsecured credit between Maxey and Citizens National Bank, "or any other bank that I know anything about," Shafer stated. Nor was the bank or anyone associated with it involved in any "dissipation" of Maxey's assets. "On the contrary," he said, "long, long after it could be expected, [the bank continued selling] those properties at the very highest price . . ."

Shafer ridiculed Bowlin's pledge to offer circumstantial evidence to prove the conspiracy allegation. "We are not going to be looking toward circumstantial evidence," Shafer said. "You are not going to have to draw any inferences . . . We will offer documented proof . . . facts and figures . . . that [Maxey's] business enterprises were operating at a loss." Even after the foreclosure, the bank had offered to discount Maxey's debt by $100,000, Shafer claimed, "but that Maxey was unable or unwilling to pay." After finishing with his prepared statement, Shafer attempted to add a few remarks as to his personal opinion of the case.[11]

Bowlin interrupted to make an objection, but Shafer kept talking. As Judge Pat Moore recognized Bowlin, Shafer attempted to continue, offering an anecdote to illustrate his point: "If I owned a horse . . ."

Bowlin cut him off. Shafer's personal opinions, he said, were not part of the defendants' pleadings and, therefore, were not admissible. The same, he said, applied to Shafer's stories about "whether or not he owned a horse."

"I sustain the objection," said Judge Moore.

Shafer still wasn't ready to give in. "I think now, Your Honor," he said, "I am probably within my prerogative to illustrate my denial . . ."

Judge Moore repeated her ruling. "I sustain the objection," she said.[12]

In the legal community in Lubbock, Pat Moore enjoyed a general reputation as a fair-minded judge. But some attorneys, including those who represented Homer Maxey, observed that whenever Charlie Jones tried a case in her court, she tended to rule in Jones's favor, resulting in the appearance of bias.[13] Moore may have been so impressed by Jones's intellect and forceful manner of argument that she gave greater deference to him without being aware of it.[14]

If Judge Moore was dazzled by Charlie Jones's brilliance, she was not alone. "Everything you heard about Charlie is true," says Carlton Dodson. As an attorney with Evans, Pharr, Trout & Jones before his 1977 appointment to the court of appeals, Dodson worked alongside Jones on many of the firm's cases or, as another colleague put it, "Carlton carried Charlie's briefcase an awful lot of the time."

"Charlie graduated from high school when he was either fourteen or fifteen," says Dodson. "He could read so fast, he would just flip the pages. A lot of times he would read through a file for the first time on the way to court. When he got there, you'd think he'd been working on that thing for months. Charlie's brilliance was such that some people would be, you know, awed by him."[15]

As the battle lines were drawn in court that day, one key personality was conspicuous by his absence—E. W. Williams, Jr., president of Citizens National Bank and first-named codefendant.

Asked by one of the authors if he incurred any negative fallout from the Maxey suit, Williams replies: "Not at all." He also denies that the suit hurt the bank's business. Facts suggest otherwise.[16]

In the aftermath of its foreclosure on Homer Maxey, depositors began moving their accounts elsewhere. On January 11, 1973, a much-weakened Citizens National Bank merged with an interstate bank holding company, Texas Commerce Bancshares.[17] The new entity, Texas Commerce Bank of Lubbock, did not fare very well, either, and on October 1, 1993, merged with First National Bank of West Texas.[18] The story of the decline of Citizens

Charlie Jones, one of
the leading attorneys in
Lubbock County, was
known for his high IQ and
confident manner. Photo
by David Tuohy. Courtesy
of the Lubbock County
Bar Association.

National Bank of Lubbock and the role played by its mismanagement of the
Maxey affair was described in great detail in a hard-hitting investigative story
in *Texas Monthly* published in 1983.[19]

Over the course of the trial, the jury would hear testimony regarding the
actions Williams had taken, the promises he was alleged to have made and
broken, and the documents he signed, as well as other information about
the man and his actions. But they would never see what the bank president
looked like nor hear his personal responses to the accusations against him.

By contrast, the jury panel would see Homer G. Maxey, red-faced and bald
as ever, every day of the trial. The lawsuit wasn't just about his legal petition
against the defendants, it was about Maxey: who he was, how he had made
his fortune, and how it was lost.

Maxey took the witness stand late in the afternoon on Tuesday, October
28, 1969. His testimony began with the most basic of questions regarding his
name, birthdate, marital status, and so forth. Maxey's answers reminded the
jurors that, despite all the wealth and power he had accumulated, he was one

of them. When Bowlin asked, "What did your father do?" Maxey said, "He was a building contractor."

The eight men and four women in the jury box had been evaluated to make sure none of them had become so familiar with the case that they had already made up their minds about it. The Maxey family name was so familiar in Lubbock, however, that it would've been quite difficult to find twelve suitable jurors in town who knew nothing about them.

Although Bowlin had carefully prepared his client, the modest, self-effacing persona he presented on the witness stand wasn't something Homer Maxey had to learn. Perhaps the jurors would have enjoyed a self-deprecating anecdote or two about working as a teenage carpenter for his father during the construction of the Texas Tech campus, but it might have come off as self-serving or, even worse, immodest.

Of all the jurors, Gwendolyn Murphy undoubtedly was the least familiar with the Maxey family.[20] Only a year earlier, her husband's employer, a manufacturer of fire extinguishers, transferred his job position from their native Rhode Island to Lubbock. Murphy says they knew virtually nothing about the area before moving there and that it took years to adjust to the change.

"Coming from New England, Lubbock was like nothing we'd ever known before," she says. "When we flew in, we looked out and saw the quilt, you know, the patchwork of colors. We thought there was nothing here. We thought we had come to the ends of the earth."

Murphy realized right away that she would be picked for the jury. "They were asking questions that I didn't know the answers to," she remembers. "I'm not a Texan and that's what they liked, somebody without any background here. But I didn't know the trial was going to take three months."

Various city directories were used to obtain additional details about the other jurors. Joyce Branhan was a schoolteacher, the only one of the female jurors listed as being employed outside the home in their listing in the city directory. Mrs. Harmon Boothe was married to the owner of a Texaco station. Harmon was her husband's first name; no first name was given for her, either in the directory or the trial records in the authors' possession. Bunny Gordon was the wife of Jay E. Gordon, curriculum director of Lubbock Public Schools. Gordon, who was seated to Gwendolyn Murphy's right, is the juror Murphy remembers best. The male jurors included Robert Lambert, a civil servant; Clarence Rice, a mechanic; B. C. Coleman, a mill worker; Charles Woodruff, an employee of the Plains Cotton Co-op; Douglas Stokes, whose occupation was listed as "carrier"; Louis Lemond, "self-employed;" Bobby J. Carroll and Earl Beesinger.[21]

His direct examination had been underway for less than two minutes before Bowlin asked Maxey how he supported himself as a student at Texas Tech once he enrolled there in 1927.[22]

> Maxey: I opened a partnership with Cecil Bickley in the grocery business on Sixteenth Street and Avenue W. . . We constructed a small grocery store and operated it while I was in college at that address.
>
> Bowlin: Do you remember what you called it?
>
> Maxey: Cash Delivery Grocery.
>
> Bowlin: I see. And your partner was Cecil Bickley?
>
> Maxey: Yes, sir.
>
> Bowlin: Did it require the investment of some money to open the store?
>
> Maxey: Yes.
>
> Bowlin: And how much money, how much money did you invest in the store?
>
> Maxey: Nine hundred and fifty dollars, as I remember it.
>
> Bowlin: Do you remember where you got the $950?
>
> Maxey: I had saved that from working as a laborer and as a carpenter for my father during the summer months of high school.
>
> Bowlin: I see. During the time that you were in high school, you worked at least during the summer?
>
> Maxey: Yes, and after hours.
>
> Bowlin: All right, sir. And the nine hundred, or $950 you invested in the store was money which you saved from that work?
>
> Maxey: It was.

During the next few exchanges, jurors learned how Maxey used his share of a drawing account to pay his expenses in college and how, after graduation, he sold the store to Cecil Bickley for $1,500. Then came the job with Waples-Platter Grocery Company, where he drove a delivery truck during the day and kept books for the company at night. Next was the Continental Oil Company, doing the same thing.

Maxey had been testifying for less than five minutes when the questions turned to his second venture into entrepreneurship, the Caprock Dry Goods and Uniform Company. Maxey stated that he had invested $2,250 in the store. Most of the money came from the sale of his grocery store; the balance, he said, was borrowed money.

Two years later, he sold his interest to his partners for approximately the amount of his original investment. The only profit, he testified, was from his "draw" during that time, which was, he added, "back during the Depression."

Then the jurors heard about Maxey's brief experience as a distributor for Continental Oil and the founding of the first Maxey Lumber Company on Eighth and Avenue Q in 1937.[23]

> Bowlin: Was that a going business already that you bought or did you just open a business?
>
> Maxey: No, I bought the real estate and built the lumber sheds and started in.

Bowlin took the opportunity to introduce some other important actors in the story of Homer Maxey's beginnings. When asked if starting the new business had required the services of an attorney, Maxey testified that he had employed William H. Evans for that purpose.[24]

> Bowlin: Is he the same William H. Evans or Bill Evans that is a senior partner in the law firm of Evans, Pharr, Trout & Jones?
>
> Maxey: Yes.
>
> Bowlin: In other words, he is the partner of Charlie Jones, Chauncey Trout, Jr., and David Hughes?
>
> Maxey: Yes.

With that fact planted in the minds of the jury, Bowlin continued the established line of questioning.

Maxey testified that his lumber company began by selling building materials to contractors and the public but soon moved into the development business, building the Maxey Place Addition, the Melba Addition, and the Green Acres Addition in Lubbock between 1937 and 1942. With the description of each enterprise founded, as well as every building or subdivision built, the addresses were given. The varied locations added a dimension of specificity to each of Maxey's achievements and helped the jurors draw a mental map of modern Lubbock—one that happened to be studded with Homer Maxey landmarks.[25]

Maxey testified that after six successful years, he sold the lumber company. "The war had been declared," he explained, "and I had accepted a commission in the United States Navy in 1942, and I liquidated the Maxey Lumber Company at Eighth and Avenue Q."[26]

When Maxey stated that he attended naval officer's training at Harvard

University, it made an impression on juror Murphy. "I never expected to hear that anybody in Lubbock went to Harvard," she remembers. "That really got my attention."[27]

Bowlin probed Maxey for details regarding his service, including whether he was in combat during the war. Maxey's answers were short and to the point, devoid of drama. "After taking command of that ship," Maxey said, "we went overseas to the Solomon Islands, through Guadalcanal and 'the Slot,' they called it, through Bougainville."[28]

There was no mention of the slaughter that took place during the amphibious invasions, the swarms of kamikaze attacks from the air and the sea, or the experience of watching fellow seamen die as their vessel blew up and sank. But, in 1969, the events of the war were recent enough that the sparse facts related in Maxey's reply still had the power to conjure such visual horrors in the minds of most people in the courtroom.

Maxey had been on the stand for less than thirty minutes. During that time, the jury had heard how he put himself through Texas Tech by running a store and then, after graduating, had worked double shifts during the Depression years, squeaking by from deal to deal. In 1937, he became a builder, like his father, until he went off to fight in World War II.

Gwendolyn Murphy remembers being impressed by the details of the plaintiff's biography, and also by the way he presented himself. "Mr. Maxey was always amicable and pleasant on the stand," she says. "He never got ruffled. He was really a good witness for himself. He didn't fumble, he just told it straight out, or the way he recalled it, anyway. We were more likely to believe him than the bank's witnesses."[29]

After the war, Maxey testified, he built up the business of the new Maxey Lumber Company and also founded Homer G. Maxey & Co.[30] The number of business ventures increased year by year, as did the amount of money they made. He testified, for example, that in 1948 he was one of ten of the original stockholders who started American State Bank. He invested $35,000 and, for the next seventeen years, he earned an annual salary of $12,000 until he sold his interest in the bank in 1963 for $350,000. It was just one of many profitable business ventures Maxey described over the next half hour, including the construction of Veteran's Administration buildings, subdivisions, apartment complexes, shopping centers, the Plainsman Hotel, and other projects.

For every business deal that Maxey described, Bowlin inquired as to the names of Maxey's partners, the percentage of their ownership, and their profit participation. Bowlin probed Maxey for details regarding the participation of attorney Bill Evans in various projects. The jurors learned that Evans not only collected legal fees for his work in setting up Maxey's numerous partnerships and corporations, but was a partner in many of them. As a partner in the Plainsman Hotel, Evans also drew a monthly salary.[31]

The last project Maxey testified about was the Pioneer Hotel, which he bought in 1960 and spent $860,000 remodeling before its opening in 1961. Bill Evans made money on that one, too.[32]

The first day of testimony ended on that note. Bowlin staged his client's time on the stand so that, in the last hour of the first day in court, the jury was introduced to a vision of Homer Maxey as a hardworking local citizen who had risen to great heights in his first fifty-eight years of life. Next would come the story of his fall.

Over the next six days, Bowlin would guide Maxey, step by step, through the story of his financial downfall. Then, under cross-examination by the defense, some of the same people accused of destroying Maxey's wealth and reputation would also attempt to dismantle his version of that story.

A short time after Maxey resumed the witness stand Wednesday morning, Bowlin guided his client through the saga of his relationship with banker E. W. Williams, Jr., which had begun on a high note in the fall of 1962, but soon adopted a downward, corkscrew-like trajectory.

When Maxey borrowed his first $200,000 from Citizens National Bank in 1962 to begin converting his urban assets into ranches, Williams well understood the course that he was taking, Maxey said.[33] He and Williams discussed the fact that the cattle industry ran in long cycles and that it would take at least six years for the venture to begin to see a profit.

During that same period, Maxey said, his daughters and sons-in-law acquired 50 percent ownership of Plaza Building Corporation.[34] Subsequent to that transaction, he began folding many of his other assets into that corporation. With the help of his attorneys, Maxey embarked on a complex series of transfers and trades.[35] Most were "tax-free" exchanges, such as the deal in which he acquired the Triple M Ranch near Tulsa from Carl Bledsoe. To acquire that ranch, Maxey traded the Plainsman Hotel and then leased the hotel back from Bledsoe for $6,000 per month. Through such transactions, Maxey stated that he continued, with guidance from his attorneys at Evans, Pharr, Trout & Jones, to swap his hotels and other real estate properties for more ranches and rural properties in Oklahoma, New Mexico, Missouri, and the Texas Panhandle.

By May 1963, Maxey's debt to Citizens National Bank had grown to

$350,000.[36] Sometime that month, Maxey testified, Williams summoned him to his office and explained that bank examiners were pressuring him to obtain a chattel mortgage on Maxey's cattle for security. Williams said he wanted to farm out the loans to other banks, which would allow Maxey's $1 million line of credit to remain open.[37]

Six months later, in January 1964, Maxey's debt to the bank had increased to $750,000 and Williams informed Maxey that the bank examiners were adamant that Maxey put up collateral to cover his loans. At Williams's insistence, he pledged a portion of his shares in Maxey Lumber Company as security for the loans.[38]

On March 30, 1964, Maxey was informed by his lawyers that he would have to obligate additional collateral or the bank would call his loan. As Maxey told it, Chauncey "Chick" Trout, Jr., prepared the new collateral agreement and relayed a dire message from the bank. "He told me to sign the instruments," Maxey testified, "or the Citizens National Bank would call my loan."[39]

W. O. Shafer objected. Maxey's conversation with Trout, he explained, "will be hearsay as to the bank and the defendants that I represent." Excluding such testimony when it involved one of the defendants but no others, he conceded, would be difficult. Charlie Jones and Barney Evans subsequently rose to voice similar objections.[40]

Judge Moore declared the court in recess until after lunch. During the first portion of the recess, a hearing was held outside the presence of the jury to discuss the defense objections.

During the hearing, Shafer explained that, from time to time, certain evidence would be presented during the trial, such as Maxey's conversation with Trout, which might be admissible as to one defendant, but not to others. Shafer asked the judge for instructions on the procedures for attorneys to enter such objections. Judge Moore answered that she had not yet made up her mind on the issue and would issue her instructions later.

"Your Honor," said Bowlin, "we are taking the position that all of this evidence is admissible under our allegation of conspiracy. It's a circumstance that happened and it is all admissible, and admissible against each one of them. We have alleged a conspiracy involving every one of them, and we have a right to prove, according to the courts, we have a right to put in all of the circumstances which tend to prove the conspiracy."

"It is my understanding," said Moore, "that when a conspiracy is shown, then every act and circumstance and words become admissible, and that is all I intend to instruct the jury about."

Jones addressed the judge, repeating his contention that testimony that involved just one defendant, such as the Maxey-Trout conversation, would be hearsay as to the others. As they listened to Moore's responses, it appeared to the plaintiffs' table that the judge was not going to allow evidence of the conspiracy until she had ruled that the plaintiffs had offered sufficient evidence that such a conspiracy actually existed.

Jim Cade rose and spoke at length on legal precedents regarding the subject of conspiracy. When Judge Moore asked for citations, Cade reminded her that he had submitted a brief on the subject. Moore did not seem to remember anything about it, so Cade presented her with another copy.

Pending a final decision on such evidence, Moore stated that she would proceed by allowing the attorneys to make running objections and exceptions to such testimony for individual clients who were not involved in a direct manner, a decision that amounted to a small victory for both sides.[41]

When then jury was called back into the courtroom and Maxey returned to the witness stand, he was asked again about the conversation with Trout. Jones then addressed the judge, registering his objection to the testimony in regard to the other defendants.

"I sustain the objection as made," said Moore. "Conversation admissible as to Mr. Trout and Mr. Maxey between them."

When Bowlin asked a follow-up question about the conversation between Maxey and Trout, Jones objected again, and Moore overruled the objection.

Instructed by the judge to answer, Maxey testified: "I explained to Mr. Trout that the Citizens National Bank apparently at that time was violating the agreement that they had made prior to my moving to the bank, and he replied that he had orders from the Citizens National Bank to prepare the instruments, and that he, as my friend and attorney, would advise that I sign the papers or the loan would be called."[42]

Maxey stated that he then signed the documents because he felt he had no choice. Asked if the new collateral agreement benefitted him in any way, such as granting an extension of time on his note or conferring any value at all, he answered, "No."[43]

Over the course of the next several hours, Bowlin introduced twenty-three individual financial documents that Maxey had signed on March 30, 1964, in Chauncey Trout's office. Plaintiffs' exhibit number one was a copy of a chattel mortgage for a $350,000 note secured by the cattle on the Triple M Ranch (a herd consisting of over two thousand cattle), payable on demand to Citizens National Bank.

Bowlin: Did you get any money from [this] note dated March the 30th, 1964,
   in the amount of $350,000?
Maxey: No.

Exhibit number one was offered into evidence and was accepted, with no objection from the defense, and Bowlin moved on to exhibit number two, setting up a pattern that would become a familiar refrain, like a hammer pounding a nail into place. Number two was another note for $350,000 payable on demand to the bank. Again, Maxey answered "No" when asked if he received anything of value when he signed the note. Maxey also read off a series of payments made on the note, setting up another one of the allegations in the petition: that Maxey made payments to the bank on various notes, yet never received any credit for them, even on notes that purported to be renewals of previous ones. In addition to notes secured by cattle on the ranches, some were secured by equipment on a ranch or farm, and others were secured by notes that were due to Maxey by other parties.[44]

Bowlin orchestrated his questioning in a way that established a sense of familiarity and pattern throughout the long presentation of new documents. He wanted the jury to remember that his client had been forced to sign agreements that conflicted with his original agreement with the bank. According to the plaintiff's version of the events, Maxey was pressured to sign agreements that restricted his options—documents that had been, he alleged, prepared without his knowledge—by his own attorneys, who also worked for the bank.

Bowlin: Had you ever seen the instrument or heard it discussed prior to the
   time you got to Mr. Trout's office?[45]
Maxey: No.
Bowlin: Did you get, give or receive anything of value for the execution of
   that instrument?
Maxey: No.
Bowlin: Is it another instrument which you executed under threat of foreclo-
   sure?
Maxey: Yes.

Writing in the next day's *Lubbock Avalanche-Journal*, reporter Kenneth May summarized Maxey's testimony in colorful terms: "Maxey painted a word picture Wednesday of a gradually tightening loan belt that finally choked him out of far flung properties in four states."[46]

Continuing his testimony on Thursday, Maxey said that after the March

30, 1964, meeting at the bank, he was upset and concerned enough to consider transferring his business to other banks. By August of that year, he testified, he "felt the situation had improved" and he stopped looking for another bank.[47] Clyde Gordon, Jr., a vice president at Citizens National Bank whom Williams tasked with much of the bank's business with agricultural accounts, accompanied Maxey on an inspection tour of his ranches in July.

In October 1964, things took a definite turn for the worse. Maxey described being summoned to Williams's office by Trout for a noon meeting.[48] When he got there, he said, the curtains were drawn and Williams had shed his coat and rolled up his sleeves. A large stack of new financial instruments was being sorted. The papers took up every inch of space on Williams's desk, and some were even stacked on the floor beside it. The documents, which had been prepared for his signature, called for additional collateral assignments that would cross-mortgage the vast majority of Maxey's assets.

Tommy Elliott had accompanied Maxey to the meeting with Williams and Trout because his signature was required on some of the documents. Other bank representatives present at the meeting were Clyde Gordon and George Atkinson, a senior vice president. In the future, Tommy was the only other person in the room Maxey would ever feel friendly toward again.

"I was shocked," Maxey said. "I thought they had all the collateral I could possibly give and operate with." It didn't make sense to him. He said he was opposed to signing.

"Sign or we will foreclose today," Williams said.

"I told them I wouldn't sign," Maxey said, "that I'd take off for Dallas to the First National Bank [where] I had done business for years . . . Mr. Williams told me my business was in such a mess and the bank in Dallas would recommend they not take my business."[49]

Trout told Maxey to cooperate with the bank. "As your attorney," Trout said to him, "I advise you to sign." It was only later, Maxey said, he found out that Trout, Charlie Jones, and Bill Evans all owned stock in Citizens National Bank.

"I was shocked and upset and I began to sign the papers," Maxey told the jury.

Once Maxey finished signing the documents, Williams told him that he was putting Clyde Gordon in charge of all of Maxey's ranching operations.[50]

"[T]here was considerable discussion," he said, "regarding . . . the extent that I was not capable of operating, in their opinion, the cattle operation or farming operation on any of my properties because I did not have the background for operating cattle and farming, ranching business . . . I was told to instruct all the employees of all properties that the Citizens National Bank was taking over the operation and was ordered to reduce all loans and to liquidate my properties."

Bowlin asked if Williams had advised or instructed him to dispose of or liquidate some of his properties at any other time.

"That was the first time, yes," Maxey said.

Maxey felt a particular animosity toward Gordon after the meeting. In the section of the plaintiffs' petition accusing the defendants of ruining Maxey's good reputation with unflattering remarks and insinuations, Gordon's name was singled out for special mention.[51]

Testimony such as the foregoing was difficult to bear for Homer Maxey's wife and daughters. They had lived through the experience; now they were hearing about each humiliating episode in excruciating detail. The previous six or seven years had been a period of escalating conflicts and financial setbacks. His anxiety and simmering anger had inflicted a great deal of collateral suffering on the very people who loved him most.

Bill Goodacre, Glenna's husband, was working for Homer on the Triple M Ranch when E. W. Williams put Clyde Gordon in charge of all Homer's ranching operations. "Bill missed out on the opportunity of running a business that Daddy started," says Glenna. "I wish we could have kept that ranch. It was the biggest one and it was a good place. Losing it was a terrible misfortune."

"We heard his side of it," says Carla. "We knew his side of the story and we believed it. But I went into the trial with an open mind because I felt like there are two sides to every story. As bad as I hated E. W. Williams, you know, just because Daddy hated him, I still wanted to know both sides. You assume it had to be a case of right and wrong, but it really wasn't that at all."[52]

The October 1964 conference with Williams, Maxey testified, was "the final blow" that precipitated his downfall. In the months that followed, the bank assumed more and more control over his businesses, and Maxey found himself unable to move in any direction. He wanted to expand his ranching business, but the bank wouldn't let him spend a dime without prior approval, and it was a rare occasion when the bank's approval was given. He wanted to refinance his debt so he could end his relationship with Citizens National Bank, he said, but the bank thwarted those efforts as well.[53]

With Bowlin and Griffin taking turns at an easel where they documented Maxey's financial rise and fall with endless columns of figures, it took until 1:30 that afternoon to examine and enter into evidence the instruments Maxey signed at the October meeting. The new notes were secured by Maxey's stock in Maxey Lumber Company, Plaza Building Corporation, and the Triple M Feeders Corporation (an entity formed a few months earlier, at the urging of Williams, to control Maxey's ranching businesses). By the end of the day's testimony, the total figure for the notes that Maxey was pressured to sign between March 30, 1964, and early 1965 totaled almost $4.8 million. Many of the instruments, it should be noted, were renewals of previous loans. This fact would help explain the $4.8 million total, quadruple the amount Maxey had borrowed. Although most of the loans were made on a six-month term, he was often required to renew the notes before the due date, oftentimes at a higher rate of interest.[54]

The overall effect, Maxey claimed, was confusion and frustration. He never understood, he said, how the bank was handling his personal accounts or the separate accounts of the corporations. Also, he testified, "They were crediting notes as they saw fit."

Bowlin continued hammering home the familiar refrain as each new document was entered into evidence:

> Bowlin: And you received no money or anything of value for signing this note?
>
> Maxey: No.

All of the documents had been prepared by attorneys at Evans, Pharr, Trout & Jones, the firm that had represented Maxey for almost thirty years. He had paid the firm "from $35,000 to $50,000 a year" to handle his affairs and, he said, "relied for protection" on them.[55]

In November 1964, Maxey sold all the cattle on the Texline farm for just over $300,000 and applied the entire amount to his debt at Citizens National Bank. According to Bowlin's calculations, the payment should have reduced Maxey's debt from $1,208,000 to approximately $900,000. According to Maxey, however, the payment was never credited.[56]

> Bowlin: You mean you never got a single note marked paid, or a single release, or anything?
>
> Maxey: No.

Later, the bank sold two thousand head of Maxey's cattle from another location. Williams had ordered the sale, but, according to usual procedure, most of the logistical end was handled by Clyde Gordon. According to Maxey, the cattle were not ready for market, thus the sale resulted in a net loss of $135,000. Charlie Jones raised an objection, stating that Maxey's figure was unsupported by evidence. Judge Moore sustained the objection and instructed the jury to disregard it.[57]

Of all the contentious meetings between Maxey and his bankers and lawyers, the one in mid-January 1965 may have been the most explosive. Tommy Elliott was again asked to accompany Maxey to Trout's office on the ninth floor of the Citizens National Bank Tower. Maxey and Elliott were presented with another stack of financial instruments that Maxey was supposed to sign. Once again, Maxey testified, he was shocked to learn that the bank wanted even more collateral.

Some of the instruments, he testified, made no sense at all to him. One of the most unusual, Maxey recalled, was a deed of trust for an additional $20,000 mortgage on the Maxey home on Vicksburg Avenue.

> Maxey: I had quite an argument with Mr. Trout in that meeting regarding
> having to sign additional papers that I didn't know the reason for signing. I
> couldn't understand taking an additional mortgage on my home of $20,000.
> They had mortgages. I discussed with him the reasoning behind making
> deeds of trust and notes payable to me and transferring them to the bank
> when there [were] no properties or money changing hands. I couldn't un-
> derstand the deal. I had an argument with Mr. Trout about some of the
> papers being back-dated so they would become due in May of 1965 . . .
> back-dated to October to make them a six-month deal.
> Bowlin: Mr. Maxey, at that time, as a matter of fact, did you completely lose
> your temper?
> Maxey: Yes.[58]

Despite his concerns, Maxey followed his attorney's instructions and signed the documents. After the meeting, Maxey and Tommy Elliott went downstairs for an appointment with Williams. Bill Evans, who followed them downstairs from the law offices, caught up with them as they exited the elevator into the bank lobby. Evans told Maxey he had heard that there had been "a little spat" between him and Trout.

Using the type of blunt language for which he was renowned, Maxey gave his old friend a first-class dressing down. They argued for a few minutes and then moved the confrontation to Williams's office, where Maxey complained to Williams that he was putting him into what he called "a financial straitjacket."[59]

> Maxey: [It] was obvious to Mr. Evans that Mr. Williams and I were falling out, and he made the statement to me that he, and to Mr. Williams, that he would be unable to represent either side in the case that I became involved in any kind of dispute with the Citizens National Bank . . .
>
> Bowlin: Would you say that that was a meeting that all of you left at least not good friends at the moment?
>
> Maxey: That is true.[60]

After the meeting, Maxey realized he needed legal advice from an independent attorney. The person he called was James Milam, one of the most respected attorneys in Lubbock. Besides being a friend and fellow member of the empire builders, Milam was also chairman of the board at First National Bank of Lubbock.

Milam agreed to represent Maxey pro bono. In the end, Milam's help wasn't enough to prevent Maxey's financial disaster, but it was important for the jury to know that he had tried. Milam's reputation lent more credibility to Maxey's version of events.[61]

On Monday, November 3, Maxey's fourth day on the witness stand, the narrative of his relationship with Williams and the bank took a more sinister turn. With increasing frequency, Bowlin butted heads with Shafer and Jones, who were determined to exclude such evidence. As a result, much of the testimony was made during hearings outside the presence of the jury, so that Judge Moore could hear arguments by the opposing counsel regarding its admissibility. Motions by Shafer and Jones to exclude evidence regarding the controversial allegations made on the day in question were often, though not always, granted by Judge Moore.[62]

The day began with Maxey testifying about his trips to Houston, Tulsa, and New York City in early 1965 to meet with other bankers and financiers in efforts to refinance his indebtedness to Citizens National Bank. At the time, the total was approximately $1.2 million.[63]

In May 1965, Maxey made arrangements with the National Cattle Feeders Association (NCFA) in Oklahoma City for a loan of $250,000, which he intended to apply to his debt at Citizens National Bank.[64] The loan would have required the release of certain chattel mortgages held by the bank; however, as Maxey testified, Williams did not even want to consider it. The banker saw the NCFA deal as an attempt by Maxey to remain in the cattle business, not to take care of his obligations to the bank.

"He refused to take the money," Maxey testified. "He told me that I was instructed to liquidate and not to refinance [and] get out of the cattle business . . ."

In June, Williams accompanied Maxey on an inspection tour of Maxey's ranches.[65] At one point during the trip, Maxey complained about the fact that his calves were being sold before they had been fattened for the market. Such an egregious waste of money galled Maxey. "I told him," Maxey testified, "that it had killed my soul."

"He made the statement to me that my soul would be killed many times before this was over . . . It was obvious I would have to dig up the money I owed them, that they wanted all of the money or none."

Around the same time, Maxey sought financial advice from Harold Taft, the well-known Fort Worth television weatherman known to his television and radio audiences as "the world's greatest weatherman" and "the dean of TV meteorologists."[66]

Harold Taft and his brother, Bob, told Maxey they had been "arranging loans for churches," and that one of their financial consultants, William Ed Drumwright, might be able to help him.

Drumwright was the president and chairman of the board at a Phoenix-based company called Century Sales & Leasing, Inc. His wife, Dorothy, was the secretary-treasurer of the company, and other board members included Clifford A. Jones, a powerful Las Vegas attorney, Floyd R. Lamb, a former Nevada state senator, and Dale Robertson, a cowboy actor and Oklahoma native.[67]

Robertson, who had expressed an interest in buying the Triple M Ranch from Maxey, was a well-known cowboy actor who began working in television and film in the 1950s and was still active in the early 1990s. Robertson often portrayed square-jawed, straight-shooting cowboy types, but over the course of his career he also played the devious villain.[68]

Clifford A. Jones was a prominent figure in Nevada business, law, and politics. A decorated World War II veteran, Jones served two terms as lieutenant governor of Nevada (1948–1954) and founded a powerful Las Vegas law firm. Jones fronted for casino owners with mob ties, helping them obtain permits and serving as a go-between with other political powers in the state. Aside from real estate, his business interests included casinos (he was a part owner of at least seven casinos), banks, and cement.[69]

Floyd Lamb was one of the biggest landowners in Nevada. He gained public recognition in 1977 when an urban desert oasis located within the Las Vegas city limits was designated Floyd Lamb State Park. In 1983 Lamb was convicted of taking a $23,000 bribe from an undercover FBI agent in a sting known as Operation Yobo. He was paroled after serving nine months in prison.[70]

During Maxey's testimony, he related the history of his association with Ed Drumwright. Their first meeting occurred in February 1965 at the Adolphus Hotel in Dallas. Drumwright's wife Dorothy was present, along with the Elliotts, the Goodacres, and Maxey's accountant, Joseph Cassel. Maxey's need for refinancing was the main subject of the meeting. Their second meeting was in April 1965, when Ed and Dorothy Drumwright flew to Lubbock in Drumwright's private plane. Maxey picked them up at the airport and took the Drumwrights on a tour of his ranch properties. A few weeks later, Drumwright made an offer to buy Maxey's ranches, plus the Texline farm, for $4.5 million. Several other parties were to be involved in the financing. One key provision of the deal was a short-term loan of $1.3 million that would allow Maxey to pay off his Citizens National Bank loans, which were secured by second liens on the ranches.[71]

The defense objected to Maxey giving the figure of $4.5 million for the proposed sale, stating that it was unsubstantiated. Judge Moore sustained the objection.[72]

Ed Drumwright died in 2007, but his widow, Dorothy Drumwright, remembers their 1965 trip to Texas to meet with the Maxeys, the Goodacres, and the Elliotts. "My husband really did like Mr. Maxey," she says. "They became good friends. My husband was basically the finder for the loan. He had found a company that was going to loan Mr. Maxey the money. I don't remember all the particulars but what I do remember is that Mr. Maxey really got a raw deal from the bank."[73]

Although Dorothy Drumwright did not testify in the trial, Ed Drumwright did, along with two of his associates involved in financing Maxey's loan (W. L. Brady and Jack Wakefield). The so-called "Drumwright deal" would prove to be a major point of contention in the trial. Strenuous objections from the defense greeted almost any reference to Drumwright's association with Maxey. Jones and Shafer raised objections to the introduction of any telegrams, correspondence, and any other written communications about terms of financial arrangements for the refinancing deals by Drumwright on behalf of Maxey. The defense maintained that such communications were inadmissible because they were hearsay. Judge Moore sustained each objection. Bowlin and cocounsels Griffin and Cade each weighed in with counterarguments. Concessions from the bench were rare. Responding to Moore's refusal to allow testimony that established the fact that a telegram had been received, Griffin said, "Your Honor, is this not a statement of fact? Now, this is not a hearsay situation. I can understand taking individually your ruling on these things. I am not saying I agree with your overall ruling, we have taken exception to that . . . but the fact that there was a letter is a fact; that is not hearsay. The fact that there was a telegram is a fact; that is not hearsay . . ."[74]

Judge Moore replied, "Well, I don't want to argue with you; I am just making my ruling." The judge also sustained objections by the defense to testimony relating to material derived from certain depositions given by the other principal parties in the Drumwright deal. According to the plaintiffs' version of the story, the Drumwright deal had been canceled by a phone call to Drumwright's associate, W. L. Brady, by a man purporting to be Maxey's attorney who said that the loan was no longer necessary because Citizens National Bank had agreed to loan Maxey the money. Brady said that the phone call came from Charlie Jones.[75] Over the days and weeks to come, the fight over the admissibility of the telegram and other related pieces of evidence continued to rage. Moore continued to rule against the plaintiffs, but by the mere act of raising the issue, Bowlin helped underscore the importance of the Drumright deal in the minds of the jurors.[76]

The plaintiffs' narrative concerning the Drumwright deal comprised what was the most damning evidence of the plaintiffs' allegations of conspiracy and fraud, and specific aspects of that story showed Charlie Jones in a very bad light. The legal wrestling match over whether the story of the Drumwright deal was supported by allowable evidence was to be one of the most contentious aspects in the first and second trials in the Maxey case.[77]

According to Maxey's testimony, it was either on the first day of July or a few days later that he came under even more pressure to make the Drumwright deal happen. He was, he said, summoned to the bank by Clyde Gordon for a meeting with Williams and then told to wait out in the lobby well past their appointed meeting time. When Williams at last emerged from his office, he thrust a document into Maxey's hands and instructed him to sign it. The document, Maxey told the jury, was a power of attorney. His signature would give Williams permission to begin foreclosure.

Jim Milam was still acting as Maxey's attorney and "as a friend and go-between . . . trying to work something out" with the bank. That evening, however, Maxey decided to reach out to another friend.

"I went home that night," he told the jury, "and around seven o'clock called Mr. Dub Rogers, our present mayor, who had had difficulties with the Citizens National Bank and had used Dallas attorneys."[78]

Shafer objected on the grounds of hearsay. Jones chimed in and moved that the jury be instructed to disregard Maxey's answer. Judge Moore sustained Jones's objection and gave the requested instruction to the jurors. Despite her instructions to disregard the comment, however, it was sure to linger in the minds of anyone who lived in Lubbock. Dub Rogers had been a well-known and popular figure there for a long time, even before he was elected mayor on a write-in ballot, and even before he owned a TV station with his name in its call sign (KDUB-TV). Another function of Maxey's statement was to remind the jury that he wasn't the only person in town who'd had trouble with Citizens National Bank. Even insiders at the bank agreed that its reputation was not good.[79]

When Maxey resumed his testimony, he told the jury that Dub Rogers had recommended hiring a Dallas attorney named Henry Strasburger.[80] Within a few days' time, Strasburger came to Lubbock and talked Williams into agreeing to a compromise in which Strasburger would sign a limited power of attorney on Maxey's behalf and the bank would delay foreclosure for six months. During that time period, Maxey, with Strasburger's assistance, would begin liquidating his properties and/or seeking alternative financing to cure his indebtedness to Citizens National Bank.

The Strasburger agreement appeared to give Maxey some breathing room, but he was still under great pressure to get his finances in order. Maxey paid $35,000 to a New York firm for the preparation of a sales brochure on the ranches, only to learn that the bank had substituted sales prices in the brochure that were far below the ranches' real market value.[81]

Under the management of Citizens National Bank's Clyde Gordon, the buildings on the ranches had been vacated and left unattended after Maxey's cattle were sold.[82] Abandoning a ranch makes it "a distressed property," Maxey told the jury, which "depreciates the value to no end." Items such as fences, pens, and erosion abatement structures were left in disrepair. Many items of equipment were removed by bank representatives or stolen by thieves. Structures were vandalized.

On Tuesday, November 4, Maxey testified at length on exhibit number 159, a list of operating expenses and financial projections from his cattle operations. Jones interrupted the examination to register an objection. The interruption came at a moment when Bowlin was preparing to ask a question. He had barely opened his mouth when Jones objected.[83]

Judge Moore immediately ruled. "Sustained."

Bowlin was flustered. Maxey had already been testifying about the document for some time and the nature of the document had already been established by his answers. Jones based his objection on his claim that Maxey lacked sufficient experience in cattle ranching, thus his estimates and income projections could not be accepted as reliable.

Bowlin stuttered for a moment, trying to get back on track, then took advantage of the opportunity to call attention to what appeared to be the judge's bias against the plaintiffs.

Bowlin: Well, may I proceed with—I wasn't asking a question. May I proceed with the questioning that I was about to pursue?

Judge Moore: All right, go ahead.

Bowlin: It's awfully hard to conduct an examination when an objection is made before a question is asked and the objection is sustained, because I don't know what question—I haven't asked a question yet. I don't know where to go.

Judge Moore: I thought I just told you, so go ahead and ask the question, the next question.

Bowlin: Mr. Maxey, the second page is entitled "Plaza Building Corporation, Projection of Yearly Estimated Cash Income and Expenses." [The figures all pertain to] ranches and farms, correct?

Bowlin resumed his examination with questions about income projections for Plaza Building Corporation. Later, with the jury panel present, a lengthy voir dire examination was conducted, the ostensible purpose of which was to establish Maxey's credibility in the ranching business.[84] The hearing was held at Jones's request. He had made repeated objections during Maxey's testimony, alleging that Maxey had no expertise in ranching, and therefore his testimony on income projections was inadmissible. Maxey sat for a detailed list of questions pertaining to the dates he began operating each ranch and various details of their finances.

Many of the trial observers (including his daughters and wife) may have agreed that Homer Maxey was not at his best when it came to running a ranching operation, but the pertinent issue before the judge was whether his testimony on the income projections from the ranching operations could be entered into evidence.

When Jones repeated his objection at the end of the hearing, asking Moore to exclude Maxey's financial projections because they "obviously [were] not based on the witness's previous experience," Judge Moore's response must have come as a surprise to him.

"Overrule the objection," she said, "Number 159 admitted."

Wednesday was a day of dramatic testimony by Maxey about the final, humiliating stages of his economic downfall. Much of the morning was taken up with testimony about the Plainsman and Pioneer Hotels.[85] As Maxey related the sequence of events, an odd detail emerged: W. E. Lavender and Edwin Nichols, the two men who bought the Pioneer from Maxey, both died within two years of the purchase. Nichols died in March 1965, at the age of 41, thirteen months after Maxey was forced to foreclose on the Pioneer because the mortgage was in default. Lavender died in November 1965 at the age of 90. Maxey foreclosed on the Plainsman in July 1965.

Maxey's testimony also addressed the reason he took out a second lien on the Pioneer Hotel. The mortgage secured cash loans Maxey had extended to Plaza Building Corporation in the amount of $550,000. Maxey testified that he used his own cash for the loans, supplemented by funds derived from the sale of bonds and life insurance policies.[86] The fact that Maxey had made a cash loan to a corporation in which he was the majority stockholder and secured that loan with a second mortgage on a financially unstable investment (the hotel) caused his bankers a great deal of concern and alarm. David Hughes (an associate of Evans, Pharr, Trout & Jones, board member at Citizens National Bank, son of former Citizens National Bank president, John Hughes, and one of the nine remaining individual defendants) views Maxey's actions in a very negative light. Taking out the second mortgage on the Pioneer, says Hughes, caused some members of the community to question Maxey's sanity. "It may have been instrumental in generating the feeling of sympathy for his wife and children by the jury," states Hughes, "but it was evident to the general community and his friends that he was, at best, vindictive."[87]

Maxey's explanation to the jury was that he took out the second lien because he felt certain the bank was about to foreclose and take over the stock in the Plaza Building Corporation. Because the hotel was owned by Plaza, he knew that the bank would try to liquidate it when they foreclosed, but with the second lien, they would have to account to him if they attempted to do so.[88]

"If [the bank] wanted to be honest and fair with you," Bowlin asked his client, "this [second lien] would not affect the bank in any way, would it?"

"No," Maxey replied.

Maxey had good reason to suspect that the bank was about to pull the rug out from under him.[89] The Strasburger agreement had expired and the bank was again pressuring him to sign a power of attorney. Discussions about revising the power-of-attorney agreement to be less restrictive went nowhere. Maxey hired another attorney, Tom Duggan, who was an old friend of the family. The arrangement, however, was short-lived. Maxey testified that he was instructed not to bring Duggan to any meetings at the bank. He didn't say why.

On December 28, 1965, Maxey had to sign loan agreements that increased the rate of interest on his indebtedness from seven to eight-and-a-half percent.

On February 15, 1966, the day after Maxey took out the second lien on the Pioneer, he was summoned to a meeting at Citizens National Bank.

Bowlin: What was that conversation?[90]

Maxey: I advised Mr. Williams that I had an appointment with Mr. Morgan and Mr. Warnicke in Los Angeles on February 16, 1966; I had my reservations made and the appointment was set up to close a loan with Mr. Warnicke to pay off the Citizens National Bank.

Bowlin: What . . . did Mr. Williams advise you?

Maxey: Mr. Williams, the afternoon of February the 15th, told me in the presence of Chauncey Trout, Tom Duggan, and other officials of the bank that if I left town, that he would foreclose while I was gone . . .

Bowlin: What happened next?

Maxey: I told him that he would just have to foreclose. Now, that was the afternoon of February 15.

Bowlin: February 15th?

Maxey: February 15th.

Bowlin: Did you hear from anybody representing the bank after that?

Maxey: At 11:30 p.m. on the night of February 15th, I received a telephone call from Mr. Harold Blank who related to me that Mr. Jones had called for him to cancel my trip to Los Angeles.

Shafer: I will object to that conversation, as that would be hearsay as to all defendants, Your Honor.

Moore: Sustained.

Jones: We ask again that the witness be instructed not to repeatedly make hearsay statements that are not even responsive to questions.

Bowlin: Homer, if you will, listen to my question and just answer the questions that I ask you.

Maxey: I'm sorry.

Maxey's allegation, that Jones had telephoned Blank on Williams's behalf, helped support allegations that the bank had interfered with his efforts to refinance his debt and with his day-to-day business operations. It would also remind jurors of the claim that Charlie Jones made the phone call that killed the Drumwright deal.

When Bowlin resumed his direct examination, he asked Maxey if he had any further conversations with anyone from the bank after the 11:30 p.m. call from Harold Blank.[91] Maxey answered "Yes," saying that Williams had called him next, at 1:10 a.m. Melba took the call. Maxey wouldn't speak to him. Williams called back five minutes later, but Maxey still wouldn't take the phone. The next morning, he canceled the trip to California.

Chauncey Trout also called that day to tell Maxey to be at the bank at 10:30 a.m. and that he wasn't to bring his lawyer, Tom Duggan. Instead, Maxey enlisted the help of another Lubbock attorney, Hugh Anderson, who accompanied him to the meeting. Bowlin asked Maxey what transpired next.

Maxey: I was instructed again to sign the power of attorney, including my wife's signature, release the second lien that I had placed on the Pioneer Hotel, [and] resign as officer and director of all corporations . . . [I was also] advised of the debts I owed Citizens National Bank.

Bowlin: Did you refuse to do the things which they demanded that you do?

Maxey: I did.

Bowlin: Did anything else happen at the meeting?

Maxey: Mr. Anderson and I left the office.

Bowlin: Did you hear anything else from that day?

Maxey: I was advised that they had a sale of my properties at 3:00 p.m. that afternoon.

Bowlin: Who advised you that they sold your properties at 3:00 p.m. that afternoon?

Maxey: Charlie Jones advised my attorney.

Bowlin: Did they advise you that they had a private sale in the office of Mr.
E. W. Williams, at which meeting only the officers and directors of the Citizens National Bank were present?

Maxey: Yes.

Bowlin: Did they advise you that they sold the properties to either themselves
or companies which they claimed were owned by the bank?

Maxey: Yes.

A few minutes later Bowlin asked Maxey about the prices that the bankers
got for his assets after the foreclosure action was initiated.[92] Plaza Building
Corporation, which owned most of the ranch properties, the hotels, and a
long list of other properties and assets, was sold for $749 to Monterey Lub-
bock Corporation, an affiliate corporation owned by the bank. The Triple M
Feeders Corporation, which controlled the ranching operations, was sold for
$1,000, also to Monterey Lubbock Corporation. His stock shares in Maxey
Lumber Company were sold for $231,000, which would seem to be a bargain
price considering that company's annual profits averaged between $75,000
and $100,000.

When Maxey Lumber was sold, several years after the foreclosure, the
purchaser was Maxey's lead attorney, Ken Bowlin. "Homer actually encouraged me to buy it," explains Bowlin.[93] "He gave two reasons: He told me it
was a great deal and that someday, when all this was over with and he got
back on his feet again, he would buy it back from me."

Another major Maxey asset, H & H Corporation, owned real estate in
Lubbock worth a total of $270,249 according to Alton Griffin's calculations.
Maxey's stock shares in H & H Corporation, which amounted to 75 percent
of the stock, were valued by his attorneys at $45,000. The stocks were sold
for $37,500.[94]

The list continued, but nothing had the impact of the $749 that Monterey
Lubbock Corporation paid for Plaza Building Corporation.[95]

Bowlin finished his line of questioning by drawing attention to a few
more examples of seeming irregularities in the bank's actions. In March 1966,
one month after the foreclosure, Maxey learned that Citizens National Bank
was about to sell the cattle on the Triple M Ranch to Lubbock cattle broker
J. E. Birdwell.[96]

The news did not sit well with Maxey. Back in 1964, Birdwell had made an offer to buy the Triple M Ranch from Maxey.[97] Williams had advised Maxey to take the offer. Maxey refused, however, saying the offer was far too low. The ranch wasn't even for sale at that time.

The bank's pending arrangement with Birdwell to buy the Triple M cattle struck Maxey as being suspect. Birdwell, an old friend of Williams, was married to the sister of Citizens National Bank director William Ellwood Keeney. The Keeneys were a blue-blooded family from New England with ancestors who had made the trip to America on the Mayflower. They had married into the Ellwood family, which owned massive tracts of ranchlands in Texas and New Mexico.[98]

Even some of the bank's supporters expressed the opinion that, at least for appearances' sake, another buyer for the cattle should have been found. Williams still insists there was nothing wrong with selling the cattle to Birdwell.[99]

"Homer had gotten a judge to put a restraining order on the cattle so they could not be sold," explains Williams. "We got it revoked and then we had to sell the cows before he got another restraining order put on them. I called Birdwell and sold the cattle right there on the phone. We were just trying to protect the bank's collateral."

Other cattle brokers, however, had made better offers for the same cattle. Emmet Marcum, who operated an auction yard in Hominy, Oklahoma, testified that he had appraised the herd at $233,000.[100] That amount was $60,000 greater than the $173,000 that the bank had accepted on the sale to Birdwell and his partner, E. C. Mullendore III.[101]

If the low sales price aroused further suspicion of conspiracy and fraud, so did the easy financing terms offered by the bank. The bank accepted a down payment of just $1,500 each from Birdwell and Mullendore and loaned the partnership the balance of $170,000.

The irksome details continued to pile up: Over the next few months, the cattle were fattened on Maxey's former ranch land, using Maxey's feed and equipment without charge, he claimed. The cattle were then sold for $320,000. The sale netted Birdwell and Mullendore a profit of $126,000. The amount, Maxey testified, should have been applied to his indebtedness to the bank, but it was not.

Also, claimed Maxey, when the bank took over the operation of his ranches (in the months before the foreclosure), the bank had continued to charge him for the salaries, motel bills, and other expenses, even though they were employees of the bank. Clyde Gordon was a vice president at Citizens National Bank, yet even the charges for his services on the ranches were billed to Maxey.[102]

Maxey was still testifying at 2:55 on the afternoon of Wednesday, November 5, 1969, when Judge Moore announced a twenty-minute break. When the court reconvened, Bowlin stood and said, "Pass the witness." Then he sat down.[103]

As the defense team began shuffling their files and shifting gears for cross-examination, Shafer asked for and was granted a ten-minute break. Just the day before, Bowlin had told the court he didn't expect to finish until Monday or Tuesday at the earliest.

When court resumed, the time was 3:35 in the afternoon. The jurors were tired and the day was almost done. Try as he might, Shafer gained little traction during his questioning of Maxey. Maxey may have been bankrupt, but he still owned the momentum in the courtroom.

The session dragged on for about twenty minutes, punctuated by uncharacteristic stumbles by Shafer and delays as his team scrambled to get their exhibits in the right order. Judge Moore banged her gavel and gave voice to the obvious. "Perhaps," she said, "if we recess until morning . . . the attorneys might have a better opportunity to organize their exhibits and present them a little bit faster."

For more than a week, Homer Maxey had been on the stand, telling a very compelling story. Tomorrow the defense team would get their chance to try to cut that story to pieces.

During the period of time that Maxey was scrambling to keep his financial empire afloat, both sons-in-law worked overtime to help him manage the hotels, ranching operations, and other properties to which Maxey still held title or some sort of leaseback arrangement. The strain of his father-in-law's predicament seems to have been more burdensome to Tommy Elliott than to Bill Goodacre. Elliott's comments about those times offer a perspective not shared by other close family members and friends.

In Elliott's point of view, the tragedy of the foreclosure was presaged as early as 1960, when Maxey purchased the Hotel Lubbock. After renaming it the Pioneer Hotel, Maxey launched on a major renovation program while at the same time scrambling to trade all his urban assets for ranch properties. Decades later, Elliott still remembers feeling as if he was being pulled in several different directions at once.[104] "I was back at the mortgage loan company," says Elliott, "working my ass off trying to support my wife and kids," when Maxey recruited him to manage the Plainsman Hotel. He had already left the mortgage company once before to assist with the opening of the Pioneer. According to Elliott, he never wanted the jobs or the pressure that went along with them. "Why would I want to manage that old hotel? I already had a good job."

Between 1962 and 1965, working for Homer Maxey could be a stressful and thankless proposition. Both hotels were in decline for various reasons that had grown out of the complex exchanges Maxey had made to obtain his ranches.

First, he had traded the Plainsman Hotel to the Bledsoe family in exchange for the Triple M Ranch. Under the terms of the exchange, as cited previously, the Bledsoes would own the hotel but Maxey would lease it back from them for $6,000 a month. Later on, he made another swap for a ranch property by trading the Pioneer Hotel plus the Plainsman lease and the shopping center at Twenty-Sixth and Boston.[105] The buyers were W. E. Lavender and Edwin Nichols. It would appear that Lavender and Nichols intended to flip the properties for a quick profit. Instead they defaulted on the mortgage payments on the Pioneer and failed to make the lease payments on the Plainsman. Maxey was forced to foreclose on both hotels.

The blow to Maxey's business operations could not have come at a worse time. With the help of his sons-in-law, Maxey resumed operating the hotels in mid-1964, but it was not a pleasant situation for anyone involved. Under pressure from Citizens National Bank, Maxey had no cash flow to make improvements or even keep up appearances. Elliott was caught in the middle doing thankless jobs, forced into a career path with diminishing prospects.

"They tell you, 'We want to keep everything in the family,' and 'Mr. Maxey wants this or that . . . ' So you try to be a good guy. I'm a good guy, but you get assassinated," he says. "That's why I quit. I told myself, I'd better get out of here, fast."[106]

Asked for his opinion of E. W. Williams, Jr., Elliott says, "I always thought a lot of him. He's a smart guy and he knew ranching business. He knew the cattle business and he knew the Tulsa ranch would be a jewel. I know he wanted it. So they got Homer under the gun, where they had him borrowing all this money. Money, money, money." Homer Maxey's downfall, according to Elliott, was a combination of poor decisions that left him vulnerable and the conflict of interest of the law firm that represented not only Maxey but also Citizens National Bank. "And of course Charlie Jones was a very ambitious, really smart guy," Elliott recalls. "I think they just saw an opportunity. They said, 'Well, the old man's going to lose those ranches anyway, why not jump in there and get them ourselves?'"[107]

An alternative spin on the narrative of Maxey's downfall—much more negative than Tommy Elliott's—is offered by Jack Flygare. Flygare was a friend and colleague to Charlie Jones and other partners and associates at Evan, Pharr, Trout & Jones. Today Jones's son is a senior partner in the firm, which is now known as Jones, Flygare, Brown & Wharton.

In addition to having been a member of the firm when the suit went to trial, Flygare knew Maxey and often saw Maxey and his brother, Robert, in the law office. When Flygare married his fiancée, Arlett Arnett, Homer and Melba threw a party for the couple. Arlett was the daughter of the Maxeys' good friends, Olga and Dr. S. C. Arnett, Jr.[108]

"Back in those days, they gave all kinds of parties," says Flygare, "and when somebody got married in your family, your friends would actually fight to be the one to give the party for your son or the daughter or whatever."

When Maxey's attorneys filed their original lawsuit in 72nd District Court, four members of the law firm were named as defendants. "Since he was pretty much gang-suing a lot of innocent people," Flygare says, "I won dered why he didn't sue me, too. I felt like the reason he probably didn't sue me was because I was Dr. Arnett's son-in-law." Then, with a chuckle, he says, "but there may have been other reasons."

Flygare remembers that Bill Evans did not want his law firm to be involved in the lawsuit. "There was no conflict of interest," maintains Flygare, "but Bill Evans felt like there was a conflict of clients." Flygare is of the opinion that the firm would have been better off if had it stayed out of the case.

"The firm got a lot of bad publicity," he says, "because everybody knew we represented Homer for years." The case also cost the firm a lot of money in lost revenue, as the time and energy of their top-earning attorney [Jones] was dominated by the Maxey case for so many years.

Flygare says that he did not work on the Maxey case, but because of his close relationship with so many of the participants, he developed strong opinions about it. There's no mistaking the anger in his voice as he asserts that Maxey's friends and trial attorneys "sold the community" on a "bullshit" version of Homer's financial collapse.

"They said that there wasn't any reason for the bank to foreclose," says Flygare, "that the bank was greedy and they just wanted his assets. That was the whole pitch that he was selling to the community. That's what his law-yers were selling to the jury, and it's actually asinine. I mean, when you think about it, all the bank wanted was its money back."

Flygare's feelings of antagonism toward Maxey seem undimmed by the passage of time. In his view, Maxey alone was to blame for his downfall, and all his wounds were self-inflicted. Then, being unable to accept failure, Maxey blamed all his problems on his bank and his former attorneys, accusing them of taking advantage of him.[109] Flygare's statements are insightful, despite the fact that some of them were refuted by evidence presented in court. Such strong opinions and impressions are reminders that the Maxeys weren't the only constituency in Lubbock who believed their reputation had been im-pugned.

Juror

Broke, Not Broken

Chapter 7

THE OTHER SIDE

OF THE STORY

Those who participated in and attended the Maxey trials still retain powerful memories of the experience. The name W. O. Shafer may not immediately spring to mind, but they remember the lead defense attorney's bent frame and caustic wit. They remember that the presiding judge was a polio survivor who wore cat's-eye glasses. J. E. Birdwell and his tobacco pipe may have made an impression. Ken Bowlin, with his good looks and suave manner, was a favorite of many. With his wide grin, broad shoulders, and oversized glasses, Alton Griffin had the look of a high school teacher. Charlie Jones bristled with self-assurance, despite the dark circles under his raptor eyes. Jim Cade was aged and cranky, but with his encyclopedic knowledge of the law, he was always ready with a case citation.

Melba Maxey, slender and well-dressed, the classic image of a Lubbock wife of a successful man, was in the courtroom every day, taking notes. Each week she wrote a letter to her sister, Doris.[1] Doris and Curtis "Jiggs" Cheaney lived in Watsonville, California, with their two girls, Jan and Kim. Their son, Chuck, was serving in the army in Vietnam. Using the salutation "Dear Family," Melba enclosed the previous week's coverage of the trial from the *Avalanche-Journal*, a collection of news clippings dated in pencil and bound together with a paper clip. In one letter, Melba enumerated her answers to Doris's queries on the previous week, commenting, "You ask more questions than Charlie Jones."

Melba, at left, poses with two unidentified friends on the Triple M Ranch near Tulsa, Oklahoma. Triple M stands for Melba Mae Maxey. Courtesy of the Maxey family.

At Melba's side were Carla and Glenna, both married with young children. The man his daughters still referred to as Daddy Maxey expected them to be there every day.

His daughters marveled at their father's performance in court. With his bald head and ruddy complexion, Homer Maxey presented a stolid forbearance on the witness stand that held steady day after day, no matter what Shafer or Jones threw at him. Once in a while, when the tone used by a defense attorney sounded snide or hectoring, Maxey would scowl at his antagonist, answering with a growl in his voice. Most of the time, however, he remained confident and imperturbable. Mafia trials have seen few witnesses as hard to crack. On the witness stand, Maxey was like a boxer who knows how to take a punch without yielding an inch of the ring to his opponent. "Homer was the most antagonistic witness in history," says Bobby Moody, a Lubbock attorney who was an associate with Evans, Pharr, Trout & Jones in the 1960s.[2]

"If Shafer or Jones asked the question, 'Did you sign this note?' Maxey would say, 'I don't know,'" recalls Moody. "They would ask him to look at it and he would stall. They'd ask if that was his signature and he would say, 'I guess it is.' He'd draw everything out, making them work for every single answer."

Moody's involvement in Maxey's affairs was limited primarily to handling title examinations. Moody did not assist the firm in the trial and was not privy to the evidence in the case. He did not testify in the trial or attend it, but he has strong opinions about it.

"Homer was a very successful businessman, and then he wasn't anymore," says Moody. "He made some bad decisions and he was gullible. He would not listen to advice that he didn't agree with. He bought a ranch in Hidalgo County that had no water rights, which meant it was basically worthless. Another time he wanted to buy this hot-sheet motel in Wichita Falls. This thing supposedly had a heliport. I went up there with him to inspect it and the heliport was just some bricks with a white circle painted on it." "Homer was a flat-out liar," adds Moody. "He did not want to be known as a failure and when he made mistakes he could not admit it."

The lawyers who represented the bank were accustomed to defending corporate clients. Insurance firms, oil companies, and other big businesses were their bread and butter. Ken Bowlin and Jim Cade, by comparison, represented a diverse clientele. Sometimes they went to court for the rich and powerful, sometimes for the little guy.[3]

One irony of the Maxey case was that, by suing his bank and his former law firm, Maxey assumed the role of the little guy in a David-and-Goliath struggle. The lawyers and their clients found such aspects of the case exceedingly frustrating.

In the media war, Maxey's side of the story appeared to have the upper hand. Daily coverage in the *Avalanche-Journal* began with his direct testimony and continued through the first day of cross-examination. With headlines such as "Defense Disputes Property Values," the reportage lacked the drama of the first seven days Maxey was on the stand.[4] Even after a day of aggressive grilling by Shafer, the coverage on Thursday, November 6, was a retread of Maxey's direct testimony earlier in the week, including Maxey's plan to meet with financiers in Los Angeles the day before the foreclosure. One article reminded readers that when Williams learned of Maxey's intentions, the banker informed him that foreclosure proceedings would be launched immediately if Maxey left for California. Maxey canceled the trip, but the bank foreclosed anyway.[5]

Throughout his vigorous and relentless cross-examination, Shafer pounced upon apparent contradictions in Maxey's previous testimony and questioned the accuracy of his financial statements.

On the subject of the Pioneer Hotel, Shafer produced a financial statement by Maxey that put the value of the hotel at $1.7 million, then asked Maxey if he could remember the price that Great Southern Life Insurance Company paid for the Pioneer after the foreclosure. Maxey said he didn't remember, but the amount was revealed to be $295,000. Great Southern later sold the hotel for $250,000 but, within a year, the buyer had defaulted and the insurance company was forced to take the property back again.[6]

Bowlin objected to the line of questioning, asserting that a forced sale at auction "on the courthouse steps" in no way proved the real value of the Pioneer Hotel. "[T]he test of the value of property," he argued, "is that price which a willing seller would sell to a willing buyer, who is willing to buy, but not compelled to buy, and the seller is not compelled to sell." Left unsaid was the fact that Maxey's $1.7 million valuation of the Pioneer Hotel was made when the hotel was open for business, and that there was nothing unusual about a defunct business property being sold at auction for a fraction of what it was worth when it was an ongoing business concern.

Judge Moore overruled Bowlin's objection and the evidence was admitted. Twisting the knife, Shafer read aloud from the writ ordering the public sale of the hotel, which took up well over five minutes' time and established little, except for giving Shafer the opportunity to point out certain parts of the document, including the $295,000 sales price. We must presume that Shafer's intent was to suggest that the hotel being sold for such a low price must have been a humiliating—and therefore, unforgettable—experience for Maxey.[7]

The strategy of the defense was to compile and present a huge list of Maxey's actions that painted a more complex and darker picture of the man than jurors had heretofore seen. Maxey, they alleged, had a long a history of giving inflated values for properties, cheating on his taxes, making false claims about the management of his accounts by Citizens National Bank, and giving false or misleading statements in his testimony. The insinuations were made in property trades that were so complex as to be almost beyond comprehension, conflicting financial statements, and tax returns that showed Maxey paid less than $200 in income tax during years in which he testified that he had made well over $200,000 in salaries alone.[8]

However, there was nothing illegal in the figures entered on Maxey's income tax returns. Nor was it unusual. To say that Maxey took advantage of all the loopholes and special advantages his CPA recommended was to say that he was pretty much like every other businessman he knew, and pretty much like any other individual in his position in America. Until the tax law was changed in 1986, a taxpayer could write off 100 percent of any depreciation of assets, even if that depreciation figure exceeded the current value of the property.

If some of the insinuations and counternarratives made by the defense failed to persuade, their hope seemed to be that the sheer collective weight of them would crush Maxey's own narrative of allegations against the bankers and their associates. Every piece of evidence that cracked Maxey's veneer of honesty and integrity was a possible opening to wider, more serious injuries to the plaintiffs' case.

Most members of the jury had probably never been involved in a financial transaction more complicated than a real estate mortgage, an automobile loan, or a small business or agricultural loan. If trading hotel deeds and leases for ranches did not strike them as being exotic, the messy details of the collapse of such deals by default were certain to raise questions and doubts.

The defense attorneys' attack on Maxey's reputation continued with the comparison of conflicting financial statements from Plaza Building Corporation. Both statements were issued on January 31, 1965, and signed by Maxey. One statement gave the value of the Triple M Ranch as $1,482,000 and the Texline farm as $580,000. The other statement posted the values as $1,750,000 for the Triple M and $650,000 for the farm at Texline.

Asked if those were his figures, Maxey replied yes. Instead of taking the opportunity to question Maxey about the discrepancies, Shafer moved on to a third document from 1964 that gave the value of the Triple M as $963,300.[9]

> Shafer: We are talking about the same ranch, aren't we, Mr. Maxey?
>
> Maxey: No, sir.
>
> Shafer: Not talking about the same ranch?
>
> Maxey: No, sir.
>
> Shafer: All right, sir. What is the difference, if you will tell me, please sir?
>
> Maxey: Well, you have the Zink lease added to this ranch; you have the Keystone Dam was completed; the lake was filled on this statement, making the shoreline, the development property, [a] valuable piece of property that [it] wasn't in 1964.

Maxey's explanation referred to the additional sixty-one hundred acres of property he leased from an adjacent landowner and friend, John Zink, and the filling of the Keystone Dam reservoir, which resulted in twelve-and-a-half miles of valuable lakefront property on Maxey's acreage. Shafer failed to score any points in the initial skirmish.[10]

Turning to the subject of the ranch near Wilburton, Oklahoma, Shafer reviewed the list of properties that Maxey had exchanged for the property. The list included a small shopping center valued at $20,000, plus $38,500 equity in residential duplexes, and a $56,000 lien on the ranch, for a total of $114,500. When those amounts were added together, Shafer asserted, the 2,060 acre ranch proved to be worth $55 an acre, yet Maxey had valued the ranch at $95 an acre.[11] Left unsaid, however, was that Shafer's mathematical calculations did not reflect the actual market value of the ranch.

Shafer next shifted to the subject of the 4,935 acre Atoka ranch, which Maxey had acquired in a much more complicated exchange. As part of the deal, Maxey had traded 243 acres of ranchland near McKinney, Texas, which he said he remembered as being "debt free." Shafer then produced a document showing a $40,000 lien on the McKinney property.[12]

Although Maxey contested it, Shafer also offered evidence that he contended demonstrated that Maxey had inflated the values of the Tucumcari ranch and the Green Acres apartments in Amarillo.[13]

As described by reporter Kenneth May in the *Lubbock Avalanche-Journal*, the defense team appeared intent on portraying Maxey as "a man whose business ventures were not always as profitable—or worth as much—as he would have liked for people to believe."[14]

Shafer and Jones strove to illustrate that, in his various real estate exchanges, Maxey had inflated the property values on his financial statements, a practice that enabled him to show a much greater net worth for Plaza Building Corporation, the umbrella company that owned or traded the assets in such transactions. The defense team contended that, after foreclosure, Citizens National Bank had merely sold those assets on the basis of their true market value and that Maxey's estimate of losses from the liquidation was a fantasy.

Maxey's attorneys were careful to emphasize, however, that in any type of forced sale, such as a foreclosure, buyers do not expect to pay the actual market value for the assets that are being sold. Therefore, the prices the bank realized when selling off Maxey's ranches could hardly be expected to reflect their true worth.

Also, in the banking industry, a lender is obligated to make a record of any perceived discrepancy or doubt as to the value of a collateralized property, particularly if the lender suspects it is worth less than the customer claims, and place such information in the customer's credit file. Under normal circumstances, such documentation would be offered as evidence in court.

The attorneys for the bank insisted that Maxey had not been mistreated or cheated in any way. After selling Maxey's assets and applying that money to Maxey's debt, the bank claimed that Maxey still owed it $300,000. To arrive at this sum, the bank used very different valuations of Maxey's properties than the amounts he claimed they were worth. Using Maxey's figures for the value of the properties, the bank had sold his assets for approximately $2 million less than their actual worth.

The defense attorneys confidently framed all the issues of the lawsuit as a simple math problem. If you accepted their calculations, then the bank had not damaged Maxey. They did not owe him any money and, by deduction, had not acted in bad faith.

Dozens of hours of testimony were expended attempting to nail down the argument. To read the transcript or follow the trial through reporter Kenneth May's twice-daily coverage is to wade through a tidal wave of details designed to support the bank's distillation of the issues into a simple mathematical formula.

The juror Gwendolyn Murphy remembers feeling that the defense attorneys were arrogant and unlikeable. "No one really discussed it until the end," says Murphy. "We were very conscientious. But it turned out that we all thought the same thing. We didn't like them to begin with and we didn't like their presentation. We found them offensive."[15]

Studying the transcript of the trial, it isn't difficult to find samples of Shafer's rhetorical tactics that could be interpreted as condescending and calculated to elicit a negative opinion of the witness. Shafer began his cross-examination of Maxey with a promise to try to keep his questions simple and clear. "I will make an effort," said the attorney, "to keep my questions so that there will be no difficulty in understanding them. Undoubtedly before I am through I will fail several times, so I will depend on you to tell me when I don't make myself clear to you. Is that fair enough?"[16]

Such statements were part of a concerted effort by the defense to humiliate and annoy Maxey, says Glenna Goodacre, by treating him as if he were befuddled or senile.

"Poor Daddy," she says, "he sat in front of that jury for days and weeks and he was constantly belittled. It was a sad state of affairs. He was on the stand for weeks identifying all these different papers and Charlie Jones would hand them to him upside-down or backwards so he had to turn each one around. They were trying to make him look like a fool."[17]

At another point in his cross-examination of Maxey, Shafer used a financial statement in an attempt to quickly knock down Maxey's $3 million valuation of Plaza Building Corporation. He began his line of questioning by getting Maxey to agree that the value of any corporation is the sum of its assets, minus its liabilities.[18]

Maxey agreed with the statement, despite the fact that the sum in the assets-minus-liabilities equation would only indicate the "book value," not the "reasonable value" of the corporation. A "no" answer to the question might have appeared argumentative, but it would not have been inappropriate.

Shafter continued. When listing Plaza's liabilities, the bank's attorney included the figure of $1,440,000, the total amount of the Plainsman lease, $6,000 a month for twenty years. When Plaza's other liabilities were added in, the corporation ended up over $700,000 in the hole. Therefore, the logic went, Monterey Lubbock Corporation paid more than the corporation was worth when it paid its affiliate Citizens National Bank $749 for Plaza.

Asked if he agreed with that conclusion, Maxey answered that Shafer's computations did not take into consideration the release agreement or income offsetting. Shafer persisted with the same line of questioning, but Maxey refused to be drawn into an argument about it. "That's your interpretation," he said, stating that he did not agree with Shafer's math.[19]

Another key allegation the defense sought to nullify was the claim that Williams had reneged on a promise to guarantee Maxey an unsecured line of credit up to one million dollars. Shafer asked Maxey, who had been a director and loan committee member at American State Bank for eleven years, if that bank had required security on their loans.

"On some we did and some we didn't," Maxey replied. Following up on that answer, he added, "We never required security after an agreement was made."[20]

Maxey refused to bow or break down when confronted with information from his income tax returns. In previous trial testimony and on financial statements, Maxey had claimed a stock value of $485,000 for the Green Acres apartments but, on one of his tax returns, the figure was $117,000.[21]

Shafer: Now, do you still say the stock was worth $485,000?

Maxey: Yes.

Shafer: But you told the government it was worth $117,000 when it came time to pay taxes on it?

Maxey: Yes.

Shafer: Did you under-report it to the government in that amount ($368,000)?

Maxey: I reported what is on the tax return.

In 1962, it was revealed, Maxey had paid a personal income tax of $166.55.[22] Shafer asked Maxey if 1962 was "the first time in five or six years" that Maxey had paid any income tax. Maxey replied that he didn't know.

Shafer: Can we agree that for the years 1960 to 65 every operation you had was showing you were losing money?

Maxey: The returns say that, yes.[23]

On Friday, the second full day of cross-examination, Shafer queried Maxey about an apartment project in Amarillo, asking if that project had been "turned back" to the mortgage holder because it was in default. Maxey testified that there had been no foreclosure proceedings, qualifying his answer with "as I remember." But Shafer produced a sale data sheet stating that "default has occurred in payment. . . ."[24]

Shafer attempted to follow up that point by questioning Maxey about a document relating to the Plaza Apartments, which Maxey built with the assistance of the FHA in 1948. As before, Maxey testified that he did not remember that project going into default with the government.

At that point, Bowlin registered an objection, stating that 1948 was long before any of the events at issue in the lawsuit and had nothing to do with it.

Judge Moore sustained the objection and advised the jury not to consider any of the questions regarding that subject.[25]

Shafer's cross-examination continued with more detailed questioning about taxes. The apparent purpose was to prove that Maxey never paid a penny more than he was legally obligated to pay. It is difficult to imagine that this tactic damaged Maxey's image in the eyes of the jury.

At the end of the day, Judge Moore announced that she was due to hear another trial in Crosbyton, and therefore court would be in recess until Wednesday. On Tuesday, however, the break was extended until the following week because of a serious illness in the family of one of the jurors.[26] When court resumed Monday, November 17, Shafer continued his cross-examination of Maxey with questions regarding the Strasburger agreement. Shafer introduced a letter from Strasburger's partner, Claude Miller, seeking payment of $25,000 for the firm's services. The bill was several months past due. Asked if he had hired the firm to help delay foreclosure by Citizens National Bank, Maxey denied that he had hired the firm for that purpose. The letter from Miller, however, stated that Maxey had, in fact, hired them when he was "about to suffer foreclosure. . . . We secured a delay . . . so we provided the services you sought."

Maxey testified that he had objected to the actions that Strasburger had taken on his behalf. One of his chief complaints was that Strasburger had settled a $130,000 debt owed to him for $50,000. The funds from the settlement were applied to his debt at Citizens National Bank.

Later during Tuesday's morning session Shafer handed off the cross-examination to cocounsel Charlie Jones. Jones began by reexamining Maxey's prior testimony, quickly building a counternarrative to the plaintiffs' allegations of a purely adversarial relationship with the bank.

March 30, 1964, had been presented as the first of many meetings between Maxey and Williams in which Maxey was pressured to sign new lending instruments against his wishes. Maxey had testified that, like many other credit agreements he had signed with the bank, he had received nothing of value in return—no money nor any notes renewed or extended. The defense produced a deposit slip dated March 30, 1964, showing that Maxey had received a new loan for $54,500 on that date. The new loan brought Maxey's total indebtedness at Citizens National Bank to $957,000.[27]

Jones asked Maxey, "Did you want the money?"

"I wouldn't have borrowed it if I hadn't wanted it," Maxey replied.

"So that's one instrument, at least, that they didn't force on you," said Jones.[28]

Jones also asserted that the collateral agreements Maxey signed on that date weren't much different from agreements he had signed on previous occasions. His contention was that much of Maxey's collateral had already been secured by previous notes.

Over the next two months after the March 30 meeting, Maxey reduced his indebtedness at Citizens National Bank to $927,970. On May 12, he borrowed an additional $400,000 from the bank.[29]

Jones: That's just a month and twelve days after all those dire claims about losing all your property?

Maxey: My records show that I borrowed $400,000 on May 12, 1964.

Jones: Did you want the money?

Maxey: Yes. I borrowed it for a purpose.

Jones had exposed several areas of weakness in Maxey's allegations. The sarcasm coloring his questions was a reminder to everyone in the courtroom that he was on a roll, and he intended to keep cutting away at what his side of the case called Maxey's "great fiction."[30] Maxey repaid the $400,000 within a short period of time, but his debt soon increased again. Jones introduced deposit slips and other records showing that, between March 30 and September 28, 1964, Citizens National Bank had advanced Maxey more than a quarter million dollars in additional loans.[31]

Jones then returned to Maxey's previous testimony regarding a meeting in Chauncey Trout's office on October 1, 1964. Maxey had stated that, at that meeting, he had been pressured to sign another set of new security agreements with the bank but had received nothing in exchange, that no previous notes were marked renewed or paid off, nor were any new loans obtained.

The counternarrative being developed by the defense was that most of Maxey's notes were payable on demand in six months. Therefore, every six months, in addition to renewing such notes, he was required to update his collateral.

Two weeks after the October 1 meeting, Maxey borrowed another $95,000, which upped his debt at the bank to $1,220,418. Under direct examination by Bowlin, Maxey had stated that he didn't recall receiving the $95,000. After reading Maxey's testimony from the transcript, Jones handed him the documents showing receipt of the funds and how they were disbursed.

Jones showed off his talent for composing a memorable refrain, asking the witness, "Did you get the money?" to which Maxey would reply, "I concede I got the money," or "Apparently I did . . ." Then came the follow-up, "Did you want the money?" to which Maxey would respond, "I did; I wanted it for a purpose," and so on.[32]

Jones also probed Maxey about his seeming lack of knowledge about his bank statements and other records, which should have told Maxey all he needed to know about whether he had received the funds from the loan, and if the loans had been renewed. Jones tried to prove that the bank was trying to help Maxey, not foreclose on him, but that notion got lost in the thicket of Maxey's noncommittal responses.

> Jones: Now, Mr. Maxey, were these instruments executed on the first of October, 1964, so far as you know?[33]
>
> Maxey: I don't know the date they were signed but the date that shows on the instrument.
>
> Jones: Were they executed the date you renewed the notes and signed the checks?
>
> Maxey: I don't know.
>
> Jones: Were they signed, Mr. Maxey, in a part of this meeting under threat of foreclosure?
>
> Maxey: I would think so, yes.
>
> Jones: Well, were the notes renewed then?
>
> Maxey: I don't know.
>
> Jones: Under threat of foreclosure?
>
> Maxey: I don't know on that date, I don't know. . . . I don't know whether it was October first or not, because I have no recollection of the exact date that I had the October meeting, when I signed so many of these instruments.

In such exchanges, Maxey and his attorneys hoped the jury would remember the plaintiff as a man who'd been under siege from his bankers and lawyers, harassed, and pressured into signing new agreements that were contrary in spirit to his original gentleman's agreement with Williams. When Maxey claimed, time after time, that he could not recall exact dates and other details, the cross-examination bogged down. Maxey was polite and made a pretense, at least, of wanting to give helpful responses, but his selective memory for dates and other details helped mute any revelations the cross-examination unearthed.

Maxey also responded to some questions with the answer, "I don't know; you have the records." The bulk of his files, he reminded the jury, were in the possession of Evans, Pharr, Trout & Jones, and they had refused to release them.[34]

The law firm had refused to turn the records over to Maxey. He was allowed to have access to them, but he could not remove anything from their offices. Making copies of the records would have cost hundreds of dollars, perhaps thousands. Maxey and his attorneys claimed they were handicapped by not having Maxey's records. If that tended to make the bank and Maxey's ex-lawyers look bad, it also begs the question: If those files were so important, why didn't he borrow the money to have them copied? When suing for millions, why be stingy about photocopies?

On the other hand, if the law firm or the bank had paid for the copies, it would support the defendants' position that they had done nothing wrong and had nothing to hide.

The combative dynamic of the trial was escalating and showed no sign of slowing down any time soon. The media always loves a good fight, and the Lubbock newspaper dutifully trumpeted the new tone with action phrases. The headlines for three successive days in November, for example, included "Defense Counter Attack Launched," "Defense Continues to Grill Homer G. Maxey," and "Trial Tempo Quickens . . ."[35]

During the afternoon session on Wednesday, November 19, Jones began hammering away at another aspect of Maxey's allegations: that after the bank took over his cattle feeding operations, its mismanagement had exacerbated Maxey's financial troubles, thereby hastening his financial ruin; and, further, that the bank continued to mismanage the ranches after the foreclosure, resulting in an even greater loss of value to those assets. During his cross-examination of Maxey, Jones produced a succession of documents, including canceled checks, that appeared to show payments for cattle feed and other expenditures. Many of the documents bore Maxey's signature or what he suggested might have been a rubber stamp of his signature.[36]

If the tactic helped widen the cracks in the plaintiffs' case, Maxey, stubborn as ever, made Jones work hard for every concession, no matter how trivial. As reporter May noted in his coverage of the trial in the late *Avalanche-Journal* edition on November 19, 1969, much of the day was taken up by a "repetitious game of 'Was that for feed?' and 'I don't know.'"[37]

Jones was the kind of person who relished detail. He enjoyed examining such evidence, tallying the figures in his head. He continued his line of questioning Thursday, but it appeared that Jones's enthusiasm for such information was not shared by the jury panel, spectators, or the press. In the Friday morning edition, May noted that Jones had gotten "bogged down" in the cattle feeding issue for a full day.[38]

"One thing about Charlie that most people didn't realize," says Carlton Dodson, "is that he was very good with the jury. He would astound them with his mind. He was one of the best civil defense trial lawyers there ever was in this country. But if you were trying a case against him, the longer you tried him, the better off you were. If there was any way to win a lawsuit in two or three days, he could do it. The only kind of cases he ever lost was whenever people would grind him out over a long period of time, like the Maxey case."[39]

If Jones was responsible for wearing out the jury with excessive accounting details, the defense faced momentum problems for other reasons. The trial marked its twelfth day on Thursday, November 20. Friday the court was in recess, and the following week would be a short one. Monday and Tuesday the court would be in recess because of scheduling conflicts. Thursday was Thanksgiving. Soon it would be Christmas.

Maxey's daughters could not have been the only trial participants daydreaming about the ski slopes of New Mexico, recently blanketed with heavy snowfalls. Jurors like Gwendolyn Murphy parked their cars on Texas Avenue before nine o'clock every morning, leaving a note on the dashboard with the words "jury duty," which allowed them free all-day parking. On windy and wet mornings, they inevitably thought about holiday preparations, the Christmas plays their children were rehearsing, and various other concerns of normal family life that become more prominent than usual during the holidays.

While her husband was concentrating all his energies on winning his lawsuit, Melba was busy documenting the family's experiences inside and outside the courtroom. The notes in her journal were not confined to the daily court sessions. She also made notations about pertinent aspects of the Maxeys' business and social world. One journal page lists the amounts of loans from various friends extended in 1968, plus the funds that had been advanced to cover court costs, including handling the appeals of the summary judgments in favor of nine codefendants before the case began in the 72nd District Court.[40]

Melba also made lists of friends and supporters, with reminders to send thank-you cards or return phone calls. One page has a list of over two dozen names, with Mary Lou and Jane Livermore at the top. There's also a running diary of telephone calls of support the Maxeys received. Dub Rushing and

Loans

Lee Fields –	3-22-68	300.00
	9-24-68	500.00
J.L. Lalkington –	3-22-68	200.00
	7-1-68	1000.00
Palutka Attorneys		4000.00
H. Blank	4-3-68	500.00

Bonds Signed

J.L. Lalkington	$2500.00	House
Harold Griffith	"	House
Harold Blank	"	House
R.P. Fuller	Main Court Cost	
Rex Fuller	" " "	
George Fields –	$2500.00	House
	Appeal Bonds Directory	

A page from Melba Maxey's journal shows her accounting of debts owed to friends for legal expenses. Courtesy of the Maxey family.

an anonymous man who said "I am 100 percent for you" called on October 30. There were seven calls the next day. Bess Vickers said the "Vickers clan is behind you. God will take care." Forrest Van Pelt called to say he had "information against CNB." Ed Drumwright's wife, Dorothy, called from Phoenix to express her support, and Mrs. Harry Newberry, employed by a Lubbock doctor, claimed to have information about a dry cleaning business that had a bad experience with the bank: "Business taken over by CNB. Not behind on payments. Will testify against CNB . . ."

On Saturday, November 1, Homer and Melba—plus Glenna, Bill, Carla, and Tommy—all pitched in to work on exhibits with the attorneys in their office until 10:15 that night, missing the football game between Rice University and Texas Tech.

Sunday, November 2, the Maxeys twice met with Homer's accountant, Joe Cassel. That same day, a woman whose husband had recently died of a heart attack told Melba that "a few hours before he died . . . [he said] he was 100 percent behind HGM."

Monday, November 3, someone called to report that a friend or relative had a "bad experience with CNB 1963–64" and that "J. W. Smith (a director of the bank) is a dog." Someone else with a complaint against Citizens offered to "come as a witness against CNB at my expense."

Another of Melba's journal pages records the names of people who brought meals to the Maxeys during the week of November 3. Elinor and James Denton, mentioned in her notes, brought chicken and rice casserole and German chocolate cake Monday night. On Wednesday, Charles Flowers brought Mexican food for Melba and Glenna when they were waiting at the beauty shop. On Sunday, several couples came over after church service. Among them were the steadfast friends Bill and Jennie Dean, who, eighteen years earlier, had dressed up in hillbilly attire to celebrate the grand opening of the Plainsman Hotel.

Veterans Day fell on the following Tuesday, when court was in recess for the week. The extended Maxey family, including the Elliotts and the Goodacres, went out to dinner and a wine tasting at the Lubbock Club.

Not everyone in Lubbock felt free about expressing his or her allegiances to the parties at trial. Several of the telephone calls to the Maxeys were from people who didn't want to give their names. At least one "anonymous female" was for the other side. "I want you to know that the people of Lubbock are sick of your trial," she said. "So are we!" said Melba. The anonymous caller said "Homer got into trouble by himself." Melba disagreed and asked the woman to identify herself. When the woman refused, Melba said, "OK, dear, see you in the funny papers," and hung up.

For Homer and Melba, the litigation had become the central event in their lives. They were surrounded by others who had, in varying degrees, been forced to put much of their normal lives on hold for the past two years. Around the same time Bowlin had taken Maxey's case, he had separated from his first wife and moved into a small apartment. Shortly before the trial got under way, one of Bowlin's clients took pity on him and suggested that he move into an apartment building that the client owned. The building had a unique and sumptuous apartment on the top floor that the owner had recently vacated.

"It had its own staircase on the outside," says Bowlin, "and it was surrounded by all kinds of trees, so they called it the Tree House."[41] Around that same time, Bowlin began seeing Jane Livermore. Jane, whom Bowlin had known "since she was a baby," had also divorced a short time before. Once the trial got underway, Jane and her mother, Mary Lou, did whatever they could to support not only the Maxeys, but Bowlin as well.

"Every day when I'd get out of trial," remembers Bowlin, "when I got home, Mary Lou and Jane would be there with dinner ready."

By the time Charlie Jones completed his cross-examination of Homer Maxey on Wednesday, the third of December, Maxey had been on the witness stand a total of seventeen days since the trial began on October 28. In the previous several days, Jones had highlighted more contradictions in Maxey's direct testimony. One of the most important came out when Jones was questioning Maxey about his contention that the conditions imposed upon him by the bank in the months leading up to foreclosure had tied his hands and made it impossible for him to sell any of his assets in order to pay his creditors or reduce his debt. Jones produced correspondence between Maxey and Strasburger showing that Citizens National Bank had, in fact, permitted sales of Maxey's cattle, feed, and equipment to help pay off creditors.[42]

Avalanche-Journal reporter Kenneth May summed up the gist of that day's testimony: "Lubbock attorney Charles B. Jones spent Monday trying to get Homer Maxey to say 'yes.'" The reporter mentioned how, once again, Jones had retraced the history of Maxey's loans and note renewals with Citizens National Bank, using twenty-one deposit slips and other documentation to show that Maxey's accounts had been credited with every penny of the $1.3 million in notes he had signed.

When asked if he agreed with that conclusion, Maxey stubbornly refused. "Testifying from notes," he said, referring to the fact that Jones's law firm still had his files, "I won't say yes and I won't say no."[43]

Despite what may have appeared to be weaknesses in Maxey's case, the story called attention to the defense attorneys' "time consuming" presentation and the overall slow pace of the proceedings since Jones had taken over the cross-examination. May observed that Maxey had been on the witness stand "longer than anyone in Lubbock County history."

The first witness to follow Maxey for questioning by the plaintiffs' attorneys was Chauncey Trout. Because Trout was an "adverse witness" (one whose relationship to the defendant implied that his testimony might be prejudiced against the plaintiffs), Bowlin was allowed more leeway in his questioning.[44]

Trout was the son of a professional golfer. Father and son both answered to the nickname "Chick." The younger Trout graduated third in his law school class at the University of Texas at Austin, and he had practiced as a partner with Jones until the two of them joined the firm of Evans, Klett & Bean in 1955. That same year Robert H. Bean (son of founding partner George R. Bean) left the firm to serve as a judge of the 140th District Court, Lubbock County. The death of Emil Klett also occurred that year. Trout was assigned many of Judge Bean's former clients. He also did some trial work but, according to a colleague, "he wasn't very good at it."[45]

Bowlin began by questioning Trout about the actual process of the foreclosure proceeding on the afternoon of February 16, 1966. As a dramatic device, the foreclosure meeting served the same function as a murder scene in a homicide trial. Bowlin wanted Trout to retrace his steps on that day, much like a detective or prosecutor revisiting the scene of a homicide.

Bowlin asked Trout to identify the individuals who were present in Williams's office during the foreclosure proceedings.[46]

Trout replied: "Mr. Williams was there, I think Mr. Barclay Ryall, I think Mr. J. W. Smith, perhaps Mr. George Atkinson, and I believe Mr. Frank Junell might have been there part of the time."

"Anybody else?" Bowlin asked.

"I can't think of anyone," he said.

An in-depth story in the *Fort Worth Star-Telegram* published during a later phase of Maxey's litigation stated that although Charlie Jones and Barclay Ryall denied being at the meeting, "others who attended the sale said both men were present."[47]

David Hughes, who was directed by Williams to type up the necessary documents for foreclosure, also remembers Jones and Ryall being at the meeting. "Charlie was there for the meeting," recalls Hughes. "Later in the day, Barclay Ryall and I worked together."[48]

Because of the serious allegations against Jones (i.e., that he made the phone call to W. L. Brady that killed the Drumwright deal) and other, more general suspicions (e.g., that he was a key part of the conspiracy against Maxey), it would be in the best interests of the defense if the jury could be persuaded that Jones was not present at the meeting.

Bowlin's underlying purpose wasn't so much to bring out new information on the events at the foreclosure proceedings, but to underscore the themes of betrayal and bad faith that were implicit in the allegations of the petition. One of the most damning was the issue of Trout's conflict of interest in representing both Maxey and Citizens National Bank. One of the least complex issues in the plaintiffs' petition, it was sure to strike a chord with the members of the jury.

Bowlin questioned Trout for several minutes on the history of Evans, Pharr, Trout & Jones and their long relationship with Citizens National Bank. During a pretrial deposition, Trout had stated that the founding members of the firm had represented the founders of the bank and had even performed the legal work of obtaining the bank's charter; however, under questioning by Bowlin, the attorney refused to go on the record about it. Bowlin probed him further.[49]

> Bowlin: I had understood, Mr. Trout, that you said that Mr. Bean or Mr. Klett one represented the bank at its inception or formed it, helped form it?
>
> Trout: That may be true. I'm not sure.

Bowlin next asked Trout if he could estimate how many times the firm had charged Maxey fees either during or after the foreclosure. Citing $10,000 in fees paid to Trout out of the Plaza Building Corporation after the foreclosure, Bowlin asked, "You weren't operating under the illusion you were representing Mr. Maxey, were you?"

"No," answered Trout.[50]

Bowlin continued to query Trout about the legal work he had done with regard to Maxey. For each specific instance, whether the work had been charged to Maxey or not, Bowlin asked a simple question: "Were you doing this work for Homer Maxey or Citizens National Bank?"[51]

Trout answered the question with difficulty, sometimes admitting that he wasn't sure which party he had been representing at the time. When Bowlin asked Trout whether it was Homer Maxey or E. W. Williams who had asked him to prepare the collateral agreements, Trout claimed he couldn't remember.

> Bowlin: Did it occur to you, Mr. Trout, that as a stockholder of the bank, there might be a conflict between your interest and Mr. Maxey's?
>
> Trout: No, no sir.
>
> Bowlin: You mean it just didn't occur to you at all because you were one of the

owners of Citizens National Bank and he was doing business with you that there could be any conflict at all?

Trout: I owned such a small portion of the bank.

Bowlin: In other words, in your opinion, whether or not there was a conflict would have depended on how much stock you owned?

Trout: No, are you saying I shouldn't represent anybody that does business with Citizens National Bank?

Bowlin: Assume, Mr. Trout, that you owned 90 percent of the stock of the Citizens National Bank. Would you have thought that there was a conflict then?

Trout: No, sir.

Bowlin: Assume you had owned all of it. Would you have thought there was a possibility of a conflict in that case?

Trout: No, sir, not in 1964; later on there might have been.[52]

The fact that the Monterey Lubbock Corporation was an affiliate corporation of Citizens National Bank (some referred to it as a "shell corporation") was another topic that Bowlin used to help draw attention to the conflict-of-interest issue. The Monterey Lubbock Corporation was the entity that purchased Plaza Building Corporation for $749 during the private sale foreclosure meeting.[53]

The corporation bore the names of the pair of rival towns that had been moved and consolidated in the late 1800s to pave the way for the modern town of Lubbock. Just as the identities of those settlements had eventually been subsumed as the new community marched on, the Monterey Lubbock Corporation existed as an ambiguous and slightly mysterious entity, even to the attorneys who owned stock in it and were assigned as its directors and officers. No one, or at least no one who testified in the Maxey suit, seemed to know much about it.

Even the name of the corporation became a running joke in the trial. When Bowlin asked Trout if it was Monterey Lubbock Corporation or Lubbock-Monterey, Trout said he didn't know; it was one or the other. Later that day, Bowlin asked the next witness, Charlie Jones, who didn't know either. Trout also appeared uncertain as to whether his law firm represented the corporation.

Bowlin: Did your firm represent that company also?

Trout: I presume we did, yes, sir.

Bowlin: Do you know whether you represented them or not?

Trout: Well, it was a company that was connected with the bank and for that
   reason I am sure we represented them.
Bowlin: Do you still represent that company?
Trout: I guess so.

When queried about the connection between Citizens National Bank and Monterey Lubbock, Trout said he believed that "the capital stock of that company is held by trustees for the owners of the capital stock of the Citizens National Bank."

"Is that something that you know or that you have just heard?" asked Bowlin.

"Well, I have heard it enough to where I think it is correct," answered Trout.

Bowlin then asked Trout what he thought of the foreclosure sale of Plaza Building Corporation to Monterey Lubbock for $749. Did he consider that to be a transaction with a "separate legal entity, another corporation, or in effect, to the bank?"

Trout answered: "Well, it was to another legal entity, but it was . . . That other legal entity was in effect owned by the bank."

"In other words," said Bowlin, "it was kind of a sale to yourselves, so to speak, wasn't it?"

"It was a sale . . . by the bank to an organization controlled by the bank," answered Trout.

Bowlin then attempted to introduce into evidence some of the answers Trout had given during his deposition, which contradicted his current testimony. Shafer objected and Judge Moore sustained the objection. Bowlin requested permission to prove up a bill of exception.[54] A bill of exception is a detailed record of evidence that a trial judge has excluded from the trial. The record may consist of the reading of a document, such as a letter that the judge has excluded, or a detailed examination of a witness on a specific subject or area of testimony that the judge has excluded. The record is preserved with the transcript of the trial so that, in case of an appeal, the appellate court can make a determination as to whether it was proper for the evidence to be excluded at trial.

The jury was excused while Bowlin questioned Trout over the discrepancies between his trial and the deposition testimonies. In his deposition, Trout had answered "yes" when asked if he had billed Maxey for preparing security agreements for Citizens National Bank. Also in his deposition, Trout replied in the affirmative when asked if he had made use of the Plaza Building Corporation files in his office while preparing the bank's defense against the Maxey lawsuit.[55]

However, when Maxey had asked Trout to turn the files over to him for help in the preparation of his lawsuit, Trout refused.

Bowlin made another motion, asking Judge Moore that the deposition be admitted as evidence. Moore denied the motion.

For a second bill of exception to Moore's ruling, Bowlin read from the State of Texas canon of ethics, chapter 3, section 6, article 13:[56]

> It is the duty of a member at the time of retainer to disclose to the client all of the circumstances of his relation to the parties, and any interest in or in connection with the controversy which might influence the client in the selection of counsel. It is unprofessional to represent conflicting interests, except by expressed consent of all concerned given after a full disclosure of the facts. Within the meaning of this rule, a member represents conflicting interests when in behalf of one client it is his duty to contend for that which duty to another client requires him to oppose. The obligation to represent the client with undivided loyalty and not to divulge his secrets or confidence forbids also the subsequent acceptance of retainers or employment from others, in matters adversely affecting any interest of the client with respect to which confidence has been reposed . . .

Bowlin underscored his point with a passage from section 34 of the same chapter, reading from a paragraph that included an admonition on the duty to preserve the confidence of a client, which "outlasts the member's employment" and that "a member shall not continue employment when he discovers that his obligation prevents the performance of his full duty to his former or to his new client."

When asked if he was familiar with the ethical rules for attorneys, Trout replied that he was "generally familiar with them." Bowlin asked if it was true that "you made available to the Citizens National Bank your files and records which Mr. Maxey had paid for, did you not?"

"Well, Mr. Maxey had paid for the legal services, yes, but he had not paid for the files and records," answered Trout. Responding to another question about the files, Trout took exception to Bowlin referring to them as "Maxey's files."

"Now, they were my files," said Trout.

After several more questions, Bowlin repeated his motion to go into the canons of ethics in testimony before the jury. Judge Moore again denied the motion. Shafer informed Moore that the defense had no questions for the witness, but would reserve the right to call him back at later time. Court was then recessed until 2:30, and when the trial reconvened, the jury was called in and Bowlin called the second adverse witness, Charlie Jones.[57]

If his barbed, combative responses were any indication, Jones may have enjoyed his turn in the witness stand more than anyone else over the course of the long trial. When answering a question, he would often answer Bowlin by name, saying, "Well, Mr. Bowlin . . ." One of Bowlin's first questions involved the amount of Citizens National Bank stock that Jones and Trout each owned. Jones said that each of them paid $2,500 for one hundred shares of stock shortly after they joined the law firm and had not purchased any additional stock since then. With dividends, each of them held a total of approximately 120 shares at the time.[58]

In answer to Bowlin's other questions about his working relationship with Citizens National Bank, Jones replied that, until Emil Klett died in the fall of 1955, Klett had handled the majority of the firm's work with the bank. For a short period of time, before Jones took over the account, "a good bit" of the bank's legal affairs had been handled by Hobart Nelson, a Lubbock attorney and former state senator.[59] Among Nelson's other well-known clients was the infamous convicted swindler Billie Sol Estes.[60]

Bowlin then asked Jones if he remembered the date he had joined the bank's board of directors. Jones answered that he was elected to the board sometime in February 1966, but he couldn't remember the exact date.[61]

"No sir," Jones answered. "I would be glad to look for you. I might ask Mr. Atkinson and find out pretty quick. I think it's the second Tuesday that the board meets."

Bowlin probed further, asking Jones if the date was "before or after the foreclosure held by the bank in connection with Mr. Maxey's properties?"

"I think it was before," answered Jones, but he wasn't sure how long before, that it could have been "ten days or eight days or seven days."

Bowlin: You didn't consider that at all a momentous event in your life?
Jones: To be elected to the board or—
Bowlin: Yes.
Jones: —to foreclose on Mr. Maxey by the bank?
Bowlin: Either one of them.

Jones: Well, no, sir, it didn't affect my relationship with my wife or family. I
had been making a living until then and it pays $50 a meeting to attend. I
probably get four hundred or five hundred dollars a year.

That Jones was elected to the bank's board of directors so near the date
of the foreclosure certainly sparked a good deal of speculation that it might
have been a reward for his contribution to Homer Maxey's financial demise.
Bowlin wanted to make sure the jury had a chance to at least entertain that
notion. With any luck, jurors would also remember Jones's flip responses to
questions on that and other topics that could have shown him in a bad light.
In a similar situation, most lawyers probably would be expected to maintain
a more formal, less loquacious manner while on the witness stand. But most
lawyers were not Charlie Jones.

Later on, Jones was given opportunities to demonstrate his vaunted skill
at complex calculations.[62] Bowlin asked Jones to check the math on certain
calculations presented as evidence. When asked to double-check the amount
of interest the bank had charged Maxey on a specific loan, Jones answered
with a figure that was actually 23 cents less than the $1,771.33 that the bank
had assessed. In a separate instance, Jones calculated that the bank had actually
undercharged Maxey by 26 cents.

In a subsequent exchange, Bowlin asked Jones if he was aware of the
allegation that the bank prevented the sale of Maxey's properties. "Yes, sir,"
Jones answered.[63]

Bowlin continued: "And you heard Mr. W. O. Shafer say in his statement
to the jury that you were going to prove that you didn't make that phone call,
did you not?"

"I don't recall that, no, sir," Jones answered.

Shafer objected, saying, "There is no evidence about a phone call in this
record. We object to the question and the answer until there is and ask that the
jury be instructed not to consider it."

Judge Moore sustained the objection.

Bowlin then reminded the court that Shafer had indeed made such a
promise in reference to the phone call when he summarized his pleadings at
the start of the trial.

"I see," said the judge. "I believe you are correct there."

"Pardon?" said Bowlin.

"I believe you are correct there," Judge Moore repeated. "Go ahead."

Maxey's side was very pleased with that ruling. The defense team, for all their professionalism and confidence, had made a serious blunder on day one of the trial when Shafer had, himself, mentioned the alleged phone call he had insisted be excluded from the testimony. Bowlin repeated the question.

Jones: Mr. Bowlin, I don't remember it. He may well have said it, I don't dispute it, if you do remember it, then he said it. I just don't remember it.

Bowlin: Did you make a phone call, Mr. Jones, that prevented Mr. Maxey from making a sale of his properties?

Jones: No, sir.

Bowlin: Do you know who did?

Jones: You will have to tell me what phone call you are talking about

Bowlin: Which phone call was Mr. Shafer talking about when he said we are going to prove he didn't make that phone call?

Jones: Mr. Bowlin, I don't recall his making the statement. You made an allegation in the pleadings. Are you talking about that?

Bowlin: Yes, sir.

Jones: No, I don't know who did it, I don't even know if it was done.

Bowlin: You don't know who made the phone call?

Jones: No.

Bowlin: But you deny that you made it?

Jones: Yes.

Bowlin: Pass the witness.

Court was adjourned for the day and Shafer conducted a short direct examination of Jones the following morning. Much of that inquiry was about the total indebtedness of Maxey to Citizens National Bank at various times between 1962 and 1966 and about the value of stock in Plaza Building Corporation and Triple M Feeders Corporation.[64] Shafer also asked Jones to clarify the relationship of Citizens National Bank with Monterey Lubbock Corporation and Citizens National Company (the other affiliate corporation named as a defendant in the case).[65] Jones answered that both corporations were affiliates, that stock in Monterey Lubbock Corporation was held by Citizens National Company, and that "if you buy stock in the bank, you own stock in Citizens National Company." Shafer asked Jones if that meant that ownership of the various affiliates and the bank itself was identical, "as far as beneficial interests are concerned."

"That is the effect of it, yes, sir," answered Jones.

Shafer then asked Jones for some perspective on the amount of stock he owned in Citizens National Bank. Jones stated that out of approximately 300,000 shares, he owned 120 shares, an amount that would work out to be one twenty-fifth of one percent. Or, as he put it, "If I had twenty-five times as much, I would have one percent."

Shafer proceeded. "If you and Mr. Trout and twenty-three persons who own the same amount of stock got together, you could control one percent, couldn't you?"

"We own it, yes, sir," replied Jones.

Later, when asked if his law firm had made it known to Maxey and his attorneys that they could come in and look at their files on Maxey at any time, Jones answered in the affirmative, adding "although I don't know about nights and Sundays."

Confusion over the name of the Monterey Lubbock Corporation continued. Shafer's cocounsel Barney Evans referred to it with the names inverted at least once and Jones, despite his well-known photographic memory, began one of his responses by referring to the Monterey Lubbock Corporation, then paused to add, "Or Lubbock-Monterey Corporation, I swear I can't ever remember which way that is."

Thursday afternoon the jury heard testimony from cattle dealer J. E. Birdwell, the third adverse witness called by the plaintiffs. Birdwell puffed on his pipe as Bowlin used his first batch of questions to establish Birdwell's many ties to Citizens National Bank, including his marriage to one of the bank's directors and his friendship with Williams.

Maxey had already testified in detail about Williams selling his cattle to Birdwell and E. C. Mullendore III for only $173,000, an amount that Maxey believed was low by at least $50,000. In his testimony, Birdwell confirmed that he and Mullendore paid $3,000 cash to the bank for the cattle and received a loan for the balance.[66] Birdwell claimed that the cattle were in poor condition when he bought them and that good rains in the spring and summer of 1966, which improved grazing conditions, contributed to a rise in cattle prices. That and proper management of the herds, he claimed, explained the large profit margin.

Birdwell's opening testimony, however, contradicted statements he had made in a deposition taken on November 30, 1967, in which he stated that equipment on Maxey's ranches had been used during the months that the cattle were being readied for market by ranch hands employed by the Birdwell-Mullendore partnership. Using that equipment for no charge had also contributed to their profit margin. As described by Kenneth May in the *Avalanche-Journal*, Birdwell "hedged" his earlier statements by saying that couldn't remember if the ranch hands had used Maxey's equipment or not.[67]

Bowlin also asked Birdwell a number of questions about his past dealings with Mullendore. Although Mullendore was the grandson of one of Oklahoma's most prominent ranching families, he had been experiencing severe financial difficulties since 1965 and perhaps earlier.[68] By the time of the Maxey trial, Mullendore's wife was in the process of obtaining a divorce, and his father was estranged from him. The unraveling of Mullendore's business and personal affairs was a popular topic of discussion in West Texas ranching circles.

In fact, Mullendore was found murdered in his ranch house in the fall of 1970, less than a year after the trial. Because of Mullendore's chaotic life and a number of associations with shady characters, the murder case sparked a great deal of speculation and rumor as to the actual cause and circumstances of his death, ranging from suspicions that it was a Mafia hit to rumors that his own father had killed him. The case would not be solved until late 2010, and there does not appear to be any connection with the Maxey case.[69]

During testimony about the Birdwell-Mullendore cattle deal, Melba Maxey made terse notations in her journal:[70]

> March 24, 1966: Ken Bowlin was hired by Bruce Gambil for a Lubbock attorney.
> March 25: EWW visited HGM in office to ask that the lawsuit be called off.
> And that they work out a settlement.
> At the same time, he sold cattle to Mullendore (E.C. III) for about $190,000.
> ECM & Birdwell of Post were at ranch branding cattle.

Later on, Shafer objected when Bowlin attempted to introduce testimony from the deposition Birdwell had given in 1967, which contained several statements contradicting his trial testimony. Judge Moore sustained the objection.[71]

After their long days in court, the Maxeys were buoyed by even more calls from friends and admirers. Monday night's notations in Melba's journal were "For you," from one friend and "Praying for you" from another.[72]

On December 8 and 9, back-to-back testimony by three witnesses—Ed Drumwright, W. L Brady, and Jack Wakefield—introduced pivotal evidence for what Bowlin had long considered "the guts of the lawsuit." The three men all played key roles in setting up a deal to refinance Maxey's debt. They linked the sale of his ranches to a short-term loan arranged so that Maxey could pay off all his indebtedness to Citizens National Bank. Maxey's allegation that the loan package, the so-called Drumwright deal, had been killed by a phone call from Charlie Jones was a powerful accusation, with negative connotations that could resonate far beyond the walls of the courtroom.

Decades later, the allegation that Jones made the phone call that killed the Drumwright deal remains a touchy subject for people on both sides of the Maxey litigation. Some believe he made the call, some do not. Not even all Maxey partisans are convinced that Jones did it.

Jones's most passionate defenders include those who worked with him at the law firm. Bobby Moody, for example, does not believe Jones made the call.[73] "Charlie would never have made that phone call," says Jack Flygare, adding that "anyone who ever knew Charlie Jones would know that."[74]

Another adamant Jones supporter is Charlie Joplin, who was a vice president in charge of the cotton department at Citizens National Bank in the 1960s. "Anyone who wants to say that will have to go through me," he says. "We played tennis together, drank good scotch together, and sang songs together, and I did and will always have a very high regard for Charlie Jones."[75]

When asked if he believed that Jones made the call that killed the Drumwright deal, Williams says: "I would say that did not happen."[76]

When asked if she believes that Jones made the call that killed the Drumwright deal, Glenna Goodacre does not hesitate. "Yes," she says, "Daddy believed it and I believed it."[77]

Over the course of two days, Bowlin skirmished repeatedly with both the defense team and Judge Moore to get testimony about the call admitted into evidence. The defense objected to almost every aspect of the testimony about the Drumwright deal.

For Bowlin, the tug-of-war over the Drumwright deal was a key part of the wider issue of fairness. The way Bowlin recalls it, Judge Moore went out of her way to exclude anything that might impugn Jones's reputation.

"I just thought she and Charlie Jones were close," says Bowlin. "Charlie was a likeable guy and before that case, he and I had been friends."[78]

Bowlin recalls that Maxey always felt certain that there was an underlying reason for what he perceived as an extreme bias by the judge in favor of Charlie Jones and Citizens National Bank.

"One time when she called me into her office," says Bowlin, "I asked her if there was anything I should know about regarding her connection with Charlie Jones and Citizens, and she said no. During the trial it was obvious she was trying to hide something, because she decided early on that we were not going to put any evidence in about Charlie. You couldn't even mention anything. I was determined that I was going to get it to the jury one way or the other. I thought it was important enough that I would risk being charged with contempt, and she threatened to have me thrown in jail on contempt of court almost every day of the trial. But I knew that would influence the jury, and they were smart enough to get it."

During his testimony, Drumwright confirmed that his company, Century Sales Inc., had been put in touch with Maxey by the Taft brothers of Fort Worth, who had helped a religious organization obtain financing for an apart ment building.[79] Drumwright related the details of the April 1965 trip in which he and his wife flew to Texas in his private plane and spent several days inspecting the ranches. On May 21, 1965, he said, he contacted Maxey with an offer to buy the ranches for $4,511,480. The sale was contingent on a short-term loan of $1.3 million to Maxey, who would use it to pay Citizens National Bank, thereby forcing the bank to release its second liens on the ranches.

Drumwright explained that he had been acting in his capacity as a broker, or as a finder, for the financial assistance that Maxey needed and that Allied Concord Financial, the "dealer," issued loans only through other approved corporate dealers.[80] A broker at Allied Concord Financial named J. W. Wakefield would handle the loan for the company. Another contingency of the deal was that the $1.3 million loan was to be secured with a "take-out commitment" that was to be arranged by W. L. Brady, a mortgage and insurance broker in Kansas City, Missouri. Brady would secure the loan with a policy from Oklahoma Standard Life & Casualty, so that if Maxey defaulted on the loan, the insurance company would assume the payment of the loan, or "take out" Allied Concord Financial.

Defense objections to Drumwright's testimony necessitated numerous hearings outside the presence of the jury, creating substantial delays. On Monday and Tuesday, the jurors spent more time out of the courtroom than inside it. Drumwright was allowed to testify about meeting Maxey and touring the ranches and making his appraisals, but each time he mentioned the agreement to buy the ranches, Shafer objected. Because the contract had not been consummated, he maintained, it was hearsay.

Judge Moore continued to sustain Shafer's objections. Each time Shafer repeated his objection and Judge Moore sustained it, Bowlin protested and requested a bill of exception. Then the jury was excused and a hearing was held during which Bowlin questioned Drumwright for more details on the purchase/loan package to show that a proper predicate had been laid for the evidence to be allowed before the jury, but Judge Moore refused to allow the testimony into evidence.

Each time the jury returned, Bowlin would continue his examination for a moment, then stop and once again ask Judge Moore to allow the initial testimony into evidence. Each time Judge Moore ruled against Bowlin outside the presence of the jury, he made sure to repeat his request once the jury returned. He never gave up.

The defense also objected to the introduction of telegrams between Maxey and Drumwright about the deal. During one of the many bill-of-exception hearings on Monday, Alton Griffin made an eloquent plea to the judge to allow the telegrams to be admitted into evidence.[81] He argued that the defense had made repeated assertions that Maxey had made no serious attempts to reduce his indebtedness to the bank. By excluding testimony about the Drumwright deal, Griffin said, the court was making it impossible for the plaintiffs to refute that allegation.

Judge Moore decided that Drumwright would be allowed to mention receiving a telegram about the deal from Maxey, but he could not divulge its contents. Testimony resumed and once that fact had been brought out in Drumwright's testimony, Bowlin passed the witness.

On cross-examination, Shafer peppered Drumwright with questions about Century Sales Inc., bringing out the fact that the company had been incorporated only eighteen months prior to the alleged deal with Maxey.[82] In addition, it had been incorporated with just one thousand shares of stock at one dollar per share, and some of its affiliate corporations had no full-time employees.

Drumwright was also asked numerous times about his role in the purchase and loan package. "You weren't going to loan Mr. Maxey this money out of your back pocket, were you?" Shafer asked. Shafer repeated the same question several more times later on.

Then Jones took his turn. Jones attempted to call Drumwright's credibility into question from several angles.[83] Why, he asked, was the value of each of Maxey's ranches in Drumwright's appraisal the exact same amount that Maxey himself had used on his financial statements? Drumwright countered that he considered Maxey's appraised values to be "conservative." For example,

Alton Griffin joined Maxcy's legal team after his term as county attorney ended. Courtesy of the Lubbock County Bar Association.

he pointed out that his own appraisal of the Triple M Ranch gave no consideration for the lakefront acreage under lease, which was, he said, "very, very valuable."

Jones next grilled the witness on his knowledge of ranching.[84] Did he know the difference between grazing land that was appropriate for steers versus "good mother cow country?" Did he know his grasses? Could he tell little blue from cheek grass? Drumwright answered no to all such questions. Jones was having fun with the witness.

Jones: Do you know which of those ranches are in bad tick country?
Drumwright: Ticks?
Jones: Ticks.
Drumwright: No.
Jones: Do you know what a tick is?
Drumwright: Oh, yeah, I know what a tick is.
Jones: Do you know which of those ranches were in bad tick country?
Drumwright: No, sir.

The defense attorneys also drew attention to the fact that Drumwright stood to make a broker's fee of $55,000 on the deal.[85] The amount of the fee might have helped undercut the credibility of the financing package if the jurors had not already heard Trout's testimony about a New York securities firm that had charged Maxey $35,000 merely to attempt to find a buyer for his ranch properties—the deal in which Trout sued to obtain a refund of $10,000, out of which he then collected $3,300 for his services.

Maxey's cause was not helped by the fact that few records of the Drumwright purchase-loan package existed. Drumwright brought the telegram and a few notes with him, but he had no written commitment from Allied Concord Financial to make the loan.

Wakefield testified next, affirming that Allied Concord Financial was ready to loan Maxey the money, but he had no written evidence to document the deal, either. However, as Wakefield's testimony revealed, Allied Concord Financial had merged with Chrysler Credit Corporation in 1965 and, at some point during the transition, the files were either lost or destroyed.[86]

Before Brady took the stand, Judge Moore convened a hearing with the jury absent. During the hearing Shafer restated his objection to any testimony regarding the alleged phone call by Jones. Judge Moore again sustained the objection.

"Your Honor," Bowlin asked, "is the court ruling that we cannot even mention a telephone call or anything?"[87]

"Yes," Judge Moore replied, "being sort of familiar with this from our past discussions on pretrial, I would like to consider all of that outside the presence of the jury."

Bowlin argued that it would pose a serious obstacle to presenting the plaintiffs' case if they were not allowed to mention the phone call. How could they relate the chronology of the deal without giving any mention of the event that caused everything to come to a halt?

Judge Moore said she didn't "see any point in it until we decide about the conversation," and that was that, at least for the moment. Although the defense team must have been relieved that Judge Moore had not changed her mind, they must have felt some apprehension as the jury was brought in and Brady's testimony began. Investigating the phone call issue was one of the first things Shafer and Jones had done as a team. It was sometime in the spring of 1966 that the two lawyers flew to Kansas City to interview Brady about the phone call allegation.[88]

About twenty minutes into Brady's testimony, Bowlin came to the discussion of the actual loan package, meaning the complete file of documents from Maxey and his accountant with details on the ranch properties, financial statements, and so forth. Brady testified that the package was quite large in size because it had to do with so many different parcels of land.[89]

> Bowlin: All right, sir. Prior to the time that the matter was concluded, did certain events occur which necessitated or which caused you to stop all of your action in connection with that loan?
>
> Brady: Yes, sir.
>
> Bowlin: And subsequent to that time, did you return the package which you had had to someone else?
>
> Brady: Yes, sir, I returned it all.
>
> Bowlin: Who did you send it to?
>
> Brady: Century Sales.
>
> Bowlin: All right, sir. Do you have anything to show that you sent it back to them?
>
> Brady: I have the receipt.
>
> Bowlin: May I see it, please, sir?

Brady handed him an air express mail receipt dated October 11, 1965. If the defense team had relaxed its guard, alarm bells now went off when Bowlin asked Brady, "Is there anything on the receipt which is in your handwriting, please?"

Shafer objected and suggested that the court might need to look at the receipt before the witness read what he had written on it. As it turned out, the handwritten portion of the receipt included the name of Charlie Jones and a notation explaining why the package was being returned.

Shafer's objection was sustained. Bowlin said he wanted to make a bill of exception.

"Right now?" asked Judge Moore.

"Yes ma'am," said Bowlin.

The jury was excused for a twenty-minute break. As Bowlin began asking questions, Judge Moore interrupted to instruct the bailiff to make certain the door to the jury room was closed. As the testimony continued, Brady testified that he wrote the notation on the receipt because he was stunned and angry about the deal being canceled in such an abrupt fashion.[90]

Brady: The telephone conversation consisted of a call from Lubbock, Texas, and in—the party said they were Charlie Jones, and they wanted [me] to send all of that information on the Maxey deal to them.

Bowlin: Now, did the man who identified himself as Charlie Jones tell you anything else to indicate or to identify to you who he was?

Brady: He was an attorney for Mr. Maxey, and he had something to do with the bank. Now, I don't know the—with the Citizens Bank. I don't know what.

Bowlin: Did he tell you that he was the attorney for the Citizens National Bank?

Brady: I believe he did.

Bowlin: All right, sir. Do you recall anything else he said about his connection with the bank?

Brady: That they were going to make the loan, and I was perturbed about that because we had worked on the situation, and [the call meant we] were out in the cold, but that is part of the business, I suppose.

Brady testified that Jones said he wanted the package returned to the bank, but Brady told him that he would only return it to Century Sales, which was the proper protocol, and would make sure that Brady had "an ironclad receipt." After further testimony, Bowlin again requested that the phone conversation be entered into evidence.

Judge Moore denied the motion, but did make a small compromise: The witness would be allowed to mention the phone call, but nothing about the conversation, including the caller's identity. Shafer objected even to the small concession, but was overruled.

Bowlin then asked additional questions to add more testimony to the bill of exception and, when finished, again requested that the air express receipt be allowed into evidence. Judge Moore denied the request.

Next, with the jury in the courtroom, Brady's testimony resumed. In a short series of questions lasting less than two minutes, the jury heard that the Drumwright deal was brought to a halt as a result of a phone call.

Announcing that he was ready to pass the witness, Bowlin once again asked that the air express receipt be admitted into evidence. The judge again denied the request, but at least Maxey's team had won one small victory that day.

"I was just thinking on my feet," says Bowlin. "I kept trying to get the phone call in evidence, but Pat Moore ruled it inadmissible. To be absolutely honest about it, it probably was inadmissible. He really had no proof that the call happened and he couldn't even give the exact date that he got the call."[91]

Bowlin remains convinced that Judge Moore was trying to protect Jones. "She thought I was trying to get Charlie disbarred," he says.

"Ordinarily, a judge will let you introduce something like that," says Bowlin, "but they'll say if you don't prove it up, they will instruct the jury not to consider it. Pat wouldn't do that, however, because she didn't want the jury to hear it. I was interested in the jury hearing it, whether it was admissible or not. Pat knew what I was doing. So she zealously tried to keep everything out. It was trial technique that a lot of plaintiffs' lawyers use, but the judges don't like it."

The defense team continued to maintain that Jones's reputation wasn't the issue at all, but that such topics were inadmissible because the financing on the Drumwright deal had never been in place and the chances of the deal ever coming to fruition were nil. Jones, therefore, would have had no reason to make a phone call to kill such a deal.[92]

In a written deposition taken before the trial, Williams stated: "I do not know and never knew that Homer G. Maxey had secured a loan commitment sufficient to pay his debts, and I do not believe that he ever had such a commitment that was genuine, true, and practical."[93]

Jack Flygare characterizes the Drumwright deal as being, at best, a shady one. "Homer kept telling E. W. Williams that he was going to get a big loan," remembers Flygare. "I think Homer paid somebody in Phoenix $50,000, or it may have been $75,000 or $100,000, I don't know. I think he borrowed the money from Citizens Bank and paid it to this loan shark out in Phoenix who guaranteed him a loan in an amount that would have paid off the Citizens Bank."[94]

Flygare's use of the inflammatory term *loan shark* should be taken with a grain of salt. Attorneys for the bank made repeated mentions of the fact that Drumwright and others associated with putting together the loan package stood to collect substantial fees for their work. No evidence was ever presented, however, suggesting that the fees were higher than normal, much less illegal or unethical.

Drumwright's widow, Dorothy, takes issue with Flygare's statements.[95] She insists that the funds were available and all the parties involved in the arrangements were committed to making it happen.

Flygare maintains that the Drumwright deal was one of the last straws for Williams. "I remember that E. W. was upset because Homer lied to him about that loan," says Flygare. "He said it was going to be made and that he had a commitment, but apparently he never had a written commitment. All the lies he would tell, you know, he had a purchaser for the cattle, he had a purchaser for the ranch, he was going to liquidate assets and pay down the loan. Months went by and he didn't sell a damn thing. And as far as I know, he didn't try to do those things or didn't have any intention to do so. But finally it got to the point where he told one too many lies to E. W. Williams and E. W. got madder than hell and decided to foreclose."

Flygare's statements that Maxey did not liquidate any of his assets or attempt to seek new financing are contradicted by evidence to the contrary which was presented during the trial and also reported in the media coverage of the trial. Correspondence and other materials entered into the record documented Maxey's efforts to obtain financing through contacts in New York, Chicago, Phoenix, and Los Angeles.

The lack of written documentation for the Drumwright deal was repeatedly underscored by the defense. On the witness stand, Brady explained that he was waiting on certain additional documents from Maxey's accountant, Joe Cassel, before finalizing the deal, but was confident, he said, that the loan would be approved.[96]

Joe Cassel, the last witness called to testify for the plaintiffs, gave his testimony on Wednesday, December 10. He was on the stand all day. As Maxey's accountant, Cassel had handled most of the negotiations on the aborted Drumwright deal.

The son of a Lubbock ginner, Cassel was a longtime friend of the Maxey family and a respected member of the community. During Maxey's term on the city commission, he was one of the CPAs hired to audit the city's finances. On that particular contract, Cassel worked with a CPA named Ed Merriman, who was also a member of the Citizens National Bank board of directors and, as such, one of the defendants in Maxey's lawsuit against the bank.

During the cross-examination of Maxey, the defense tried to show that Maxey's wealth and income had been exaggerated for many years. In contrast, Cassel testified, Maxey's corporations—Plaza Building Corporation and Triple M Feeders—showed a gain in net value of $415,534 from 1963 to 1965.[97]

During that time, Plaza had total funds of $3,267,249, including a $1.3 million loan to buy ranches and $1 million borrowed from Maxey. The following amounts had been spent: $1,151,956 to buy land, $494,868 for buildings and equipment, $616,658 to reduce notes payable, and $848,580 to reduce mortgages payable. Deducting those amounts left a total of $89,805.

Bowlin asked if Cassel could say whether those figures meant that Maxey's net worth had increased or decreased between 1963 and 1965. "It increased," Cassel replied, stating that Maxey's total net worth had gone up by $211,726.

When Jones began his cross-examination, he attacked Cassel's "net worth" conclusion. He wanted to know, he said, "if a man can have a cash flow gain every year while he's going broke?"

"I don't know that he could," answered Cassel.

Jones continued by offering a scenario: A man borrows $300,000 but loses $150,000 in his business. At year's end he shows a cash flow gain of $150,000 but, in reality, he is $300,000 in the red.

Cassel conceded that, under that scenario, Jones was correct. When Jones went on to question the accountant about Maxey's income and losses, the jurors heard that $300,000 figure again. In 1963, Jones pointed out, Maxey had disposed of $882,051 in capital assets, and $300,000 of that money was used to cover losses.

Jones then asked Cassel to calculate how much money Plaza Building Corporation would have had left over if all Maxey's ranches had been sold, using sales prices that were below the appraisals that Maxey had used on financial statements, but somewhat higher than the values the defense claimed they were worth. After paying all the mortgages and taxes, Cassel testified, there would be $481,000 left over.

However, Jones showed by his calculations that Maxey would still be in debt, because he owed an additional $1,024,000 to creditors other than Citizens National Bank. He would need another $383,000 just to break even.

Bowlin took over on redirect and had Cassel do the math again, using the appraisals from the Drumwright deal that totaled over $4.5 million. Under that scenario, after paying all his debts, Maxey would have $917,000 left over, and the bank would have been off his back.

The trial had been under way for six weeks. Bowlin made a final attempt to convince Judge Moore to admit testimony and evidence regarding the Drumwright deal into evidence, which she again denied. The plaintiffs now rested their case.[98] The date was the tenth of December, 1969, almost four years since the bank foreclosed on Homer Maxey.

Shafer indicated that his side would not be able to begin its case in chief that afternoon. After stating that she, too, needed time to go over some aspects of the case, Judge Moore announced that it was a good time to begin the Christmas recess.

No objections were raised.

Judge Moore informed the jurors that they would not need to return until 9:15 a.m. Monday, January 5, 1970. "And of course," she said, "I hope all of you have a very merry Christmas and that you get your shopping done before Christmas Eve, and you are excused at this time."

As the courtroom emptied and people filed down the steps of the courthouse to face a cold wind and light rain, the anticipation of a three-week holiday break undoubtedly struck a harmonious chord with everyone involved. Such moments were rare.

Throughout the last weeks of 1969, Melba Maxey carefully noted every gift and holiday party contribution made by friends and family, a long list that documents a season of rich food and strong spirits.[99] In the glow of the Christmas tree lights and spiked eggnog, to the tune of Christmas carols and playing grandchildren, the Maxeys toasted the future, confident that the jury would rule in their favor. In private moments, they wished for a return to a less complicated time, when Homer's integrity and status were unquestioned.

Christmas had always been an extra-special time in the Maxey family. Work came to a halt, the kids came over, and the grandkids ran loose. Melba—who always kept a home with a cozy hearth, decorations everywhere, and enough food to feed an army—pulled out all the stops. There were bouquets of flowers, special linens, the Sunday china and silver, candles, and various artistic decorations, many of which she had crafted and painted herself.

For Harold Blank, Melba wrote a special thank-you note. Blank brought cake for dessert. He had also remembered a favorite hobby of hers (and Homer's), carving wooden game birds, and he brought new kits for them. A local artisan produced the kits for making the birds, which the Maxeys chiseled, sanded and painted, and then presented to family members and friends as gifts.

"They're really well done," says Bill Goodacre. "I still have a couple of them and I cherish them."[100]

For Carla, the birds are reminders of her father's personality quirks. "Mother loved carving them, especially the feathers," she says. "She was always fiddling with something. She started doing it first, then Daddy butted in and he started doing it. He had to show he could do it faster and better. So that kind of squelched Mother's interest in it and she didn't go on with it."[101]

No one could have appreciated the holiday break in the Maxey trial more than the jurors. Gwendolyn Murphy appreciated Judge Moore's thoughtfulness when the jury panel was released early for both Thanksgiving and Christmas.[102]

"We had a very enjoyable Christmas holiday," she says. "I remember it well because we drove to Dallas so we could see Notre Dame beat Texas in the Cotton Bowl."

The Murphy family's wish did not come true. Before a crowd of seventy-three thousand (which included former President Lyndon B. Johnson), Notre Dame went down in defeat to the Texas Longhorns, 17–14.[103]

When the trial recommenced on Monday morning, January 5, 1970, the zero in the new decade was mirrored by zero temperatures in the Texas Panhandle. An arctic storm steamrolled across the entire continent, bringing freezing temperatures all the way to south Florida. Snow flurries and lows in the teens were predicted for the next few days.

But the North Pole was not the only source of the chill in the courtroom as the proceedings resumed. On Tuesday, December 23, 1969, Judge Moore had announced her ruling in favor of the defense on their motion for summary judgment for ten of the eleven defendants. The effect of the early Christmas present to the defense was the exoneration of all the individuals named in Maxey's suit—E. W. Williams, Jr., Clyde Jordan, George Atkinson, J. W. Smith, Barclay Ryall, Charlie Jones, Chauncey Trout, Jr., David Hughes, and J. E. Birdwell (all other individual defendants had already been dismissed from the case during appellate court proceedings).

The bank's two affiliate corporations, Monterey Lubbock Corporation and Citizens National Corporation, were also relieved of liability. The sole defendant now was Citizens National Bank.[104]

Judge Moore's ruling stated that the evidence presented by the plaintiffs was "wholly insufficient" to prove the conspiracy allegation against the ten defendants; therefore, "the only question is whether or not Citizens National Bank disposed of Plaza Building Corporation's properties for inadequate amounts."[105]

The ruling was a serious blow to the Maxey family, and it could very well have destroyed their chances of winning the case. Each side had argued their case before Judge Moore in advance of the ruling. Taking the lead for the plaintiffs, Alton Griffin had enumerated every overt act by the defendants that tied Maxey's hands and led to the foreclosure, after which the bank had disposed of his assets in a manner that, according to Maxey's allegations, involved conspiracy and fraud.

In contrast to Griffin's detailed presentation of allegations and the evidence supporting them, Shafer presented a much more streamlined argument, holding that, during a foreclosure, a bank was not required by law to get "the last dollar" of value for assets, but only to collect an amount that is not "grossly inadequate."

That morning, as they left for the courthouse, Melba reminded Homer of the prayer she had clipped from the newspaper.

Lord,

Because we trust You, we can climb the hill and go down the valley singing. You give us songs in darkest nights and make us joyful in spite of all conditions.

Amen.[106]

Having won an instructed verdict for the ten codefendants in the case, the bank's attorneys came into the courtroom Monday morning feeling a tailwind. Freed of the burden of disproving the conspiracy allegations, they streamlined their presentation and focused on knocking out the remaining pillars of Maxey's petition with testimony from a total of five witnesses.

The entire presentation by the defense, from first witness to last, would take less than three days.

Former Citizens National Bank vice president Barclay Ryall, a one-time bank examiner from Williams's hometown of Post, was the first witness. His testimony lasted all day Monday and much of Tuesday.[107]

Ryall, a young protégé of Williams, had not been on the Christmas list of anyone on the Maxey side. He was present during the dissolution of Maxey's assets on February 16, 1966. Maxey's attorneys had also connected Ryall with various acts of alleged chicanery by the bank during his tenure as president of Plaza Building Corporation, a position he assumed after the foreclosure. W. O. Shafer's questioning of the witness took up the entire day. Ryall was E. W. Williams's right-hand man at Citizens National Bank and had direct involvement in the accounting of every last cent that Maxey and his corporate entities owed the bank and other creditors.

Under questioning by Shafer, each credit to Maxey's accounts was identified and tallied, beginning with the amounts given for the stock in the corporations on February 16, 1966, through the crediting of the proceeds of sales of assets, some of which had been parceled out between accounts.

Everything seemed to add up for Citizens National Bank and, although the narrative was already a familiar one, it was a logical way to support the bank's claim that it handled the foreclosure in what it assured the court was "a fair and orderly" manner.

According to the figures testified to by Ryall, as of February 16, 1966, Plaza Building Corporation owed a total of $481,777.10 on its notes at Citizens

National Bank. Maxey's personal account owed $495,988.10, and the total due from Triple M Feeders Inc., was $389,074.24.

From there, Ryall identified every credit to those accounts, down to the balance of Maxey's personal checking account, $50.59.

The liquidation of stock, ranches, other real estate, livestock, equipment, and credit notes continued until the last one, on February 28, 1969, with the sale of a small farm in Missouri for $27,408.89.

After that last credit, Plaza was still in debt to the bank to the tune of $91,446.91, plus interest. Counting the balances due from Maxey's personal notes and Triple M Feeders Inc., Maxey's accounts with Citizens National Bank ended over $300,000 in the hole, according to the bank's analysis. Vaughn Hendrie, the *Avalanche-Journal* reporter covering the trial that day in place of Kenneth May, was not impressed. Hendrie referred to the "long procedure of detailing every receipt of cash and every check."[108]

Tuesday morning Shafer guided Ryall through the sales of Maxey's ranches and the crediting of the proceeds to his accounts. Bowlin objected, complaining to the judge that it was pointless to go through the same material once again.

> Bowlin: Your Honor, Mr. Jones already testified about this in great detail. I object to it on the grounds that it is repetitious, it is already in the record, and then yesterday [Ryall] testified to the credits given on all these transactions, which was repetitious at that time, and this will be the third time that I can recall this was gone into, and we object to it for that reason.
>
> Judge Moore: Overruled.

It was before the noon break when Shafer passed the witness. Bowlin began his questioning of the witness with a simpler, more dramatic line of questioning.[109] First of all, Bowlin brought up the fact that Ryall was in the room when Maxey's assets were disbursed to the bank's affiliated entities and associates (including Birdwell). It took less than a minute for him to ask Ryall about the paltry $749 the bank gave for the Plaza Building Corporation.

> Bowlin: All right. The position has been taken here that Plaza's assets were worth $749 on that day. Was that your position also, that day?
>
> Ryall: No, Sir.
>
> Bowlin: In other words, at the time that the Plaza stock was sold, you knew it was worth more than $749, did you not?
>
> Ryall: No, sir.

Bowlin: Did you think it was worth $749?

Ryall: The stock?

Bowlin: Yes.

Ryall: No.

Bowlin: You didn't think it was worth anything?

Ryall: I didn't know at that time.

Bowlin: Then you were not one of the men who decided what it was worth, obviously?

Ryall: No, sir.

Bowlin: All right. Did you—anybody ask you your opinion of it?

Ryall: I don't recall if they did.

During the deposition given by Ryall prior to the trial, Bowlin had asked numerous questions about how the banker had come to be president of Plaza.[110] According to Ryall's statements, he had been informed in a rather offhanded manner that he had been elected president of Plaza on February 17, 1966, the day after the foreclosure. There had been no advance notice, no discussion of salary or responsibilities. Williams told him he had the job with no preamble whatsoever. Bowlin asked Ryall if Williams had said anything else.

Ryall: Merry Christmas.

Bowlin: Merry Christmas? Is that the extent of it?

Ryall: Just about.

Bowlin: Does *merry Christmas* have some significance concerning your election as president of Plaza?

Ryall: No.

Bowlin: What did he mean by that, then?

Ryall: I don't know. That's just what he said.

The testimony was painful for the Maxeys to hear. A multimillion-dollar corporation, created to help manage a significant portion of the postwar building boom that had reshaped Lubbock, had been sold for the paltry sum of $749 during foreclosure. After that, it was handed off to a young executive as if it were the punch line of a joke.

Bowlin's first two questions for Ryall established that Ryall was deeply involved in the foreclosure and secret sale of Maxey's assets, yet his position at the bank was so lowly that no one bothered to ask his opinion about the corporation of which he was appointed president. The inference is that E. W. Williams and the other top executives at Citizens National Bank were at best acting in a blithe and careless manner as they disposed of Homer Maxey's properties and companies.

As Williams himself later described the private stock sale, "It doesn't sound good, but it was legal."[111]

Charlie Joplin has only good things to say about Ryall and Williams. "Barclay Ryall and I were young vice presidents at the same time. We took care of one another's customers when the other was out. We played tennis together and were good friends."[112] Joplin admits that he has a "very biased viewpoint," one reason being that Williams gave him his first banking job in 1955, when Williams was at First National Bank.

Later, when Joplin was at Citizens, he remembers the morning Williams announced that he had talked to Maxey the night before and that Maxey was going to move all his business to Citizens National Bank. Williams was excited but, at the time, Joplin knew little about Maxey. "They told me he was a big deal in Lubbock, but I didn't know, I just ran the cotton department," says Joplin.

"Barclay Ryall was the one Mr. Williams got to do the details and carry all the water on the Maxey case. I did a few things on it, mostly clerical things, more or less." Speaking from his present office in the Lubbock National Bank Building, the admission elicits a chuckle from Joplin, a pleasant, smiling, white-haired banker. "You know, Mr. Maxey named everybody in the lawsuit, but probably the reason he didn't sue me was that he never could remember my name."

Ryall was not so lucky. His employment at Citizens National Bank began in 1965. Maxey's relationship with Williams had already soured. The Maxeys and their attorneys held Ryall in very low regard.[113]

Bowlin cross-examined Ryall for under an hour, but he made the most of every minute. He hit Ryall with questions about various apparent irregularities in the bank's handling of the Maxey affair.[114]

Later, Ryall conceded that one month after the foreclosure, Citizens National Bank had increased the value of properties owned by Plaza by almost $600,000. What Bowlin wanted the jurors to hear was that, once Maxey filed his lawsuit against Citizens National Bank, the bank decided that Plaza was worth at least $599,251 more than the bank's valuation at the time of foreclosure.

Bowlin seemed determined to portray Ryall as a bank officer who did whatever he was told, and that, most of the time, his orders came from Williams and Jones.

Bowlin: Now, subsequent to that time, and in your actions as president of Plaza, all of the actions which you took were those actions which Citizens National Bank advised you to take, were they not?

Ryall: Yes, sir.

Bowlin: In other words, you didn't run Plaza Building Corporation as the . . . principal executive officer, having made the decisions about what would be done, did you?

Ryall: No.

In follow-up questions, Ryall conceded that the decisions were made by Williams and, "frequently, Mr. Jones."

When Bowlin asked Ryall if he had been an officer of the Monterey Lubbock Corporation, Ryall said he didn't think so, but he couldn't remember.

Bowlin next led the witness through some of the bank's questionable actions in handling Maxey's accounts after the foreclosure. Ryall admitted that the bank had continued to charge Maxey for expenses incurred after it had taken possession of his properties, even though it was not supposed to.

The biggest issue of contention raised by Bowlin was the way the bank had handled two cashier's checks made out to Maxey, which had been received in early February 1966. One check, in the amount of $75,000, was for the sale of property owned by Maxey on College Avenue; the other, for $50,000, was for the payment on a note owed to Maxey.

The plaintiffs' petition maintained that the bank had waited until after the foreclosure to deposit the funds, which had the effect of reducing the apparent value of Plaza by $125,000 prior to the foreclosure, an assertion that was hotly contested by the defense. The much more crucial issue, however, was the manner in which the funds were credited. Ryall testified that the $125,000 had been credited to Maxey's indebtedness to Citizens National Bank.

One of the linchpins of the plaintiffs' case was that because Plaza Building Corporation owed Homer Maxey an amount greater than $125,000, the proceeds from those checks should have credited Plaza's indebtedness to Maxey by that amount. Instead, the bank took the money and applied it to Maxey's loans. The net effect, Bowlin argued, was that the bank still counted the $125,000 in the liabilities column for Plaza Building Corporation.

Ryall didn't see it that way. Bowlin used several different examples to illustrate the logic behind his assertion, but Ryall stuck with his original answer.

After consulting Ryall's deposition, Bowlin referred to the answers Ryall had given on the subject of the two checks. Bowlin reminded Ryall that when asked if the $75,000 check should have been credited for $150,000, Ryall had replied, "Yes."

On the stand however, Ryall said, "I believe I was in error then."

After grilling the witness about the handling of other checks made out to Maxey, Bowlin pivoted to the subject of an arrangement the bank made with a man named Steve Gose to lease the Triple M Ranch, with an option to purchase. Under the terms of the deal, Gose paid $3,000 the first month and $6,000 each month thereafter, for a total of $75,000 profit to the bank in just over a year's time.

The terms also included, as Bowlin phrased it, "some sort of a deal where he was going to pay the bank a couple of hundred thousand dollars more than was owed on it, and share any profit above that," alluding to the allegation of kickback agreements that Citizens National Bank had made with various purchasers of Maxey's ranch properties. The allegation was that the bank would only credit Maxey with the amount received on the first sale and, thereafter, would pocket 50 percent of the profit when the property was flipped to the next buyer.

Shafer rose and said, "We object, Your Honor, to an unconsummated transaction, not being evidence of value or relating to any issue now in the lawsuit."

Judge Moore sustained the objection.

Today E. W. Williams says he has no recollection of such deals, which he prefers to call "participation in profit." "When a property sells within a certain time period, you get a percentage of the profit," he says. "That's legal and it would not be uncommon. It is not a kickback."

Bowlin was undeterred. He asked several questions about the Birdwell-Mullendore cattle deal, probing for reasonable explanations as to why Birdwell, who had close personal and familial ties with the board of Citizens National Bank, and his friend, Mullendore, were able to obtain a loan to buy Maxey's Triple M cattle on such generous terms as they were, making a quick profit as the reins were tightened on Maxey.

Bowlin passed the witness, and after a short recess, Shafer questioned Ryall for a little over two minutes on the topic of the $125,000 in payments which had been a key subject of Bowlin's cross-examination. Bowlin then rose for a last recross. He began by asking Ryall a few details about the handling of Maxey's account after the foreclosure, after which he asked the big question.

Bowlin: Mr. Ryall, did you make a telephone call to Mr. Brady?

Ryall: No, sir.

Bowlin: Do you know who did?

Ryall: No, sir.

Bowlin: Do you know whether or not Mr. Jones made a telephone call to Mr. Brady?

Ryall: No, sir.

Bowlin: Pass the witness.

Next, the jury heard from four defense witnesses who all testified as to the values of the ranch and farm properties.[115] Three of them were appraisers and one was a geologist. The witnesses supported their testimony with aerial photographs, which they used to point out facilities and features on the land, describing in detail the geography, the types of soil, and economic potential of the properties. That, according to their opinions, ranged from the Tucumcari ranch, at $26 to $30 per acre, to upward of $250 an acre for the Texline farm.

Bowlin objected to the 1963 appraisal of the Texline farm by the first witness, Melvin Moore, on the grounds that Moore's appraisal predated Maxey's ownership of the farm. Subsequent to that date, Maxey had acquired the property and made numerous improvements on it. Judge Moore overruled the objection.

D. K. Swan, an appraiser, realtor, and rancher from Muskogee, Oklahoma, gave some of the most entertaining testimony of the trial. While describing the relative merits of the Oklahoma ranches, he stated that they were in rough country and some of the geographic features detracted from their utility. The Atoka property he said, was located in what "is sort of the widow woman part of the state, primarily very rough mountainous country . . . some boulders as large as that desk there . . ."

Getting around on the Wilburton ranch was difficult, he said, because of the "hogback mountain" that had the effect of splitting the ranch into north-south sections. "About the only way you can get over it is in a jeep or horseback," he said. "I have driven a car over it, but much to my sorrow."

After the lunch break, the defense called Claude Keeton, who testified regarding the physical condition of the cattle at the Triple M Ranch before their sale to Birdwell and Mullendore.[116] Keeton claimed fifty years' experience in cattle trading, feedlot operation, meat packing, and other beef-related enterprises. He said he had appraised the cattle at $275,000 in July 1965, but when he returned the following February, their condition was not as good.

Bowlin struck sparks when he took over the questioning of W. E. Medlock, a Lubbock native who claimed some forty-three years of experience farming on the southern plains.[117] No simple dirt farmer, Medlock was a large-scale cotton grower, rancher, and developer who had served on the Lubbock City Council from 1964 to 1968.

Medlock was the purchaser of Maxey's Texline farm after the foreclosure. As the owner of a farm of several thousand acres near Texline, he had prior experience farming in that area and, therefore, felt qualified to make accurate appraisals of farmland in the region.

Medlock's career as a farmer began, he said, with a one-hundred-acre farm just north of Lubbock. The year was 1944 and he was eighteen years old. By the age of twenty-one, he owned forty-five thousand acres and rented roughly the same amount, for a total of about ninety thousand acres. He also attended seminary school in Fort Worth, graduating in 1952. Fort Worth is over 320 miles from Lubbock.

During cross-examination, Bowlin asked, "Did you farm it by long distance when you were down [at seminary school]?"

"I attended the seminary on weekends, and . . . Fridays and Saturdays and Sundays," Medlock replied.

Bowlin then asked about his purchase of Maxey's Texline property. Earlier, Medlock had testified that he paid $275 an acre for the Texline farm, even though he believed it was only worth $250.

In connection with his purchase of the farm from Citizens National Bank, Bowlin asked, did Medlock also agree that if he sold a portion of the land for a profit, or more than $275 an acre, that he would split the profit with the bank?[118]

Medlock answered "No."

Bowlin pressed him again, asking whom he had agreed to split the profit with.

"No one," said Medlock.

Bowlin then showed Medlock an agreement and then read from the document:

> It is further understood and agreed by and between us that should we sell the northeast quarter of Section 3, Block 5, FDW Sub-Division, within five years for more than $275 an acre, we shall divide all above the amount of $275 with the Citizens National Bank.

"Did you sign that?" Bowlin asked.

"Yes, sir," answered Medlock.

"Pass the witness."

Bill Goodacre remembers being disgusted with the former city council member.[119] "I'm just looking at it from one side of the story," he says, "but they caught him in a lie, and it just showed how there was a lot of rottenness going on that was not right. If the bank had done all this in the right way, that would've been something else, but they didn't."

Jones examined the next witness, George D. Ray, focusing his questions on the less-than-ideal condition of the cattle on the Triple M Ranch after the winter of 1965–66. As a cattle trader born and raised in Pawhuska, Oklahoma, the witness's authority on that part of the country, the cattle trade, or the people involved in it would seem to have been implicit. When Ray inspected the cattle in April 1966, he observed that they appeared to have been "poorly wintered."[120]

Ray had gone to the ranch to place a bid for the herd. He offered $150 a head for the cows and $200 for the bulls. He had planned to turn the cattle for a quick profit of between $7,000 and $15,000. His bid, however, was not accepted.

Under cross by Bowlin, Ray confirmed that, for a quick sale, $10 profit per head would be the "top profit" one could expect. Bowlin asked if the cattle were in such bad shape that he expected to make less profit than usual. Ray answered, "No, I wouldn't have termed them that way."

Bowlin wanted to know how long Ray had known E. C. Mullendore III. Had he known him "many, many years?" "Yes, sir," responded Ray.

Author Jonathon Kwitny relied a great deal on Ray for information and insight about Mullendore and his untidy life when researching his book, *The Mullendore Murder Case*. The cattle salesman is quoted countless times throughout the book, and his appearance in the opening paragraph, where Mullendore's murder is first mentioned, has implications of shady behavior of which Maxey's attorneys may have been aware.[121]

[O]f the people he saw gathered at the mall for the funeral, Ray figured he knew E. C. as well as anyone. The slender, graying salesman had worked cattle with E. C. when the Mullendore boy was still in school. . . . Ray had sold for E. C. in the good years. He also had sold for E. C. in the last year, at significant risk to himself, when E. C. rapidly was losing access to other old friends. Now there was talk that those cattle sales had been illegal, and that the federal prosecutor was investigating. Ray was, frankly, a little nervous. But if anybody came around asking him questions, he would just tell the truth: he had done what his friend asked him to; if the cattle sales were crooked, well, that was a matter E. C. had resolved for himself. Ray certainly hadn't coaxed anybody into selling anything. Despite what he knew about the cattle sales, and despite all the rough characters he had seen around E. C. that summer, George Ray certainly hadn't figured to become a pallbearer for the young man so soon.

"Did you know him when he was out in Hollywood?" Bowlin asked the witness. "You knew he was an actor, did you, out there sometime?"[122]

"No, sir," answered Ray.

Asked if he knew that Mullendore and Birdwell had made a net profit of $126,000 on their purchase of Maxey's cattle from the Triple M Ranch, Ray said he had not heard that. Would he say that $126,000 was a "reasonable profit?" He responded: "I think it would be a good profit."

Bowlin drew out the fact that Mullendore was the person who had suggested that Ray offer a bid on Maxey's cattle. By that time however, it was later revealed, Mullendore and Birdwell had already bought the herd from the bank (making a down payment of $3,000 with the rest financed by a $167,000 loan). Ray offered no explanation for the strange sequence of events, nor did he provide any additional commentary or observations regarding other unusual details of the Triple M cattle deal.

Bowlin asked Ray if he had ever heard of anyone making $126,000 on a herd of that size. "Not that exact figure," he answered, "but I have heard of some big profits."

"Have you ever had anything like that happen to you, Mr. Ray?" asked Bowlin.

"No," he said, adding "I don't run cattle at all; I turn cattle."

The last witness for the defense, Marvin Hugley, was a farm and ranch broker from Clovis, New Mexico. Hugley had sold Maxey's Tucumcari ranch to a buyer named E. P. Tixier of Logan, New Mexico, in December 1968 at a price of $516,760, or $29.06 an acre. In Hugley's evaluation, the land was worth about $26 to $30 an acre.[123]

During his testimony, the jurors were treated to a good bit of information about geography and the economics of cattle raising. Handling the examination on direct, Jones seemed to enjoy showing off his knowledge in those fields. Hugley rated the ranch at forty acres per "cow unit," meaning that forty acres of pasture on the land was required to support each grazing cow. At a price of $29.06 per acre, that worked out to $1,160 per cow unit.

The name of the ranch was somewhat misleading, as it was located forty miles west of Tucumcari, on the west side of the Conchas Lake reservoir in San Miguel County. As seen from the air, State Highway 104 cut through the southwestern edge of the ranch, and, as the reservoir backed up behind Conchas Dam, the ranch dipped southward into the mesas on the extreme northeastern portion of the property.

According to Hugley, there were some decent grasslands atop the mesa, while the steep walls of the red-rimmed canyons served as natural boundaries. The land was rugged, however, and anyone had to know that ranchland in that area was at the mercy of flooding and erosion. Hugley also testified that, while the reservoir was "a pretty lake to look at" and did not detract from the value of the ranch, the fluctuations between its high and low water levels created "a considerable area of boggy, muddy conditions." Therefore, in his opinion, it had no potential as lakefront property for vacation cabins or recreation.

By the time Jones finished examining the witness, the jurors were given the impression that the bank had been lucky it didn't have to take even less than Hugley got for it. Also, the implication was that Maxey had inflated its value on his financial statements and in the plaintiffs' petition, and that when he purchased it for $746,440 (which included livestock), he had grossly overpaid.

Bowlin's first question for Hugley concerned the gigantic Bell Ranch, which was located on the opposite side of Conchas Lake from the Tucumcari ranch. The ranch was one of the largest and most famous in the Southwest. In 1947 Harriet Keeney and her family acquired ownership of 130,000 acres of the ranch, plus the ranch headquarters, name, and brand. At the time of the Maxey trial, the Keeneys were in the process of selling the Bell Ranch to a Chicagoan named William N. Lane II, the CEO of General Binding Corporation, a manufacturer of office supplies and equipment.[124]

"Mr. Hugley, are you familiar with the Bell Ranch?" asked Bowlin.

"Not too familiar," answered the witness. "I have driven through it several times."

Bowlin reminded Hugley that the Bell Ranch adjoined Maxey's ranch and that it was owned by the Keeney family, as in William Ellwood Keeney, one of the directors of Citizens National Bank. "Are you familiar with the sale of it recently, around the time this one sold?" Bowlin asked. "Did you sell it?"

"No, sir," answered Hugley. "I wasn't aware that any of it had sold at the time this one had sold."

"You were not aware that it sold for $40 an acre about the same time this one sold?"

"No, sir."[125]

Bowlin wanted jurors to consider the possibility that acreage on the Tucumcari ranch might have been equal in value to that of the nearby Bell Ranch, but a secondary strategy was to question the credibility of the witness for the defense. It strains credulity that a real estate broker or anyone with any interest in ranching in that area would be unaware of the sale of large parcels of such a historic ranch. The Bell Ranch was one of the most famous and largest ranches in the Southwest. A good many of the richest families in Lubbock had either once owned a piece of it or still did. During the 1960s and 1970s, members of those same families were still well represented on the board of Citizens National Bank.[126]

After foreclosing on Maxey's Tucumcari ranch, Citizens National Bank leased it to Birdwell and his friend Mullendore, who ran one thousand head of cattle on it for three years. That was four hundred head more than Maxey's largest herd. As a result, the pastures were overgrazed. Also, as Maxey had related in his testimony, the facilities had been vandalized. Thieves helped themselves to equipment and supplies.[127]

The defense offered no testimony or other evidence to contradict the assertions that the ranch properties formerly owned by Maxey had deteriorated under the management of the bank, or that Birdwell in particular was responsible for various types of destructive abuse and neglect on the Tucumcari ranch.

Under Birdwell's watch, many earthen dams Maxey had erected on the ranch were allowed to deteriorate. The rains came and washed out pastureland downstream. Where Maxey had cleared the mesquite brush from grasslands, the hardy invader was again allowed to run wild.

Bowlin asked Hugley if Birdwell's neglectful treatment of the ranch had contributed to the low price when the ranch was sold.[128] Hugley's reply was evasive. Bowlin tried again. If he was honest about it, Bowlin said, would Hugley admit that "it certainly didn't help" to abandon the work Maxey had done on the ranch, did it?

"No, sir," answered Hugley, "it never helps to stop the erosion control."

Bowlin tried to pin Hugley down on a few other questions and then announced that he had nothing else to ask. Shafer had no further questions, either. The witness was excused.

The jurors had heard new revelations about Birdwell, whose family ties to the bank went back to the horse-and-buggy days and whose murky deal to snap up a foreclosed cow herd for a fat profit would be a vivid reminder of the backroom dealings that had dispersed Maxey's other assets. For all the flaws in Hugley's testimony, at least he had not been caught lying about signing a kickback agreement, as had Medlock.

Shafer informed Judge Moore that the defense had no more witnesses. The date was Wednesday, January 7, 1970. The trial, which had begun at the end of October, was near the end.[129]

Chapter 8

TWISTS AND TURNS

Judge Moore gave everyone Thursday and Friday off, and the trial resumed the following Monday morning, January 12, 1970. The attorneys for both sides took full advantage of the two hours allowed for final arguments. After enduring twenty-eight days of testimony in the longest trial in the history of Lubbock County, the jurors could see the light at the end of the tunnel. They had even been treated to an increased rate of compensation to $10 per day, instead of the usual $4.

In his opening argument for the plaintiffs, Alton Griffin related once again the history of Homer Maxey's relationship with the bank.[1] As a prosecutor, Griffin was practiced in the art of telling stories about relationships gone awry. The relationship between his client and the banker, he said, began with a gentleman's handshake agreement in the fall of 1962. At that time Maxey was one of the most important businessmen in town. E. W. Williams, Jr. was an ambitious young bank president looking to land fat new accounts for his bank. The promises sealed by that handshake, Griffin contended, were just a come-on, a lure thrown out to hook a big customer. The bank, Griffin said, "closed a bear trap" on Maxey.

Griffin, now deceased, is remembered by family, friends, and colleagues as a very effective attorney, whether working as a county prosecutor or as a defense attorney. "Alton was a fantastic orator," says his widow, Jo Anne Griffin, "and he was very, very passionate about this case. He had known Mr. Maxey forever."[2]

Homer and Melba Maxey during happier times, in their home on Vicksburg Avenue, before Citizens National Bank took it from them. Courtesy of the Maxey family.

Griffin pointed out that Maxey's former attorneys had negotiated the deals for Maxey's ranches and other properties. Now those attorneys were in court representing the bank, calling those deals into question. What did that say about their arguments? What did that say about their ethics?

Williams had lured Maxey to Citizens National Bank, Griffin told the jury, with the promise of an unsecured line of credit, then tied up his assets with cross-mortgages and interfered in his business operations, making it impossible to repay his debts to Citizens either by making a profit or by refinancing his loans. "You haven't heard one word to refute it," said Griffin. "You haven't seen E. W. Williams on the stand."[3]

In the argument for the defense, presented by W. O. Shafer, the lead defense attorney again attempted to show that the numbers alone told the tale: During the years of his association with the bank, Maxey's businesses were all losing money, his debts were greater than his assets, and his assets were not worth the values listed on his financial statements.

The financial broker Ed Drumwright also came under heavy scrutiny. Shafer told the jury that the financier didn't know cow country from steer country. He also underscored the fact that Drumwright was earning a five-figure fee for his services, failing to mention that there was nothing unusual about the practice.[4]

Bowlin wrapped up the final argument for Maxey's side. "The question in this case, really, when you get down to it, is whether or not the bank was fair with Homer Maxey," he said. "[The bank] got caught with their hand in the till . . . I'm telling you, they ain't been fair to Homer Maxey."[5]

In his rebuttal, Shafer maintained that the bank had "gone as far as they could go and it was time to foreclose." After foreclosure, the bank had even offered to discount Maxey's debt by $100,000 and release all his collateral, if he would agree to their other terms. "Is that evil intent, or is it a creditor that would like to get partly paid?"[6]

By the end of the final arguments, it was late afternoon. Before sending the jury members out to begin their deliberations, Judge Moore gave them instructions. Among the most important pertained to a list of special issues regarding the individual allegations in the plaintiffs' petition. The issues were presented in a series of questions, and each had to be answered separately, with unanimous agreement as to guilt or innocence. The jury was also responsible for computing the amount of damages to be awarded. The first issue to be determined was whether Citizens National Bank was at fault. If the answer to that question was no, most of the rest of the questions would be moot. If answered in the affirmative, the jury was required to determine whether Maxey's assets had been liquidated for amounts that were "grossly inadequate," a term defined by the court as being so low that it would "shock the sense of justice and is extremely unreasonable." A yes answer meant the plaintiffs were entitled to exemplary (punitive) damages.

The jurors deliberated for seventy minutes before being excused for the day. On Tuesday, they met again and deliberations continued. Blair Cherry, the Lubbock County district attorney, gave Homer and Melba a deck of cards to help pass the time while they waited.[7] Almost six hours passed before Foreman Clarence O. Rice, who had missed more than two months' work in his job as a mechanic for the highway department, sent a message to the bailiff that the jury had reached a verdict.[8]

That the verdict would be in favor of the Maxeys must have been rather obvious as Judge Pat Moore, having adjusted her cat's-eye glasses, began reading the jury's verdict.[9]

To the question "Do you find from a preponderance of the evidence that Citizens National Bank held the sale on February 16, 1966, without having exhibited the property to be sold to any prospective purchaser other than itself and companies controlled by it?" The answer was "yes."

The jurors also agreed that the bank held the sale "without notice to any prospective purchaser other than itself and companies controlled by it," and purchased the properties without opening the bidding to any outside parties.

The jury also agreed that a preponderance of the evidence showed that when Citizens National Bank sold Plaza Building Corporation to Monterey Lubbock Corporation, the $749 purchase price was a "grossly inadequate amount." Instead, the jury determined the fair market value of Plaza Building Corporation to be $1,051,516.02.

The bank's position was that the value of Plaza's assets, $3,619,617 (a figure that defense witnesses had sometimes disputed during the trial), was exceeded by its liabilities, which they argued were $3,897,678, leaving a deficit of $278,061. The jurors disagreed.[10]

The jury also found the bank's credit for the Maxey Lumber Company stock to be grossly inadequate. The bank had appraised the value at $231,000; the jury said $370,000.

On the issue of exemplary damages, the jury found the plaintiffs were entitled to $1.5 million.

The total sum of the actual damages (the differences between the jury's valuation of Maxey's assets and the amounts credited to him by Citizens National Bank) came to just under $1.2 million. After adding in the award of $1.5 million for exemplary damages, the total amount of the judgment was $2,689,767.[11]

Maxey was jubilant. "We did it," he said. "I feel great. If I'd won a dollar, I'd have won."

Kenneth May, writing for the *Avalanche-Journal*, wrote that Melba, Carla, and Glenna were "wet-eyed and joyous."

The jurors made a point of shaking hands with the Maxeys. Several of them were crying, too. Some of them struggled to explain how they felt about the experience. Glenna said that several of the jurors told them they tried their best, but "felt so inadequate."

Bill Goodacre's sister, Mooney, was there on the last day, too. She had come for Christmas but stayed on ten days beyond her vacation time just to see the family through the trial.

May approached Bowlin with what would seem to be a rather obvious question: "Are you happy with the verdict, Ken?"

"I'm not happy with it," he replied, "but I'll take it."

Like a sports reporter visiting the locker room of the losing team, May next approached the official spokesperson for the bank. The new president, who happened to have the ironic name of Willard Paine, was ready with a prepared statement.

"We intend to pursue every available legal avenue with confidence that ultimately the bank's position will be vindicated," Paine told the reporter. The bank was "gravely concerned," he said, "about the future effect of this decision on all banking and lending institutions—not only in the Lubbock area but throughout Texas and the nation. Certainly all borrowers will feel the effect."

Paine issued a few more dire warnings about the possible extinction of the banking industry if the Maxey verdict was allowed to stand, but he also wanted to reassure the bank's customers that "a majority of the bank's stockholders have already come forward to assure us that the strength of the bank will not be affected."

Paine's promise to soldier on in the courts was more than just bluster. Among other tactics, the bank's owners planned to enlist the help of the Texas Bankers Association, which later filed an amicus brief echoing the gloomy tone of Paine's prediction that the impact from the Maxey case would be imposed "not only on the litigants but upon all creditor-debtor relationships."[12]

Jim Cade countered that such legal moves represented a "blatant and unsupported claim of power and influence" that pretended to speak for "the entire banking industry of this state." Quoted in the *Lubbock Avalanche-Journal*, Cade acknowledged that the board of Citizens National Bank represented a group of West Texas's wealthiest, most powerful families.[13]

"We cannot match the great accumulation of power and influence with what remains of the wreckage of the life work of Homer G. Maxey," said Cade, "but we are assured by many of our friends in the banking world that what the jury has done, after hearing evidence for three months, is a boon to all honest bankers and they compose a majority of that business."

In reality, the most observable outcome of the Maxey trial was that Citizens National Bank saw its depositors leaving in droves to do business with other local banks. As for Maxey, he pinned his hopes on starting over again with the money he received from his successful lawsuit. He knew it wouldn't be easy. A friend offering encouragement reminded him that he'd made a fortune once and he was confident that he could do it again. Maxey told his friend, "I used to have people waiting outside my office waiting to see me. Now, I've got to go see them. It's harder to make your fortune the second time than the first time."[14]

The night after the verdict, the Maxeys celebrated with a victory party at a steak house. The guest list included more than thirty people. Joining the Maxeys and their attorneys and wives were their closest friends—the Fullers, the Talkingtons, the Cassels, and Dr. Olan Key and his wife.[15]

According to Melba's journal, at least half a dozen people called to congratulate them. The entries for the next two days recorded another two dozen phone calls. Friends came over with food and other presents, and a note at the bottom of the page for January 14, 1970, says "Rev. Hollis—'many prayers,'" with a mailing address for the thank-you card Melba would be sending out.

Some of the friends who called with congratulations were members of families whose ties to the Maxey family went back fifty years or more and who were, in one way or another, also associated with the opposing parties in Maxey's lawsuit. Russell Bean, for example, was the son of the late District Judge George R. Bean, who was one of the founding members of the firm that became Evans, Pharr, Trout & Jones.

Next to some of the names on Melba's list were quotes such as "Happy Days" and "Prayers answered." Dub Rogers and Dub Rushing both called to relay their congratulations.

By Melba's count, the number of congratulatory calls reached over one hundred by the end of the week. In a note prefacing Melba's letter to her sister, Doris Cheaney (enclosed with a packet of the most recent clippings from the trial), Homer wrote: "Melba and I are *tired* . . . It will be a long time before we receive any money, from appeals, etc. However we have done all we can do ourselves and will have to get some kind of job to make our living."[16]

The next day the Maxeys left for Dallas to visit friends for the weekend. Melba told Doris they just needed to get away from Lubbock for a few days. "We are still sort of numb . . . People have been wonderful to us but we need a change."

She closed her letter saying how thankful she was that "a lot of good prayers were answered," and that "Homer had the strength to fight for so long—and most of this is behind us."

The Maxeys were also encouraged by the next major developments in the litigation. The attorneys for the bank asked Judge Moore to declare a mistrial, which was denied. Next the attorneys filed a motion for a judgment non obstante veredicto, or JNOV, which means that the judge would enter a verdict for the losing party, notwithstanding the jury findings.[17] It's an intervention that is often requested, but not often granted. On January 26, two weeks after the jury verdict, the judge denied the defense's motion for a JNOV.

In their motion, the lawyers had asserted that the verdict was "contrary to the undisputed evidence in the case," alleging that the jury's finding "was without authority in law or in the evidence." Bowlin told the *Avalanche-Journal* that such motions were to be expected from the losing party in a lawsuit.[18]

Bowlin was correct. He might as well have added, however, that there would be many more such legal maneuvers yet to come from the defense.

During the last weeks of January and into February, the Maxeys had time to enjoy a sigh of relief and recuperate from the trial. Melba was taking two-hour naps every afternoon and still, each time she stretched out in Homer's big chair, she fell fast asleep. Carla came down with the flu. Bill Goodacre was limping around after tearing a ligament playing hockey.

Homer and Melba were aware that the bank would appeal the verdict, but if the appellate court upheld the jury's findings, they expected the money from the judgment to be forthcoming within a year or so. Another factor: the bank would owe an additional six percent interest on the judgment after it became final. (In Texas state courts, the judgment becomes final thirty days after being signed by the judge.) Therefore, it seemed logical that the bank would want to pay up or settle for a compromise amount.

But during the month of March, the legal seesaw would begin tipping up and down in earnest. On March third, Judge Moore signed the judgment of the jury, and nine days later, attorneys for the bank filed a motion for a new trial, citing the same allegations mentioned in their motion for JNOV.

On the fourteenth, Homer celebrated his fifty-ninth birthday with more than enough cake to go around, as there was still a trickle of friends coming over with presents, food, and liquor. Carla and Glenna bought their dad a pair of slip-on loafers. Homer, however, couldn't help feeling uneasy about wearing laceless shoes (a trait he shared with many such men of his era, including Richard Nixon). Melba told Doris that Homer thought the shoes were "a little gay for him," but that he would keep them "as they are his first new shoes in six years."[19]

Melba also enclosed a small note thanking Doris for the spinach salad recipe her sister had shared with her. Melba had just attended a "marvelous cooking class" at the gas company and was energized by the new recipes she had learned—in particular, the diet recipes that called for using a blender. The Elliotts were using them in their new diet regime to great success. "Carla has lost eleven pounds," she wrote, and "Tommy has lost twenty . . . Now that's a lot of lard!"

Despite the Maxeys' falling out with Bill Evans, Melba's feelings for him were still mixed enough to mention to Doris that he was "in the hospital again . . . not doing any good."

But there was still plenty of good news. It was snowing in Lubbock and even more in the mountains. Homer and Melba were going up to Oklahoma to file some papers on the Triple M Ranch, then to New Mexico to join the Elliotts at the family cabin near Cowles.

Glenna was busy painting portraits, working to raise the money for a three-week trip to Europe in June. Months earlier, she had finished her first bronze sculpture, a seven-inch tall ballerina figure modeled after her daughter, Jill. She had reached a pivotal point in her art career.

"Daddy was always encouraging me to do better and figure out ways of getting ahead," she recalls. "Not necessarily just making money, but always trying something different. That's what he taught me."[20] Once Glenna tried her hand at clay-mashing and bronze casting, she was hooked. Over the next ten years, as she intensified her studies and experimentation in the art form, she began earning recognition and acclaim in the art world. One lucrative commission followed another, and she embarked on a path to becoming one of America's best-known sculptors.

On the surface, Glenna's chosen field couldn't have been more different from that of her father the builder, developer, and dealmaker. Glenna not only created works of art that demonstrated great talent and skill, she produced work that satisfied the needs of the public. She also coordinated the structural, logistical, and financial support essential for producing that work, as well as its marketing and promotion. With further consideration, it's easy to see that Homer, the hustler and builder, and Melba, the creative, artistic type, provided fine role models for their daughter, an artist with hard-headed business instincts.

The people of Lubbock, who turned out to be "surprisingly cultured and sophisticated," as Glenna says, were always enthusiastic in their support of her career. Many became collectors. For Glenna's star to be rising at the same time she was sitting in a courtroom, watching her father endure week after week of humiliation and frustration, however, was colored with dark irony. Glenna says she had "always admired the growth and achievements of my hometown and I have always been very proud to be from Lubbock, with one bad exception."

Carla, Homer, and Melba sharing a moment with *Girl with Ribbons*, Glenna's first life-size sculpture. Courtesy of the Maxey family

That "exception" began in 1966, with the foreclosure proceeding against her father, and it continued for the next decade and a half. It troubled Glenna to realize that some of the people who had become collectors of her work were on the opposing side of the lawsuit. "I couldn't believe," she says, "that some of them had done this to Homer."

The 1960s was a decade of tumult and change for most of the world, with momentous events in politics, culture, war, and civil rights. For the Maxey family, the turmoil in the outside world must have felt like a strange manifestation of the roller coaster ride they had experienced in their own lives. After twenty-five years of great success in business, Homer Maxey began the decade with the purchase of a downtown hotel that was doomed to fail, and at the same time, began moving from urban builder and investor to cattle producer. By mid-decade, that venture, too, was failing. He spent the last years of the sixties fighting to regain his fortunes in court. The year 1970 began with a jury verdict in his favor.

On May 11 of that year, real physical turmoil in the form of an F5 torna-

Like much of downtown Lubbock, Fields & Company (the former H. G. Maxey & Company) was completely destroyed by the F5 tornado that struck on May 11, 1970. Photo by B. C. and Conny Martin. Courtesy of the City of Lubbock.

do struck Lubbock, doing its best to erase from the map the downtown area, the Tech campus, and various other sections of town. More than two dozen powerful tornados had struck the downtown areas of US cities since the late 1800s. Few were category F5. Category F5 tornados are officially referred to in the scientific community as *incredible* and can carry with them wind speeds of up to 318 miles per hour.

By some strange coincidence, an F5 had plowed through Waco, Texas, killing over one hundred people, seventeen years before the one that hit downtown Lubbock.[21]

Dan Law was coaching Little League practice at a field on Nineteenth Street that evening, unaware of the impending danger. When he got home, his wife, Jean, told him about the tornado alert. "There was a builder named Bill Burden who lived across the street from me, over here by Higginbotham Lake," says Dan. "We went over there to get in his basement. I had no idea of the seriousness of it. I mean, how could you?"

When the racket died down, Dan Law emerged from the basement and told Jean he'd better get over to the store. By *the store* he meant Fields & Co., which began its life as Homer G. Maxey & Co.[22]

"I got in my car but you could only drive as far as the football stadium at

Broke, Not Broken

Fourth and University," recalls Law. "The street was blocked with debris. So I had to walk quite a ways to get there."

The devastation was so great that Law still finds it difficult to describe. "Your mind just can't comprehend something like that," he says. "One of the things I remember most was a gas supply line coming into the back of the warehouse that was broken and spewing gas. It was just, things were everywhere."

The Living Center, the showcase room of the store, was demolished and scattered to kingdom come. There was still a great deal of valuable merchandise and hardware in the facility, however. Law found a telephone that worked and then called up his old football buddy for help.

"Dan Law called me and said, 'Tommy, Tommy, Tommy, hey, I need some help!'" recalls Tommy Elliott. "I went over there and it was just wiped out. When that place was built, there was nothing better in the state of Texas. But it was just destroyed. I went and got some people to go over there. We had guards out there packing Winchesters, keeping an eye on things. It was something else."[23]

The destruction covered at least twenty-five square miles, or one-quarter of the town of Lubbock. The number of dead totaled twenty-six. Hundreds of residences of all kinds were obliterated. More than 250 businesses, plus many schools and government offices, were severely damaged or destroyed. Not a single motel between Fourth and Tenth Street on Avenue Q escaped major damage.

The 271-feet-tall Great Plains Life Building was twisted and full of cracks, but it would be repaired and saved, making it the tallest building to survive a direct hit from an F5 tornado.

Carla remembers her father wanting to pitch in and help out after the tornado. "Daddy went up in a helicopter with Mayor Granberry to survey the wreckage," she says. "He wanted to do whatever he could to help his town recover, because he just loved Lubbock."[24]

Carla also recalls that her parents spent the night in Margaret's dress shop on Broadway to keep the looters away. "People were just running rampant up and down Broadway, going through everything and just hauling it off any way they could," she says.

"We were in New York at Market when the tornado hit Lubbock," said Margaret Talkington. "What happened to the store was just terrible, but my friends, people like Homer and Melba, all went down there and sat in the store to keep people from coming in to steal from it."[25]

In stark contrast to all the other ravaged buildings on Broadway, the Pioneer Hotel, which had suffered so much public humiliation in recent years, stood there tall and solid after the tornado had roared past, peeling concrete and bricks and timber from surrounding churches, schools, and office buildings. The old hotel had refused to yield any of its red brick or white lattice work to the caprice of nature.

In the aftermath of the tornado, Lubbock found itself at a crossroads. To recover and move forward again, it would require the leadership of people like Homer Maxey, who had built the city and kept the wheels of progress turning during good times and bad. As good as Maxey's intentions were, however, he was still engaged in the fight of his life: the bank's attorneys were determined to get the jury verdict overturned.

Ken Bowlin, who had promised himself he would retire by the age of forty-five, was burned out after the trial. Now that he had tried the Maxey case and marked his forty-fifth birthday, he wanted to get married to Jane Livermore, quit working, and move to a ranch on the lake by Del Rio, although not in that order. Bowlin didn't exactly cut himself off from friends and associates in Lubbock, nor did he actually quit practicing law, but he did marry Jane and move with her to Del Rio.[26]

Bowlin received an offer from W. O. Shafer to settle the Maxey lawsuit for $1 million. Although Maxey had earlier said he would have felt like he had won the case if he had only been awarded one dollar, the settlement offer lacked one vital element.

"I conveyed that offer to Homer," says Bowlin, "and without hesitation, Homer said, 'No, I want a public apology from Charlie Jones.' I told him Charlie would never apologize, and I was correct. Charlie refused."

At the beginning of Bowlin's involvement with Maxey, Maxey had promised to pay him by the hour and borrow the money to pay the expenses. However, at this point he was unable to fulfill his promise, as he was completely broke. Bowlin said he had spent about $80,000 "out of my own pocket" on expenses, and had personally worked more than seventy-three hundred hours on the case (a number that does not include the number of hours worked by Bowlin's partners, James Cade and Alton Griffin).

Although Maxey wanted Bowlin to continue working on the case, Bowlin insisted that his decision to withdraw was final. "I told Homer that I would not change my mind," says Bowlin, "I told Homer he'd have to talk to my partners about the money, but that I was through with the case, and that he could have my share."

Bowlin's partners weren't very happy that he had, on Maxey's behalf, turned down the bank's offer to settle the lawsuit for $1 million. Cade told Bowlin he was "a damn fool."

"At least I didn't have a bad conscience," says Bowlin. "I never talked to them about it again and I have no idea what happened."

By the end of the summer of 1970, Maxey had also lost several other legal battles. All the codefendants who were granted pleas of privilege were exonerated, including E. G. Rodman, E. G. Rodman, Jr., and W. D. Nöel, the majority owners of the bank.

By the fall of 1970, as the date approached for the Amarillo Court of Appeals to hear the bank's motion for overturning the jury verdict, Maxey decided to turn up the heat. He had his attorneys file a written brief to the court asking for a larger award than the $2.6 million awarded in the district court case. Now he was asking for $2,126,950 actual damages for himself, plus $904,904 for each of his daughters and their husbands, along with the original $1.5 in exemplary damages awarded by the jury.[27]

Maxey seemed to be sending a message to Charlie Jones: the cost of not saying you're sorry has just doubled.

Gwendolyn Murphy, a juror in the 1969 Maxey trial, knew that her next-door neighbor, David Hughes, was married to a woman from Sweden and that their little boy enjoyed playing with her grandson. She also knew that he was a lawyer. But it wasn't until sometime during the trial that she realized he worked for Evans, Pharr, Trout & Jones, the firm that represented Citizens National Bank.[28]

A native of Lockney, Texas, John Hughes moved the family to Lubbock in 1948, after being hired as a vice president at Citizens. According to David Hughes, his father had previous experience running other small-town banks in West Texas, including one in Petersburg, where he and another partner owned controlling interest. In later years, he would be named to the board of the Continental Bank of Chicago.

John Hughes was described by Jack Flygare as "tall and trim, kind of an elegant man," which may have been an unintentional reference to a "kinder, gentler" approach in comparison to that of E. W. Williams, Jr., Hughes's successor. Hughes was replaced by Williams when Rodman and Nöel bought Citizens National Bank in 1961 and began a concerted effort to rebuild the market share of the bank.[29]

One evening a week or so after the verdict was reached in the Maxey case, David Hughes was taking out the garbage when he saw his next-door neighbor. He asked if she had enjoyed her experience as a juror. According to Hughes, Murphy said it was "a very big ordeal," and that the jurors had difficulty comprehending all the complex financial aspects that had been offered as evidence.

Murphy also confided that the jurors had sympathy for the Maxeys, but the bank "had a nice new office tower and bank downtown, and they could afford to pay something." Wasting no time, Hughes reported Murphy's comments to Charlie Jones and W. O. Shafer. Jones and Shafer asked Hughes to see if Murphy would sign a statement. Hughes asked, but Murphy refused.

Murphy was offended by the request. "I didn't think that was right that they came knocking on the jurors' doors after the trial and asking questions," she says. "We had given a verdict and here it turned out they didn't believe us. They didn't get me, though. I left town. It just so happened that one of my daughters who lived in Georgia was expecting. So I went there."

The lawyers for the bank found a juror who was willing to sign an affidavit. Bobby J. Carroll corroborated Murphy's statement that the "bank had a nice new building downtown" and also commented on certain other elements of the deliberations, including his assertion that when ascertaining the market value of Plaza Building Corporation stock, the jurors had not factored in the indebtedness of Plaza to creditors other than Citizens National Bank, nor had they considered Maxey's personal indebtedness to other creditors.[30]

The new allegations were cited as points of error in the bank's pleadings to the appellate court. Rather than being heard in Amarillo, where most cases are argued before the court of appeals, the hearing was conducted on the campus of Texas Tech for the benefit of students at the new law school. The hearing was attended by a large number of local citizens as well as law students.[31]

The decision by the Amarillo Court of Appeals was published on December 7, 1970. The opinion, written by Associate Justice James G. Denton, stated that the jury should not have been permitted to determine the market value of Plaza Building Corporation without considering the debts owed to creditors other than Citizens National Bank. The ruling also opined that the amount the bank had given for Maxey Lumber Company stock was over 60 percent of fair market value and, therefore, was "not grossly inadequate and did not warrant imposition of exemplary damages" against the bank. Because these points of error were sufficient to reverse the verdict and send it back to the district court for a new trial, the allegations of jury misconduct brought by the defense were deemed "unnecessary to discuss."

The practical import of the court of appeals ruling was that the initial decision as to whether there would be a second trial was up to Judge Pat Moore, who granted a summary judgment in favor of Citizens National Bank, handing the bank, its directors, and their team of attorneys the outcome they had predicted all along.[32]

In December of 1972, the appellate court in Amarillo affirmed Judge Moore's summary judgment ruling. But much more devastating to the plaintiffs' cause was the appellate court's further decision that the judgment issued by Judge Moore in December 1969, which held that the bank's representatives were not at fault in the allegations brought against them, "prevents plaintiffs from proceeding against the bank for damages based on the same acts."[33]

In other words, because E. W. Williams, Jr., Clyde Gordon, and all the other codefendants—who were named in Maxey's allegations because of their roles as agents employed by or otherwise associated with Citizens National Bank—had been found blameless, the bank itself could not be sued again for the same allegations.

The legal terms used by the appellate court were *res judicata*, which applies to "claim preclusion," and *collateral estoppel*, which has to do with "issue preclusion." Under res judicata, which is Latin for "the matter has been decided," a final judgment on the merits of an action precludes the parties from relitigating the same issues that were (or could have been) raised in the original lawsuit. The doctrine of collateral estoppel is applied in cases where the cause of action is different, but decisions as to an issue of fact or law necessary to its judgment preclude relitigation of that particular issue.

These legal concepts are used to protect the defendant in a civil litigation case in the same way that "double jeopardy" protects the accused in a criminal case. Under double jeopardy, a person may not be tried again on the same charges after having already been found not guilty in a previous trial. By logical extension, it seemed to suggest that a corporate entity was only capable of wrongdoing through the derivative actions of its corporate officers. If individuals working on behalf of the corporation were accused of wrongdoing but found blameless by a court of law, then the corporation itself could not be held liable for those actions, either. Bringing the issue back full circle, then, under the doctrines of res judicata and collateral estoppel, the corporation could not be sued.

Maxey's options were limited in part because of errors committed during the past two years. Various deadlines for filing appeals had been missed by Maxey's attorneys. Since Maxey had no money to pay his attorneys, certain aspects of the case requiring follow-through were neglected. As a result, the case suffered.

In late 1972, a Fort Worth law firm called Simon & Simon began representing Maxey. The firm assigned the case to a partner named Harold Hammett, who had grown up in Lubbock and attended high school with Glenna. During the hearing of Maxey's appeal of Judge Moore's summary judgment for the bank, Hammett argued that the judge should have disqualified herself from the case because of her relationship to Citizens National Bank.

By means which have never been made public, Maxey obtained an incriminating document—a deed of trust and other financial documents pertaining to a note that was held by Citizens National Bank and that was secured by a cotton gin co-owned by Patricia S. Moore and her brother, Jean David Smith. The judge had cosigned the loan for her brother. The amount of the loan was over $116,000, and it was delinquent.[34]

"Before we went to trial, I asked Pat if there was any reason we shouldn't file this case in her court and she said no," recalls Ken Bowlin. "She told me she did business with First National. Homer and I always thought that there was something between her and Charlie Jones and that was why she was so unfair."

"Judge Moore refused to recuse herself, claiming no conflict of interest," says attorney Mike Liles, who joined Harold Hammett on the Maxey case in 1975. "The fact that [Bowlin] couldn't at least get a grievance filed against Pat Moore just goes to show you how crooked things were in this case."

As Hammett argued before Amarillo Court of Appeals, he cited the Code of Judicial Conduct, whose guidelines for the conduct of judges had been adopted by the American Bar Association. The appellate court responded, however, that the code did not have the status of law in Texas. The ruling also opined that "alleged bias or prejudice of a judge does not disqualify a judge," and that "while delicate discretion might indicate a judge's withdrawal from a case in a contentious situation, there is no compulsion to step aside when the judge is not legally disqualified."

The ruling also called attention to a major oversight committed by Maxey's previous legal team, which had failed to appeal the summary judgments in favor of the individual defendants in the lawsuit:

The March 3, 1970, judgment disposed of all remaining parties and issues, and, although it did not refer to nor incorporate the prior judgments, they became merged into the last judgment and constituted a final judgment in the case. *Zachry Co. v. Thibodeaux*, 364 S.W.2d 192 (Tex. Sup. Ct. 1963). As the final judgment was cast, plaintiffs recovered from the bank, but were adjudged to take nothing by their cause of action asserted against all other defendants.[35]

The ruling concludes with what appeared to be very bad news for Maxey:

The judgment in favor of the bank's representatives being final as to plaintiffs, the query then turns to whether it possesses the requisite elements to bar or estop plaintiffs from proceeding against the bank As plaintiffs' pleadings were drafted, the culpability of the bank, if any, depended solely on whether the actions of its representatives were tortuous; that is, upon the culpability of the representatives. *Whether they were culpable in fact has been foreclosed by the judgments of absolution plaintiffs permitted to become final.* (Emphasis added.)

Regarding the defenses of res judicata and collateral estoppel, the judges state that, in such circumstances:

. . . a final judgment on the merits in favor of an agent acting for his principal is conclusive in a subsequent suit brought against the principal for derivative liability determined in the former litigation. . . . It follows that the final judgment exculpating the bank's representatives from any liabilities for their actions taken on behalf of the bank prevents plaintiffs from proceeding against the bank for damages based on the same acts.

And so, as Maxey's new attorneys, Harold Hammett and J. Michael Liles, took on the case, there was a lot of skepticism as to their chances of success. Hammett was a member of Lubbock's Monterey High School graduating class of 1956, where he was voted "Mr. Monterey" during his senior year. Hammett wore glasses, smoked a pipe, and was just as smart as he looked. He had a BA from Yale and earned a law degree from the University of Texas at Austin in 1964. Hammett's knowledge of the law and his ability to cite precedents was formidable, but he was also erudite in person and in print. The American Bar Association recognized his essay writing with at least two awards.

Liles was Hammett's opposite in several ways. Dark-haired and handsome, Liles was a charming pugilist in court who knew how to talk to a jury and how to wring the drama out of a dry or very complex session in court with an obfuscating witness. Instead of being intimidated by the avowed brilliance of Charlie Jones, Liles relished the idea of going head-to-head with one of Lubbock County's most formidable barristers.

In early 1974, around the same time that Hammett appeared before the Texas Supreme Court to argue for a reversal of the Amarillo Court of Appeals ruling against Maxey, the Junior League of Lubbock bestowed a special honor on Judge Pat Moore by making her the first recipient of a new, annual award that had been created in her honor.

A statement from the organization, in which Moore had been an active member, described the award as being a recognition of individuals who have provided "outstanding inspiration to others, service to the community, and . . . qualities of integrity, morality, loyalty, humility, compassion, and courage."[36]

The statement mentioned Moore's many admirable achievements, which had been accomplished despite great physical handicaps, and also her charity work, such as her role in the founding of the Texas Boys Ranch. It did not, however, offer an explanation for her failure to disclose her relationship with Citizens National Bank prior to the Maxey trial or her refusal to disqualify herself from the case.

Nor did the award mention that the first female district judge in Lubbock County had been diagnosed with cancer. Moore succumbed to the disease in January 1975, not long after being honored at a banquet where she was given the award that bore her name.[37]

By the time of Judge Moore's death, however, her rulings in the Maxey case had been put through the wringer. On March 20, 1974, the Texas Supreme Court reversed and remanded the lower court's ruling, sending it back to the 72nd District Court for a new trial. In an amazing coincidence, the justice who wrote the opinion was none other than James Gray Denton, who had written the appellate court opinion that ruled against the Maxeys in December 1970.

Denton's influence over the course of the Maxey case was substantial. Born in 1917 in Bonham, Texas, Denton completed his undergraduate studies at Texas Tech and then attended law school at the University of Texas at Austin.[38] According to his son, Tommy, the elder Denton was a year away from graduating from law school when the Japanese bombed Pearl Harbor. He joined the navy and served the duration of World War II on a minesweeper, the USS *Surfbird*, in both the Atlantic and the Pacific.

Denton began his law career in Lubbock in 1947, opening an office with A. W. "Shorty" Salyers. "To make ends meet, he also taught government at

Tech for a year or two," says Tommy. In 1950, Denton was appointed as the judge of a newly created court at law in Lubbock County and was then elected judge of the 99th District Court in 1952. Four years later, Governor Price Daniel appointed him as chief justice of the Seventh Supreme Judicial District Court of Civil Appeals in Amarillo. He was elected to Texas Supreme Court in 1970 and was sworn in on January 4, 1971. During his time as an associate justice, Denton wrote the opinions in *Southwestern Bell v. Public Utility Commission* and *Railroad Commission v. Entex,* which are considered landmark decisions in the area of public utility law.

In a brief to the Texas Supreme Court on the Maxey case, Hammett underscored certain new allegations of misconduct by the bank. By selling Maxey's stock in a secret sale, Hammett wrote, the bank had "breached its duty to plaintiffs . . . by failing to exercise the standard of care required of the Bank as chattel mortgagee because the Bank became, by its act of foreclosure, a constructive Trustee for the benefit of its debtors." The bank, Hammett asserted, was under contractual obligation to obtain fair market value for the property foreclosed on, and when it failed to do so, each sale of stock was "an illegal conversion of plaintiffs' property."[39]

"The basic duty of the Bank," Hammett argued, "was to exercise good faith and fairness with respect to the conduct of the sale of the common stock pledged by plaintiffs. The Bank violated such duties and also violated its duty to plaintiffs to make a sincere effort to obtain full market value."

The Supreme Court's opinion, written by Justice Denton, stated that the main question to be addressed by the court was whether the liability of the bank was derivative of its officers.[40] The lower court ruling had maintained that it was. Denton, however, wrote that the "liability of the bank was independent and direct and not derivative of the acts of the bank's agents."

And because the bank was a "contracting party to chattel mortgagees, pledge agreements and deeds of trust," it owed the plaintiffs certain duties that were separate and distinct from those of its officers and directors. Those duties would include, by inference, making a sincere effort to obtain full market value for Maxey's assets during foreclosure.

The court ruled that because the bank's liability was *not* derivative of its agents, it was, therefore, not entitled to a summary judgment under the doctrines of res judicata and collateral estoppel. In a stunning victory for the plaintiffs, the case was remanded and sent back to district court for a new trial.

Maxey had his rematch coming. With the death of Judge Moore, there would be a new referee and new corner men for both combatants, but the ring was the same and the opponents were more or less the same (even though the individual defendants were not named in the suit, their reputations were still on the line). By the time the case came to trial again, Maxey would be ten years older than he was when the fight first began, but he was still tough. He was still the local favorite, too.

The boxing metaphors are appropriate and timely. Just a few weeks after the Texas Supreme Court decision set the stage for a new trial in the Maxey case, Muhammad Ali flew to Zaire to begin training for the Rumble in the Jungle, his epic fight against George Foreman. Ali would defeat the much younger Foreman in eight rounds, regaining the heavyweight title, which had been stripped from him seven years earlier after he refused to register for the draft in protest of the war in Southeast Asia. It was a matter of principle for the former and future boxing champ.

Considering Homer's background and the general attitudes of his generation on racial politics, religion, and patriotism, we might assume that he was not a fan of Muhammad Ali, and that is unfortunate. The two of them had a lot in common.

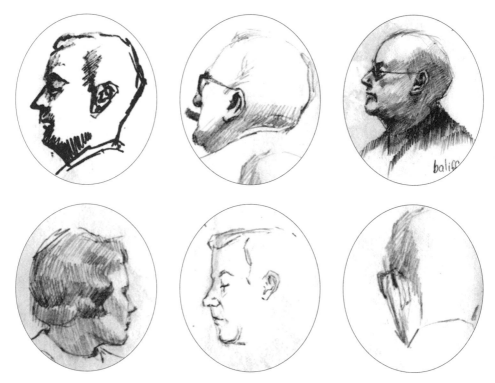

Chapter 9

BEHIND CLOSED DOORS

The death of Bill Evans on March 27, 1970, touched a large cross section of Lubbock's citizenry. In addition to being an elder statesman of the legal community and a businessman, Evans was a leader in civic affairs, Texas Tech, his church, and the public school system.[1] The crowd at the funeral also included a good number of the thirty-something individuals who, like Evans, had been sued by Homer Maxey.

At the time of Evans's death, Maxey was still enjoying a moment of triumph, but in every appellate court hearing for the next four years, the bank's side won out. Even in the Texas Supreme Court ruling in March 1974, which reversed the district court verdict and sent the case back for a new trial, the individual defendants remained absolved of blame.

Former defendants David Hughes and his father, John A. Hughes, felt little sense of elation, however. The two men had been involved in the drama of the Maxey case from its inception.[2] John Hughes had never been a big fan of Williams or his aggressive style. Nor had the elder Hughes approved of the bank becoming so involved with Maxey. Speaking as a board member, John Hughes went on record as opposing the extension of a $1 million line of credit to Maxey. His advice went unheeded.

Although David Hughes was not involved in any of the actions that led up to the bank's foreclosure proceedings against Maxey, he was in a position to witness many of the pivotal events as Maxey's relationship with the bank and his attorneys became more and more strained, to the point of bitterness and acrimony. Today David Hughes refers to the Maxey case as "a debacle," "a fiasco," "a nightmare for the family," and "a tumultuous experience in my life as a young lawyer."[3]

Even before the foreclosure proceedings, David and his father had good reason to worry that severe collateral damage could result from the way Citizens National Bank and their attorneys were handling the Maxey situation. David remembers the day of February 16, 1966. Charlie Jones summoned him to the second floor boardroom in the bank building to a meeting that was presided over by E. W. Williams and included Jones, Barclay Ryall, and Chauncey Trout. The purpose of the meeting was "to prepare foreclosure papers for the bank to take over Maxey properties, including Maxey Lumber Company, Plaza Building Corporation, and stock in Triple M Feeders," says Hughes. Williams, who asked Hughes to prepare many of the necessary documents, told Hughes that those present in the boardroom "thought it was about time you got involved in this case."

Although he did not mention it at the time, Williams's statement reminded David of his father's warning *not* to get "dragged into the Maxey case." And as David returned to the law office to begin preparing the foreclosure documents, he could not help thinking about Bill Evans's strong objections to the manner in which the bank was handling the Maxey affair. Evans was a longtime friend of John Hughes and a mentor to David. His words carried great weight with them.

In a period spanning almost thirty years, Evans had worked with Maxey on the lion's share of his successful business ventures. In the 1950s, Evans moved from litigation to other areas of legal work at the firm. In 1955, when Charlie Jones and Chauncey Trout, Jr., joined the firm, most of the work on the Maxey account was assigned to Jones and Trout.

Evans and Maxey remained friends, however, so when Evans learned of Maxey's intention to buy the old Hotel Lubbock and return it "to its former grandeur," Evans met with Maxey to share his point of view on the subject. The attorney told Maxey he thought that the hotel was a bad investment and urged his friend not to go through with the purchase. Maxey was determined, however, and could not be talked out of the idea.

In late 1962, Evans learned that Homer was trading his urban properties for ranchland and feedlots, which he believed to be a foolish idea. According to David Hughes, Evans was worried that his old friend had lost his sense of judgment. Evans told Maxey that in his opinion, big cattle ranches were just fine as tax shelters, but they were not solid investments for making money. As a counter suggestion, Evans pleaded with Maxey to consider retiring and enjoying the fruits of his labors instead of putting his family fortune at risk.

Maxey responded to Evans's entreaty by saying, "I have never failed in anything, and this time is no exception."

The troubles Bill Evans faced worsened during the weeks leading up to foreclosure proceedings against Maxey. The attorney was suffering from the compounded burdens of lung cancer and the associated cobalt treatments. David Hughes recalls a disturbing conversation with Evans at the office water cooler, in which Evans admitted that he felt as bad as he looked, and that his physical condition was only part of the problem.

Evans went on to confide in Hughes that he was upset that Charlie Jones and E. W. Williams had decided to foreclose on Homer Maxey and liquidate his assets in a private sale. Evans called it "the biggest mistake ever made by the firm and the bank."

Evans recommended that the bank pursue a judicial foreclosure instead. That way, the sale would be conducted before a judge in open court, with both sides presenting evidence as to the value of the properties being liquidated. Williams and Jones disagreed.

David Hughes says the conversation with Evans left him feeling "startled, alarmed, and fearful." In a meeting with Jones and Trout, Hughes expressed his concerns and asked the reason for their opposition to judicial foreclosure. Jones answered, "It would cost too much."

After the board room meeting on February 16, 1966, Hughes set about preparing the security agreements and financing statements for the foreclosure, filling in the values he was given, including the $749 for the stock of Plaza Building Corporation.

"It was the worst feeling," he says, "doing a job that should not have been done privately, irrespective of the values and liabilities of the properties." Despite those feelings, Hughes believed and still believes that the bank's appraisals of Maxey's properties were correct.

When John Hughes learned that his son had been "dragged into the disaster in progress," he was furious. The elder Hughes agreed with Evans that the move could end up bringing about the demise of the bank, and that it could also destroy the law firm.

Indeed, once Homer Maxey filed the lawsuit, people like John and David Hughes ran into awkward situations in public on numerous occasions. Maxey's supporters weren't the only aggressors. Many of David's friends, for example, enjoyed giving him a hard time for "trying to collude with the bank to steal worthless property." The satire was carried even further by his colleagues in a Junior Bar skit that awarded David Hughes the dubious distinction of being "the youngest member of the bar ever to be sued for $30 million." (Maxey had asked for a mere $20 million.)

The publicity was devastating for Evans, Pharr, Trout & Jones as well as Citizens National Bank. The conflict-of-interest issues so central to the lawsuit reinforced the prejudices of people who were already suspicious of lawyers. At the same time, the private foreclosure sale reinforced stereotypes and negative associations people often held against banks and bankers.

In Hughes's opinion, Kenneth Bowlin exploited such prejudices in his "clever and innovative portrayal of Maxey as a victim and innocent debtor," ruined by a bank that was depicted as "an evil villain bent on ruining Maxey."

The way David Hughes sees it, the bank had nothing to hide. By conducting the sale in secret, however, shielding their actions from public view the way a burglar or an embezzler would, they made it look as though they were conspiring to commit fraud. The jury's conclusion that the bank's credit of $749 for Plaza Building Corporation stock was "grossly inadequate" came as no surprise to Hughes.

"The perception was that the bank had hidden the truth by having a private sale behind closed doors," he says. "This hurt me a great deal. It could have been avoided."

Hughes attended the court of civil appeals hearing of the Maxey case in the fall of 1970. "I came away feeling that the law was on our side," he says, "but it was painful to sit and listen to the recital about the big elephant that was in the room, the private foreclosure sale of Maxey's properties."

Even after the ruling of that court, which sent the case back to 72nd District Court, where Judge Moore issued a summary judgment that exonerated the bank, Hughes felt saddened because the new rulings did not garner the same kind of front-page headlines as when the jury ruled against the bank. He was, however, consoled by what he felt was a gradual change in public perception about the case. "We stopped hearing about 'poor old Homer,'" he says, "and how the bank and their lawyers conspired to take his property."

David Hughes never quite felt the same about working at the law firm after Bill Evans died. In 1973 he moved to Austin and joined John Hill, the former Texas attorney general. He did not follow the subsequent appeals or the second jury trial that would commence in October 1976.

The Texas Supreme Court ruling in March 1974 held that a bank has responsibilities to its clients that are unique from those of the individuals who work for it, one of those responsibilities being to act in good faith. In various different court settings in the years ahead, the bank's attorneys would continue to argue that the bank had acted in good faith in its dealings with Homer Maxey. Alongside such arguments were so-called "alternative" arguments, which were based on the logic that a bank is not a person, but a corporate entity, and as such, its actions are all derivative of its agents. All those individual agents had been exonerated by the courts, and thus the bank had been found innocent. That legal issue, argued the attorneys for the bank, had been settled, and could not be relitigated.[4]

And so, as the case went back to trial again in October 1976, seven years after the first trial, the bank's attorneys were still confident of the potency and rightness of those same arguments. In their opinion, the State Supreme Court's interpretation of corporate responsibility, which figured prominently in its ruling on the Maxey case, made no sense. One man who agreed with them was Denzil Bevers, the new 72nd District Court judge. Bevers wasn't a big fan of Homer Maxey, either.

Chapter 10

REMATCH

Between the cloud of vague suspicions and rumors surrounding the Homer Maxey case and the cold, hard facts, Mike Liles did not lack for incentive. He believed that the case reeked of judicial impropriety, going all the way back to Judge Pat Moore and her relationship with Citizens National Bank. As a young lawyer he was, as he describes himself, cocksure, arrogant, and somewhat of an egotist.[1]

Born in Tyler, Texas, Liles grew up in the Texas City-Lamar area and was still in grade school at the time of the Texas City explosion in 1947, when two ships loaded with ammonium nitrate exploded and killed 581 people. He decided at an early age that he wanted to become a lawyer. After finishing law school at Baylor University, he practiced law in Brownfield for a year and then moved to Galveston where he was mentored by the famed Texas attorney and former Democratic legislator A. R. "Babe" Schwartz. Liles moved to Fort Worth in 1966 and went to work for the Simon & Simon firm in 1975.

"Simon & Simon was primarily a business firm and I was a trial lawyer," says Liles. "The Simon firm had handled the appeal on the Maxey case when it got remanded by the State Supreme Court. That's when I got involved with the Simon firm and we started preparing the case for the last trial."

The senior partners at the firm were less than encouraging. In fact, they told Liles that the case was hopeless. "They said to me, 'Here's the case of Homer Maxey, it cannot be won . . . nobody can win it,'" recalls Liles. "They had a lot of correspondence from West Texas attorneys saying there was no way that we could win this case."

Being paired with Hammett gave Liles additional confidence. "Harold was

Mike Liles, who joined Maxey's legal team in 1975, described himself as being cocky and combative. Courtesy of the *Fort Worth Star-Telegram* Collection, Special Collections, University of Texas at Arlington Library, Arlington, Texas.

Harold Hammett, a Lubbock native, took the lead on arguing Maxey's case before the appellate courts in 1974.Courtesy of the *Fort Worth Star-Telegram* Collection, Special Collections, University of Texas at Arlington Library, Arlington, Texas.

a book man, and he is one brilliant lawyer," says Liles. "He's the kind you love to try a case with. He knows the law and there's practically nobody who can write a brief like Harold."

Liles also enjoyed the prospect of brawling in a courtroom with the legendary Charlie Jones. The conflict-of-interest issue had already been decided in the courts and decided in favor of the defendants. It was still a troublesome aspect of the case for the defense, however, and, as the litigants returned to court, Liles and Hammett planned to make the most of it.

Hammett and Liles were confident of their case and impressed by their client. They were also moved by thoughts of what might have been if Maxey's original plans had not been derailed in 1966.

"Mr. Maxey was a visionary," says Liles. "All of those ranches he acquired in the early 1960s had lakes on them. The Triple M Ranch near Tulsa on the Keystone Reservoir had twelve miles of lake frontage. He was going to develop all those properties into subdivisions. He realized that the economy was going to change in the next decade, and he projected that around 1970, 1971, people would start becoming attracted to moving to subdivisions with lakes and recreation and everything. That was his vision."

Although the cattle business was not one of Homer Maxey's areas of expertise, he did have vast experience in building subdivisions. "Mr. Maxey went to E. W. Williams and laid out all his plans, how Maxey Lumber Company would build these subdivisions," says Liles. "He discussed it all with E.W., how it was going to take a few years, and in the meantime he was going to feed out the cattle on the ranch land and produce a certain number of calves every year. That was his plan. It was very insightful."

Others saw the story in a different light. While admitting that Maxey had been very successful in the past, they felt that he had gotten involved in a field where he had no experience. They believed that Maxey had made questionable business decisions and that he, alone, was to blame for the collapse of his financial empire.

Although Maxey did have his detractors in Lubbock, there was still a great reservoir of good will for Maxey and his family.

"You would not believe the number of letters Homer got from people around West Texas," says Liles. "These people would enclose a dollar saying, 'This is all I can afford, I wish you the best.' Sometimes it was just a quarter. Hundreds and hundreds of those letters came in. I always thought it was an amazing thing."[2]

. . .

On Sunday, October 3, 1976, the day before the second trial began, readers of the *Avalanche-Journal* were treated to a front-page story on Homer Maxey titled "Once-Wealthy Maxey Broke, Not Broken," written by staff reporter Frank Patrick.[3] The subtitle on the page 12 continuation was another complimentary phrase: "Loss of Wealth Fails to Dim Life's Achievements for Maxey." An additional sidebar to the story gave a concise history of the litigation.[4]

The article began with Maxey recounting how he and Melba had moved away from Lubbock after the bank foreclosure because he was "just too embarrassed" to face everyone as a pauper. "I just couldn't live here," he told the reporter, "not being able to pay my own way." Maxey's face was "twisted with emotion" as he described their decision to exile themselves to Dallas.

In reality, Homer and Melba Maxey had spent a great deal of time in Lubbock over the preceding decade, including several years before and during the first trial in which, according to Ken Bowlin, "Maxey basically moved into our law office."[5]

After the trial, however, the Maxeys had, indeed, been spending most of their time in Dallas, where they lived in an apartment just off the North Central Expressway. The Maxeys adapted, more or less, to a downsized lifestyle, subsidized in part by the generosity of the Elliotts and the Goodacres, and, later on, by Social Security payments. After Homer obtained a real estate license, Tommy Elliott attempted to steer some business to his father-in-law.[6] However, the first commission didn't work out so well. According to Elliott, who was representing commercial properties at the time, he let Maxey sit in with him on a series of meetings with a client who was considering buying a chain of department stores. When he closed the deal, Elliott told the buyer that Maxey expected a six percent commission.

"These guys told me, 'Why? He didn't do anything,'" says Elliott. "We're not going to pay him anything."

Elliott convinced the client to agree to pay Maxey $100,000, a lesser amount than the full commission, but still a significant payday. Maxey, says Elliott, "just went ballistic" when informed of the compromise.

"I'm going to sue those sons of bitches," Maxey said.

"Look, Homer," Elliott said, "you're going to get me fired."

"I don't give a shit, Tommy," Maxey said. "I want my money."

Elliott met with attorney Jim Milam and pleaded with him to convince Maxey to accept the lower fee. In the end, Maxey accepted the $100,000.

Meanwhile, Melba joined the ranks of the working class, toiling away as a clerk in a department store for $2 an hour.[7]

"It is always a sad spectacle when the mighty have fallen," wrote Patrick in the Sunday feature, "but the poignancy runs deeper in Maxey's case." The highlights of the Homer Maxey story, as related in the article, included how the family had moved to Lubbock because of Texas Tech and, "while a boy of 14, Maxey helped put up the first structure at Tech," earning about $12 a week. During a recounting of his early career as a builder in the 1930s, when his father was still very active, the article quotes Maxey on the difference between business in that era and modern times. Maxey related an anecdote about when his father had paid the deposit on a winning bid that had been submitted by a rival contractor because the contractor had been prevented from attending the bid meeting by rain.

"I want to tell you a little about the type of people who were working then, the sort my father did business with," Maxey said. "In those days, a man's word was his bond."

Maxey's allegations against the bank always made reference to such unwritten ethical codes, gentleman's agreements, and transparency in dealings. The theme had been established during the first trial, and it was reprised again during the second.

"They took my home, everything I had," Maxey told the reporter.

When Maxey was asked how difficult it had been adjusting to his reversal of fortune, he seemed anxious to downplay his background as the son of a wealthy and successful businessman. "Not as much as you might think," answered Maxey. "It would be different if we hadn't started poor. When we got married, my wife had to make her own dresses."

The biographical article distilled the subject of the lawsuit to one basic question: whether Maxey's millions had evaporated "because he was over-extended and couldn't pay his debts, as his bank said, or, as Maxey insists, through the chicanery of others."

Homer and Melba had returned to Lubbock, the story continued, driving their battered old 1967 Dodge. With its windshield shattered from the 1970 tornado, the car was a visual reminder of the devastation visited upon the city by that storm, and the fact that natural catastrophes sometimes bring rich and poor down to the same level. Six years after the tornado, despite heroic, ongoing efforts to recover and rebuild the town, there were still gaping wounds and ugly scars wherever you looked. To the people of Lubbock, that shattered windshield was a reminder that even if Homer Maxey had exiled himself to Dallas, he was still one of them.

The sixty-five-year-old former millionaire returned to Lubbock with new physical scars as well. He made frequent trips to the dermatologist to have skin cancer lesions removed, the legacy of light skin pigmentation and long days out in the West Texas sun.[8] And, earlier in the year, Maxey underwent major surgery to have a large section of his colon removed. Cancer was suspected, but the pathology tests found no malignancy, prompting the biggest celebration in the Maxey family since the jury award in the first trial. Maxey made a quick recovery after the surgery and threw himself into the pretrial preparation with great enthusiasm, but he tired more easily and lost his temper with greater frequency. His limp was more pronounced and he suffered cramps in his legs when seated for long periods of time.

But Maxey's faith—in himself and in his religion—never wavered. "Even as Homer went through all these difficulties, he remained very active in his church, just like his daddy," recalls Rex Fuller, a longtime friend and one of the townspeople who contributed gifts and support during the first trial. "Homer and Melba were there at First United Methodist Church every Sunday."[9]

And as they read the newspaper feature on Homer's trials and tribulations that Sunday morning, the Maxeys must have taken heart in the prayer for the day, which appeared on page one, adjacent to the "Broke, Not Broken" story: "Help us, Father," the prayer began, "to realize that with You, all things are possible. Thank you for challenges, for it is through our challenges that we rise above ourselves and learn Your highest truth. Amen."

Someone like Maxey, who said his mother taught him "a Maxey never starts anything he doesn't finish," could not have asked for a more appropriate pleading to the Almighty. As his old friend and kindred spirit, Dub Rushing said of Maxey, "That's the reason he's still fighting this thing. He's not going to quit as long as he's alive."[10]

As David Hughes tells it, some people in Lubbock were saying it was time for Maxey to give up on the lawsuit.

If Maxey entered the courtroom this time looking a little more beat-up and battle-scarred than in 1969, the opposition was also worse for wear. Charlie Jones still stood tall and lean, but the crevices in his face had grown deeper and his dark hair had gone gray. Citizens National Bank, meanwhile, was never able to recover the customers who had quit banking with them after Maxey filed his lawsuit. In addition to the Maxey suit, the public relations nightmare associated with E. W. Williams's term as president had been compounded by at least two other lawsuits in which Williams was named as a defendant.[11] One of the suits was filed against the Amarillo National Bank, where Williams had gone to work as a vice president prior to the first trial, alleging various irregularities involving the handling of a large trust fund. The other was brought against Williams by a former employee of his at another bank, who alleged that Williams had fired him for divulging information about the payment of kickbacks.

The *Avalanche-Journal* article of October 3, 1976, relating the legal history of Maxey's feud with Citizens National Bank included a statement that Maxey's lawsuit had been filed almost seven years before Citizens was sold to Texas Commerce Bancshares and that "neither that holding company nor Texas Commerce Bank is involved in the suit." This statement was repeated in each day's coverage of the trial.

Over the ten-and-a-half years after Citizens National Bank pulled the plug on Homer Maxey's businesses, the bad blood between the two sides had not mellowed a bit. Raw nerves and deep grudges exposed during the first trial had metastasized. Tempers erupted every day of the second trial, a fact that surprised no one who was familiar with the personalities of the respective lead attorneys, Charlie Jones and J. Michael Liles.

Charlie Jones's decision to represent the bank for the second jury trial precluded the involvement of W. O. Shafer. As Mike Liles put it, "Jones was a big deal in Lubbock, but W. O. Shafer was one of the preeminent attorneys in the state; there was no way he would serve second chair to Charlie Jones."[12]

Nonetheless, Jones's reputation was formidable enough. Many insiders believed that Maxey's defeat was certain this time. Liles remembers being told that the Maxey case was "unwinnable," and that trying the case would not do any good for his law career.

"Some people tried to warn me off," says Liles. "They said, 'Boy, Charlie Jones is one of the best trial lawyers anywhere in the country and you really got your hands full.' Homer got letters and phone calls from attorneys, saying there was no way that we could beat Charlie Jones in Lubbock. And there was a lot of discussion by some people in the firm, saying we just had to get Charlie Jones disqualified. I said, 'Why in the hell would you want to disqualify him?'"

The way Liles saw it, Jones was a far greater liability for the defense than asset. He was not only Maxey's former attorney, but also a director of the bank that he had represented at the same time he was representing Maxey. On top of that, he had already tried the case once in front of a jury and lost.

"I understood that, around Lubbock, Charlie Jones was considered a genius," says Liles, "but I'm sorry, I disagree. How on God's green earth did

Charlie Jones decide that he should be the one to try that case again? I was so happy about that."

Liles cited a number of issues regarding Jones's prior association with the case—and with Homer Maxey—that he believed worked against Jones. And Liles would make reference to every one of those issues as often as possible during the trial. One of his favorites was the fact that Jones was at the private sale where the bank divvied up Maxey's assets. "I was able to wag my finger in front of his nose in court about things like that," remembers Liles. "To me, that's not a genius."

Perry Davis, who was a partner at Shafer, Gilliland, Davis, Bunton & Mc-Collum, served as second chair for Jones. Davis had a reputation as one of the better trial lawyers in the region. "Davis was a very smart lawyer, and an honest lawyer, too," says Liles. "I had no complaint with him."

On Monday morning, October 4, 1976, Judge Denzil Bevers called the 72nd District Court of Lubbock County to order in the second jury trial in the Maxey case, officially styled as *Homer G. Maxey et al. v. Texas Commerce Bank of Lubbock, Texas (formerly Citizens National Bank of Lubbock)*, 72nd District Court of Lubbock County, 1976 (hereafter referred to as *Maxey v. TCB*). The first sparks in the trial flew during testimony by Joe Cassel, the first witness to take the stand, and one of the most important for the plaintiffs' case. As Maxey's former accountant, Cassel was a logical choice to testify first because the lawsuit was still a debate over whether, at the time of foreclosure, the value of Maxey's assets exceeded his liabilities.[13] In the first trial, Cassel was the last witness called by the defense.

Liles's direct examination began with questions about Maxey's assets, debts, and exchanges of properties. Cassel admitted that in the years from 1963 to 1965, Maxey's business operations were losing money, but at the same time they had viable cash flows and the assets of the various corporations had increased, not decreased, in value.

Charlie Jones would, of course, challenge Cassel's answers to the questions during cross-examination, but he found no reason to interrupt the proceedings until Liles asked the witness if he was aware of any correspondence between Ed Drumwright of Century Leasing, Inc., and Maxey concerning Drumwright's offer to buy six of Maxey's ranches for $4.5 million.

Jones objected. The Drumwright offer was hearsay, Jones asserted. Also, he added, offers of purchase were not admissible evidence of property value unless a deal had been consummated.

"We contend that the deal was consummated," responded Liles, "but it was blocked by the bank."

Judge Bevers sustained the objection. Liles asked for a bill of exception, and the judge excused the jury so that Cassel's testimony and arguments by opposing counsel could be heard outside their presence. However, because the *Lubbock Avalanche-Journal* reported on the highlights of each of the hearings, it was quite easy for the jurors to find out what the fuss was about, despite the fact that the judge admonished them *not* to follow media coverage of the trial. Today Mike Liles says he was counting on the jurors being sufficiently curious that they would disobey the judge's admonition.[14]

Liles sensed that several of the jurors were charmed by his manner and receptive to his arguments. With his dark hair, impish grin, and flair for dramatic presentation, he cut an impressive figure in the courtroom. Judge Denzil Bevers, however, did not think very much of Liles or the plaintiffs' case.[15]

Liles was not enamored of Bevers, either. In his opinion Bevers was underqualified for the job of district judge.[16] The Maxey case would be the most significant of Bevers's judicial career.

During the bill-of-exception hearing, Liles argued that the jury should be allowed to hear Cassel's testimony and examine the evidence, such as the letters between Maxey and Drumwright. The bank's attorneys, Liles reasoned, had "represented that Mr. Maxey was unable to find a buyer for his property," a contention offered as proof that Maxey's values for his properties were exaggerated; the Drumwright deal, however, was proof that Maxey's values were correct.[17]

Judge Bevers had already ruled in a pretrial hearing that evidence concerning the Drumwright deal was not admissible. The way the judge saw it, evidence of that nature spoke to the conspiracy allegations from the last trial and, according to the Texas Supreme Court, that issue had been settled when the individual defendants were all exonerated.

The arguments were featured in the *Avalanche-Journal* coverage in its Tuesday morning and evening editions. The articles, written by staff reporter Frank Patrick, also reminded readers that, in the previous trial, Maxey alleged that the bank had blocked the Drumwright deal. Although evidence relating to that allegation was inadmissible, Maxey's attorneys wanted the jury to hear about it anyway—one way or the other.

Throughout the trial, Mike Liles and Harold Hammett would continue fighting to get certain facts entered into evidence or covered by the media. It helped that Liles had befriended Frank Patrick when the reporter was living in Fort Worth. One day at the Fort Worth Press Club, Patrick announced that he was moving to Lubbock to work for the *Avalanche-Journal*. "He told me he was grateful for my friendship," says Liles.

"Frank Patrick attended the trial every day," recalls Liles, "and he reported on all the evidence that Bevers disallowed. It was important that we get that evidence into the record because that was our best shot at winning punitive damages."

In the hearing on Monday morning outside the presence of the jurors, Liles resumed his questioning of Joe Cassel regarding Drumwright's offer to purchase six of Maxey's ranches for a total of $4.5 million, a purchase predicated on a $1.3 million short-term loan to be arranged with the assistance of two other financial consultants, W. L. Brady of Kansas City and Jack Wakefield of Los Angeles. Jones took the witness on cross, repeating, as always, questions as to whether the deal was ever finalized and other pointed inquiries regarding the legitimacy of the offer.[18]

After Jones finished his examination, Liles again asked Judge Bevers to admit the testimony and the letters into evidence. The judge again denied the request.

That scenario would be repeated throughout the trial. Maxey's attorneys fought daily skirmishes with the judge to get evidence before the jury and, in some respects, the opening days of the second trial resembled a replay of the first. Judge Bevers was adamant about excluding evidence about the Drumwright deal—including any evidence purporting to suggest that Charlie Jones made the phone call that killed that deal.

Liles and Hammett were unsurprised and undeterred. Judge Bevers had made his positions clear earlier in the year at a motion in limine hearing. (A *motion in limine* is a request to the judge to exclude evidence that one of the parties in a case believes would prejudice a jury against it and, it can be argued, is not relevant to the issues in the case. In a criminal trial, for example, the defense might move to have evidence of previous crimes excluded.)

In the Maxey case, the bank's attorneys had filed a pleading entitled "Defendant's Fifth Amended Answer to Plaintiff's Petition" in which twenty-seven objections, or exceptions, were made in response to various allegations in the petition filed by Hammett and Liles.

Many of the exceptions listed in the bank's amended answer objected to any evidence relating to the Drumwright deal and allegations that Jones made a telephone call that canceled that deal. Others concerned certain allegations against the bank that could be construed as being derivative of the actions of its individual agents—allegations such as those that had been dismissed against the individual defendants in the first trial.[19]

In his ruling, Judge Bevers granted twenty-five of the twenty-seven exceptions requested by the bank. Liles and Hammett knew then that they would face an uphill battle in the courtroom.

On Tuesday, October 5, the second day of the trial, Jones's cross-examination of Cassel continued. The attorney got Cassel to agree that by the fall of 1965, the Plainsman and Pioneer hotels were so encumbered with debt that they had become major stumbling blocks to any proposed restructuring of Maxey's finances.

> Jones: You were of the opinion that the Plainsman and Pioneer hotels would sink the corporation, regardless of what the ranches sold for?
> Cassel: Not regardless of whatever price they sold for, but it was a stone around our neck.[20]

After several exchanges of a similar nature, Jones passed the witness and, on redirect, Liles attempted to query Cassel about the bank's promise to Maxey regarding an unsecured line of credit. The question sparked an objection from the defense and a recess was called, during which the attorneys debated the point in the judge's chambers. "We feel that Mr. Jones has opened the door," Liles argued. The defense had "represented to the jury that Plaza was unable to pay its debts. We think because of that we should be allowed to bring out the facts that Mr. Maxey was promised a revolving line of credit by the bank for five to six years."

Jones repeated his side of the argument, stating that the alleged promise of a line of credit, like all the other allegations of broken promises and bad behavior on the part of individual agents of the bank, had already been litigated and deemed off limits, not only during pretrial hearings, but by the Texas Supreme Court's 1974 decision. Judge Bevers agreed. The plaintiffs' motion was overruled—again, and not for the last time.

Homer Maxey took the stand on day three. In the first trial, Ken Bowlin used his examination of Maxey to relate Maxey's life story, from his birth in Plainview through his youth and education in Lubbock, his start in business, his military service, and each of his major business deals, slowly constructing an image of Maxey as a man who had built an empire through hard work, instinct, ethics, and experience. Examining such an extensive business history had taken up the better part of two hours.

Liles spent all of fifteen minutes covering the same story. Maxey acquitted himself well under Liles's guidance, but under cross-examination by Jones the following day, Maxey appeared much more susceptible to the defense attorney's aggressiveness and sarcasm than in the first trial. Jones reread Maxey's responses on direct examination in which Maxey claimed that, before the foreclosure, Citizens had sold at least two of his properties without his permission. Then he asked Maxey to look at his signature on a document showing that he had, indeed, given his permission. Jones's tactics "appeared to have left the witness floundering" for explanations, said the *Avalanche-Journal*.[21]

Another allegation in Maxey's testimony regarding the sale of the two properties, which occurred five days before the foreclosure, was just as serious as the first: according to Maxey's records, the bank had failed to credit his account with the proceeds of those sales (an amount of over $200,000) until after the foreclosure. Therefore, on Monday, February 15, 1966, when Citizens National Bank notified Maxey that his notes would be called the following day unless they were paid off, Maxey's indebtedness was overstated by that same amount. The alleged misstatement was offered as additional evidence of bad faith and misconduct by the bank.[22]

On Thursday, day four of the trial, Jones asked Maxey to explain why he had increased the value of the Triple M Ranch on a Plaza financial statement by more than $150,000. The second statement had been prepared just two months after the first.[23] Jones told Maxey to "turn to the jury and tell them what you did in those two months to increase the worth of that property by $150,000."

Maxey did not do as Jones ordered him but, instead, responded, "I just thought it was worth that amount."

On that same day, Judge Bevers allowed the introduction of the schedule of property values developed by Henry Strasburger's firm, overruling Harold Hammett's strenuous objections that the values set forth by Strasburger were not reflective of the actual market values of the properties. Hammett argued that Maxey had signed the agreement under duress and the prices were the equivalent of a fire sale.

Bevers denies that he played favorites in the trial. During the first half of the trial, it was pointed out by Maxey's attorneys and the daily media coverage, Bevers allowed the defense considerably more leeway in presenting evidence regarding property values—an issue of singular importance in the case.[24] In the end, neither the question of Bevers's impartiality nor his rulings in favor of the defense appeared to have an effect on the verdict of the jury.

Maxey offered a credible rebuttal for the defense accusation that he had submitted two conflicting financial statements for the Triple M Ranch on the same day. The larger figure on one of the statements, Maxey pointed out, included the value of fourteen thousand acres of leased property adjacent to the ranch; the smaller valuation did not.

Overall, however, Thursday did not go well for Maxey's side. No surprise, then, that later in the day, Liles and Hammett decided to put Drumwright on the stand the next morning. They were depending on Drumwright's impassioned testimony, followed by corroboration from W. L. Brady and Jack Wakefield, to revive the momentum on their side.

In the newspaper coverage of Fridays' proceedings, reporter Patrick described the testimony of the three witnesses as "explosive," and yet, like so much of the testimony already given, it was delivered outside the presence of the jury. Patrick's recounting of the Drumwright deal, as well as the alleged phone call by Charlie Jones that killed the deal, was certain to draw the attention of any jurors who picked up the newspaper that weekend.

Saturday and Sunday, Hammett and Liles huddled in the offices they had rented to prepare for the coming week. Representing Homer Maxey in the town where he was once a king was an exhilarating, but arduous, undertaking. "You'd think it's the sort of trial you'd be dying to be part of," says Liles, "but I lost twenty-five pounds just from stress. And you'd want to go have a steak and a glass of wine to unwind but you couldn't, because everywhere you went, people would come up and want to talk to you because you're Homer Maxey's attorney."[25]

Still, Liles and Hammett were touched by the depth of Maxey's support in Lubbock. "The motel where we stayed, which was just a few blocks from the courthouse, had a big marquee out front that said, 'Welcome Mike Liles and Harold Hammett, Homer Maxey's Attorneys.' The people there were very, very nice to us. Every morning they would bring us a newspaper and orange juice, without asking."

When the attorneys first arrived in Lubbock, however, they got a different kind of welcome. After arriving at their motel from the airport, they realized that the bags they had picked up from the luggage carousel did not belong to them. After a phone call to the airport and a long delay before their actual baggage was located, Liles and Hammett came to the conclusion that the mix-up had been intentional. After a substantial delay, their bags were delivered to their office but, by that time, says Liles, "certainly they'd had enough time to go through them."

If that reaction sounds paranoid, plenty of other things happened during the trial to make it clear that the attorneys' feelings of suspicion were not unwarranted. "Early on, we realized that our phones were tapped," says Liles. "So we started conveying false information over the phone about who we would be calling to testify the next day at trial. It kind of got comical for a few days. They'd have their books laid out and everything for cross-examination and we'd call somebody they weren't expecting. Harold and I had a hard time not laughing. Eventually they caught on."

"At that time," Liles explains, "we didn't have the discovery the way we do now, where you are required to tell the other side every witness you are going to call. It was more trial by ambush."

At one point, Liles was going out one evening to interview a surprise witness at a rental property that had once belonged to Maxey. Liles had driven to Lubbock in his Lincoln Mark IV, a two-door luxury model with a gold paint job and a powerful 460-inch V8 engine under the hood.

"It was a nice car," says Liles.

As he was driving to his meeting with the witness, Liles was heading into a sharp turn when the car's power steering failed. "I barely missed some gas pumps and wound up in a field right next to the service station," he says. "Several people saw it and were quite scared. They put my vehicle on the rack to check it out and said 'Here's the problem.' I could see that my power steering line had broken. The guy said, 'That's no break, it's been cut.' To this day, I am convinced that my power steering line was cut. They were going to try to do something. Kill me, injure me, or whatever."

It's impossible to say whether such incidents were actually caused by sabotage. However, Liles was also the target of another strange incident that inspires comparisons with pulp fiction novel intrigue.

On one of his trips to Lubbock before the second trial, Liles was sitting in a cafeteria with three other men when he was approached by an attractive young woman. He was surprised that he would be the object of her attention. "The three girls that were with her left, and when I went to pay the bill, she came up and asked if I was Mike Liles," he said. "I was single at the time. She asked if I would meet her for a drink, and I told her I had a plane to catch at seven. She named a [motel bar] that was on the way to the airport and I met her there. I knew it was probably a put-up."

In 1976 establishments in Lubbock that served liquor by the drink were not common. The motel also provided the ideal accommodations for the type of proposition the woman had in mind. Sparked by curiosity and the usual male urges, Liles went through with the rendezvous and the predictable follow-through. It was no surprise to him that, before and after he and the mystery woman engaged in consensual intercourse, the purported former Maid of Cotton peppered him with questions about the Maxey case. For Liles, it was both humorous and frightening to realize that he and his crusty, bald-headed client were the subjects of intrigue worthy of a James Bond movie.

"She said she had access to a villa in Acapulco, and she was going to invite me down there," recalls Liles, "but instead of going to Acapulco, she came to see me in Fort Worth and kept asking all these questions. I didn't pass up the opportunity to have horizontal calisthenics with her, but she didn't get any information out of me."

Whether his seducer was in fact a spy for the other side, Liles enjoyed her attentions sufficiently that on a subsequent trip to Lubbock, another tryst was arranged. "She tried to get information out of me and I played along without telling her anything. She claimed that she was a former Maid of Cotton. I don't know if she was or not, but she was a pretty girl."

During their second liaison, Liles told her he was married and found her reaction interesting. "She was disappointed. She never called me back after that."

On a darker note, Hammett and Liles were shocked to hear Ed Drumwright describing how he narrowly escaped death when his Bonanza Beechcraft crashed near Indio, California, on April 4, 1966.[26] Today, Liles says he can't be certain about the timing, but he believes that Drumwright had been scheduled to give his deposition in the case later that week. Maxey filed his original lawsuit against the bank on March 16, 1966.

Drumwright, who died in 2007, mentioned the crash during his testimony in the first trial, in response to a question about the reason he had closed his offices for a number of months that year.[27]

> Drumwright: I was in a private airplane crash April the fourth of 1966, and since I was the executive officer of three corporations, the activity of the corporations were curtailed quite a bit until I was out of the hospital.
> Bowlin: How long were you in the hospital?
> Drumwright: Well, I was in the hospital practically ten days, but I was in a full body cast for several days, and I was six months before the doctor would allow me to go back to the office full time.

Bowlin: Was anybody else in the plane with you, except you when you had the crash?

Drumwright: There was one business associate and another gentleman.

Bowlin: And did that crash occur in California?

Drumwright: Yes, sir, right out of Palm Springs.

Today Bowlin cannot recall any details of his discussions with Drumwright about the plane crash. In any event, it's clear from testimony he gave during the second trial that he was convinced that the crash was no accident.

Mike Liles states that he remains one hundred percent convinced the plane crash was the result of sabotage. Asked if Ed Drumwright felt that way as well, Liles answers, "absolutely, beyond the shadow of a doubt."[29]

In a feature about the Maxcy case published in the *Fort Worth Star-Telegram* in 1979, Drumwright was quoted as saying that his Bonanza Beechcraft had a new engine with 160 hours of flying time, that it had been checked out by a mechanic just before take-off, but the engine failed once the plane reached an altitude of two hundred feet.[29] Forced to make a hard landing near the airport, Drumwright suffered a broken back and nearly lost an eye in the crash. His two passengers were less seriously injured.[30]

The *Star-Telegram* quotes Drumwright with a cryptic statement regarding the actual cause of the crash: "I'm sure there's a lot of people connected in and around that bank that would have felt it easier if I wasn't around."

The accident report from the National Transportation Safety Board states that the cause of the accident was "engine failure or malfunction," and that the probable cause was due to the fact that the pilot "attempted operation w/ known deficiencies in equipment . . ." Elsewhere it says, "landed at [airport] due to [engine] malfunction, [pilot] made take-off without any corrective action to engine."[31]

Dorothy Drumwright says she will never forget her husband's plane crash. She does not, however, remember any discussion that it may have been caused by sabotage related to the Maxey case.[32] It is difficult to reconcile that with her husband's comments to Liles and the newspaper. Two possibilities come to mind: she forgot, or Drumwright managed to keep his suspicions secret from her. The latter seems plausible, except for the fact that Drumwright mentioned his suspicions in at least one newspaper story about the case.[33]

Liles says he is convinced "beyond a shadow of a doubt" that Drumwright's plane crash was a murder attempt, and that Drumwright thought so as well.

"I believe if you told him that if he said it was sabotage but it really wasn't, you'll go to hell, he would have said, 'It was sabotage.' I'm that certain."[34]

Liles also offers a plausible explanation for Dorothy's saying she doesn't remember her husband fearing his life was in danger. "If he had he told his wife that, then she would be screaming and hollering that he couldn't go [testify against the bank]."

Also contributing to the sensational elements of the trial were the sordid rumors about E. C. Mullendore III, who, in partnership with J. E. Birdwell, had bought Maxey's cattle after foreclosure in a deal that had been set up by Citizens National Bank President Williams and that was the subject of a great deal of criticism and suspicion during the first trial.[35]

At the time that Mullendore and Birdwell were involved in the cattle deal arranged by E. W. Williams, Mullendore was in deep trouble. His finances and personal life were in disarray. He consorted with a number of shady characters. Month by month, his situation became more perilous. When Mullendore was murdered in 1970, it began a morbid guessing game indulged by those who knew the victim.[36] Mullendore's financial straits were worse than Maxey's and the details more bizarre. Stories that Mullendore had borrowed large sums from the Mafia fueled speculation that his death was a mob hit.

Mike Liles is certain that Mullendore gave a deposition to Ken Bowlin and Jim Cade before his death, and that his deposition included statements of fact that bolstered Maxey's most serious allegations of fraud and conspiracy, as well as addition allegations of conspiracy and illegal deeds.[37] "Harold and I were told that Mullendore told everything about private planes landing on dirt landing strips out in the country and dividing up cash from the kickbacks, and things like that," says Liles. "He told the whole nine yards."[38]

Monday morning, the beginning of week two of the second trial, Jones made a motion that any testimony given before the jury regarding Drumwright's $4.5 million offer for Maxey's ranches be stricken from the record. Judge Bevers sustained the motion, echoing Jones's contention that unconsummated deals were not evidence of value, and he issued the appropriate instructions to the jurors.[39]

Maxey's attorneys felt that the ruling was unfair and unreasonable. Judge Bevers had no problem accepting the property values listed under the Strasburger agreement, despite the fact that they reflected minimum values only. Maxey's attorneys insisted that the Strasburger prices were not at all representative of market value and that Maxey had agreed to them because he was

Homer buying stock for his cattle yards in Denver, early 1960s. Courtesy of the Maxey Family

under pressure from the bank. (The court of appeals in Amarillo sided with the plaintiff. The decision, issued September 18, 1978, stipulated that "Generally, a landowner's offer to sell his land for a certain price has been considered an admission of value of his land." "[T]his general rule is applicable only if the proposed offer was freely and openly made. The offer is not an admission if made under circumstances of economic duress . . . The record shows that the Strasburger agreement was not made freely and openly. There is evidence that Maxey was under pressure from the bank to enter into the Strasburger agreement or face immediate foreclosure on chattel mortgages.")[40]

Later that morning, Maxey returned to the stand and Jones continued his cross-examination. When Jones inquired about the purchase price of the ranch near Atoka, Oklahoma, Liles objected, stating, "Trades of property for like property are irrelevant as to value, and the court has ruled such outside the presence of the jury."

Jones rose and approached the bench, addressing Judge Bevers in a voice that was inaudible to the jury. Judge Bevers excused the jury and, after the jurors filed out of the courtroom, Jones asked for a mistrial.

"Mr. Liles has made reference three or four times to rulings made outside the jury's presence, and the defense has made repeated objections," said Jones to the judge. "We ask the court to instruct counsel not to do so. In fact, we . . . told the court on the last occasion that if it happened again we would ask for a mistrial."

The next statements made during Jones's tantrum revealed the underlying reason for his irritation. "The jury has repeatedly been informed," he elaborated, "that there is testimony going on outside their presence, to the prejudice of the defense."

Liles apologized for mentioning the ruling, but he also corrected Jones, stating that he had mentioned the court's ruling and said nothing about any testimony.

The motion for a mistrial was denied. Maxey remained on the witness stand for the rest of the day. His physical discomfort and pain manifested itself in his appearance and his behavior. He was impatient and irritable under Jones's questioning. The following day his performance was no better.

After the lunch recess on Monday, Jones showed Maxey two financial statements. The first statement, dated June 20, 1964, valued the Pioneer Hotel at $1.3 million. The second statement, filed with the bank on January 31, 1965, showed a figure of $1.7 million.[41]

"What increased the value of the Pioneer from $1.3 million to $1.7 million in just seven months," asked Jones, "except the typewriter?"

"That question just makes it sound like I'm just making things up," replied Maxey, adding that the hotel was worth "a whole lot more than it brought on sale at the courthouse steps."

Jones pounced on Maxey's response. "What was that value?" he asked.

Liles objected, stating that the "price of a forced sale at foreclosure is not a true gauge of market value," a rationale that had been cited by the appellate courts in the Maxey case. Judge Bevers, however, overruled the objection, reasoning that Maxey himself had opened the door to further testimony on the subject.

Jones repeated the question. Maxey, his face going from its usual reddish hue to crimson and purple, remained silent. Judge Bevers instructed him to answer the question.

"Three hundred thousand dollars, including furniture," Maxey responded.

The answer was a damaging blow to the plaintiffs. In a case built on conflicting assessments of value, Maxey had just made a touchdown for the other team. Sitting in the courtroom, Melba, Carla, and Glenna, the three most important women in Homer's life, keenly felt his embarrassment and humiliation.

Liles asked for a short recess.[42] After the jury was excused, Liles addressed Judge Bevers, reminding him of his client's various health issues, some of which were causing him a great deal of discomfort during long periods of testimony. The explanation was unnecessary, however, due to Maxey's flushed complexion and other signs of physical discomfort.

Liles asked the judge if it would be all right to allow Maxey a day or two to rest, after which he could complete his testimony. Liles also suggested that Maxey be allowed to stand while testifying, which would be much easier on him than being seated for long periods of time. Although reluctant to do so, Judge Bevers agreed to Liles's requests.

While Maxey's health problems were real, Liles and Hammett were relieved to have an excuse to shake things up. They knew that if they didn't regain the momentum of the trial soon, their case was as good as lost.

The next morning, Liles called George Atkinson as an adverse witness. Atkinson, a Lubbock native, had been with Citizens National Bank going back to the Hughes's regime and had been a senior vice president with the bank during the run-up to the Maxey foreclosure. During the second trial, Atkinson sat at the defense table as the official representative of Texas Commerce Bank of Lubbock (the new name of the bank after the takeover by Texas Commerce Bancshares) and its stockholders.

Calling Atkinson as a witness caught the defense off guard, recalls Liles. "Atkinson was none too bright," he says, "and apparently, he had not been woodshedded by the bank's lawyers on what to say and what not to say."

Liles began his examination by asking Atkinson a series of questions about the secret sale of Maxey's assets during the foreclosure.[43] He also queried the banker about the manner in which Maxey's assets had been cross-pledged to the bank. Since the first day of the trial, Liles had taken every opportunity to mention the bank's secret sale and the fact that the cross-pledging of Maxey's properties effectively set up Maxey's financial empire, ready to fall "like a row of dominoes."

Atkinson affirmed the fact that, during the secret foreclosure sale, Plaza Building Corporation was deemed worthless and that the bank's affiliate corporation, Monterey Lubbock Corporation, was allowed to acquire all the stock shares in Plaza for a total of $749.

Liles repeated that figure, enunciating every syllable: "Seven hundred and forty-nine dollars?"

"Yes," answered the witness.

Liles then asked a series of questions regarding the procedures employed by the bank in reporting the value of collateralized assets to national bank examiners. Atkinson told the jury that, in addition to lending applications, financial statements, and credit memos, the opinions of the bank officers are also taken into consideration by the bank examiners.

Liles next asked Atkinson to examine a series of credit memos, including some that had been initialed by E. W. Williams. The internal bank documents, which Maxey had obtained by secret means, gave the value of Plaza Building Corporation as $1,784,000.

"You could hear the gasps in the courtroom," recalls Liles. "The feeling of shock and outrage was palpable."[44]

Atkinson sensed it, too. He tried backtracking, explaining that the $1.7 million figure had come from one of Maxey's own financial statements.

"Haven't you already told this jury that banks make their own evaluations?" Liles asked.

The damage was done. The headline in the *Avalanche-Journal* seemed to trumpet the shift in momentum: "Banker Affirms $1.7 Million Maxey Appraisal."[45]

During his examination of Atkinson the following day, Jones did his best to repair the damage. Jones solicited testimony from Atkinson affirming that when Citizens National Bank disposed of Maxey's ranch properties, the bank received less money than it had loaned Maxey. Liles objected, again arguing that what happened to the ranches after foreclosure was irrelevant to the actual market values of the properties on the date of foreclosure. Judge Bevers overruled Liles's objection.

Liles launched a quick counterattack when the witness was passed back to him. Reporter Patrick described the scene in the *Avalanche-Journal*:[46]

... Liles paced the courtroom floor, glowering.

"On the Texline farm, didn't that contract have a kickback agreement?" he shot suddenly.

Atkinson indicated he did not know what supposed contract Liles was asking about.

Almost in the same breath, the lawyer asked if a contract between CNB and an individual buyer whom he named was not an agreement under which the prospective buyer would refund money to the bank if he later sold the property for a larger sum than he paid.

"That contract was never consummated," Atkinson said at one point, apparently in reference to negotiations on the Tulsa ranch which was later foreclosed.

The stormy interchange ended as quickly as it began when Liles turned the subject to the Tulsa ranch's possible value, and, after a moment, said he had no more questions.

The issue of kickback agreements had emerged during the first trial, when witnesses for the bank appeared reluctant to admit their existence. One witness, Marvin Hugley, denied that such agreements existed until Ken Bowlin produced one bearing Hugley's signature.[47]

Today, E. W. Williams shrugs off any inference of impropriety regarding what he says are referred to as "profit-sharing agreements."[48]

"Yes, that's really what they were," says Liles today, "I called them kickbacks because I liked that better than profit-sharing. It sounds more evil. And it was. If you sell something for a good price, which the bank was obligated to try their best to do, you don't expect it to sell for a better price a little while later."[49]

After his annihilation of Atkinson, Liles made another good point for Maxey's case during his examination of a real estate appraiser named Harold Chapman, who refuted a contention by Jones that Maxey had exaggerated the value of some duplexes he had traded for other properties.[50]

On Friday, Maxey returned to the witness stand rested and refreshed. Continuing his cross-examination, Jones pointed out that just one section of the Texline farm had been included in the alleged kickback agreement testified to by Atkinson. Maxey reluctantly agreed that the statement was true.

Jones also pointed out that Maxey, acting as a representative of Plaza Building Corporation after the foreclosure, had spoken to a prospective buyer of the Triple M Ranch and had full knowledge of the profit-sharing plan in advance.

"Now it seems everybody's had a lot of fun talking about 'kickbacks,'" said Jones. "Now is it good or bad?" Jones asked. "Why use the word 'kickback'?"

Maxey's reply was loud enough to be heard down the hall. "Because that's exactly what it was," he shouted at Jones. "I say a kickback is a rotten deal no matter whether it's Plaza or whether it's you."[51]

Chauncey Trout, Jr., was the next witness. Liles asked Trout numerous questions about his role at Evans, Pharr, Trout & Jones, representing both Citizens National Bank and Maxey.[52] Liles wanted to know the exact date that Trout was named to the bank's board of directors and how many shares of stock he owned in the bank. He also asked about the mood in the law office when it became obvious that Maxey and Citizens National Bank were on a collision course.

Trout responded: "I know that it was suggested to Mr. Maxey that he might retain other counsel."

"You had a choice of not representing either one of them, didn't you?" asked Liles.

"Yes," answered Trout.

Liles said he had no other questions.

After Jones finished asking Trout a few cursory questions, court was adjourned until Monday morning. Again, the big theme in the news coverage over the weekend was the subject of kickbacks. No one could say it had been a good week for the defense.

Monday morning, October 18, 1976, the plaintiffs called Charles Osenbaugh, their last witness. Liles had first met Osenbaugh when he was practicing law with Babe Schwartz.[53] "Charlie was an expert in evaluating corporations and determining what they were truly worth," says Liles. "We were trying a lawsuit over the construction of Interstate 45 through Houston. Charlie testified for the other side, for the defendant, but afterwards we became friends."

After being sworn in, Osenbaugh replied to a series of questions about his areas of expertise and experience.[54] Next, Liles asked Osenbaugh to give the name of his biggest client. The answer was Texas Commerce Bancshares, the holding company that now owned the institution formerly known as Citizens National Bank of Lubbock.

Osenbaugh's testimony buttressed two of the most important contentions of the plaintiffs' case. First, that Maxey's assets were worth much more than the amounts for which they were sold by the bank; and, second, that the $1.2 million debt owed to Maxey by Plaza Building Corporation had not been credited to Maxey's indebtedness. Maxey's loan to the corporation should have been shown as one of his personal assets, or treated as what Osenbaugh termed "a meaningless debt." The bottom line, Osenbaugh asserted, was that the bank owed Maxey $1.2 million.

Osenbaugh estimated that the value of the stock shares in Plaza Building Corporation, for which the bank had paid $749, was $911,994 on the date Citizens National Bank had foreclosed on Maxey. Osenbaugh also testified that, considering its potential for lakeshore development, the Triple M Ranch was worth $1.8 million.

Some of Osenbaugh's estimates, however, were not much higher than those of the bank. In several instances, his estimates were lower than Maxey's.

During cross-examination, Jones took the witness back through each estimate, probing for contradictions, juggling figures in his head and zooming in on minute details. One of Jones's friends and admirers, Charlie Joplin, recalls having dropped in to watch the progress of the trial.

"I remember Charlie Jones was trying to explain a financial statement," says Joplin, "and there were a couple of fellows up on the back row [of the spectators' gallery] sound asleep. I thought to myself, 'Well, that's a hell of a trial.'"

Later that day, Jones asked Osenbaugh if his evaluation of the Triple M Ranch was based on any comparable land sales in the area. Osenbaugh answered that the only sales during that time period had involved smaller aggregates of property. "The only comparable sale I know of is of the same property," said Osenbaugh, "the subject property we're talking about, of $4.5 million when it was sold later."

Writing in the *Avalanche-Journal*, reporter Patrick described Jones's reaction to Osenbaugh's answer as one of "chagrin."[55]

A vexed Jones stalked to the witness stand. "Have you testified in court before?" he asked Osenbaugh. After chiding the witness for another few seconds, he asked Judge Bevers to instruct Osenbaugh to answer questions as they were asked.

Later, ruling on a motion by Jones, Judge Bevers ordered that Osenbaugh's answer giving the $4.5 million sale price of the Triple M be stricken from the record on the grounds that it was an unresponsive answer and, also, because the sale had occurred in 1972, six years after the foreclosure.[56]

At the conclusion of Osenbaugh's testimony, Liles rose and addressed the bench, "Your honor, at this time, the plaintiffs rest their case."

If Liles's announcement exuded an air of confidence, it failed to intimidate Charlie Jones. When the judge asked if the defense was ready to proceed, Jones requested that the jury be excused and then moved for an instructed verdict in favor of the bank, arguing that Maxey's attorneys had not presented enough credible and relevant evidence to merit the continuation of the trial. Maxey's case, he said, was so weak it would be a waste of time to argue against it.

"They allege breach of contract," Jones said, "then rely on us to show that the breach did not occur . . . Plaintiff has alleged there was something wrong with foreclosure, but has not shown what was wrong."

After Jones finished, Judge Bevers asked the attorneys at the plaintiffs' table if they wished to respond to Jones's arguments. Their answer was no.

Judge Bevers denied the defense motion. "In view of the Supreme Court decision, I feel obligated to overrule defendant's motion," he said. "But I do not do so with any great confidence."[57]

The diminutive man in the black judicial robes had never agreed with the 1974 ruling of the Texas Supreme Court in the Maxey case. But the opinion stated that a corporation owes its customers a responsibility to act in good faith and that Citizens National Bank had responsibilities to Homer Maxey that were not derivative of its agents.[58]

The way Judge Bevers saw it, the Maxey case was simple: "A bank loaned a fellow too much money and he couldn't pay it back, so he got mad."[59]

Bevers was well aware that some people in Lubbock felt that he was biased in favor of the bank, and that his great admiration for Jones clouded his judgment. Today the former district judge responds to such accusations by offering a humorous anecdote of his own. He says that in a deposition for the Maxey case, Jones was asked if it was true that his father, a prominent physician, had paid Denzil Bevers's way through law school, to which Jones responded: "Well, not to my knowledge, but I'm sure as heck going to ask him about that because he sure didn't help me any."

On a more serious note, Bevers says that the 1974 Supreme Court ruling never made sense to him. "In the second Maxey trial, they didn't have anybody directly involved in the damned controversy that was still party to the lawsuit," says Bevers. "How can a corporation be responsible except through its agents?"

"I wanted the appellate courts to tell me, if they're going to reverse, here's what you have to do if you're going to stick the corporation," complains Bevers. "They never did say how you ought to charge the jury. In view of the fact that there was no damn agent to represent the corporation, how in hell do you stick it to the corporation?"

However, according to David Hughes, Judge Bevers's unsympathetic view of Maxey predated the trial over which he presided.[60] One day, when Bevers was a county court-at-law judge and the first Maxey trial was under way in Judge Pat Moore's 72nd District Court, Hughes dropped by his office for a casual visit. Bevers inquired about the Maxey case. At some point in their conversation, says Hughes, Bevers asked if he thought Homer Maxey was "crazy." Hughes says that he told Bevers he thought Maxey wasn't "crazy in the usual sense," but "deluded" and "obsessed."

The briefs filed by the attorneys for the bank during the appellate battles also seem to reflect a lack of regard for the Denton ruling on corporate responsibility. One argument offered to the appellate courts asserted that Maxey's attorneys were attempting to relitigate the original fraud and conspiracy allegations of the first trial, and that the plaintiffs were attempting to disguise a tort case as a breach-of-contract suit.[61]

Testimony by the witnesses for the defense began on Wednesday, October 20, 1976, and concluded early the next day.[62] As in the first trial, five witnesses were called. Three of them, Barclay Ryall, Clyde Gordon, and George Atkinson, the latter of whom had already testified earlier in the trial to the great dismay of the defense, had been executives at Citizens National Bank during the tenure of E. W. Williams. The other two witnesses, Marvin Hugley and Fred Foley, were real estate appraisers. All but Atkinson had testified in the first trial.

The testimony given by the appraisers was a condensed version of what was heard by the jury in the first trial, while the bank executives were called upon to recite figures regarding Maxey's assets, liabilities, loans, and credits given by the bank after the foreclosure. There were, to be sure, some dramatic moments, such as when Liles and Jones went at each other during objections, or when Liles took one of the defense witnesses to task.

Liles expressed his outrage when, on cross-examination, Barclay Ryall revealed that the bank had subtracted more than $89,000 in real estate commissions from the credits given to Maxey's accounts for the properties that were sold, even though no real estate agents were involved in the transactions, which consisted of transferring deeds from Maxey's corporations to the affiliate corporate entities of Citizens National Bank.

As in the first trial, Atkinson's testimony provided some of the most dramatic moments in the courtroom. When called as an adverse witness by Maxey's attorneys the week before, Atkinson's testimony had inflicted serious damage to the defense. Liles had hammered the banker about credit memos in the bank's files that gave the value of Plaza Building Corporation as $1,784,000. Now, however, Atkinson returned to the witness stand armed with internal documents showing that the bank considered Plaza Building Corporation to be worthless.

Reporter Patrick characterized Atkinson's testimony as a successful effort at damage control:

> Throughout the trial, Liles had used the bank's own records, in the form of credit memorandums, to try to demonstrate CNB had consistently and officially valued Plaza's net worth at $1.7 million until foreclosure.

Atkinson's testimony therefore helped shore up a seeming gap in bank defenses by citing a bank record which stated Plaza's value as zero.

The record was an assessment of Maxey's holdings reportedly compiled after a September, 1964 tour of Plaza-owned ranches by a bank appraiser.

"What does it show as the value of Plaza stock?" bank attorney Charles Jones asked.

"None," Atkinson said.

The cross-examination of the bank's witness, however, was described by Patrick as "a jury-riveting attack."[63] Liles challenged the banker to defend the legitimacy and relevance of the credit report. Why were there so many erasures on the report, he asked Atkinson. Why were several of Maxey's properties, including the Pioneer Hotel, not listed on the report? How could the bank arrive at a total value of the corporation if they didn't list all its assets?

Atkinson's answer to the last question was simple: the properties left off the report were ones in which the bank did not hold collateral.

Today, Liles views the belated introduction of the credit report as yet more proof of chicanery by the officers of the bank. "Why did they have two sets of books?" says Liles. "I asked Osenbaugh that same question on the stand. His reply: 'There's no reason, not an honest reason, anyway.'"[64]

After both sides had completed their examinations of the final witness for the defense, Liles informed Judge Bevers that the plaintiffs wished to exercise their right to call a rebuttal witness.

The witness called to testify was G. C. Walters, a real estate appraiser from Oklahoma who specialized in selling real estate at auction.[65] After being sworn in and asked a few introductory questions, Liles asked Walters to tell the jury about a meeting with Citizens National Bank President Williams in the fall of 1966.

Walters said he met with Williams to discuss the possibility of selling the Triple M Ranch. As Walters described it, Williams did not seem very impressed by Walters's interest in the property. Williams did, however, tell him to go ahead and appraise the property, which he did. Liles asked Walters to describe Williams's response to the appraisal in his subsequent meeting with the bank president.

Walters: I told him I thought it would bring, on a conservative basis, $3 or $3.5 million.

Liles: What did Mr. Williams say?

Walters: He told me he appreciated my services, appreciated what I had done.

Williams's lukewarm response was puzzling to Walters. The appraiser was even more puzzled when he learned that the bank had sold the Triple M Ranch for a mere $1.8 million.

In 1973, however, Walters had a second opportunity to handle the property when the new owner asked him to put the ranch up for auction. Walters conducted the auction before a "motel room full of people—thirty or forty of them," he said, and the ranch sold for $4,560,000.

On a previous occasion, when Charles Osenbaugh cited the figure, Jones had objected, explaining that sales after foreclosure were not true evidence of property value. Bevers had sustained the objection, despite having allowed the same sort of evidence when it was offered by the bank. This time, however, judge overruled Jones's objection. The testimony would be allowed.

Taking Walters on cross, Jones tried hard to nettle the witness, but there was no way to make that $4.56 million figure go away or become less impressive.

The bank's witnesses had insisted that the Triple M was worth, at the most, a little over a million dollars. In contrast, Walters's testimony added powerful evidence to the claim that Maxey's properties were, in fact, worth considerably more than the prices for which they had been sold after the foreclosure.[66]

The Maxey team arrived at the courthouse Friday morning, October 22, 1976, spoiling for a fight.[67] Throughout the trial, the odds had been stacked against them in many different ways but, now and then, Maxey had an ace up his sleeve. Several of the important documents Liles and Hammett had relied upon for evidence had materialized in mysterious ways. In all likelihood, the credit memorandum that had caused George Atkinson so much grief during his testimony had been smuggled out of the building by a bank employee who was sympathetic to Maxey and his family. Liles says that there were several other occasions in which Maxey presented them with a piece of important evidence, such as the credit memorandum, and said, "You probably don't want to know how I got this, but . . ."

Another inside contact had helped Maxey gain what could have been termed "home field advantage," that is, the better of the two counsel tables in the courtroom.

"It was a very poorly designed courtroom," recalls Liles. "During all the pretrial hearings, Charlie Jones kept getting the good table. We were able to get the good table just one time."

The way the courtroom was laid out, with the jury box on the side, perpendicular to the counsel tables and the judge's bench, the counsel table nearest the jury box blocked the jurors' view of the other table. Liles and Hammett wanted the jurors to be able watch Maxey and his reactions when he was seated with them. They wanted the table next to the jury box.

"On one of the last of the hearings," Liles recalls, "we talked and I said to Bevers, 'Judge, I guess tomorrow morning at the trial we'll establish these tables, who will sit where for the rest of the trial,'" to which Bevers agreed. Liles smiles and explains that that Maxey had a friend who was employed at the courthouse, and that unidentified individual loaned Maxey the keys to the courtroom. "The morning of the trial," Liles says, "Homer got there before anybody else. He went in and put his books on the table we wanted and just waited. So, Homer's sitting there, the courtroom is dark, and when Denzil comes in and turns on the light and sees Homer, it scares the crap out of him." And that's how the Maxey team got the "good table" for the trial.

Arriving at the courtroom on the morning of the last day of trial, however, it was Liles who had an unpleasant surprise. "I walk by Bevers's office and he's having a closed-door meeting with Charlie Jones and Perry Davis," says Liles. "It wasn't the first time, and I was fed up with it."

For a judge to engage in such contact—meeting with one or more attorneys without a legal representative from the opposing side present—which is referred to as an ex parte communication—is regarded as unethical behavior on both the part of the judge and any attorney involved. *Ex parte* in Latin means "from one party," and is antithetical to fair representation in a lawsuit.

Liles says he was already boiling mad when he opened the door to the judge's chambers. What Bevers said to him enraged him further.

"He told me, 'Here's what we're going to do, Mike,'" remembers Liles. "Bevers says, 'Charlie's going to put E. W. Williams on the stand as a rebuttal witness to deny what the auctioneer said about his meeting with E. W., but I'm not going to let you cross-examine him.'"

Liles says he went ballistic: "I said, 'You goddamn, motherfucking, crooked, no-good son-of-a-bitch.' Bevers comes from around his desk and goes nose to nose with me and says, 'You say that again and I'll hold you in contempt and put you in jail.' So I said: 'You goddamn, motherfucking, crooked, no-good son-of-a-bitch. Go ahead and hold me in contempt and put me in jail. All the reporters out there will know why you did, too.'"

Liles says he was ready to go to jail, and also ready to punch the judge in the face. Bevers, however, suddenly appeared anxious to defuse the situation. After a short conference between Davis and Jones, the judge announced that Williams would not be called as a rebuttal witness after all.

When asked about the incident, Bevers replies, "I know Liles got mad at me, but don't recall him cussing me out." When asked about several other, well-documented aspects of the trial, Bevers could not recall those details, either.[68]

During the previous three weeks of the trial, E. W. Williams had been in Amarillo, tending to his duties as president of Amarillo National Bank. However, he states that he traveled to Lubbock on the last day of the trial so that he would be available in the event that he was called as a rebuttal witness. Which meant he could have been in the courtroom for the final arguments, had he wished to hear them.[69]

"Neither Harold nor I had ever seen E. W. before," says Liles. "And you might think this is strange, but when I was giving my final argument, I saw a face in the audience, and I knew it was him. I could just feel it. I had this powerful sense of who he was."[70] The authors felt it was important enough to ask Williams about this again in a second interview. Jesse Sublett asked Williams if he was present in the courtroom for the final arguments. After a moment of hesitation, Williams said, "I may have been there."[71]

Liles still had a fire in his belly from his heated exchange with the judge when he began to address the jury for the first part of his final argument. He began with a deliberate pace, treating the jurors to a short biographical sketch of Homer Maxey and his rise in the business world, accentuating his business acumen and vision.[72] Such talents served Maxey well when he was starting out, establishing Maxey Lumber Co., H. G. Maxey & Co., building subdivisions and shopping centers. The same talents came into play, Liles contended, when Maxey laid out his long-range plan to buy vast tracts of ranch lands, with the end goal of subdividing them years later when the market was ready. (Liles says that Maxey discussed his long-range plans in detail during the many hours they spent together preparing to try the case. The attorneys did not, however, mention Maxey's long-range plans in their own closing arguments.)

As he related the story of Maxey's relationship with E. W. Williams and Citizens, Liles underscored the idea that, beginning in 1964, when Maxey was vulnerable and needed a continued source of financing until the cattle ranching enterprises became profitable, the bank had backed Maxey into a corner. In order to keep his plans going, Maxey had to sign over all his collateral, which later became completely cross-pledged. Here Liles used one of his favorite metaphors, asserting that his client was "set up like a domino; if one thing fell, everything fell at once."

As to the endless debate over the true value of Maxey's assets, Liles posed the following question: "If the properties weren't worth what he said they were on the financial statements he gave to the bank, why would they want him to give it to them? Why? If it was worthless, then why did the bank want to own it?"

At times, Liles admitted to the jurors that he might be getting carried away with his rhetoric. "I do submit," he said to the jury, "I'm not trying to be overdramatic, but February 16, 1966, was one of the blackest days that ever occurred, when you look at all of the facts."

Years later, Liles recalls being "overdramatic" and even a little clownish during the Maxey trial.[73] "One day I was being very dramatic and I took my pen and I put it into my pocket, just being a ham," remembers Liles. "Then I was standing at the counsel table and one of the lady jurors said, 'Mike, Mike . . . ' and Bevers pounded his gavel and said, 'What's going on here?' She said, 'Look at Mike's shirt!' I hadn't put the top back on my pen and ink was going all down the front of my shirt. Denzil wanted to call a recess, but it was late in the afternoon, so I suggested that we just continue because the shirt was already ruined. But that little lady on the jury said, 'Mike, you haven't ruined it. I'll take it home and wash it for you.'"

Neither Judge Bevers nor the bank's attorneys were very amused by the juror's kind-hearted gesture, says Liles. "Ordinarily, you'd move for a mistrial or take some other measure when something like that happens," he says. "But the bank didn't do that, they just wanted to get the trial over with. The publicity during the trial was very, very bad for the bank. So they just let it go."

Liles says that while he is not proud of some of his tactics, he says he felt obligated to "fight every way I could" to counteract the judge's bias against Maxey.

"Bevers would act like he was about to fall asleep whenever I was questioning a witness," he says, "but when Charlie was asking questions or arguing, he'd sit up there and look really interested. You know, jurors notice this. So a lot of times when Charlie was asking questions, I would keep getting up and going around my chair to distract from what Charlie Jones was doing. One time, when they were mowing the grass outside the courtroom, I went over and opened the window so all that noise would come in. I couldn't resist it."

Toward the end of Liles's final argument, Jones rose to make an objection, asserting that no testimony had been given to support Liles's previous statement.

Liles blew his top. "I literally put my finger right up against his nose and argued with him," he says. "I was such a smart ass."[74]

Liles studded his final argument with questions about a long series of thorny issues for the defense. Was it fair, he asked, for the bank to dispose of Maxey's assets in a secret sale? To give no advance notice to potential buyers? For the bank to sell Maxey's properties to its affiliates and, in at least one case, to a brother-in-law of a director?[75]

"Thirty minutes was all it took," he asked. "What did they take? Maxey Lumber Company . . . the Tulsa ranch [Triple M] . . . Plaza Building Corporation for $749 . . . Fair? Let's talk about fairness . . ." Attacking the bank's evaluation of Plaza, Liles insisted that the bank had appraised Maxey's assets piecemeal, disregarding the value of the corporation as an intact entity. Using an automobile as an analogy, he said, "You can't take bits and pieces off. When you take a tire off and you say, OK, what's that worth? What is the radiator worth by itself? . . . and so on. The value of the car is what it is when it is intact and all together."

Attorney Perry Davis gave the first part of the final argument for the bank. Davis had a less flattering version of the Homer Maxey story. The plaintiff, he said, "had become a wealthy man due to the building boom . . . [and] for reasons best known to him, . . . he decided to get into some businesses in which he had no experience, the ranching business and the cattle business. And he started borrowing large sums of money. We told you, ladies and gentlemen, that we thought the evidence would show, and that we could agree on, the fact that, as of February 16 of 1966, Mr. Maxey owed $1,226,000."

Davis made some good points in his presentation. Liles, he asserted, had attempted to create the impression that Maxey had taken out long-term notes with the bank but, instead, in borrowing money on a line of credit, he had signed notes that were payable on demand. Indeed, Maxey had signed many such notes over the years of his business career before he became a customer of Citizens National Bank.

"A bank is in business to try to make loans," Davis told the jury, "and to make money off of loans. That's the bank's business. We suggest to you that there is not anything unusual about a business transaction where the bank says, 'Well, Mr. Maxey, if you're willing to sign these notes then we are willing to loan you $1,227,000.'"

Addressing the math of the case, Davis claimed that the statements by Osenbaugh that the bank should have paid Maxey the $1.2 million debt owed to him by Plaza Building Corporation were nonsensical. "Liles gets up there and says it's only $1.2 million going from one pocket to another," Davis said. "It just doesn't make sense, not in anybody's language."

The last thing any bank wants to do, Davis argued, is to foreclose on a customer. In his view, Citizens had been very lenient with Maxey by not foreclosing in July of 1965. "The choice was Citizens National Bank's," he said. "They agreed to six months." During the six-month grace period granted under the Strasburger agreement, none of Maxey's properties were sold, even at the prices that Maxey claimed were far below market value. What, asked Davis, did that say about the true value of these properties? If they failed to find buyers even at unfairly distressed prices, how much more could they possibly be worth?

Neither Maxey nor his attorneys ever gave a satisfactory response to that question. Davis continued, raising questions as to the credibility of the plaintiffs' witnesses, in particular, Ed Drumwright and Charles Osenbaugh, the latter of whom had "never even driven by a comparable ranch" before coming up with his appraisal of the Triple M Ranch.

Regarding the testimony of G. C. Walters, Davis asked the jurors: "Would anybody believe . . . that if Mr. Walters made that statement, that Mr. Williams or any other bank president, would say, 'Oh no, we don't want to sell the property for that. We'd rather get out [and foreclose on Maxey] and lose $333,000.'"

Jones followed Davis's presentation with a rebuttal to each of Maxey's allegations against the bank. Despite Jones's legendary rhetorical skills, however, he labored to present all his arguments in the allotted time slot. Jones found himself pressed for time because of a tactic employed by Liles in his previous presentation.[76]

Liles had raised more than two dozen nagging questions for the defense, beginning with every allegation of impropriety against the bank listed in the plaintiffs' petition, followed by specific instances in which Liles alleged that witnesses for the bank had lied or fudged the truth on the stand. For each of these points, Liles had written a question on a three-by-five inch index card such as: "Why did Marvin Hugley deny that there was a kickback agreement on the Texline farm?" Before moving on to the next question, Liles placed the card on the railing of the jury box, leaving it for the defense team to answer. By the time the defense attorneys rose to present their side, the cards stretched from one end of the railing to the other.

"I think there were twenty or more of those cards, a whole pack of them, as I recall," says Liles. "I turned around and pointed my finger at Charlie

Jones and said, 'I'm going to leave these cards here to see if he can explain why they told so many untruths.' You never use the term lie. Why were they so untruthful? Charlie had to spend all of his time defending the cards rather than arguing for their point of view."

Nevertheless, Jones still found time to get in some powerful points. Jones underscored the fact that, with the exception of Maxey Lumber Company, all of Maxey's businesses were losing money after 1963.[77]

According to Jones's figures, after all Maxey's assets were liquidated and his accounts credited, the bank still lost $330,000. Jones suggested that that fact alone was sufficient to prove that Citizens National Bank had not conspired to take Maxey's properties or acted in bad faith. Jones asserted that Maxey's attorneys were trying to convince the jury that "everybody who had occasion to foreclose on any of Mr. Maxey's properties rushed right out and sold them so that they could take a bigger loss."

Continuing, Jones reminded the jurors that Great Southern Life Insurance Company had also taken a loss after financing Maxey's renovation of the Pioneer Hotel. Maxey bought the hotel in 1960 for $450,000 and spent $860,000 renovating it. Of that amount, $1.2 million was financed by Great Southern. By the date of foreclosure in 1966, the debt had been reduced to $450,000[78] and, according to Maxey's financial statements, the hotel was valued at $1.7 million.

After calling Maxey's loan, the insurance company sold the Pioneer Hotel, which had been shut down, during a public auction for $250,000. "I expect they were glad to get that much for it," Jones told the jury.[79] "Were they also just out, for some reason, to get Mr. Maxey? Mr. Liles speaks here about what all they did to Mr. Maxey. All they did was take a whopping big loss."

Returning to the subject of Maxey's relationship with Citizens National Bank, Jones said that, even after it had informed him in December of 1964 that the bank could no longer continue loaning Maxey large sums of money, "they kept on advancing additional funds for him to pay his mortgages to other people . . . Was that part of their scheme to hurt him?"

Reaching the conclusion of his argument, Jones stated that "Maxey was a fifty percent owner of [Maxey Lumber Company] . . . and so was the bank. *We* had a little more equity, he had the control. And *we* only sold that fifty percent and *we* had $276,000 in it. . . . I would appreciate your fair consideration in that." (Emphasis added.) Jones announced that he had reached the limit of his allotted time, thanked the jury again, and sat down.

The fact that Jones used the pronoun "we" in connection with actions taken by the bank ("*We* had a little more equity . . . *we* only sold that fifty percent . . .") did not escape the attention of Maxey's attorneys.

Liles rose and began his rebuttal argument by telling the jurors that he had had trouble sleeping the night before. As he lay in bed, he said, he saw his father, who had died in May of 1976. Liles's father, he said, wanted to offer him his support and encouragement for the next day in court.

Today, the attorney is still humbled and awed by the dream visit from his father. "He was standing right there," says Liles. "I saw his face looking down at me and he said, 'Don't worry son, everything's going to be fine.' I actually saw that vision. I am not sure that I even believe in this kind of thing, but this vision was very, very clear."[80]

After a brief preamble, Liles reminded the jurors of Jones's last statements, in which he had spoken, consciously or not, of his own business relationship with the defendant in the case. In a highly emotional appeal, Liles said he had felt "a burning sensation all over" as Jones asked them to "look what *we* did, what *we* did with Mr. Maxey's property . . ."[81] (Emphasis was added to Jones's statement and also added here for clarity. Whether Jones's use of the pronoun "we" was intentional or a slip of the tongue, Liles used it to full advantage.)

Liles soon segued to the issue of the $1.2 million debt that Plaza Building Corporation had owed to Maxey. That debt, Liles argued, was a stockholder's equity and a personal asset of Homer Maxey. Therefore, he said, the bank should have paid Maxey for it.

In his conclusion, Liles told the jurors he wanted them to think about how it might feel to be in Homer Maxey's shoes. He reminded them that defense attorney Charlie Jones, who had formerly been Maxey's attorney, was one of the codefendants in the original lawsuit. How would it feel, he asked, to be cross-examined by your former attorney, friend, and trusted confidant?

"For thirty-five years that trust had been there and then it was turned," Liles told them. "Jones's law partner said, 'We have a choice, we can represent Homer Maxey or represent the bank.' And they chose the bank. Was that fair?"

"I could not be more proud than to represent a man and his family that have stood by him through these trials," Liles continued. "He knows his rights. He knows that those properties have those values, and he is entitled, under all of this evidence, to his recovery, at long last. And with everything I have, I am not ashamed, but proud, and I ask that each of you see your intentions to right this wrong, wrong injustice. Thank you."

It was early afternoon by the time the jurors retired to begin their deliberations. The panel of eight women and four men elected Victor Pellini as their foreman.

Liles learned of some of the discussion during the deliberations when he interviewed several of the jurors after the verdict had been returned.

"Pellini had been a sergeant in the army so he was kind of used to giving orders," says Liles. "When they went in to deliberate, Pellini said, 'I want to give Maxey every penny they're asking for.' Two of the women on the jury said, 'No, if you will find damages of only $2.2 million, the bank will not appeal the verdict.'"[82]

Liles had been concerned about those same two women during the jury selection process, but Hammett liked them, so they ended up on the panel. The significance of the $2.2 million figure mentioned by the two jurors was that, years earlier, during its negotiations with Texas Commerce Bancshares, the owners of Citizens National Bank had set aside $2.5 million in an escrow fund which was referred to in internal documents under the title "The Maxey Claims."

"That they had that amount of money in escrow was not public knowledge," says Liles. "Which makes it interesting that these women came up with that number, doesn't it?"

Liles and Hammett were convinced that someone from the bank got word to some of the potential jurors, and that the two women were among that group.

According to Liles, Pellini queried the rest of the jury panel and was pleased to learn that the two women who suggested limiting the judgment to $2.2 million were the only ones in favor of it. The other jurors regarded the proposal as being unworthy of further consideration. The jurors who proposed it were regarded with disgust. Maxey was going to get more than $2.2 million; the only question was, how much more?

Waiting for the jury to return with a verdict is the most stressful part of any trial. Hammett and Liles sat in the room with their clients waiting for the deliberations to end. After many months of trial preparation, filing briefs and outlining strategy, followed by intense legal sparring and rhetorical gamesmanship, the decision was in the hands of the jury. Waiting was not easy.

Everyone was nervous and exhausted. Time slowed to a crawl. "Harold decided to go out and get a sandwich," recalls Liles. "He asked if I wanted one and I said no, I wasn't hungry, but he brought me one anyway and I ate it in two or three bites. It dawned on me that I hadn't eaten in two or three days."

Around that time, the bailiff escorted the jurors out for a coffee break.

Liles watched the jurors as they walked out. "Pellini was the last one to come out," he says. "The jurors have their heads down and they're not looking at us. Normally, that's not a good sign. But when Pellini walked out, he walked a little ways past me without looking at me, then he backed up, came back and winked at me. That made me feel good."

Tommy Elliott thought some of the jurors were smiling. "I think they're trying to decide how much to give us," he told a reporter. Other members of the Maxey team were more pessimistic, but the former college football star predicted victory.[83]

Around five p.m., Pellini sent a message to the judge that the jury was ready to deliver the verdict. Deliberations had taken a little less than three hours.

When court was reconvened, Judge Bevers cautioned everyone in the courtroom against any verbal reaction during the reading of the verdict. "As if he could do anything about it," says Liles.[84]

As in the first trial, the jury had been charged with addressing a list of specific issues in arriving at the verdict. Regarding the question as to whether the bank had "failed to exercise good faith" in its dealings with Maxey and if the amounts the bank had credited Maxey for his stock in Plaza Building Corporation and Maxey Lumber Company were "grossly inadequate," the jury answered "Yes."

Homer Maxey leaned toward Liles and asked what he thought. "It's fantastic," Liles told him. Glenna let out an audible gasp. Maxey listened and, by the time the entire decision had been read aloud, he was almost beside himself. He took Liles in a bear hug and wept.

"The court reporter came up and gave Homer a cassette tape," recalls Liles. "She told him she thought my final argument would be great, so she made an extra copy of it for him. Homer made a copy for me but I've never wanted to listen to it."

The verdict was a substantial one. Until that day, the $2.6 million award in the 1969 Maxey trial had been the largest award on record in Lubbock County. Depending on the way the courts ruled regarding the prejudgment interest Maxey could collect, Liles predicted that the 1976 verdict would end up being at least one million dollars more than one in the 1970.

The jury found that, on the date of foreclosure, the value of Plaza Building Corporation was $3,040,599.31. The value of Maxey's 23,125 shares of Maxey Lumber Company was estimated at $689,541.22. Those amounts added together came to a judgment totaling $3,730,140.53, just as Liles had predicted. It was assumed that Maxey would also be awarded prejudgment interest between six and ten percent. Maxey's attorneys were pushing for ten percent. Six percent interest over ten years would add $2,238,080, for a total of $5,968,220, and ten percent would be double the amount, for a net recovery of $7,308,204.80. Adjusted for inflation, the $3,730.140.53 would be equivalent to $15,092,382 in 2012 dollars.[85] With six percent interest over ten years, the 2012 equivalent would be $24,147,796, and with ten percent added, $30,184,765.

The Lubbock Club was the scene of a big victory party that evening. "There must've been two hundred people at the Lubbock Club," says Liles. "The word just kind of got around very quickly and people went down there to meet and celebrate the verdict. Later on we went to a nightclub. They stopped the music and made an announcement about the Maxey case. It was a big, big deal in Lubbock."

Liles and Hammett stayed over that weekend and went down to the courthouse for the reading of the judgment on Monday morning. They had prepared themselves for some kind of push-back from Judge Bevers, the bank's attorneys, or both.

"We were entitled to prejudgment interest," says Liles. "Denzil said, 'I know you're entitled to it, but I'm not going to give it to you.' Which just proves how crooked he was. I'll say this about him: Bevers was absolutely crooked."

The bank's attorneys filed a motion for a mistrial and also filed a motion for judgment non obstante veredicto. Judge Bevers overruled both motions, and, in seeking a sort of compromise, issued a decision that pleased no one.[86]

Judge Bevers ruled that the jury's estimation of the value of Plaza Building Corporation was in error and should, therefore, be disregarded. Bevers disagreed with Osenbaugh's explanation that the $1.2 million debt Plaza owed to Maxey should have been credited to him. The judge instead gave the value of Plaza stock as $1.7 million and awarded the plaintiffs a total judgment of $1,961,936.60.

The bank's attorneys gave notice that they would appeal. Judge Bevers's decision to substitute his own values for the jury's finding on the value of Plaza Building Corporation was one of their top points of error. In their own brief to the Amarillo Court of Appeals, Maxey's attorneys also singled out that same decision. The bank's attorneys thought that the substitution made by the judge was too much; Maxey's attorneys thought it was too low.[87]

Chapter 11

"A MAXEY NEVER STARTS ANYTHING HE DOESN'T FINISH."

T he Amarillo Court of Appeals took its time rendering its decision on the bank's petition to overturn the verdict. Final briefs were filed in May 1977, and oral arguments were heard in Amarillo on October 4, 1977. The court was composed of a chief justice and three associate justices. Mary Lou Robinson, appointed to the court in 1973, had been appointed chief justice earlier in 1977.[1]

The newest justice on the panel was from Lubbock. Carlton Dodson, who received his appointment in September 1977, asked to be disqualified from the Maxey case because of his prior association with Evans, Pharr, Trout & Jones. "That was my first official act on the court of appeals," remembers Dodson. "I had been a member of the firm representing the bank, and I wasn't about to get involved in that thing."[2]

A former Texas Tech professor who knew Dodson when he was legal counsel for the university used a colorful saying to describe Dodson's decision to disqualify himself from hearing the case. "What Dodson did," said the former colleague, "reminds me of the old saying, 'Don't take too long to look at a hot horseshoe.'"[3]

The decision in *Maxey v. TCB* was announced August 16, 1978. The jury's verdict and the trial court's judgment were again reversed and the case was remanded to the 72nd District Court. The bank and Homer Maxey were right back where they started in the fall of 1969.[4]

The reversal came as a bitter disappointment for the Maxey side. "By this time, Homer was pretty well spent," says Mike Liles. "He was sixty-seven years old and his health wasn't great. We worried that this was his last time at bat."

In their brief to the court, defense attorneys listed numerous points of error, including their objection to Judge Bevers' substituting his own figure for the jury's finding on Maxey's $1.26 million advance to the Plaza Building Corporation. Chief Justice Robinson granted the point of error, stating that there was "insufficient evidence" for the jurors' decision on that issue, and that Judge Bevers had erred in not granting the defense motion for a mistrial.

In every other argument between the two sides, including the validity of the jury's finding that Citizens National Bank had failed to exercise good faith, that Osenbaugh was a qualified expert, that Maxey was qualified to estimate the value of his own properties, that Citizens National Bank's valuation of Maxey Lumber Company stock was grossly inadequate, and whether the case fell under the concept of res judicata and collateral estoppel, the chief justice denied relief to the defense.

However, because of Judge Bevers's attempt at compromise, ignoring the jury's figures and substituting his own, the appellate court reversed the verdict and sent the case back to district court for a new trial.

For Maxey, the worst part of the ruling was that the Texas Supreme Court had no jurisdiction over appellate court decisions based on insufficient evidence. Liles and Hammett appealed the decision to the Supreme Court anyway but, as expected, the court refused to hear the case.

Two juries had ruled in Maxey's favor. Did the bank's stockholders want the lawyers to try their luck again with another jury?

Charlie Jones was discouraged and depressed by losing the case twice. After the Robinson opinion, however, Jones was in a more upbeat mood. With a sly grin on his face, Jones explained to a fellow attorney that he had just been asked to give an address to a defense lawyers' group. "They want me to speak to them," Jones said. "I guess it's because they think that I know how to lose a big case."[5] E. G. Rodman and William Nöel realized that a new approach was called for as well. They contacted attorney S. Tom Morris in Amarillo and asked him to evaluate the case for the defendants.

"When I came into the picture," recalls Morris, "I talked to Charlie Jones and he asked me to come down and take a look at the case.[6] Charlie said, 'Tom, I just don't think I can win this case, and I probably ought to disqualify. Why don't you come down and take a look at it and see if you can take over for us.'"

Morris remembers finding a "mass of background papers" to go over when he arrived in Lubbock. "It was pretty obvious to me that there was some merit to Maxey's allegations," Morris says, "but his case was puffed up way beyond what it was worth. He wanted millions and it didn't have that kind of value at all. So it was an obvious case for settlement. The bank had some risk, and the question was how much, but I definitely felt that this case should be settled. I met and conferred with Charlie Jones, Pat Maloney, Homer Maxey, and the bankers, and told them we ought to get this case settled if we can."

Pat Maloney, an outstanding and prominent trial lawyer in San Antonio, was hired by Maxey in the early part of 1980. Liles and Hammett were preparing for the next trial when a series of disagreements between Maxey and his attorneys came to a head, and they decided to part company. One of their main points of contention was the issue of taking a new deposition from E. W. Williams. Maxey kept insisting on it; Liles and Hammett were firmly against it.[7]

"Homer could never understand why it would've been a mistake," says Liles. "A deposition from E. W. wasn't going to help us because he would just deny everything. We knew the other side wasn't going to bring him in to testify, and that way, there was nobody to refute Homer's version of what went on. It would have been absolutely ridiculous to have that guy testify."

The disagreement led to a falling out between Maxey and his Fort Worth legal team. Liles and Hammett say there were other disagreements, but the one over deposing Williams was the most important. The attorneys cite it as the reason they were terminated by Maxey.

Liles and Hammett filed a motion for leave to withdraw on April 21, 1980. Maxey then hired Maloney, who had a reputation as a "gunslinger" who scored big judgments for his clients. "He was one of the early personal injury lawyers that got big verdicts," says Morris. "He was a good, effective lawyer and a good friend of mine. I knew him before he started law school."[8]

Maloney promised Maxey that he would get a deposition from Williams and he did follow through. Although E. W. Williams says he doesn't remember it that way, a notice of deposition was filed with the court and scheduled for July 25, 1980.[9]

Morris, meanwhile, met with Williams for the first time and came away impressed. Williams, he decided, was a "very fine banker and a fine person."

Morris also concluded that some of Maxey's allegations against Williams "were not correct."

"When Mr. Maxey got down," says Morris, "he had his gun out for everybody. He was shooting for anybody he thought might have some money that he might be able to get his hands on."

Although Morris believed that Maxey's case was "overblown" and that he had unfairly made a scapegoat of Williams and others, it was clear to him that the bank had made some serious mistakes and that Maxey's petition for relief had merit.

People in Lubbock had come to the conclusion that the bank was wrong long ago. Even under a new name and new ownership, the bank that foreclosed on Homer Maxey never recovered its reputation. Public relations campaigns emphasized that the bank was under new management, but that didn't help much, either. And the fact that it was owned by a Houston-based holding company probably did not work in its favor during the second trial.[10]

A casual encounter with a Texas Commerce executive in Houston gave Rex Fuller an insider's point of view. "He asked where I was from," says Fuller, "and I kind of smarted off to him. I said something about 'Maxey National Bank,' and the guy laughed and said, 'That experience taught us two things: One, don't go a long ways out of your territory when you buy a bank, and two, don't buy a bank that has a troubled image.'"

The fact that Citizens National Bank was damaged goods at the time it was acquired by Texas Commerce was acknowledged in internal documents obtained by Hammett before the second trial. Seeking additional documents, Hammett had subpoenaed several current and former bank officials, requiring them to appear in district court for oral depositions and bring with them all "minutes, reports, memoranda, letters, business records, and any other documents" in possession of Texas Commerce Bank similar to those that had been provided to the Federal Reserve relating to the acquisition of Citizens National Bank. A series of excerpts from the original documents were provided so that there would be no doubt as to the type of materials Maxey's lawyers wanted to see.

Page 6:[11]

After the Bank had begun to deteriorate in the mid-1950s, control was acquired by non-resident owners in 1961. Shortly thereafter, top management was replaced, investment and operating policies were changed, and the Bank adopted a flamboyant approach to business development and lending.

... 1964, the Bank had become adversely involved with three different individuals who owned sizable, uncollectible loans.

... and the third (Maxey), which has been given statewide publicity for over six years, has damaged the Bank far more than the loan of $1.25 million which has been written off (See pages 12–19)

Page 7:

On February 16, 1966, the Bank foreclosed on the Maxey properties which had been mortgaged as collateral for the loan. Immediately thereafter, a suit was filed against the Bank which later was amended to include several of its officers, all of its directors, some of its attorneys and even some of its customers, alleging total damages in excess of $30 million. The allegations of the Plaintiffs, given wide publicity in the area, included the charge that the Bank had conspired to purchase very valuable properties at the foreclosure sale at a small fraction of their value. This suit took three months to try beginning in October 1969. The trial ended with the jury awarding a judgment against the Bank for approximately $2.5 million. This was reversed by the court of civil appeals, with the decision of this court being upheld later by the Supreme Court of Texas in June 1971. A subsequent proceeding in district court resulted in a summary judgment being granted in favor of the Bank. This latter action is now on appeal.

Regardless of the merits of this suit, the Bank has suffered severely from the adverse publicity given to the litigation over the years and will have difficulty in regaining its reputation for fair dealing with its customers."

Page 10:

... Moreover, the larger and more knowledgeable shareholders have agreed to continue in escrow $8 of the per share price of $28 to provide for the contingency of an adverse settlement of the Maxey suit. Finally, as a further indication of the difficulty which the present shareholders have had in managing the Bank, it is noted that the selling price of $28 represents the exact price paid by the controlling shareholders 11 years ago.

Pages 46–47:

The statements made in Article IV of the Stock Purchase Agreement made as of March 1, 1972 between Texas Commerce Bancshares, Inc. and E. G. Rodman and W. D. Nöel, such Article IV entitled "Maxey Claims," and providing, among other things, for the delivery by Rodman and Nöel to Texas Commerce Bancshares, Inc., of the value of at least $2.5 million for the purpose of holding Citizens National Bank of Lubbock harmless from the "Maxey Claims."

Pages 49–50:

Such Security Agreement-Pledge, being Exhibit A to the above-mentioned Stock Purchase Agreement entered into as of March 1, 1972.

Pages 51–52:

The Stock Purchase Agreement entered into as of March 6, 1972, between Texas Commerce Bancshares, Inc., and the stockholders of Citizens National Bank of Lubbock signing such Agreement, providing for, among other things, the pro rata part of such signing shareholders in the liability of said Bank arising out of the "Maxey Claims."

Attorneys for Rodman and Nöel filed a motion to quash the subpoena that contained the above excerpts. At the time of the hearing in 72nd District Court, Judge Pat Moore was in deteriorating condition due to ovarian cancer. Moore signed the motion to quash the subpoena on October 16, 1974, which was one of her last official acts before her death the following January.

A subpoena ordering Thomas McDade, an attorney for Texas Commerce Bank, to give an oral deposition was also quashed; however, in response to written interrogatories provided by Hammett, McDade provided answers to some, but not all, questions. When contacted for an interview, McDade wrote that the events of the case returned to him "vividly." McDade maintained that although Texas Commerce Bank was not liable in the case and had no financial exposure from the outcome, "we had great concern over its effect on the public image and acceptance of us in the Lubbock market. At the time, it seemed that we could not shake the stigma that it attached to the bank and we felt handicapped for a number of years."

McDade represented Texas Commerce Bank during the negotiations with Rodman and Nöel for the acquisition of Citizens National Bank in a package deal that also included San Angelo National Bank and Permian National Bank & Trust in Odessa. "We viewed [Rodman and Nöel] as men of the highest integrity and very fair," wrote McDade. "Without hesitation, they accepted and retained any liability that the Maxey matter carried."[12]

Of all the bad press the bank received during the Maxey case, a feature in the *Fort Worth Star-Telegram* probably collected the largest amount of negative information into one place. Published November 4, 1979, just two months before the third Maxey trial was set to begin, the article set a dramatic tone with its headline: "Golden Fleece or Just Yarn? Homer Maxey's Story One of Rags to Riches to Rags."[13]

The article suggests that some effort was made to present both points of view. Early in the piece, the reader learns that the *Amarillo Globe-Times* voted E. W. Williams as its Man of the Year in 1976, the year that his former employer lost the verdict in the second Maxey jury trial. In the same paragraph, Williams is described as "a multimillionaire . . . regarded by his associates as one of the most successful and ruthless bankers in West Texas."

The article said that Barclay Ryall blamed Maxey's problems on poor financial judgment, not any capriciousness on behalf of the bank. Despite the fact that Williams was the man who gave Ryall his job at Citizens National Bank, the banker had some criticism for his former boss, saying that he had taken on more responsibility than he could handle. "Some guys can handle a lot of loans and others cannot," Ryall was quoted as saying. "If he had had more time, he would not have been so badly fooled by Mr. Maxey's problems."

The article had both Ryall and Chauncey Trout scoffing at the legitimacy of the Drumwright deal. Ryall was quoted as saying that the bank would have been "overjoyed" if Maxey had turned up a genuine offer on his properties, and that the notion that Charlie Jones would make a phone call canceling the deal was "absurd."

Several quotes were attributed to an anonymous "longtime Lubbock attorney" whose favorable impression of Maxey was quite evident. At one point, the anonymous lawyer professed the opinion that most people in Lubbock felt that "Homer just ran into a little bad luck and the bank took advantage of it."

Sam Levenson, who was a vice president at Citizens during the Maxey foreclosure, sprinkled his words with bitterness as he voiced the opposite point of view. "The Maxeys were the financial aristocracy of Lubbock County," Levenson said. "The name Maxey was like King Kong in Lubbock." Levenson's quotation could have served as a caption for the photo on page one, which superimposed a close-up of Homer's face on the side of the Texas Commerce Bank Tower, taking up at least five stories of the building. If some magical transformation had caused Homer Maxey to balloon to the same proportions, he would have been even bigger than King Kong himself. Perhaps the *Fort Worth Star-Telegram* photo editor was inspired by the thought that

Sam Levenson's nightmares were haunted, not by a giant gorilla scaling the Empire State Building, but a giant Homer Maxey shaking down the Texas Commerce Bank building.

The article also quoted another former director of Citizens National Bank, Dub Rushing, who had known Maxey since childhood.

> Rushing said anyone without Maxey's determination would have given up on the lawsuit years ago. He recalled, however, that Maxey's mother had always taught her son that "a Maxey never starts anything he doesn't finish."

Maxey, he said, was "a man of the highest integrity . . . always way ahead of his times." "If he had been able to have lasted six months or one year longer," Rushing said, "the properties he bought would have turned to gold. They'd probably be worth $40–$50 million today."

The reporters also sought the opinion of Retha Martin, another entrepreneurial giant of the South Plains who was, like Williams, known for his aggressive streak. Martin was a former chairman of Citizens National Bank's board of directors and had been Williams's friend for many years. Despite those ties, Martin said that Williams's handling of the Maxey affair reflected poor judgment.

The *Star-Telegram* feature states that Williams had told the paper that the Maxey suit was the only time he had ever been individually named in a lawsuit. The article pointed out, however, that Williams had failed to mention a suit filed in New Mexico involving kickback allegations as well as one brought against Amarillo National Bank (in which he was the only named individual) alleging mishandling of trust accounts to his own advantage. At least one other lawsuit had been settled by the time the article went to print. Because one of the provisions of the settlement was that neither party discuss it in public, no details were provided, other than Williams's being named as a defendant.

The *Star-Telegram* reporters made an effort to give Williams an opportunity to acquit himself and the bank in the arena of public perception. It can be assumed that the banker had been advised by Texas Commerce's attorneys (as well as his own) to curtail his statements. Even bearing that in mind, it can be said that Williams's pungent responses did not do much to improve his characterization as the villain of the piece. Typical of these is Williams's aforementioned description of the private foreclosure sale. "It doesn't sound good, but it was legal," he said.

Another action by Williams in the "doesn't sound good" category was the sudden notice given to Maxey—late on the night before—that foreclosure proceedings would commence the following afternoon. Williams said he was justified because he had just learned that Maxey was diverting his assets. "That's the thing the juries have never understood," Williams said. However, if this accusation is true, it appears that the attorneys for the bank did not think it was important to bring up in either of the jury trials or in any of the many briefs filed in Lubbock County District Court or any other court in the appellate chain.

Later in the article, the writer repeated Williams's claim that bankers were not often sued for their business decisions, but with the rise of "consumerism," it was becoming much more common. "You don't have these [legal] problems when you've made a good deal," Williams said. "It is unfortunate that business morals are such today that people don't want to pay their just debts."

Williams admitted to the reporters that Maxey's lawsuit was a continuing "source of irritation." The banker told the newspaper it was "a shame, a disgrace" for Maxey, with all his experience and talents, to spend thirteen years on "this magnificent obsession." Williams did not comment on the accusations and rumors that someone connected with the defendants' side of the case were behind suspected acts of sabotage against the plaintiffs. But Ed Drumright did have something to say about it.

> An indication of the strong feelings aroused by all the financial and legal maneuvering is Drumwright's suspicions about a plane crash he was involved in April 4, 1966. . . . "I'm sure there's a lot of people connected in and around that bank that would have felt it easier if I wasn't around," Drumwright said, because of his key testimony in Maxey's behalf.[14]

The *Star-Telegram* article also pointed out the synchronicity between the murder of E. C. Mullendore III and the pretrial investigation into the Maxey case: "Mullendore's deposition in the case was taken at the Osage County Courthouse in Pawhuska, Oklahoma, about a year later. A few days after Mullendore gave his deposition, he was murdered."

At the time the Maxeys were interviewed for the *Fort Worth Star-Telegram* piece, they were preparing to move to a condominium in Granbury, a location chosen because it was closer to Liles and Hammett's office. Homer was packing up his voluminous files. Melba was worried about his health and finding it hard to avoid being consumed with bitterness. "I wonder sometimes if he'll ever live through it," she was quoted as saying. "You can see the palsy in his hands. He's been under such tremendous pressure . . . I'm sure the bank would like to know it's about to kill him."

Later, she added: "He is so determined, he'll do what he has to do. It may kill him but he'll do what he has to do. It's my job to try to take care of him. Even after fifteen years I don't understand it all, but I'll stick by him."[15]

Melba Maxey wasn't the only person worried about Homer's health. His daughters began to notice, too. "At first we didn't realize how much the lawsuit had taken its toll on him," says Carla. "He was beyond repair, you know."[16]

Maxey's health was also on the minds of his former attorneys, Liles and Hammett. As much as they were saddened and frustrated by the falling out with Maxey, they wished him well. "He deserved to win that case and we didn't want him to end up dying before he got there," says Liles. "He was under a terrible amount of stress for a long time. Just in the three years or so that Harold and I represented him, you could see how much he had aged."[17]

Maxey's new attorney, Pat Maloney, was joined in the case by attorneys from Bayne, Snell & Krause, also of San Antonio. The new petition Maloney filed in 72nd District Court not only pleaded for financial recompense for the plaintiffs but also sought damages for pain, suffering, and mental anguish for a total sum of $41.76 million.

In comparison to previous petitions filed in the case, the narrative history of Maxey's adversarial relationship with Citizens National Bank is stripped down in the Maloney petition, and the tone is more dramatic. Morris drafted an answer to the original petition, asking that many of the statements and allegations be stricken and numerous parts revised. A number of the allegations in the petition seemed to confuse the lawsuit with a tort action, and Morris knew that the law would not allow such a combination.[18]

A date was set for E. W. Williams to give a deposition, although Williams says he doesn't remember a thing about it, and no deposition notice can be found in the records of the district clerk's office in Lubbock County.[19] Maxey's determination to have Williams deposed again continues to puzzle Mike Liles, Harold Hammett, and Ken Bowlin. None of them can offer any reasonable explanation for what Maxey hoped the deposition might reveal. Whether coincidence or not, rapid progress was made toward resolution of the lawsuit within days of the date that Williams was to be deposed.

Legal representatives of both parties met and signed the legal documents

Left to right: Bill Goodacre, Melba Maxey, Jill Goodacre, Glenna Goodacre, Tim Goodacre, and Homer Maxey, in 1977. Courtesy of the Maxey family.

agreeing to settle the case for $2.2 million on September 22, 1980. Adjusted
for inflation, the amount of the settlement would be $6,146,677 in 2012 dol-
lars.[20]

Homer and Melba Maxey would live in comfort for the rest of their lives. A
portion of the settlement went to pay attorney's fees. Many other debts accumulated over the past fifteen years were loans from friends and family members, a good many of which had been long since written off. The Maxeys also
enjoyed the largess of their younger daughter, Glenna Goodacre. By 1980,
Glenna's art had brought her great fame and fortune, and she was happy to
extend financial support to the parents she adored. That they had achieved a
measure of vindication and peace in their long struggle coincident with her
own success was a sweet synchronicity.

When the Maxeys were ready to buy a new residence in Lubbock, they
hired Bobby Day, a longtime friend of the family. Day, who had been Bill
Goodacre's partner in a real estate agency until the Goodacres moved to Boul-
der, Colorado, was an outgoing type, a former college basketball player and an
avid supporter of Texas Tech sports. "Homer had seats on the fifty-yard line
for Red Raider games," says Day. "When he finally quit buying them, I got
his seats."

Day found a comfortable townhome for the Maxeys in northwest Lubbock, just north of Fourth Street at Slide Road. As Day remembers it, the home sold for about $400,000.

Just shy of his seventieth birthday, Homer Maxey had no plans to spend his remaining years in quiet retirement.

"Homer had rented these offices in the First National Bank Building," says Day. "We went to the Lubbock Club for dinner with Homer and Melba, Glenna and Bill, and some other people, and after we ate everybody went downstairs to have a look at the offices. Everything was first class. They were really, really nice. I was thinking it was probably a lot more than he really needed. So, I made a statement, kind of joking, 'Goddamn, Homer, I think you missed the runway.' or something. Boy, he got mad."

Despite having well-appointed offices, Maxey no longer seemed to have the Midas touch. "He hired some of the top mortgage people in town to run the office," recalls Day. "I think he had too much expense. Sometimes I'd ask him how it was going and he'd say, 'Bobby, used to, I'd have people coming to me. I'd have people waiting outside my office waiting to see me. Now, I've got to go see them.' I'd tell him, 'Well, you made it the first time, didn't you?' and he'd say, 'Yeah, Bobby, but it's a whole lot harder to make the second time.'"[21]

But Maxey kept plugging away. Ken Flagg, who had numerous building projects in Dallas at the time, remembers regular encounters with Maxey on Southwest flights to and from Dallas. "He would be there with his briefcase and he'd have four or five projects that were supposed to be absolute winners, and he was going to finance them and make them work. He didn't quit trying. Boy, he was gung-ho, he was always going to make something happen."

Despite his much-reduced financial stature and clout, Maxey still carried himself with an air of authority. "He was very demanding of anybody who knew him," says Flagg, "He'd expect you to do things for him, get information for him and things like that. He just took it for granted that you wanted to do it, and I did."[22]

In the last decade of their lives, Homer and Melba Maxey saw their daughter, Glenna Goodacre, enjoy the kind of success and acclaim most creative individuals only dream about. She had become an internationally recognized artist, with her works exhibited in galleries and museums around the world and in public places in almost every state in the country.

Glenna's longtime studio manager, Dan Anthony, always made certain that Homer and Melba were kept apprised of the latest developments in their daughter's career. In 1988, for example, Homer and Melba basked in reflected glory during the public dedication of five new bronzes at the Sea World sculpture garden in San Antonio. Glenna had been commissioned to do bronze sculptures of Scott Joplin, Katherine Anne Porter, Barbara Jordan, Stephen F. Austin, and William B. Travis.

"I was always in touch with Homer and Melba," says Dan. "I always sent them clippings and info and invitations to Glenna's shows. Homer always called me 'My man Dan.' They were so thrilled about her success."[23]

It is not clear just when Homer realized he could no longer justify leasing the offices at First National Bank, but by the late 1980s he rented a much more modest storefront location in Winchester Square, a shopping center at Fiftieth Street and Indiana Avenue. According to Bobby Day, Maxey spent his time at his office continuing to study the files and records he had amassed since the foreclosure. "Homer was writing a book about his lawsuit," says Day. "He told me it was going to blow the lid off everything. That's all Homer did his last years, working on that book."

Day was disappointed to learn that neither of Maxey's daughters had possession of the manuscript. Glenna remembers that, after her father's death, her mother fretted over what to do with Maxey's huge archive.

"She had a warehouse full of this stuff," says Glenna. "Daddy was so meticulous. Everything had to have a file with a number and the right color label and everything. There were boxes and boxes of records and files, transcripts, and everything. She asked me, 'What are we going to do with all this stuff?' Finally she burned it."[24]

"Homer was obsessed about this book he was writing," says Day. "Toward the end he was getting paranoid. He was afraid someone was going to come kill him in the office, knock him in the head or something. All because he was writing this book."

"Daddy was losing his cognizance toward the end of his life," says Glenna. "He wanted to go with us to meet with a banker about a loan. The banker said, 'Well, what about all this other money you owe?' We didn't know he still owed debts."

Homer turned seventy-nine on March 14, 1990. At a testimonial dinner, I. A. Stephens delivered a speech singing the praises of his two longtime friends and kindred spirits, Homer Maxey and Dub Rushing. In a twenty-minute speech, Stephens condensed the past sixty years of the three men's lives into a highlight reel of business deals, marriages, the war, the Depression, and the building boom that came afterward. "Remember all the fun we had blow-

The obverse of the Sacagawea coin, designed by Glenna Goodacre. Sacagawea was the Native American woman who helped Lewis and Clark find their way through the mountains. Copyright U.S. Mint.

Melba and Homer Maxey, at Sea World of San Antonio in 1984, with Glenna's bronze portrait of Scott Joplin in the background. Courtesy of Dan Anthony.

A Maxey

ing and going?" he said at one point. The text of Stephens's speech isn't just a tribute to the virtues of two good friends, but to the joys of making deals, building, and wildcatting in the oil fields of West Texas.

Stephens made it clear that the men didn't just love money, they loved the art of the deal, including taking on risk. Some of the oil wells they invested in turned out to be dry holes, but their profits on other drilling projects were more than sufficient to let them laugh about their failures.

"A group of business people used to meet at noon at Homer's Plainsman Hotel on Avenue Q," Stephens said. "The manager always had a round table ready for us. At these luncheons, we discussed the local and national events and often made deals. We didn't need a contract, only a handshake to seal a deal."

Stephens had moved from Lubbock decades before, but he and Maxey and Rushing always remained in touch. "Business deals are simply part of life's game," Stephens said, "but true friendships are life's reward and God's blessing. I have been blessed . . . with friends such as Homer and Dub, whose support and constancy have strengthened me and given me courage and faith for sixty years."

Stephens summed up Homer's decade-and-a-half legal battle in just a few words. Maxey's ranching venture, he explained, "required a large line of bank credit; no problem unless the bank is crooked. In 1966, without sufficient reason, the bank demanded full payment of the entire loan. Homer found himself tied up in court for the next fifteen years . . ."

Then Stephens announced that "Homer is now involved in what he thinks may be his final venture; a new bank for Lubbock, in the best possible location. He has honored me by asking me to be a director and I have accepted." Stephens held great admiration and affection for Rushing and Maxey, who had also honored him at a luncheon two years earlier. In his conclusion, Stephens said "Dub and Homer have helped to make Lubbock the great city it is today and they will live forever through their contributions to 'the Hub of the Plains.'" If that line sounded elegiac, it was a hint of the somber subtext of the occasion. Maxey had been diagnosed with terminal cancer. He had only a few months to live.[25]

A lesion on one of his eyelids had proven to be the primary site of melanoma, which had metastasized. Maxey made frequent visits to his dermatologist to have lesions checked and removed, yet the site on his eyelid had been discovered too late for effective treatment.

"Homer called me," remembers Ken Bowlin, "and he said, 'I have cancer and they say it's terminal.' I asked him what I could do for him and he said, 'Nothing, just come see me,' and I promised I would, but I didn't make it in time. I never talked to Homer again."

The same dermatologist also treated Bowlin. Bowlin says that during one of his exams, he asked the doctor why he hadn't found the lesion on Maxey's eye sooner. The dermatologist explained, "When he came to see me, he always had his eyes wide open and he was always talking. With his eyelid open you couldn't see it. I never thought to tell him to close his eyes."[26]

Homer Maxey died on July 28, 1990. At seventy-nine, he had outlived his brothers by decades, defying the odds, accomplishing more, fighting harder, too stubborn to quit and too tough to die. With his quick wit and earthy sense of humor, Homer might have cracked an inappropriate joke or two if he had realized in advance that his childhood friend, Dub, who died in 2007, would outlive him by almost seventeen years. Rushing played tennis every day into his nineties and remained active in business and civic affairs.[27]

After Homer's death, Dan continued to drop in to see Melba whenever he came back to Lubbock. "She was a lovely person," he says. "She'd always whip up something, like deviled eggs, and we'd drink tall vodka and Diet Cokes and smoke Virginia Slims."

Melba Maxey died on January 26, 1995, at the age of eighty-three. She was buried alongside Homer in the City of Lubbock Cemetery. In February, the Texas State Senate passed S.R. 229, Senate Resolution in Memory of Melba Maxey. The resolution was sponsored by State Senator John T. Montford, whose political career prior to being elected state senator included four years as Lubbock County district attorney. The resolution praised Melba Maxey for being "an exemplary lady and a leader in her community" and "a woman of integrity, strength, and generosity [who] gave unselfishly of her time to others . . . Melba Maxey was a devoted wife, mother, and grandmother, and she leaves behind memories that will be treasured forever by her family and many friends."[28]

EPILOGUE

Homer Maxey would have turned one hundred on March 14, 2011. If he had returned home for a centennial visit, he would have found a city that has continued to grow in size and influence. By comparison with Homer's second decade, 1920–1930, when the population increased fivefold, growth has slowed somewhat, but the 80 percent increase in the preceding twenty years is still quite impressive.

Many changes in Lubbock have occurred since Homer's time. Most surprising, perhaps, is the lifting of the ban on packaged alcohol and liquor by the drink. The vote to "go wet" countywide passed by a margin of two to one in 2009. Homer and Melba would have approved.

Texas Tech, the campus Homer first visited with his father when it was a raw construction site, continues to progress in both size and prestige. As a dedicated booster of all things related to Tech, and football in particular, Homer would be sure to arrive in time for the first game of the season. At Jones Stadium, however, it might take a moment for him to find his bearings. After inspecting the new façade and other renovations, his attention would be drawn to the adjacent Marsha Sharp Freeway, formerly the Brownfield Highway. On the other side of the freeway there was once a town called Monterey, one of two rival towns whose residents had the wisdom and foresight to join forces and work together as a single community.

Homer would find some contemporary sights less pleasing to the eye than others. As of 2011, the once impressive headquarters of Homer G. Maxey & Co. (later, Fields & Co., then Ferguson's), remained a derelict compound of vacant buildings. The Plainsman Hotel on Avenue Q, hailed as a modernistic gem a half-century ago, was serving as a retirement home—a function not

The Vietnam Women's Memorial by Glenna Goodacre, on the National Mall in Washington, D.C. Photo by Gregory Staley. Copyright Vietnam Women's Memorial Foundation, Inc.

Attorney C. L. Mike Schmidt, who married Glenna Goodacre in 1995. Courtesy of Mike Schmidt.

Broke, Not Broken

The Irish Memorial, by Glenna Goodacre, dedicated at Penn's Landing in Philadelphia in 2003. The work stands twelve feet high. Photograph by Marcia Ward/ImageMaker Denver CO.

quite as glamorous as its first decade of existence, but a useful purpose nonetheless.

Homer's heart would swell with pride as he drove the length of Glenna Goodacre Boulevard, the street named in her honor in 2005. Among the other highlights of Glenna's success and acclaim in recent years, her design for the Sacagawea dollar coin was minted in 2000, and in 2003 she unveiled her largest piece to date: the massive Irish Memorial at Penn's Landing, Philadelphia.

In March 2007 in Santa Fe, where Glenna has lived since 1983, she suffered a near-fatal and mysterious brain injury. Her fight to survive and recover reminded family and friends of the famous Maxey stubborn streak, as it took a tremendous amount of strength and willpower—a different kind, perhaps, than her father had summoned during his own struggles, but as Glenna likes to say, "I'm an exact replica of Homer."

Homer's long fight to regain his fortune and his reputation ended at the county courthouse in 1980. From the outside, the building itself looks much the same, although Avenue H, which ran along the east side of the courthouse, was renamed Buddy Holly Avenue in 1996. Time has been less kind to the former home offices of the defendants in the Maxey case, the high-rise tower at the corner of Avenue K and Fourteenth Street, the Omni building, which began its life as the headquarters of Citizens National Bank of Lubbock. After

Epilogue

Lubbock developer Delbert McDougal says he wanted the Overton Hotel design to echo the look of the old Pioneer Hotel on Broadway, as a nod to that historic structure. McDougal is also respectful of Homer Maxey's legacy to the city. Photo by O'Jay Barbee, used with his permission.

Homer and Melba, at home, looking fairly contented. Courtesy of the Maxey family.

Broke, Not Broken

standing vacant for years, its floors and walls spattered with pigeon droppings and feathers, the building began shedding its marble siding slabs, becoming a safety hazard. In 2012 a contractor was hired to remove the entire marble skin. As of this writing, there does not seem to be a future for the structure other than condemnation and demolition.

Another downtown site of interest to Homer Maxey and his partisans is over on Broadway just north of the old bank—the Pioneer Hotel building, a structure that suffered years of decay and indignity, but with a happier outcome. The downtown landmark was purchased in 2005 by McDougal Properties and, over the next half-dozen years, renovated from the ground up, with the final touches on high-end condominiums and retail spaces nearing completion in 2012. Delbert McDougal, the man responsible for converting the North Overton neighborhood from slum to urban showcase of mixed-use development, was hired by the city as its "master developer" and placed in charge of renovating the entire downtown area.

Homer would no doubt appreciate the fact that, as Glenna Goodacre Boulevard traverses Overton Park, it connects the Texas Tech campus on its western end to the downtown business district at Avenue Q. The coming of the university in 1924, which brought the Maxeys to Lubbock, ensured the future growth and prosperity of the young town and the region as a whole. Homer also dreamed of bringing new life to the downtown area when he bought the Pioneer Hotel in 1960. As with many of the projects planned and built during his heyday, his thinking was ahead of its time.

Someday, when downtown Lubbock resumes the role as the vibrant heart of commercial and cultural activity, some occasion will see an assemblage of dynamic individuals from various areas of expertise and concern, and as they discuss their ideas and develop action plans, someone will utter the terms "empire builders" or "king makers," remembering that the Pioneer was one of the places Homer Maxey, Dub Rushing, Dub Rogers, Charles Maedgen, Charlie Guy, and others had their round-table meetings, discussing the needs and problems of the day and then deciding how they were going to resolve each one.

Somewhere, Homer Maxey is smiling.

Acknowledgments

The authors express their gratitude to those persons who have co-operated and assisted by contributing background information, assisting in research, and helping authenticate factual content for this book. It is inevitable that the names of some individuals who helped us reach our goals may have temporarily slipped our minds; but even if it was only to remind us of the name of one last person whom we should approach for an interview, we sincerely appreciate your efforts. Some who have provided vital information have asked that they not be recognized for privacy reasons.

Glenna Goodacre, the younger of Homer Maxey's two daughters, initiated the idea of writing this book. First, she answered Broadus Spivey's entreaties to talk about Homer with so many intriguing anecdotes that Broadus eventually suggested, "Glenna, you ought to write a book about Homer." Later, responding to Broadus's further entreaties to tackle the project, she said, "Broadus, you knew Daddy, why don't *you* write the book?"

As the project got under way, our many interviews with Glenna about her father not only helped fill out our narrative of what this man did but helped reveal who the real man was, in addition to the public persona described in the news media and throughout the litigation.

Glenna's husband, C. L. Mike Schmidt, her studio manager, Dan Anthony, and Matt Suhre of Matt Suhre Photography were vital in helping make this project a reality. They helped locate interview subjects and provided documents and photographs of the family and of Glenna's works of art.

Homer's eldest daughter, Carla Maxey Elliott, who died in 2013 at the age of seventy-seven, was a very energetic and valuable contributor. Carla shared memories of her father and was excited to know that his full story would finally be told. Had it not been for Carla and her extended family, we would not have located the scrapbook chronicling his experiences in the Pacific theater of war during World War II.

The mass of material furnished by Carla, along with the boxes of photos, documents, journals, newspaper collections, and other items from Glenna, allowed us to assemble an impressive archive of Homer Maxey biographical materials.

Other members of the Maxey family generously shared their time and stories with us. Kathleen Maxey Luther, Marcia Abbott, DeEtte Maxey Cobb, Bill Goodacre, and Tommy Elliott shared with us their many amazing and amusing stories about tense times in the Maxey family. They told of Homer having his sons-in-law working overtime to keep his empire afloat, with Tommy scrambling to manage two financially ailing hotels, and with Bill hauling cattle at the same time that he was managing apartment complexes.

Patricia "Pat" Hall, wordsmith and grammarian of immense talent and personal friend of Broadus and Ruth Ann Spivey since the 1960s, has played an important and indispensable role in researching, constructing an outline of these complicated events, writing and critically reviewing materials pertaining to the story of the bank, Homer, the trials, and the appeals.

Pat Hall and Broadus were in the Lubbock County district clerk's office studying the microfilm records of the two jury trials when they discovered the actual file of the first jury trial was scheduled to be shredded. Barbara Sucsy, the elected and popular District Clerk of Lubbock County and friend of the legal community, allowed Pat and Broadus to retrieve those files to study and copy portions. They were vital to obtaining an accurate and complete verification of the testimony, exhibits, court rulings, and jury summations in the first jury trial.

The files containing the documentation of the second jury trial had apparently already been shredded. Pat and Broadus had to settle for the meticulous review of microfilm for similar documentary information from the second trial.

The second greatest fortune was in locating and being able to personally interview three lawyers who actually participated in the jury trials. The only three of these still living were Ken Bowlin, Harold Hammett, and Mike Liles. We were also fortunate to be able to interview S. Tom Morris, another great lawyer. Morris took over as lead counsel for Texas Commerce Bank in 1980 and convinced his client that a third trial would be ill-advised. Morris brokered a settlement with Maxey later that year.

Ken Bowlin, a longtime friend of Broadus from his days (1962 to 1971) as a member of the Lubbock County Bar Association, was living in Del Rio and San Antonio. Along with Jim Cade and Alton Griffin, Ken tried the first case to a successful conclusion. That experience, though highly rewarding, was a financial disaster for these lawyers as their representation of Homer was on a contingent fee basis. When that verdict was appealed, it was not financially possible for them to continue giving their full time to this once-in-a-lifetime case, so they withdrew as counsel for Homer Maxey.

Then Mr. Maxey located Harold Hammett and Mike Liles in Ft. Worth. They were intrigued with Homer's recitation of his plight and their study of the documents in the case, and they signed on to represent Homer—also on a contingent fee basis, as Homer had very little money to support his battle.

Denzil Bevers, who was judge of the 72nd District Court, and who presided over the second trial, was cooperative in sharing his recollection of the facts, though his memory of the trial events varies considerably from that of Mike Liles. Denzil and Broadus have been friends since the sixties, long before he became a judge.

Broadus introduced Jesse to Forrest Bowers, under whose tutelage Broadus literally learned the art of practicing law and became a trial lawyer. Forrest is recognized as one of the all-time greatest and most respected trial lawyers of Texas, although he practiced primarily in the Lubbock–South Plains area. Forrest knew, remembered and shared his observations of all the key players. He was an especially close friend of Charlie Jones, Denzil Bevers, Alton Griffin, and Ken Bowlin. Ken and Forrest grew up just a few miles from each other—Forrest near Dunn, and Ken from nearby Hermleigh. Both were close to Snyder, Texas, and both were World War II heroes. Like Homer Maxey, they would also deny the hero appellation, but they were heroes.

Flo Schubert did an awesome amount of typing and organizing information fed to her by Jesse and Broadus, and Elizabeth Denson was a proofreader of rough drafts and storage specialist with a talent for finding and retrieving documents and news articles that otherwise might have been lost to the ages.

John Higgs, who is clerk for and grandson of Broadus, is entitled to recognition and appreciation because he was a tremendous help to both Broadus and Jesse. John was responsible for indexing and categorizing every document and copying the almost-forty-year-old case files. John has worked closely with Broadus in his law firm for almost fifteen years, but this was one of the greatest undertakings he had ever faced. Reviewing the files and piecing together the fragments from the trial documents was both tedious and fascinating, as John has a detective's disposition.

The staff at the Southwest Collection at Texas Tech University is entitled to special thanks for helping the authors utilize their amazing and extensive historical archives. The Dolph Briscoe Center for American History at the University of Texas at Austin was another invaluable resource.

Roger Carl Schaefer, a retired political science professor at Texas Tech, read an early draft of the manuscript and offered comments and encouragement.

Historian and bookseller Len Ainsworth was generous with his time, expertise, and careful eye, finding copies of the books and loaning them to us with lightning speed.

At Lubbock City Hall, Sally Still Abbe and Sarah Hensley guided us through city planning archives and other records, helping us with many questions and needs. City Secretary Rebecca Garza, Deputy City Secretary Thomas Harris III, and other staff members helped us track down answers to several esoteric historical questions.

The authors' personal meetings with various individuals often gave us more detailed and nuanced information than could be gleaned through hours of the traditional type of research. A luncheon with Jane Livermore Wofford and Johnny Hughes, for example, enriched this book immensely.

Marci Morrison, Gretchen Otto, and numerous others helped copyedit early drafts of the manuscript and assisted in other ways.

Jesse Sublett wants to thank attorney Craig Barker for handling a copyright infringement case for him during the summer of 2009, which prompted Craig to introduce and recommend Jesse to Broadus. Thank you, Catherine Keeney Bonner, for a timely communication about the Keeney family.

Tony Privett introduced the authors to Lubbock developer Delbert McDougal, who generously shared his thoughts on the legacy of Homer Maxey. O'Jay Barbee contributed the great photo of the Overton Hotel, built by Delbert McDougal in a style that consciously echoes that of the historic Pioneer Hotel, which also plays an important role in the Homer Maxey story.

The authors consulted Don Abbe on a number of issues. Tommy Denton provided biographical details about his father, the late Texas Supreme Court Justice James G. Denton. Phyllis Brown, City of Lubbock Community Development, shared generously of her time and knowledge.

Dan Law, Roy Middleton, Rex Fuller, Bobby Day, Charlie Joplin, William R. Shaver (retired US district judge), and Ken Flagg enriched this narrative considerably. Ken, for example, shared his unforgettable image of an aging Homer, ever the go-getter, with his briefcase and "four or five projects that were supposed to be absolute winners . . . he was gung-ho, he was always going to make something happen."

Meredith McClain, Jane Holden Kelly, Don Bundock, and Berwyn Tisdel all helped us track down the real story behind the adobe house ban legend in Lubbock. Jo Anne Griffin, Jo Love Nelson, and the late Margaret Talkington shared their extensive personal recollections, which added realism and flavor to our history of Maxey family.

Gwendolyn Murphy served on the jury during the first trial, and she vividly described the tension in the courtroom during those long weeks, along with her overall impression of the opposing sides: Maxey and his attorneys seemed credible and likeable; the bankers and their attorneys came off as arrogant and unlikeable. Dorothy A. Drumwright recalled significant and important details to round out our account of one of the murkiest aspects of the Maxey case, the so-called "Drumwright deal."

Special appreciation goes to all those individuals who had close ties—either personal or professional—with the defense side of the case who took the time to assist us anyway. We sincerely appreciate the fact that E. W. Williams, Jr., was willing to answer our questions and offer his version of the events. Our special thanks also go out to S. Tom Morris, Jack Flygare, Jack Tidwell, Carlton Dodson, Bobby Moody, and Thomas McDade.

David Hughes, who had actually been sued by Maxey, went the extra mile, in the interest of accuracy, sending follow-up messages and a written chronology of the case from his point of view. David's recollections included the role of his father, who served as president of Citizens National Bank in a calmer era—before E. W. Williams, Jr., took over. David and Broadus have also been friends since the sixties, and both practiced law during the same period of time in Lubbock.

Finally, the authors want to thank Texas Tech University Press, particularly editor Judith Keeling and series editor Gordon Morris Bakken, for believing in this book and playing the final role in bringing Homer Maxey's story to the public.

Appendix 1:

A Chronology

of the Maxey

Litigation

1. *Homer G. Maxey v. Citizens National Bank of Lubbock, Texas, et al.*, filed in US District Court for the Northern District of Oklahoma, March 15, 1966. Dismissed for want of prosecution November 2, 1970.
2. *Homer G. Maxey, et al. v. Citizens National Bank of Lubbock, Texas, et al.* (No. 51,441), filed in the 72nd District Court of Lubbock County, Texas. Original petition filed July 11, 1966. Amended Original Petition filed September 29, 1966. Trial began October 28, 1969, ended January 14, 1970, Judge Patricia S. Moore. Final judgment signed March 3, 1970. Verdict for Maxey, $1.2 million actual, $1.5 million exemplary damages.
3. *Melba Maxey, et al. v. Citizens National Bank of Lubbock, et al.*, 432 S.W.2d 722, May 27, 1968. Amarillo Court of Appeals, Northcutt. Affirmed denial of injunction, temporary restraining order affirmed trial court.
4. *Homer G. Maxey, et al. v. E. G. Rodman*, 444 S.W.2d 353, Amarillo Court of Appeals, Ward. July 9, 1969. Affirmed trial court granting of directors' summary judgment regarding conspiracy and fraud.
5. *Homer G. Maxey, et al. v. T. J. Goad*, San Antonio Court of Appeals, Cadena. 451 S.W.2d 763, March 4, 1970. Affirmed El Paso trial court in Rodman case.
6. *Homer G. Maxey, et al. v. J. L. Irish, et al.*, 457 S.W.2d 87, May 15, 1970, Eastland Court of Appeals.
7. *Citizens National Bank of Lubbock, Texas v. Homer G. Maxey, et al.*, 461 S.W.2d 138, December 7, 1970, No. 8096. Amarillo Court of Civil Appeals, Denton. Affirmed

bank directors entitled to summary judgment. Reversed jury verdict against bank, remanded for new trial.

8. *Homer G. Maxey v. Citizens National Bank of Lubbock, Texas*. April 18, 1972. US Fifth Circuit Court of Appeals, New Orleans. Dismissed without prejudice.

9. *Homer G. Maxey, et al. v. Citizens National Bank of Lubbock, Texas, et al.*, 489 S.W.2d 697, December 27, 1972. Amarillo Court of Appeals, Reynolds. Affirmed final judgment excusing bank's representatives from liability prevented plaintiffs from proceeding against bank for damages.

10. *Homer G. Maxey, et al. v. Citizens National Bank of Lubbock, Texas, et al.*, 507 S.W.2d 722, May 20, 1974. Texas Supreme Court, Denton. Reversed and remanded.

11. *Homer G. Maxey, et al. v. Texas Commerce Bank of Lubbock, Texas, et al.* (No. 51,441). Fifth Amended Original petition filed September 8, 1966. Trial began October 4, 1976, ended October 22, 1976, Judge Denzil Bevers. Final judgment signed December 15, 1976. Verdict for Maxey, $3.7 million actual damages.

12. *Homer G. Maxey, et al. v. Texas Commerce Bank of Lubbock, Texas et al.*, 571 S.W.2d 39, August 16, 1978. Amarillo Seventh Court of Appeals, Robinson.

13. Final settlement in the above styled case: $2 million, Judge Denzil Bevers, signed September 22, 1980.

APPENDIX 2:

SUMMARY OF

THE MAXEY

APPEALS

Homer Maxey did not merely leave a heritage of buildings, homes, and parks for the future generations of Lubbock and for Texas. He left the permanent impact and memory of two lengthy jury trials (which resulted in two of the largest verdicts in the history of the South Plains at that time) and nine appellate decisions (three of which are particularly significant), all of which have a perpetual presence in the jurisprudence of the State of Texas. Appendix 1 lists all the Maxey appellate cases.

The court system for civil cases in Texas consists of three levels: trial courts (district or county court at law), courts of appeal (formerly identified as courts of civil appeals) and the Supreme Court. There is a right of appeal of any civil case from the trial court to the court of appeal, but review by the Supreme Court is limited to those cases that the Supreme Court deems significant enough to merit review. At the time Maxey's cases were litigated, the decision of the Supreme Court was limited to either the granting of a writ (the appeal) or denying the application for writ of error (refusal to consider the case).

Two of the most important and interesting decisions in the Maxey cases were written by James G. "Jim" Denton, and those two opinions appear to be, but are not, diametrically opposed to each other. Prior to being appointed Chief Justice of the Seventh Court of Appeals in Amarillo in 1959, Judge Denton had served as county court-at-law judge and then district judge in Lubbock. He was then elected as a justice of the Supreme Court of Texas, serving from January 4, 1971, until his death on June 10, 1982.[1]

As a court of appeals justice, Denton wrote the opinion that reversed the first jury verdict in favor of Maxey in late 1970.[2] Later, as a justice on the Supreme Court of Texas, Denton reversed the Amarillo Court of Civil Appeals decision that had, in turn, reversed the second jury verdict in favor of Maxey. This second ruling has been relied upon by appellate courts, trial judges, and lawyers for its holding that a bank (corporation) can be liable for acts and misconduct by its agents, directors, shareholders, or employees, even though those individuals may not be legally liable themselves.[3]

The third significant Maxey appellate opinion was one authored by Judge Mary Lou Robinson. Prior to prior to being appointed to the US District Court for the Western District of Texas, Amarillo Division, Judge Robinson had served as judge of the county court at law and district court (in Amarillo) and a judge on the Seventh Court of Appeals.

While she was on the Seventh Court, Judge Robinson wrote the opinion that reversed the second verdict by a Lubbock County jury. At first glance, Judge Robinson's opinion appears to be essentially a reversal of the verdict of the jury. But a closer reading of that opinion confirms that some of the findings of the trial judge that were adverse to Maxey were also reversed by Judge Robinson's opinion, and she ordered that the case be remanded for a new (third) trial.

Judge Robinson rejected the bank's persistent claim that the 1976 and 1970 trial verdicts (both in Maxey's favor) were in error because the "officers, agents and employees of the bank are res judicata to any suit by Maxey based on their acts" and that "any act of bad faith by the corporation would have required an affirmative act by these individuals." Robinson agreed with the Supreme Court of Texas ruling on that issue and again overruled the bank's contention, citing the opinion written by Denton in 1974, which stated in part: "The bank as a contracting party to chattel mortgages, pledge agreements and deeds of trust owed the plaintiffs duties which were separate and distinct from the duties owed the plaintiffs by the bank's individual officers, directors, shareholders or employees."

Robinson also agreed with the jury finding in 1976, which found that "the bank had failed to act in good faith in the sale of the of both Plaza Building Corporation and Maxey Lumber Company, that the consideration paid for the collateral was grossly inadequate [and] . . . that the failure to exercise good faith at the foreclosure [the secret sale of Maxey's assets] was a cause in fact of the sale of stock for a grossly inadequate consideration."

It might strike some legal experts as surprising, upon reading the Robinson ruling, that the bank's legal team would even consider going for a third trial on this case without making a concerted effort to reach an out-of-court settlement, which they did on September 22, 1980, after fourteen years and seven months of litigation.

NOTES

Foreword

1. See David P. Szatmary, *Shays' Rebellion: The Making of an Agrarian Insurrection* (Amherst: University of Massachusetts Press, 1984).

2. Thomas K. McCraw, *The Founders and Finance: How Hamilton, Gallatin, and Other Immigrants Forged a New Economy* (Cambridge: Harvard University Press, 2012), 115.

3. Charles R. Morris, *The Dawn of Innovation: The First American Industrial Revolution* (New York: Public Affairs, 2012), 165.

4. Ibid., 166.

5. See Scott Reynolds Nelson, *A Nation of Deadbeats: An Uncommon History of America's Financial Disasters* (New York: Vintage, 2013). Bray Hammond, *Banks and Politics in America: From the Revolution to the Civil War* (Princeton: Princeton University Press, 1991).

6. Jonathan Levy, *Freaks of Fortune: The Emerging World of Capitalism and Risk in America* (Cambridge: Harvard University Press, 2012), 161.

7. Gordon Morris Bakken, *Practicing Law in Frontier California* (Lincoln: University of Nebraska Press, 1991), 51–71.

8. John A. Fliter and Derek S. Hoff, *Fighting Foreclosure: The Blaisdell Case, the Contract Clause, and the Great Depression* (Lawrence: University Press of Kansas, 2012), 167.

9. Ibid., 182.

Introduction

1. US Inflation Calculator, http://www.usinflationcalculator.com.

2. Nicholas Lemann, "Taking Over," *Texas Monthly,* October 1983.

3. Frank Patrick, "Once Wealthy Maxey Broke, Not Broken," *Lubbock Avalanche-Journal,* October 3, 1976, Sunday morning edition.

4. Delbert McDougal, telephone interview with Jesse Sublett, August 2, 2010.

5. US Inflation Calculator, http://www.usinflationcalculator.com.

6. *Homer G. Maxey, et al. v. Citizens National Bank of Lubbock, Texas, et al.*, 507 S.W.2d 722 (Tex. Sup. Ct. 1974), 15–27. Case cited hereafter as *Maxey v. CNB*; Johnson and Scott, "Golden Fleece or Just Yarn?"

7. Glenna Goodacre, e-mail correspondence with Jesse Sublett, June 15, 2011.

Chapter 1

1. Johnson and Scott, "Golden Fleece or Just Yarn?"; Nicholas Lemann, "Taking Over," *Texas Monthly*, October 1983.

2. "Civic Leader Homer Maxey Dies at 79," *Lubbock Avalanche-Journal*, July 20, 1990.

3. Glenna Goodacre, interview with Jesse Sublett, October 20, 2009.

4. US Inflation Calculator, http://www.usinflationcalculator.com.

5. Johnson and Scott, "Golden Fleece or Just Yarn?"

6. Robert Carl Schaefer, "Law and Politics in Lubbock: 1945 to the Present," in *Lubbock: from Town to City*, Lawrence L. Graves, ed. (Lubbock: West Texas Museum Association, 1986), 167.

7. Kenneth Bowlin, interview with Broadus A. Spivey, June 14, 2008.

8. Ibid.

9. Johnson and Scott, "Golden Fleece or Just Yarn?"; Kenneth Bowlin, interview with Broadus A. Spivey, June 14, 2008.

10. W. G. McMillan, Jr., interview with Sally Still Abbe, September 21, 2010, audio, City of Lubbock Archives.

11. Plaintiffs' Third Amended Original Petition, *Maxey v. CNB*, 9, 15, 27.

12. *Maxey v. CNB*, 22A–23A.

13. Glenna Goodacre, interview with Jesse Sublett, October 20, 2009.

Chapter 2

1. Lewis E. Hill, "Industry, Transportation and Finance," in Graves, *Lubbock: From Town to City*, 56.

2. Art Leatherwood, "Llano Estacado," *Handbook of Texas* (Austin: Texas State Historical Association, 1996), 4:250–2.

3. Ellysa Gonzales, "Senate Proclamation Hails Cotton-Tech Ties," LubbockOnline, *Lubbock Avalanche-Journal*, http://m.lubbockonline.com/local-news/2012-09-14/senate-proclamation-hails-cotton-tech-ties.

4. Leatherwood, "Llano Estacado."

5. Duane F. Guy, ed., *The Story of Palo Duro Canyon* (Lubbock: Texas Tech University Press, 2001), 103.

6. Donald R. Abbe and Paul H. Carlson, *Historic Lubbock County: An Illustrated History* (San Antonio: Historical Publishing Network, 2008), 16–19.

7. Lawrence L. Graves, "Lubbock County," *Handbook of Texas* (Austin: Texas State Historical Association, 1996), 4:322–24.

8. Ibid.

9. Charles G. Davis, "Estacado, Texas," *Handbook of Texas* (Austin: Texas State Historical Association 1996), 2:897.

10. W. C. Holden, *Rollie Burns, or, An Account of the Ranching Industry on the South Plains,* (College Station: Texas A&M University Press, 1932), 147–55; W. C. Holden, "IOA Ranch," *Handbook of Texas Online,* http://www.tshaonline.org/handbook/online/articles/api01.

11. Abbe and Carlson, *Historic Lubbock County,* 16–17.

12. Holden, *Rollie Burns,* 194–96.

13. Abbe and Carlson, *Historic Lubbock County,* 16–19.

14. Seymour V. Connor, "Ellwood, Isaac L.," Handbook of Texas (Austin: Texas State Historical Association 1996), 2:836.

15. L. Ford Davis, *The Last Cowboy* (Austin: Eakin Press, 2002), 130–41.

16. J. B. Maxey, James Barney Maxey Papers, microfilm at Southwest Collection, Texas Tech University.

17. Ibid.

18. Ibid.

19. Glenna Goodacre, interview with Jesse Sublett, October 20, 2009.

20. Charles A. Guy, The Plainsman Says, *Lubbock Evening Journal,* January 23, 1951.

21. Lawrence L. Graves, "Texas Tech University," *Handbook of Texas* (Austin: Texas State Historical Association, 1966), 6:436.

22. "Looking Back: Plainview Just Missed Out on Landing Texas Tech," *Plainview Herald,* http://www.myplainview.com/news/article_cd33d8fa-b4a2-58ad-8c40-6f579c3983d6.html.

23. "Lubbock Gets Tech!" *Lubbock Centennial Edition,* 2009, *LubbockOnline, Lubbock Avalanche-Journal,* http://www.lubbockcentennial.com/Section/1909_1933/Tech.shtml.

24. Ibid.

25. Ibid.

26. Freda Marie McVay, "Charles A. Guy, the Paradoxical Plainsman" (master's thesis, Texas Tech University, 1979), http://repositories.tdl.org/ttu-ir/bitstream/handle/2346/11163/31295001800753.pdf?sequence=1.

27. "Original Picture of 'Plainsman' to Hang in New Hotel," *Lubbock Morning Avalanche,* August 14, 1951.

28. McVay, "Charles A. Guy."

29. J. B. Maxey Papers; "Contractor and Leader, J. B. Maxey Dies after Heart Attack," *Lubbock Morning Avalanche,* April 9, 1953.

30. J. B. Maxey Papers.

31. "Lubbock Gets Tech!"

32. J. B. Maxey Papers.

33. Kathleen Maxey Luther, phone interview with Jesse Sublett, December 16, 2009.

34. Marcia Abbott, phone interview with Jesse Sublett, February 24, 2010.

35. J. B. Maxey Papers.

Chapter 3

1. Frank Patrick, "Once Wealthy Maxey Broke, Not Broken," *Lubbock Avalanche-Journal,* October 3, 1976, Sunday morning edition.

2. Glenna Goodacre, interview with Jesse Sublett, October 20, 2009

3. *Maxey v. CNB,* 13A–16A.

4. Ibid.

5. J. B. Maxey Papers.

6. "Miss Melba Mae Tatom and Homer Maxey Have High Noon Nuptial Ceremony," *Lubbock Daily Journal,* June 21, 1932.

7. *Maxey v. CNB,* 13A–16A.

8. I. A. Stephens, "Two Special Friends," transcript of speech, March 1990, collection of the authors.

9. Ibid.

10. Ibid.

11. *Maxey v. CNB,* 13A–16A.

12. Ibid.

13. Patrick, "Once Wealthy Maxey."

14. *Maxey v. CNB,* 15A–23A.

15. Abbe and Carlson, *Historic Lubbock County,* 34–35.

16. "Homes Being Rushed Here," *Lubbock Morning Avalanche,* January 5, 1942.

17. *Maxey v. CNB,* 15A–23A.

18. Anthony Bruce and William Cogar, *An Encyclopedia of Naval History* (New York: Facts on File, Inc., 1998), 277–78.

19. *Maxey v. CNB,* 26A.

20. *Maxey v. CNB,* 27A–28A; Navy Department Bureau of Naval Personnel, letter to Homer G. Maxey dated August 20, 1942, in "Homer Maxey World War II Scrapbook," collection of the authors.

21. *Jane's Fighting Ships of World War II* (New Jersey: Crescent Books, 1996), 303–05.

22. James M. Morris and Patricia M. Kearns, *Historical Dictionary of the United States Navy* (United Kingdom: Scarecrow Press, 2011), 377.

23. Marcia Abbott, telephone interview with Jesse Sublett, February 24, 2010.

24. DeEtte Maxey Cobb, telephone interview with Jesse Sublett, July 26, 2010.

25. Craig L. Symonds, *The Naval Institute Historical Atlas of the U.S. Navy* (Annapolis: Naval Institute Press, 1995), 140–54.

26. Ibid.

27. *Jane's Fighting Ships of World War II,* 303–05; "Navy's Changelings," *Time,* May 31, 1945; Frank D. Morris, "Bazooka Boats," *Collier's Magazine,* November 11, 1944, on NavSource Online, http://www.navsource.org/archives/10/15/15000032.htm.

28. George C. Dyer, Vice Admiral, USN (RET), *The Amphibians Came to Conquer: The Story of Admiral Richmond Kelly Turner II*, 457–532, eBook, http://www.archive.org/stream/amphibianscameto017723mbp#page/n7/mode/2up.

29. Ibid.

30. Stephens, "Two Special Friends."

31. Patrick, "Once Wealthy Maxey."

32. *Maxey v. CNB*, 27A.

33. *Jane's Fighting Ships of World War II*, 303–05.

34. *Maxey v. CNB*, 27A.

35. Dyer, *The Amphibians Came to Conquer*, 457–532.

36. Symonds, *Historical Atlas of the U.S. Navy*, 162–89.

37. Ibid.

38. Homer G. Maxey, letter to Melba Tatom Maxey, June 2, 1945, in "Homer Maxey World War II Scrapbook."

39. Homer G. Maxey, letter to J. B. and Effie Maxey, in "Homer Maxey World War II Scrapbook."

40. Dan Anthony, phone interview with Jesse Sublett, December 7, 2009.

41. Glenna Goodacre, interview with Jesse Sublett, October 20, 2009; Captain W. Dalton Davis (MC), U.S.N., letter to Melba Mae Maxey, June 30, 1945, in "Homer Maxey World War II Scrapbook."

42. "Frequently Asked Questions," *Radiation Effects Research Foundation* (RERF), http://www.rerf.or.jp/general/qa_e/qa1.html.

Chapter 4

1. Stephens, "Two Special Friends."

2. Ibid.

3. *Maxey v. CNB*, 28A–33A.

4. Ibid.

5. Ibid., 51A–52A.

6. Margaret Talkington, interview with Jesse Sublett, February 25, 2010.

7. *Maxey v. CNB*, 51A–52A.

8. S. Tom Morris, interview with Jesse Sublett, November 27, 2009.

9. *Maxey v. CNB*, 34A–37A.

10. Abbe and Carlson, *Historic Lubbock County*, 103.

11. "Oil Fever Hits Grayson County," *Lubbock Avalanche-Journal*, December 18, 1949, Sunday edition.

12. Stephens, "Two Special Friends."

13. Ibid.

14. *Maxey v. CNB*, 28A–72A.

15. "Plainsman Hotel Holds Formal Public Opening Today," *Lubbock Morning Avalanche*, August 14, 1951.

16. "Original Picture," *Lubbock Morning Avalanche.*

17. Roy Middleton, interview with Jesse Sublett, November 13, 2009.

18. Roger Carl Schaefer, "Law and Politics in Lubbock: 1945 to the Present," in *Lubbock: From Town to City*, 133–47.

19. Letters to members of First United Methodist Church of Lubbock, reproduced in *First Methodist News*, a bulletin of First Methodist Church of Lubbock, date unknown, collection of the authors.

20. "Civic Leader Homer Maxey Dies at 79," *Lubbock Avalanche-Journal*, July 20, 1990.

21. "In Memory of Melba Maxey," Senate resolution SR 229, February 16, 1995.

22. Glenna Goodacre, interview with Jesse Sublett, October 20, 2009; Carla Elliott, interview with Broadus A. Spivey, July 10, 2007; Carla Elliott, interview with Jesse Sublett, October 22, 2009.

23. Jim Harper, "Sports in Lubbock 1950–1984," in Graves, *Lubbock: From Town to City*, 386.

24. Lawrence L. Graves, *A History of Lubbock*, (Lubbock: West Texas Museum Association, 1962), 528.

25. Art Gatts, "Jack Davis Elected President of Matador Club," *Lubbock Evening Journal*, May 27, 1953.

26. Lubbock City Commission minutes, May 10, 1956, 179–81, 238–42.

27. Ruth Horn Andrews, *The First Thirty Years: A History of Texas Technological College 1925–1955* (Lubbock: Texas Tech Press, 1956), 1–5.

28. "City of Lubbock History of Annexation by Decade," City of Lubbock Archives.

29. Lawrence L. Graves, "Lubbock, TX," *Handbook of Texas* (Austin: Texas State Historical Association, 1996), 4: 320–21.

30. Lubbock City Commission minutes for December 6, 1956, 68–75; Lubbock City Commission minutes for August 22, 1957, 413–14.

31. Phyllis Brown, City of Lubbock Community Development, interview with Jesse Sublett, February 27, 2012.

32. Hank Murphy, "LISD Learns from Desegregation Case," *Lubbock Avalanche-Journal*, April 25, 1999, http://lubbockonline.com/stories/042599/cel_042599011.shtml.

33. Glenna Goodacre, e-mail to Jesse Sublett, February 28, 2012.

34. Meredith McClain, phone interview with Jesse Sublett, March 7, 2012.

35. Jane Holden Kelly, e-mail to Jesse Sublett, February 28, 2012.

36. Don Bundock, e-mail to Jesse Sublett, March 9, 2012.

37. Berwyn Tisdel, telephone interview with Jesse Sublett, March 16, 2012.

38. Roger Carl Schaefer, "Law and Politics in Lubbock: 1945 to the Present," in Graves, *Lubbock: From Town to City*, 133–47.

39. Ibid.

40. Ibid.

41. "Days of Lubbock's 'empire builders' have faded," *Lubbock Avalanche-Journal*,

March 25, 1999. http://lubbockonline.com/stories/032599/cel_032599018.shtml.

42. "James H. Milam," *Lubbock Avalanche-Journal*, http://www.lubbockcentennial.com/citysmost/040608.shtml.

43. Glenna Goodacre, e-mail to Jesse Sublett, February 28, 2012.

44. Martin Donnell Kohout," Charles Hardin Holley," *Handbook of Texas* (Austin: Texas State Historical Association, 1996), 3: 666–67; Philip Norman, *Rave On: The Biography of Buddy Holly* (New York: Simon & Schuster 1996), 23, 59–61, 192–93.

45. Marcia Abbott, telephone interview with Jesse Sublett, February 24, 2010.

46. Kohout, "Charles Hardin Holley."

47. Glenna Goodacre, interview with Jesse Sublett, October 20, 2009. Carla Elliott, interview with Jesse Sublett, October 20, 2009.

48. DeEtte Maxey Cobb, telephone interview with Jesse Sublett, July 26, 2010.

49. Carla Elliott, interview with Jesse Sublett, October 20, 2009.

50. Tommy Elliott, interview with Jesse Sublett, November 27, 2009.

51. Glenna Goodacre, telephone interview with Jesse Sublett, December 7, 2009.

52. Margaret Talkington, interview with Jesse Sublett, February 25, 2010.

53. DeEtte Maxey Cobb, telephone interview with Jesse Sublett, July 26, 2010. The Denton family to which Cobb refers was James and Elinor Denton, not to be confused with James Gray Denton, also mentioned several times in the book. James Gray Denton was a District Judge in Lubbock County (1952–1959), chief Justice on the Texas Court of Appeals (1959–1970), and member of the Texas Supreme Court (1971–1982).

54. Glenna Goodacre, interview with Jesse Sublett, October 20, 2009.

55. Johnson and Scott, "Golden Fleece or Just Yarn?"

56. Davis, *The Last Cowboy*, 130–41.

57. Glenna Goodacre, interview with Jesse Sublett, July 29, 2010.

58. Carla Elliott, interview with Broadus A. Spivey, July 10, 2007.

59. Tommy Elliott, interview with Jesse Sublett, November 27, 2009.

60. Dan Law, interview with Jesse Sublett, November 30, 2009.

61. "Hundreds Attend Pioneer Hotel Opening Here," Lubbock newspaper clipping, c. 1961, edition unknown.

62. J. B. Maxey Papers.

63. Clifford E. Hunt, "Historical Diary of Lubbock County," http://swco.ttu.edu/reference/Collections/ReferenceList/Pages/HuntDiary.htm; Lewis E. Hill in Graves, *Lubbock: From Town to City*, 73.

64. *Maxey v. CNB*, 70A–72A.

65. Carla Elliott, interview with Jesse Sublett, October 20, 2009.

66. C. W. Ratliff, "Pioneer Hotel Slates Formal Opening Today," *Lubbock Avalanche-Journal*, April 16, 1961.

67. Charles A. Guy, The Plainsman Says, *Lubbock Morning Avalanche*, October 1960.

68. Thomas Thompson, "The Turnstile," *Amarillo Globe-Times*, August 10, 1960.

69. Tommy Elliott, interview with Jesse Sublett, November 27, 2009.

70. William Kerns, "Road to the Top; Renaming of Street Spotlights Sculptor's Resounding Success," *Lubbock Avalanche-Journal*, August 13, 2005, http://lubbock online.com/stories/081305/loc_0813050033.shtml; Chris van Wagenen, "N. Lubbock Ripe for Growth Apurt, McDougal Says Rising Enrollment at Tech Major Factor in Downtown Area," *Lubbock Avalanche-Journal*, May 8, 2003, http://lub bockonline.com/stories/050803/loc_050803039.shtml.

71. Delbert McDougal, telephone interview with Jesse Sublett, August 2, 2010; Tony Privett, *Failure Is Not an Option: Delbert McDougal: A Developer's Unconventional Wisdom* (San Antonio: Historical Publishing Network, 2007), 53–69.

72. J. Michael Liles, interview with Broadus A. Spivey, August 9, 2006; J. Michael Liles, interview with Jesse Sublett, October 18, 2009.

73. Glenna Goodacre, interview with Jesse Sublett, October 20, 2009.

74. David A. Remley, *Bell Ranch: Cattle Ranching in the Southwest, 1824–1947* (Albuquerque: University of New Mexico Press, 1993), 1324, 102, 294–305.

75. Plaintiffs' Third Amended Original Petition, in *Maxey v. CNB*.

76. Glenna Goodacre, interview with Jesse Sublett, October 20, 2009.

77. Johnson and Scott, "Golden Fleece or Just Yarn?"

78. Tommy Elliott, interview with Jesse Sublett, November 27, 2009.

79. Glenna Goodacre, interview with Jesse Sublett, October 20, 2009.

80. Kenneth Bowlin, interview with Jesse Sublett, September 26, 2009.

81. Marcia Abbott, telephone interview with Jesse Sublett, February 24, 2010.

82. Glenna Goodacre, interview with Jesse Sublett, October 20, 2009.

83. Bill Goodacre, telephone interview with Jesse Sublett, October 20, 2009.

84. Ibid.

85. Glenna Goodacre, interview with Jesse Sublett, October 20, 2009.

86. Glenna Goodacre, interview with Jesse Sublett, July 29, 2010.

87. Johnson and Scott, "Golden Fleece or Just Yarn?"

88. E. W. Williams, Jr., interview with Jesse Sublett, October 21, 2009.

89. Johnson and Scott, "Golden Fleece or Just Yarn?"

90. E. W. Williams, Jr., interview with Jesse Sublett, October 21, 2009; Kenneth Bowlin, interview with Broadus A. Spivey, June 14, 2008.

91. Johnson and Scott, "Golden Fleece or Just Yarn?"

92. Kenneth Bowlin, interview with Broadus A. Spivey, June 14, 2008.

93. *Maxey v. CNB*, 18–20, 25–29.

94. E. W. Williams, Jr., interview with Jesse Sublett, October 21, 2009.

Chapter 5

1. Johnson and Scott, "Golden Fleece or Just Yarn?"

2. E. W. Williams, Jr., interview with Jesse Sublett, October 21, 2009.

3. Kenneth Bowlin, interview with Broadus A. Spivey, June 14, 2008.

4. E. W. Williams, Jr., interview with Jesse Sublett, November 20, 2009.

5. "Bank Deals, Operations Spark Suit," *Lubbock Avalanche-Journal*, November 5, 1969, morning edition.

6. "Maxey Tells of Efforts," *Lubbock Avalanche-Journal*, November 3, 1969, evening edition.

7. *Maxey v. CNB*, 47A, 59A–64A, 34.

8. Ibid., 46A–47A.

9. *Maxey v. CNB*, 1918–22.

10. David Hughes, e-mail to Jesse Sublett, June 10, 2010.

11. Ibid.

12. "Maxey Accuses Bank of Putting Him in 'Financial Straitjacket,'" *Lubbock Avalanche Journal*, October 31, 1969, evening edition.

13. *Maxey v. CNB*, 1911–73.

14. E. W. Williams, Jr., interview with Jesse Sublett, October 21, 2009.

15. The information in the statement was obtained from an interview with a longtime Lubbockite who wishes to remain anonymous, hereafter referred to as "Resident," in an interview with Broadus A. Spivey and Jesse Sublett, November 11, 2009.

16. Jo Love Nelson, telephone interview with Jesse Sublett, February 12, 2010.

17. Johnson and Scott, "Golden Fleece or Just Yarn?"

18. Ibid.

19. Ibid.

20. "Maxey Files Suit against CNB, Others," *Lubbock Avalanche-Journal*, March 18, 1966, evening edition.

21. Carla Elliott, interview with Jesse Sublett, October 20, 2009.

22. Bobby Moody, telephone interview with Jesse Sublett, November 18, 2009.

23. Glenna Goodacre, interview with Jesse Sublett, October 20, 2009.

24. Dan Law, interview with Jesse Sublett, November 30, 2009.

25. Ken Flagg, telephone interview with Jesse Sublett, December 17, 2009.

26. Margaret Talkington, interview with Jesse Sublett, February 25, 2010.

27. E. W. Williams, Jr., interview with Jesse Sublett, October 21, 2009.

28. Johnson and Scott, "Golden Fleece or Just Yarn?"

29. Ibid.

30. E. W. Williams, Jr., interviews with Jesse Sublett, October 21, 2009, and May 7, 2010.

31. Ibid.

32. "Maxey Files Suit."

33. Patrick, "Once Wealthy Maxey."

34. Carla Elliott, interview with Jesse Sublett, October 20, 2009, and February 24, 2010.

35. Kenneth Bowlin, interview with Broadus A. Spivey, June 14, 2008; interviews with Jesse Sublett, September 26, 2009, and March 9, 2010.

36. Ibid.

37. Jane Livermore Wofford, interview with Jesse Sublett, March 5, 2010.

38. Glenna Goodacre, interview with Jesse Sublett, October 20, 2009.

39. Ibid.

40. Kenneth Bowlin, interview with Jesse Sublett, September 26, 2009, and March 9, 2010.

41. Tommy Elliott, interview with Jesse Sublett, November 27, 2009.

42. Forrest Bowers, interview with Jesse Sublett, February 25, 2010.

43. Kenneth Bowlin, interview with Broadus A. Spivey, June 14, 2008; interviews with Jesse Sublett, September 26, 2009, and March 9, 2010.

44. Ibid.

45. Ibid.

46. Jo Anne Griffin, telephone interview with Jesse Sublett, March 9, 2010.

47. Ibid.

48. Plaintiffs' Third Amended Original Petition, in *Maxey v. CNB*.

49. Grace King and Gem Meacham, "Rodman, Earl George, Sr.," *Handbook of Texas* (Austin: Texas State Historical Association, 1996), 5:650–51.

50. Grace King and Gem Meacham, "Nöel, William Douglas," *Handbook of Texas* (Austin: Texas State Historical Association, 1996), 4:1024.

51. David Hughes, e-mail to Jesse Sublett, June 10, 2010.

52. J. Michael Liles, interview with Jesse Sublett, October 18, 2009; Johnson and Scott, "Golden Fleece or Just Yarn?"

53. "Resident," interview with Broadus A. Spivey and Jesse Sublett, November 11, 2009; telephone interview with Jesse Sublett, December 9, 2009.

54. Ibid.

55. Johnson and Scott, "Golden Fleece or Just Yarn?"

56. Davis, *The Last Cowboy*, 130141; Steve Kelton, *Renderbrook, A Century Under the Spade Brand* (Fort Worth: TCU Press, 1989), 170–71, 182, 192.

57. E. W. Williams, Jr., interview with Jesse Sublett, October 21, 2009, and May 7, 2010.

58. Homer G. Maxey, et al. v. E. G. Rodman, 444 S.W.2d 353, (Amarillo Ct. App. 1969) (No. 6045); William R. Shaver, phone interview with Jesse Sublett, March 12, 2010.

59. *Maxey v. CNB*, 507 S.W.2d 722 (Tex. Sup. Ct. 1974).

60. Plaintiffs' Third Amended Original Petition, in *Maxey v. CNB*.

61. "Pat S. Moore Award," Junior League of Lubbock, http://www.jllubbock.com/?nd=moore_award.

62. Jack Flygare, interview with Jesse Sublett, September 10, 2009.

63. David Hughes, e-mail message to Jesse Sublett, June 10, 2010.

64. *Maxey v. CNB*, 54–60.

65. Ibid.

66. Kenneth Bowlin, interview with Broadus A. Spivey, June 14, 2008; interviews with Jesse Sublett, September 26, 2009, and March 9, 2010.

67. Ibid.

68. Kenneth Bowlin, interview with Broadus A. Spivey, June 14, 2008; interviews with Jesse Sublett, September 26, 2009, and March 9, 2010.

69. Forrest Bowers, interview with Jesse Sublett February 25, 2010.

Chapter 6

1. Bobby Day, interview with Jesse Sublett, February 25, 2010.

2. Plaintiffs' Third Amended Original Petition, in *Maxey v. CNB*.

3. Kenneth May, "Testimony to Begin, Legal Battle Lines Drawn in Lawsuit," *Lubbock Avalanche-Journal*, October 28, 1969, evening edition.

4. Glenna Goodacre, interview with Jesse Sublett, October 20, 2009.

5. Ibid.

6. Kathleen Maxey Luther, telephone interview with Jesse Sublett, December 16, 2009.

7. Marcia Abbott, telephone interview with Jesse Sublett, February 24, 2010.

8. Jack Tidwell, telephone interview with Jesse Sublett, July 8, 2010.

9. Jack Flygare, interview with Jesse Sublett, September 10, 2009.

10. *Maxey v. CNB*, 1970, 5A–12A.

11. Ibid.

12. Ibid.

13. Kenneth Bowlin, interview with Broadus A. Spivey, June 14, 2008; Kenneth Bowlin, interviews with Jesse Sublett, September 26, 2009, and March 9, 2010; J. Michael Liles, interview with Broadus A. Spivey, August 9, 2006; J. Michael Liles and Harold Hammett, interview with Jesse Sublett, October 18, 2009.

14. Broadus Spivey, interview with Jesse Sublett, February 22, 2010.

15. Carlton Dodson, telephone interview with Jesse Sublett, Feb 17, 2010.

16. E. W. Williams, Jr., interview with Jesse Sublett, October 21, 2009.

17. Nicholas Lemann, "Taking Over," *Texas Monthly,* October 1983.

18. Texas Department of Banking, *State Banks: Bank History*, http://www.dob.texas.gov/pubs/stbks.pdf.

19. Lemann, "Taking Over."

20. Gwendolyn Murphy, interview with Jesse Sublett, November 30, 2009.

21. *Lubbock City Directory*, 1969, n.p.

22. *Maxey v. CNB*, 14A–22A.

23. Ibid., 22A.

24. Ibid.

25. *Maxey v. CNB*, 24A–60A.

26. Ibid., 26A.

27. Gwendolyn Murphy, interview with Jesse Sublett, November 30, 2009.

28. *Maxey v. CNB*, 14A–27A.

29. Gwendolyn Murphy, interview with Jesse Sublett, November 30, 2009.

30. *Maxey v. CNB*, 29A–72A.

31. Ibid., 51A–60A.

32. Ibid., 70A–72A.

33. *Maxey v. CNB*, 13–26.

34. Ibid., 9–13.

35. Ibid., 41–76.

36. Ibid., 76.

37. Ibid., 76–80.

38. Ibid., 79–80.

39. Ibid., 81–82.

40. Ibid., 81–86.

41. *Maxey v. CNB*, 97.

42. *Maxey v. CNB*, 89–92.

43. *Maxey v. CNB*, 99–121.

44. Ibid., 121–41.

45. *Maxey v. CNB*, 121.

46. "Witness Outlines Bank Loan Deals on Stand Here, Bank Loan Dealings Described," *Lubbock Avalanche-Journal*, October 30, 1969, morning edition.

47. *Maxey v. CNB*, 163–64.

48. Ibid., 205–07.

49. Ibid., 207.

50. Ibid., 264–65.

51. Plaintiffs' Third Amended Original Petition, in *Maxey v. CNB*.

52. Carla Elliott, interviews with Jesse Sublett, October 20, 2009, and February 24, 2010.

53. *Maxey v. CNB*, 206.

54. *Maxey v. CNB*, 206–66.

55. *Maxey v. CNB*, 5.

56. *Maxey v. CNB*, 280.

57. Ibid., 269.

58. *Maxey v. CNB*, 317.

59. Ibid., 317–21.

60. Ibid., 318–19.

61. Ibid., 321.

62. Ibid., 402–54.

63. Ibid., 335.

64. Ibid., 472–75.

65. Ibid., 476.

66. Johnson and Scott, "Golden Fleece or Just Yarn?"; Tom Dodge, "The Man Who Lives on Weather," in *Literary Fort Worth*, Judy Alter and James Ward Lee, eds. (Fort Worth: TCU Press, 2002), 155–56.

67. *Maxey v. CNB*, 219–394; Dorothy A. Drumwright, interview with Jesse Sublett, December 23, 2009.

68. J. Michael Liles, interview with Broadus A. Spivey, August 9, 2006; Barry Monush, *Encyclopedia of Film Actors from the Silent Era to 1965* (New York: Applause Theater and Cinema Books, 2003); "Dale Robertson," IMDb, http://www.imdb.com/.

69. Erin Neff, "Political, Business Leader Erin Neff Jones Dies at 89," *Las Vegas Sun*, Nov. 19, 2001, http://www.lasvegassun.com/news/2001/nov/19/political-business-leader-jones-dies-at-89/; Sally Denton and Roger Morris, *The Money and The Power: The Making of Las Vegas and Its Hold on America* (New York: Knopf, 2001), 101–03, 107–09, 112–14, 153–54, 199, 204, 261.

70. Rob Miech, *The Last Natural: Bryce Harper's Big Gamble in Sin City and the Greatest Amateur Season Ever* (New York: Thomas Dunne Books, 2012), 114–15.

71. *Maxey v. CNB*, 400–14; 456–61.

72. Ibid., 2198–209.

73. Dorothy A. Drumwright, interview with Jesse Sublett, December 23, 2009.

74. *Maxey v. CNB*, 448–63.

75. Ibid., 2331–61.

76. Ibid., 171.

77. Kenneth Bowlin, interview with Broadus A. Spivey, June 14, 2008; interviews with Jesse Sublett, September 26, 2009, and March 9, 2010; J. Michael Liles, interview with Broadus A. Spivey, August 9, 2006; interview with Jesse Sublett, October 18, 2009; Glenna Goodacre, interview with Jesse Sublett, October 20, 2009; Johnson and Scott, "Golden Fleece or Just Yarn?"

78. *Maxey v. CNB*, 477–81.

79. Roger Carl Schaefer, "Law and Politics in Lubbock: 1945 to the Present," in Graves, *Lubbock: From Town to City*, 133–47.

80. *Maxey v. CNB*, 482–84.

81. Ibid., 273–74.

82. Ibid., 495–99.

83. Ibid., 507.

84. Ibid., 529–46.

85. *Maxey v. CNB*, 670–703.

86. Ibid., 667–76.

87. David Hughes, e-mail message to Jesse Sublett, June 10, 2010.

88. *Maxey v. CNB*, 670.

89. Ibid., 733–47.

90. Ibid., 739.

91. Ibid., 740–44.

92. Ibid., 747–63.

93. Ken Bowlin, interview with Broadus A. Spivey, June 14, 2008.

94. *Maxey v. CNB*, 750–55.

95. Ibid., 747.

96. Ibid., 756–57.

97. Ibid., 201–3.

98. "Paul Lange's Genealogy Home Page," http://www.langeonline.com/; Catherine Keeney Bonner, e-mail to Jesse Sublett, May 13, 2010.

99. E. W. Williams, Jr., interviews with Jesse Sublett, October 21, 2009, and May 7, 2010.

100. *Maxey v. CNB*, 2164–92.

101. Ibid., 2109–13.

102. *Maxey v. CNB*, 755–57.

103. Ibid., 764–87.

104. Tommy Elliott, interview with Jesse Sublett, November 27, 2009.

105. *Maxey v. CNB*, 322–29.

106. Tommy Elliott, interview with Jesse Sublett, November 27, 2009.

107. Ibid.

108. Jack Flygare, interview with Jesse Sublett, September 10, 2009.

109. Ibid.

Chapter 7

1. Melba Maxey journal, collection of the authors.

2. Bobby Moody, telephone interview with Jesse Sublett, November 18, 2009.

3. Kenneth Bowlin, interview with Broadus A. Spivey, June 14, 2008; Kenneth Bowlin, interviews with Jesse Sublett, September 26, 2009, and March 9, 2010.

4. Kenneth May, "Defense Disputes Property Values," *Lubbock Avalanche-Journal*, November 6, 1969, evening edition.

5. Ibid.

6. *Maxey v. CNB*, 766–67, 788–94, 818.

7. Ibid.

8. *Maxey v. CNB*, 1063–65.

9. Ibid., 777–87.

10. Ibid.

11. Ibid., 827–31.

12. Ibid., 883–87.

13. Ibid., 1035–39.

14. Kenneth May, "Trades by Maxey Are Targets for Defense," *Lubbock Avalanche-Journal*, November 7, 1969, evening edition.

15. Gwendolyn Murphy, interview with Jesse Sublett, November 30, 2009.

16. *Maxey v. CNB*, 764.

17. Glenna Goodacre, interview with Jesse Sublett, October 20, 2009.

18. *Maxey v. CNB*, 764–87.

19. Ibid.

20. Ibid., 892–93.

21. Ibid., 1035–40.

22. Ibid., 1063–66.

23. Ibid.

24. Ibid., 894–902.

25. Ibid., 904–34

26. "Judge Extends Maxey Recess," *Lubbock Avalanche-Journal,* November 12, 1969, morning edition.

27. *Maxey v. CNB,* 1204–10.

28. Ibid.

29. Ibid., 1213–14.

30. Jack Flygare, interview with Jesse Sublett, September 10, 2009.

31. *Maxey v. CNB,* 1200 37.

32. Ibid., 1204–15, 1362–74.

33. Ibid., 1248–49.

34. Ibid., 93–96, 279–81.

35. Kenneth May, "Maxey Still on Stand, Defense Counter-Attack Launched," *Lubbock Avalanche-Journal,* November 19, 1969, morning edition; Kenneth May, "Checks Set Off Dispute, Defense Continues to Grill Homer G. Maxey," *Lubbock Avalanche-Journal,* November 20, 1969, evening edition; Kenneth May, "Attorneys Clash, Trial Tempo Quickens in Maxey Case Here," *Lubbock Avalanche-Journal,* November 21, 1969, morning edition.

36. *Maxey v. CNB,* 1342–92.

37. Kenneth May, "Cross-Examination Hits Cattle Feeding Claims in Bank Suit Here," *Lubbock Avalanche-Journal,* November 20, 1969, morning edition.

38. Kenneth May, "Attorneys Clash, Trial Tempo Quickens in Maxey Case Here," *Lubbock Avalanche-Journal,* November 21, 1969, morning edition.

39. Carlton Dodson, phone interview with Jesse Sublett, February 17, 2010.

40. Melba Maxey journal, collection of the authors.

41. Kenneth Bowlin, interview with Broadus A. Spivey, June 14, 2008.

42. *Maxey v. CNB,* 1296–360; 1640–71.

43. Kenneth May, "Trial's Progress Slow as Testimony Resumes," *Lubbock Avalanche-Journal,* December 2, 1969, morning edition.

44. *Maxey v. CNB,* 1918–2054.

45. Jack Flygare, interview with Jesse Sublett, September 10, 2009.

46. *Maxey v. CNB,* 1939–41.

47. Johnson and Scott, "Golden Fleece or Just Yarn?"

48. David Hughes, e-mail message to Jesse Sublett, June 10, 2010.

49. *Maxey v. CNB,* 1920.

50. Ibid., 1924–27.

51. Ibid., 1927–83.

52. Ibid., 1972–73.

53. Ibid., 1991–94.

54. Ibid., 2005–10.

55. Ibid.

56. Ibid., 2005–13.

57. Ibid.

58. Ibid., 2013–17.

59. Ibid.

60. Jo Love Nelson, telephone interview with Jesse Sublett, February 12, 2010.

61. *Maxey v. CNB*, 2013–17.

62. Ibid., 2022–33.

63. Ibid., 2051–55.

64. Ibid., 2057–87.

65. Ibid., 2087–93.

66. Ibid., 2106–23.

67. Kenneth May, "Cattle Brought Profit, Rancher Says," *Lubbock Avalanche-Journal*, December 5, 1969, morning edition.

68. Jonathon Kwitny, *The Mullendore Murder Case*, (New York: Amereon House, 1974), 9–19.

69. "The Mullendore Murder: All Done with Death of Prime Suspect, Says Retired Sheriff George Wayman," *The Bigheart Times*, December 4, 2010, http://barnsdall times.com/news/2010/12/the-mullendore-murder-all-done-with-death-of-prime-suspect-says-retired-sheriff-george-wayman.html.

70. Melba Maxey journal, collection of the authors.

71. *Maxey v. CNB*, 2157–60.

72. Melba Maxey journal.

73. Bobby Moody, telephone interview with Jesse Sublett, November 18, 2009.

74. Jack Flygare, interview with Jesse Sublett, September 10, 2009.

75. Charlie Joplin, interview with Jesse Sublett, October 20, 2009.

76. E. W. Williams, Jr., interviews with Jesse Sublett, October 21, 2009, and May 7, 2010.

77. Glenna Goodacre, interview with Jesse Sublett, October 20, 2009.

78. Kenneth Bowlin, interview with Jesse Sublett, March 9, 2010.

79. *Maxey v. CNB*, 2199–209.

80. Ibid., 2214, 2220–27, 2250–54.

81. Ibid., 2212–14.

82. Ibid., 2241–48.

83. Ibid., 2277–91.

84. Ibid., 2282–89.

85. Kenneth May, "Judge Sustains Objections of Defense Attorneys, Jury Misses Por-

tions of Testimony in Maxey-CNB Suit Here," *Lubbock Avalanche-Journal*, December 9, 1969, morning edition.

86. *Maxey v. CNB*, 2312–16.

87. *Maxey v. CNB*, 2329–30.

88. Kenneth May, "Crucial Telephone Call Cited in Maxey Case Denied by Attorney," *Lubbock Avalanche-Journal*, December 9, 1969, evening edition.

89. *Maxey v. CNB*, 2345–54.

90. Ibid., 2331–62.

91. Kenneth Bowlin, interview with Jesse Sublett, March 9, 2010.

92. Jack Flygare, interview with Jesse Sublett, September 10, 2009.

93. "Oral Deposition of E. W. Williams, Jr.," pp. 1–4, August 29, 1969, in *Maxey v. CNB*.

94. Jack Flygare, interview with Jesse Sublett, September 10, 2009.

95. Dorothy A. Drumwright, interview with Jesse Sublett, December 23, 2009.

96. *Maxey v. CNB*, 2331–62.

97. Ibid., 2380–419.

98. Ibid., 2501–94.

99. Melba Maxey journal.

100. Bill Goodacre, telephone interview with Jesse Sublett, October 20, 2009.

101. Carla Elliott, interviews with Jesse Sublett, October 20, 2009, and February 24, 2010.

102. Gwendolyn Murphy, interview with Jesse Sublett, November 30, 2009.

103. Lou Maysel, *Here Come the Texas Longhorns* (Fort Worth: Stadium Publishing Company, 1970), 358–63.

104. "Court Rules against Maxey; Evidence of Plot Lacking; Bank Must Still Justify Prices," *Lubbock Avalanche-Journal*, December 23, 1969, evening edition.

105. "Order and Judgment," n.p., issued and signed January 5, 1970, in *Maxey v. CNB*.

106. Melba Maxey journal.

107. *Maxey v. CNB*, 2595–749.

108. Vaughan Hendrie, "Bank Tells of Deals," *Lubbock Avalanche-Journal*, January 5, 1970, evening edition.

109. *Maxey v. CNB*, 2722–50.

110. "Deposition of Barclay Ryall," pp. 23–24, in *Maxey v. CNB*.

111. Johnson and Scott, "Golden Fleece or Just Yarn?"

112. Charlie Joplin, interview with Jesse Sublett, October 20, 2009.

113. Glenna Goodacre, interview with Jesse Sublett, October 20, 2009.

114. *Maxey v. CNB*, 2722–50.

115. Ibid., 2751–822.

116. Ibid., 2831–50.

117. Ibid., 2851–69.

118. Ibid., 2868–69.

119. Bill Goodacre, telephone interview with Jesse Sublett, October 20, 2009.

120. *Maxey v. CNB*, 2870–83.

121. Kwitny, *The Mullendore Murder*, 11–12.

122. *Maxey v. CNB*, 2874–83.

123. Ibid., 2939–58.

124. David A. Remley, *Bell Ranch: Cattle Ranching in the Southwest, 1824–1947* (Albuquerque: University of New Mexico Press, 1993), 294–305; "The Bell Ranch," http://www.thebellranch.com/.

125. *Maxey v. CNB*, 2939–58.

126. "How Trial Court Calculated Judgment Supplement to Application for Writ of Error by Homer G. Maxey et al.," filed in the Supreme Court of Texas, November 1, 1978, Homer G. Maxey et al., v. Texas Commerce Bank of Lubbock, Texas, et al., 571 S.W.2d 39 (Amarillo 7th Ct. App. 1978). Hereafter referred to as *Maxey v. TCB*. Citizens National Bank of Lubbock merged with Texas Commerce Bancshares of Houston in 1973 and reopened as Texas Commerce Bank of Lubbock.

127. *Maxey v. CNB*, 496–500.

128. Ibid., 2939–58.

129. Ibid., 2963–64.

Chapter 8

1. Kenneth May, "Final Arguments; Marathon Maxey Case Heading toward Jury," *Lubbock Avalanche-Journal*, January 12, 1970, evening edition.

2. Jo Anne Griffin, telephone interview with Jesse Sublett, March 9, 2010.

3. May, "Final Arguments."

4. Ibid.

5. Kenneth May, "Start Deliberations; Maxey Trial Jury Studies 10 Issues," *Lubbock Avalanche-Journal*, January 13, 1970, morning edition.

6. Ibid.

7. Melba Maxey journal.

8. May, "Start Deliberations."

9. "Judgment," n.p., in *Maxey v. CNB*, signed and entered May 3, 1970.

10. "Bank Motion Asks Change in Finding," *Lubbock Avalanche-Journal*, January 26, 1970.

11. Kenneth May, "Award Totals $2,689,767; Value of Plaza Stock Big Issue; Bank Announces Appeal Plans," *Lubbock Avalanche-Journal*, January 14, 1970, evening edition.

12. Kenneth May, "Arguments Slated Over Maxey Case," *Lubbock Avalanche-Journal*, October 6, 1970.

13. Kenneth May, "Bank-Maxey Case Aired for Court," *Lubbock Avalanche-Journal*, October 7, 1970, morning edition.

14. Bobby Day, interview with Jesse Sublett, February 25, 2010.

15. Melba Maxey journal.

16. Letter to Doris Cheaney, in Melba Maxey journal, dated January 17, 1970.

17. Judgment, in *Maxey v. CNB*, signed and entered May 3, 1970.

18. "Maxey Case: Bank Motion Asks Change in Finding," *Lubbock Avalanche-Journal*, January 26, 1970.

19. Letter to Doris Cheaney, dated March 19, 1970, in Melba Maxey journal.

20. Glenna Goodacre, telephone interview with Jesse Sublett, December 7, 2009.

21. Lewis E. Hill, "Industry, Transportation, and Finance," 83–87; James E. Jonish, "Population Growth and Expansion," 120–21, and Roger Schaefer, "Law and Politics in Lubbock, 1945 to the Present," 172. All in Graves, *Lubbock: From Town to City*.

22. Dan Law, interview with Jesse Sublett, November 30, 2009.

23. Tommy Elliott, interview with Jesse Sublett, November 27, 2009.

24. Carla Elliott, interviews with Jesse Sublett, October 20, 2009, and February 24, 2010.

25. Margaret Talkington, interview with Jesse Sublett, February 25, 2010.

26. Kenneth Bowlin, interview with Broadus A Spivey, June 14, 2008; Kenneth Bowlin, interviews with Jesse Sublett, September 26, 2009, and March 9, 2010.

27. Kenneth May, "Arguments Slated over Maxey Case," *Lubbock Avalanche-Journal*, October 6, 1970, morning edition.

28. Gwendolyn Murphy, interview with Jesse Sublett, November 30, 2009.

29. Jack Flygare, interview with Jesse Sublett, September 10, 2009.

30. Kenneth May, "Bank Seeks New Trial in Maxey Damage Suit, Jury Actions Hit," *Lubbock Avalanche-Journal*, March 13, 1970; Written Interrogatory of Bobby J. Carroll, in *Maxey v. CNB*.

31. Citizens National Bank of Lubbock, Texas v. Homer G. Maxey, et al., 461 S.W.2d 138 (Amarillo Ct. Civil App. 1970). Hereafter *CNB v. Maxey*.

32. *Maxey v. CNB*, 489 S.W.2d 697 (Amarillo Ct. App. 1972).

33. Ibid.

34. Kenneth Bowlin, interview with Broadus A. Spivey, June 14, 2008; Kenneth Bowlin, interviews with Jesse Sublett, September 26, 2009, and March 9, 2010; *Maxey v. CNB*, 489 S.W.2d 697 (Amarillo Ct. App. 1972); Deed of Trust from Bill Smith Gin, Inc. to Citizens National Bank of Lubbock, April 24, 1972, Lubbock County Deed of Trust Records, Vol. 71645–47.

35. *Maxey v. CNB*, 489 S.W.2d 697 (Amarillo Ct. App. 1972).

36. "Pat S. Moore Award," Junior League of Lubbock, http://www.jllubbock.com/?nd=moore_award.

37. Ibid.

38. Tommy Denton, e-mail message to Jesse Sublett, May 18, 2010.

39. *Maxey v. CNB*, 507 S.W.2d 722 (Tex. Sup. Ct. 1974).

40. Ibid.

Chapter 9

1. "Wm. F. Evans, Former School Board Member Dies in City," *Lubbock Avalanche-Journal*, March 28, 1970, Saturday morning edition.
2. David Hughes, e-mail message to Jesse Sublett, June 10, 2010.
3. Ibid.
4. *Maxey v. TCB*, 571 S.W.2d 39 (Amarillo 7th Ct. App. 1978).

Chapter 10

1. J. Michael Liles, interview with Jesse Sublett, October 18, 2009.
2. Ibid.
3. Patrick, "Once Wealthy Maxey."
4. "Maxey-Bank Litigation Has Marathon History in Courts," *Lubbock Avalanche-Journal*, October 3, 1976, Sunday morning edition.
5. Ken Bowlin, interview with Broadus A. Spivey, June 14, 2008.
6. Tommy Elliott, interview with Jesse Sublett, November 27, 2009.
7. Patrick, "Once Wealthy Maxey."
8. J. Michael Liles, interview with Jesse Sublett, October 18, 2009; Glenna Goodacre, interview with Jesse Sublett, October 20, 2009.
9. Rex Fuller, interview with Jesse Sublett, November 27, 2009.
10. Johnson and Scott, "Golden Fleece or Just Yarn?"
11. Ibid.
12. J. Michael Liles, interview with Jesse Sublett, October 18, 2009.
13. Frank Patrick, "Ranch Property Offer Aired by Maxey Aide," *Lubbock Avalanche-Journal*, October 5, 1976, morning edition. Regarding the second jury trial in the Maxey case, the daily transcript, more properly referred to as "Statement of Facts," could not be located, and it was the opinion of the Lubbock County district clerk that it and certain other portions of the records had been destroyed. After an exhaustive search, the authors concluded that this was the case. Certain other documents, including briefs, depositions, and various documents from the pleadings in 72nd District Court as well as the appellate courts, however, were located and preserved. Such documents have been supplemented with interviews with surviving attorneys, the presiding judge, and other credible sources, in an effort to produce a reliable and vivid chronicle of the trial and the most important developments during the appeals. Quotations from the trial proceedings were taken directly from the coverage in the *Avalanche-Journal*.
14. J. Michael Liles, interview with Jesse Sublett, October 18, 2009.
15. Denzil Bevers, interview with Jesse Sublett, October 23, 2009.
16. J. Michael Liles, interview with Jesse Sublett, October 18, 2009.
17. Patrick, "Ranch Property Offer"; "Order on Defendant's Special Exceptions," in *Maxey v. TCB*.
18. Patrick, "Ranch Property Offer."

19. "Order on Defendant's Special Exceptions," pp. 1–4, in *Maxey v. TCB.*

20. Frank Patrick, "Defense Attacks Maxey Estimate," *Lubbock Avalanche-Journal,* October 5, 1976, evening edition.

21. Frank Patrick, "Bank Attorneys Rebut Maxey Sale Accusations," *Lubbock Avalanche-Journal,* October 8, 1976, morning edition.

22. "Plaintiffs' Fifth Amended Original Petition," in *Maxey v. TCB.*

23. Patrick, "Bank Attorneys Rebut."

24. Denzil Bevers, interview with Jesse Sublett, October 23, 2009.

25. J. Michael Liles, interview with Broadus A. Spivey, August 9, 2006; J. Michael Liles, interview with Jesse Sublett, October 18, 2009.

26. National Transportation Safety Board, accident report, http://www.ntsb.gov/ntsb/brief.asp?ev_id=70251&key=0.

27. *Maxey v. CNB,* 2292–98, 2369–74.

28. J. Michael Liles, interview with Jesse Sublett, August 4, 2010.

29. Johnson and Scott, "Golden Fleece or Just Yarn?"

30. *Maxey v. CNB,* 2292–98, 2369–74.

31. National Transportation Safety Board, accident report.

32. Dorothy A. Drumwright, interview with Jesse Sublett, December 23, 2009.

33. Johnson and Scott, "Golden Fleece or Just Yarn?"

34. J. Michael Liles, interview with Jesse Sublett, October 18, 2009.

35. Kwitny, *The Mullendore Murder,* 919.

36. Ibid.

37. J. Michael Liles, interview with Jesse Sublett, August 4, 2010.

38. The authors could not find a copy of a deposition by Mullendore. As previously noted, numerous other files relating to the second trial, including the transcript, have either been misplaced or destroyed.

39. Frank Patrick, "Demand for Mistrial in Maxey Suit Fails," *Lubbock Avalanche-Journal,* October 11, 1976, evening edition.

40. *Maxey v. TCB,* 571 S.W.2d 39 (Amarillo 7th Ct. App. 1978).

41. Frank Patrick, "Maxey Reply Broaches Delicate Subject in Trial," *Lubbock Avalanche-Journal,* October 13, 1976, morning edition.

42. J. Michael Liles, interview with Broadus A. Spivey, August 9, 2006; J. Michael Liles, interview with Jesse Sublett, October 18, 2009.

43. Frank Patrick, "Banker Affirms $1.7 Million Maxey Appraisal," *Lubbock Avalanche-Journal,* October 14, 1976, morning edition.

44. J. Michael Liles, interview with Broadus A. Spivey, August 9, 2006.

45. Frank Patrick, "Banker Affirms Appraisal."

46. Frank Patrick, "'Kickback' Issue Raised by Attorney for Maxey," *Lubbock Avalanche-Journal,* October 14, 1976, evening edition.

47. *Maxey v. CNB,* 2939–58.

48. E. W. Williams, Jr., interviews with Jesse Sublett, October 21, 2009, and May 7, 2010.

49. J. Michael Liles, interview with Jesse Sublett, August 4, 2010.

50. Patrick, "'Kickback' Issue."

51. "Length of Trial Concerns Jurors," *Lubbock Avalanche-Journal*, October 15, 1976, evening edition.

52. Frank Patrick, "Only Two Hours' Testimony Given As Maxey Trial Quits Till Monday," *Lubbock Avalanche-Journal*, October 16, 1976.

53. J. Michael Liles, interview with Jesse Sublett, October 18, 2009.

54. Frank Patrick, "Appraisal of Maxey Enterprises Hits Trial," *Lubbock Avalanche-Journal*, October 19, 1976, morning edition.

55. Ibid.

56. Frank Patrick, "Call for Instructed Verdict Rejected as Maxey Case Rests," *Lubbock Avalanche-Journal*, October 20, 1976, morning edition.

57. Ibid.

58. *Maxey v. CNB*, 507 S.W.2d 722 (Tex. Sup. Ct. 1974).

59. Denzil Bevers, interview with Jesse Sublett, October 23, 2009.

60. David Hughes, e-mail message to Jesse Sublett, June 10, 2010.

61. *Maxey v. CNB*, 507 S.W.2d 722 (Tex. Sup. Ct. 1974).

62. Frank Patrick, "Banker Says Maxey Firm Thought Worthless," *Lubbock Avalanche-Journal*, October 21, 1976, morning edition.

63. Frank Patrick, "Bank Says Maxey Given Plan to Save Holdings," *Lubbock Avalanche-Journal*, October 21, 1976, evening edition.

64. J. Michael Liles, interview with Jesse Sublett, October 18, 2009.

65. Frank Patrick, "Final Arguments Expected," *Lubbock Avalanche-Journal*, October 22, 1976, morning edition.

66. Ibid.

67. J. Michael Liles, interview with Broadus A. Spivey, August 9, 2006; J. Michael Liles, interview with Jesse Sublett, October 18, 2009.

68. Denzil Bevers, interview with Jesse Sublett, October 23, 2009.

69. E. W. Williams, Jr., interviews with Jesse Sublett, October 21, 2009, and May 7, 2010.

70. J. Michael Liles, interview with Broadus A. Spivey, August 9, 2006; J. Michael Liles, interview with Jesse Sublett, October 18, 2009.

71. E. W. Williams, Jr., interviews with Jesse Sublett, October 21, 2009, and May 7, 2010.

72. J. Michael Liles, Transcript of Final Arguments, in *Maxey v. TCB*, collection of the authors.

73. J. Michael Liles, interview with Broadus A. Spivey, August 9, 2006; J. Michael Liles, interview with Jesse Sublett, October 18, 2009.

74. J. Michael Liles, interview with Broadus A. Spivey, August 9, 2006; J. Michael Liles, interview with Jesse Sublett, October 18, 2009.

75. Transcript of Final Arguments, in *Maxey v. TCB*, collection of the authors.

76. J. Michael Liles, interview with Jesse Sublett, October 18, 2009.

77. Transcript of Final Arguments, in *Maxey v. TCB*, collection of the authors.

78. *Maxey v. CNB*, 71.

79. Transcript of Final Arguments, in *Maxey v. TCB*, collection of the authors.

80. J. Michael Liles, interview with Jesse Sublett, October 18, 2009.

81. Transcript of Final Arguments, in *Maxey v. TCB*, collection of the authors.

82. J. Michael Liles, interview with Jesse Sublett, October 18, 2009.

83. Frank Parrick, "Jury Gives Maxey $3.7 Million," *Lubbock Avalanche-Journal*, October 23, 1976, Saturday morning edition.

84. J. Michael Liles, interview with Jesse Sublett, October 18, 2009.

85. US Inflation Calculator, http://www.usinflationcalculator.com

86. *Maxey v. TCB*, 571 S.W.2d 39 (Amarillo 7th Ct. App. 1978).

87. Ibid.

Chapter 11

1. "Mary Lou Robinson," *The Texas Legal Directory* (Dallas: Legal Directories Publishing Company, Inc., 2010), 1:66.

2. Carlton Dodson, telephone interview with Jesse Sublett, February 17, 2010.

3. "Resident," interview with Broadus A. Spivey and Jesse Sublett, November 11, 2009; "Resident," telephone interview with Jesse Sublett, December 9, 2009.

4. *Maxey v. TCB*, 571 S.W.2d 39 (Amarillo 7th Ct. App. 1978).

5. Broadus A. Spivey, conversation with Charles Jones.

6. S. Tom Morris, interview with Jesse Sublett, November 27, 2009.

7. J. Michael Liles, interview with Broadus A. Spivey, August 9, 2006, and interview with Jesse Sublett, October 18, 2009.

8. S. Tom Morris, interview with Jesse Sublett, November 27, 2009.

9. "Notice of Deposition of E. W. Williams, Jr.," July 14, 1980, in *Maxey v. TCB*.

10. Lemann, "Taking Over."

11. "Subpoena for Deposition of Thomas B. McDade," filed November 1, 1974, in *Maxey v. TCB*. The page numbers cited in the text refer to the original correspondence between Texas Commerce Bank and the Federal Reserve.

12. Thomas McDade, letter to Jesse Sublett, February 1, 2010.

13. Johnson and Scott, "Golden Fleece or Just Yarn?"

14. Ibid.

15. Ibid.

16. Carla Elliott, interview with Broadus A. Spivey, July 10, 2007.

17. J. Michael Liles, interview with Jesse Sublett, October 18, 2009.

18. Plaintiffs' Seventh Amended Original Petition, filed April 21, 1980, in Homer G. Maxey et al. v. Texas Commerce Bank of Lubbock, Texas, District Court, 73rd Judicial District, Lubbock County, Texas (No. 51,441), hereafter referred to as *Maxey v. TCB, 1980*.

19. Notice of Deposition, filed July 14, 1980, *Maxey v. TCB, 1980*.

20. Final Judgment of Dismissal with Prejudice, *Maxey v. TCB, 1980*; US Inflation Calculator, http://www.usinflationcalculator.com.

21. Bobby Day, interview with Jesse Sublett, February 25, 2010.

22. Ken Flagg, telephone interview with Jesse Sublett, December 17, 2009.

23. Dan Anthony, telephone interview with Jesse Sublett, December 7, 2009.

24. Glenna Goodacre, interview with Jesse Sublett, October 20, 2009.

25. Stephens, "Two Special Friends."

26. Kenneth Bowlin, interview with Jesse Sublett, September 26, 2009.

27. "W. B. 'Dub' Rushing 19102007," *Rawls College Newsletter*, http://www.rawlsnews. ba.ttu.edu/index.php/2007/01/wb-dub-rushing-1910-2007-32-architecture/.

28. SR 229: "Senate Resolution in Memory of Melba Maxey," 74th Legislature, Regular Session, Texas Legislature Online, at http://www.legis.state.tx.us/billlookup/text.aspx?LegSess=74R&Bill=SR229.

Appendix 2

1. Tommy Denton, e-mail message to Jesse Sublett, May 18, 2010.

2. *CNB v. Maxey*, 461 S.W.2d 138 (Amarillo Ct. Civil App. 1970).

3. *Maxey v. CNB*, 507 S.W.2d 722 (Tex. Sup. Ct. 1974).

SOURCES

The process of researching and writing the story of Homer Maxey created a large collection of newspaper articles, court documents, trial transcripts, interview transcripts, photographs, family records, and other documents. In the final stages of preparing the manuscript for publication, the authors began the process of organizing these materials with the intention of establishing a permanent home for them, a place where they would be preserved and also made available to researchers, historians, and others. The final decision has not been made, but the logical choice appears to be the Southwest Collection at Texas Tech University.

Books

Many books were essential sources of information and background, but few compared with *Lubbock: From Town to City* (Lubbock: West Texas Museum Association, 1986), edited by Lawrence L. Graves. This book was never far from the authors' desk during the final four years of the book's production. The chapter "Law and Politics in Lubbock: 1945 to the Present," written by Robert Carl Schaefer, helped shape our understanding of the role of the Empire Builders in the history of Lubbock. Periodically, after making significant advances in research of the Homer Maxey story, and after reading more recent articles and interviews on the topic, the authors would return to Schaefer's writing with deeper understanding and appreciation. Schaefer also read and commented on an early draft of the book.

Historic Lubbock County: An Illustrated History, by Donald R. Abbe and Paul H. Carlson (San Antonio: Historical Publishing Network, 2008), was also a reliable source of information about the South Plains and the origins of Lubbock and Lubbock County. The book is also an enjoyable read, and the authors of this book also consulted Abbe and Carlson during the very early stages of researching our book.

Abbe, Donald R., and Paul H. Carlson. *Historic Lubbock County: An Illustrated History.* San Antonio: Historical Publishing Network, 2008.

Andrews, Ruth Horn. *The First Thirty Years: A History of Texas Tech Technological College 1925–1955.* Lubbock: Texas Tech University Press, 1956.

Bruce, Anthony, and William Cogar. *An Encyclopedia of Naval History.* New York: Facts on File Inc., 1998.

Connor, Seymour V. "Ellwood, Isaac L." In *Handbook of Texas.* Austin: Texas State Historical Association, 1996.

Davis, Charles G. "Estacado, Texas." In *Handbook of Texas.* Austin: Texas State Historical Association, 1996.

Davis, L. Ford. *The Last Cowboy.* Austin: Eakin Press, 2002.

Denton, Sally, and Roger Morris. *The Money and The Power: The Making of Las Vegas and Its Hold on America.* New York: Knopf, 2001.

Dodge, Tom. "The Man Who Lives on Weather." In *Literary Fort Worth,* edited by Judy Alter and James Ward Lee. Fort Worth: TCU Press, 2002.

Dyer, Vice Admiral George C., USN (RET). *The Amphibians Came to Conquer: The Story of Admiral Richmond Kelly Turner II.* Washington, D.C.: U.S. Government Printing Office (e-book at http://www.archive.org/stream/amphibianscameto017723mb p#page/n7/mode/2up), n.d.

Graves, Lawrence L., ed. *A History of Lubbock.* Lubbock: West Texas Museum Association, 1962.

———. "Lubbock County." In *Handbook of Texas.* Austin: Texas State Historical Association, 1996.

———, ed. *Lubbock: From Town to City.* Lubbock: West Texas Museum Association, 1986.

———. "Lubbock, TX." *Handbook of Texas.* Austin: Texas State Historical Association, 1996.

———. "Texas Tech University." In *Handbook of Texas.* Austin: Texas State Historical Association, 1996.

Guy, Duane F., ed. *The Story of Palo Duro Canyon.* Lubbock: Texas Tech University Press, 2001.

Harper, Jim. "Sports in Lubbock 1950–1984." In *Lubbock: From Town to City.* Edited by Lawrence L. Graves. Lubbock: West Texas Museum Association, 1986.

Hill, Lewis E. "Industry, Transportation and Finance." In *Lubbock: From Town to City.* Edited by Lawrence L. Graves. Lubbock: West Texas Museum Association, 1986.

Holden, W. C. "IOA Ranch." In *Handbook of Texas Online.* http://www.tshaonline. org/handbook/online/articles/api01.

———. *Rollie Burns, or, An Account of the Ranching Industry on the South Plains.* College Station: Texas A&M University Press, 1932.

Jane's Fighting Ships of World War II. New Jersey: Crescent Books, 1996.

Jonish, James E. "Population Growth and Expansion." In *Lubbock: From Town to City.*

Edited by Lawrence L. Graves. Lubbock: West Texas Museum Association, 1986.

Kelton, Steve. *Renderbrook, A Century Under the Spade Brand*. Fort Worth: TCU Press, 1989.

King, Grace, and Gem Meacham. "Rodman, Earl George, Sr." In *Handbook of Texas*. Austin: Texas State Historical Association, 1996.

————. "Noel, William Douglas." In *Handbook of Texas*. Austin: Texas State Historical Association, 1996.

Kohout, Martin Donnell. "Charles Hardin Holley." In *Handbook of Texas*. Austin: Texas State Historical Association, 1996.

Kwitny, Jonathon. *The Mullendore Murder Case*. New York: Amereon House, 1974.

Leatherwood, Art. "Llano Estacado." In *Handbook of Texas*. Austin: Texas State Historical Association, 1996.

Lubbock City Directory. Lubbock: Hudspeth Directory, 1969.

"Mary Lou Robinson." In *The Texas Legal Directory*. Dallas: Legal Directories Publishing Company, Inc., 2010.

Maysel, Lou. *Here Come the Texas Longhorns*. Fort Worth: Stadium Publishing Company, 1970.

Miech, Rob. *The Last Natural: Bryce Harper's Big Gamble in Sin City and the Greatest Amateur Season Ever*. New York: Thomas Dunne Books, 2012.

Monush, Barry. *Encyclopedia of Film Actors from the Silent Era to 1965*. New York: Applause Theater and Cinema Books, 2003.

Morris, James M., and Patricia M. Kearns. *Historical Dictionary of the United States Navy*. United Kingdom: Scarecrow Press, 2011.

Norman, Philip. *Rave On: The Biography of Buddy Holly*. New York: Simon & Schuster 1996.

Privett, Tony. *Failure Is Not an Option: Delbert McDougal: A Developer's Unconventional Wisdom*. San Antonio: Historical Publishing Network, 2007.

Remley, David A. *Bell Ranch: Cattle Ranching in the Southwest, 1824–1947*. Albuquerque: University of New Mexico Press, 1993.

Schaefer, Robert Carl. "Law and Politics in Lubbock: 1945 to the Present." In *Lubbock: From Town to City*. Edited by Lawrence L. Graves. Lubbock: West Texas Museum Association, 1986.

Symonds, Craig L. *The Naval Institute Historical Atlas of the U.S. Navy*. Annapolis: Naval Institute Press, 1995.

Periodicals

Newspaper articles have been organized in chronological order. The *Lubbock Avalanche-Journal* provided daily coverage of both Maxey trials and also reported on all major developments in the case, including each notice of appeal and the decision of the appellate court. Such detailed reportage was indispensable in writing the book. If the edition (day of the week, morning or evening) could be determined, it is included here.

"Miss Melba Mae Tatom and Homer Maxey Have High Noon Nuptial Ceremony." *Lubbock Daily Journal,* June 21, 1932.

"Homes Being Rushed Here." *Lubbock Morning Avalanche,* January 5, 1942.

"Navy's Changelings." *Time,* May 31, 1945.

"Oil Fever Hits Grayson County." *Lubbock Avalanche-Journal,* December 18, 1949, Sunday edition.

Guy, Charles A. "The Plainsman Says." *Lubbock Evening Journal,* January 23, 1951.

"Plainsman Hotel Holds Formal Public Opening Today." *Lubbock Morning Avalanche,* August 14, 1951.

"Original Picture of 'Plainsman' to Hang in New Hotel." *Lubbock Morning Avalanche,* August 14, 1951.

"Contractor and Leader, J. B. Maxey Dies after Heart Attack." *Lubbock Morning Avalanche,* April 9, 1953.

Gatts, Art. "Jack Davis Elected President of Matador Club." *Lubbock Evening Journal,* May 27, 1953.

Thompson, Thomas. "The Turnstile." *Amarillo Globe-Times,* August 10, 1960.

Guy, Charles A. "The Plainsman Says." *Lubbock Morning Avalanche,* October 1960.

"Hundreds Attend Pioneer Hotel Opening Here." Lubbock newspaper clipping, c. 1961.

Ratliff, C. W. "Pioneer Hotel Slates Formal Opening Today." *Lubbock Avalanche-Journal,* April 16, 1961.

"Maxey Files Suit Against CNB, Others." *Lubbock Avalanche-Journal,* March 18, 1966, evening edition.

May, Kenneth. "Testimony to Begin, Legal Battle Lines Drawn in Lawsuit." *Lubbock Avalanche-Journal,* October 28, 1969, evening edition.

"Witness Outlines Bank Loan Deals on Stand Here, Bank Loan Dealings Described." *Lubbock Avalanche-Journal,* October 30, 1969, morning edition.

"Maxey Accuses Bank of Putting Him in 'Financial Straitjacket.'" *Lubbock Avalanche-Journal,* October 31, 1969, evening edition.

"Maxey Tells of Efforts." *Lubbock Avalanche-Journal,* November 3, 1969, evening edition.

"Bank Deals, Operations Spark Suit." *Lubbock Avalanche-Journal,* November 5, 1969, morning edition.

May, Kenneth. "Defense Disputes Property Values." *Lubbock Avalanche-Journal,* November 6, 1969, evening edition.

———. "Trades by Maxey Are Targets for Defense." *Lubbock Avalanche-Journal,* November 7, 1969, evening edition.

"Judge Extends Maxey Recess." *Lubbock Avalanche-Journal,* November 12, 1969, morning edition.

May, Kenneth. "Maxey Still on Stand, Defense Counter-Attack Launched." *Lubbock Avalanche-Journal,* November 19, 1969, morning edition.

Sources

———. "Checks Set Off Dispute, Defense Continues to Grill Homer G. Maxey." *Lubbock Avalanche-Journal*, November 20, 1969, evening edition.

———. "Attorneys Clash, Trial Tempo Quickens in Maxey Case Here." *Lubbock Avalanche-Journal*, November 21, 1969, morning edition.

———. "Cross-Examination Hits Cattle Feeding Claims in Bank Suit Here." *Lubbock Avalanche-Journal*, November 20, 1969, morning edition.

———. "Attorneys Clash, Trial Tempo Quickens in Maxey Case Here." *Lubbock Avalanche-Journal*, November 21, 1969, morning edition.

———. "Trial's Progress Slow as Testimony Resumes." *Lubbock Avalanche-Journal*, December 2, 1969, morning edition.

———. "Cattle Brought Profit, Rancher Says." *Lubbock Avalanche-Journal*, December 5, 1969, morning edition.

———. "Judge Sustains Objections of Defense Attorneys, Jury Misses Portions of Testimony in Maxey-CNB Suit Here." *Lubbock Avalanche-Journal*, December 9, 1969, morning edition.

———. "Crucial Telephone Call Cited in Maxey Case Denied by Attorney." *Lubbock Avalanche-Journal*, December 9, 1969, evening edition.

"Court Rules against Maxey; Evidence of Plot Lacking; Bank Must Still Justify Prices." *Lubbock Avalanche-Journal*, December 23, 1969, evening edition.

Hendrie, Vaughan. "Bank Tells of Deals." *Lubbock Avalanche Journal*, January 5, 1970, evening edition.

May, Kenneth. "Final Arguments; Marathon Maxey Case Heading toward Jury." *Lubbock Avalanche-Journal*, January 12, 1970, evening edition.

———. "Start Deliberations; Maxey Trial Jury Studies 10 Issues." *Lubbock Avalanche-Journal* January 13, 1970, morning edition.

———. "Award Totals $2,689,767; Value of Plaza Stock Big Issue; Bank Announces Appeal Plans." *Lubbock Avalanche-Journal*, January 14, 1970, evening edition.

"Bank Motion Asks Change in Finding." *Lubbock Avalanche-Journal*, January 26, 1970.

May, Kenneth. "Bank Seeks New Trial in Maxey Damage Suit, Jury Actions Hit." *Lubbock Avalanche-Journal*, March 13, 1970.

"Wm. F. Evans, Former School Board Member Dies in City." *Lubbock Avalanche-Journal*, March 28, 1970, Saturday morning edition.

May, Kenneth. "Arguments Slated Over Maxey Case." *Lubbock Avalanche-Journal*, October 6, 1970.

———. "Bank-Maxey Case Aired for Court." *Lubbock Avalanche-Journal*, October 7, 1970, morning edition.

Patrick, Frank. "Once-Wealthy Maxey Broke, Not Broken." *Lubbock Avalanche-Journal*, October 3, 1976, Sunday morning edition.

"Maxey-Bank Litigation Has Marathon History in Courts." *Lubbock Avalanche-Journal*, October 3, 1976, Sunday morning edition.

Patrick, Frank. "Ranch Property Offer Aired by Maxey Aide." *Lubbock Avalanche-Journal*, October 5, 1976, morning edition.

———. "Defense Attacks Maxey Estimate." *Lubbock Avalanche-Journal*, October 5, 1976, evening edition.

———. "Bank Attorneys Rebut Maxey Sale Accusations." *Lubbock Avalanche-Journal*, October 8, 1976, morning edition.

———. "Demand for Mistrial in Maxey Suit Fails." *Lubbock Avalanche-Journal*, October 11, 1976, evening edition.

———. "Maxey Reply Broaches Delicate Subject in Trial." *Lubbock Avalanche-Journal*, October 13, 1976, morning edition.

———. "Banker Affirms $1.7 Million Maxey Appraisal." *Lubbock Avalanche-Journal*, October 14, 1976, morning edition.

———. "'Kickback' Issue Raised by Attorney for Maxey." *Lubbock Avalanche-Journal*, October 14, 1976, evening edition.

"Length of Trial Concerns Jurors." *Lubbock Avalanche-Journal*, October 15, 1976, evening edition.

Patrick, Frank. "Only Two Hours Testimony Given As Maxey Trial Quits Till Monday." *Lubbock Avalanche-Journal*, October 16, 1976.

———. "Appraisal of Maxey Enterprises Hits Trial." *Lubbock Avalanche-Journal*, October 19, 1976, morning edition.

———. "Call for Instructed Verdict Rejected as Maxey Case Rests." *Lubbock Avalanche-Journal*, October 20, 1976, morning edition.

———. "Banker Says Maxey Firm Thought Worthless." *Lubbock Avalanche-Journal*, October 21, 1976, morning edition.

———. "Bank Says Maxey Given Plan to Save Holdings." *Lubbock Avalanche-Journal*, October 21, 1976, evening edition.

———. "Final Arguments Expected." *Lubbock Avalanche-Journal*, October 22, 1976, morning edition.

———. "Jury Gives Maxey $3.7 Million." *Lubbock Avalanche-Journal*, October 23, 1976, Saturday morning edition.

Johnson, Barbara, and Michelle Scott. "Golden Fleece or Just Yarn? Homer Maxey's Story One of Rags to Riches to Rags." *Fort Worth Star-Telegram*, November 4, 1979.

Lemann, Nicholas. "Taking Over." *Texas Monthly*, October 1983.

"Civic Leader Homer Maxey Dies at 79." *Lubbock Avalanche-Journal*, July 20, 1990.

"Days of Lubbock's 'Empire Builders' Have Faded." *Lubbock Avalanche-Journal*, March 25, 1999. http://lubbockonline.com/stories/032599/cel_032599018.shtml.

Gonzales, Ellysa. "Senate Proclamation Hails CottonTech Ties." *Lubbock Avalanche-Journal*, September 19, 2012. http://m.lubbockonline.com/local-news/2012-09-14/senate-proclamation-hails-cotton-tech-ties.

Murphy, Hank. "LISD Learns from Desegregation Case." *Lubbock Avalanche-Journal*, April 25, 1999. http://lubbockonline.com/stories/042599/cel_042599011.shtml.

Wagenen, Chris van. "N. Lubbock Ripe for Growth Spurt, McDougal Says Rising Enrollment at Tech Major Factor in Downtown Area." *Lubbock Avalanche-Journal*, May 08, 2003. http://lubbockonline.com/stories/050803/loc_050803039.shtml.

Kerns, William. "Road to the Top: Renaming of Street Spotlights Sculptor's Resounding Success." *Lubbock Avalanche-Journal*, August 13, 2005. http://lubbockonline.com/stories/081305/loc_081305033.shtml.

"Looking Back: Plainview Just Missed Out on Landing Texas Tech." *Plainview Herald*, September 8, 2008. http://www.myplainview.com/news/article_cd33d8fa-b4a2-58ad-8c40-6f579c3983d6.html.

Lubbock Avalanche-Journal 2009 Centennial Series

To help commemorate the Lubbock centennial in 2009, the *Lubbock Avalanche-Journal* published a series of articles on the history of the city. This material served as an excellent starting point for research on a number of topics treated in this book.

"James H. Milam." *Lubbock Centennial*. http://www.lubbockcentennial.com/citysmost/040608.shtml.

"Lubbock Gets Tech!" *Lubbock Centennial*. http://www.lubbockcentennial.com/Section/1909_1933/Tech.shtml.

Other Online Sources

Hunt, Clifford E. "Historical Diary of Lubbock County." http://swco.ttu.edu/reference/Collections/ReferenceList/Pages/HuntDiary.htm.

IMDb. "Dale Robertson." http://www.imdb.com/find?q=dale+robertson&s=all.

Junior League of Lubbock. "Pat S. Moore Award." http://www.jllubbock.com/?nd=moore_award.

McVay, Freda Marie. "Charles A. Guy, the Paradoxical Plainsman." Master's thesis, Texas Tech University, 1979. http://repositories.tdl.org/ttu-ir/bitstream/handle/2346/11163/31295001800753.pdf?sequence=1.

Morris, Frank D. "Bazooka Boats." *Collier's Magazine*, November 11, 1944. http://www.navsource.org/archives/10/15/15000032.htm.

National Transportation Safety Board. "Accident Report." http://www.ntsb.gov/ntsb/brief.asp?ev_id=70251&key=0.

Neff, Erin. "Political, Business Leader Erin Neff Jones Dies at 89." *Las Vegas Sun*, November 19, 2001. http://www.lasvegassun.com/news/2001/nov/19/political-business-leader-jones-dies-at-89/.

"Paul Lange's Genealogy Home Page." http://www.langeonline.com/.

Radiation Effects Research Foundation (RERF). "Frequently Asked Questions." http://www.rerf.or.jp/general/qa_e/qa1.html.

Rawls College Newsletter. "W. B. 'Dub' Rushing 19102007." http://www.rawlsnews. ba.ttu.edu/index.php/2007/01/wb-dub-rushing-1910-2007-32-architecture/.

Texas Department of Banking. "State Banks: Bank History." http://www.dob.texas. gov/pubs/stbks.pdf.

Texas Senate, SR 229: "Senate Resolution in Memory of Melba Maxey." 74th Legislature, Regular Session, Texas Legislature Online, at http://www.legis.state.tx.us/ billlookup/text.aspx?LegSess=74R&Bill=SR229.

US Inflation Calculator, at http://www.usinflationcalculator.com/.

Unpublished Papers and Public Collections

As described in the text, the "James Barney Maxey Papers" is a scrapbook assembled by J. B. Maxey during the last year of his life. He moved to the South Plains in 1906 and died in 1953. The book is a treasure trove of photos, memories, newspaper clippings, and assorted ephemera on the history of Lubbock and Plainview between 1906 and 1953. The selected newspaper clippings tell the story of Lubbock and Plainview in their formative years. And because J. B. Maxey was so deeply involved in the building of these towns (and numerous others in the region), also serving in various leadership roles (from president of the chamber of commerce to volunteer roles including founding charities and promoting city parks), it's almost coincidental that the name "J. B. Maxey" appears in almost every article. There are also dozens of articles about J. B. Maxey's sons, Homer, Robert, Carl, and Herschel, who followed in J. B.'s footsteps—primarily as builders, but also as civic leaders. In ways that cannot be adequately conveyed in words, the Maxey scrapbook attests to the Maxeys' dedication to their church (First Methodist Church of Lubbock), work ethic, modesty, and community spirit. But there are also weird and wonderful things, such as faded snapshots of J. B. indulging his passion for fishing (always attired in suit and tie), and notes about playing dominoes. There are also funky cartoons, pictures of the grandchildren, correspondence between J. B. and his colleagues (including Charlie Guy, who addressed J. B. as "My Dear Barney"), and photos from Maxey family road trips in the 1920s and 1930s. The authors' personal favorite is probably the shot of the young Maxey boys (plus little Dub Rushing, who always tagged along), riding in an ostrich cart. Holding the reins is J. B., at six foot four tall enough to look down at the giant bird, with, as always, a stoic expression on his face.

James Barney Maxey Papers, microfilm at Southwest Collection, Texas Tech University, Lubbock.

W. G. McMillan Jr. Interview with Sally Still Abbe, September 21, 2010, audio, City of Lubbock Archives.

Deed of Trust from Bill Smith Gin Inc. to Citizens National Bank of Lubbock, April 24, 1972, Lubbock County Deed of Trust Records, vol. 71645-47.

Lubbock City Commission minutes, in the office of the city secretary, Lubbock City

Hall. Minutes cited were in the volumes documenting city commission meetings on the following dates: May 10, 1956; December 6, 1956; August 22, 1957.

Unpublished papers, authors' collection

As explained in the text, the authors were fortunate to obtain several priceless sources of information from the Maxey family. A scrapbook of Homer Maxey's military service with the US Navy in World War II filled in many gaps in Homer's biography. Photographs from combat zones in the Pacific are interspersed with photos of the young lieutenant commander's visits home on leave. He celebrated Christmas 1944 with Melba and their two young daughters—Carla and Glenna (then known as Glendell)—then returned to the war. The stress on their faces speaks volumes.

Upon our first reading, a fifteen-page document titled "Two Special Friends, by I. A. Stephens," seemed as full of mysteries as facts. No one in the Maxey family could remember when or how the speech was delivered, but they did verify that I. A. Stephens, better known as "Steve," was a very close friend of Homer Maxey and Dub Rushing (the "two friends" of the title). After much study, however, the authors were able to sort out nearly every detail, beginning with the fact that the occasion for the speech was Homer's seventy-ninth birthday: March 14, 1990.

Stephens had befriended Homer Maxey and Dub Rushing in the early 1930s, and the trio remained friends for life. Through careful reading of the speech, it becomes apparent that Homer's cancer diagnosis was known to his friends and family by this time, and the fact of it weighed heavily on their minds. Homer died four months later, on July 28, 1990.

The collection of items we call "Melba Maxey's Journal" was located by Glenna Goodacre and loaned to us during our correspondence with Glenna. Melba collected newspaper clippings during the trials and shared them with other members of the family. She also took notes, and on some days, she used her journal for other purposes, such as compiling a list of people to send thank-you notes or invitations to a Christmas party during the holiday recess in the first trial in 1969. There were also letters, clippings of articles from *Readers Digest*, and a recipe for spinach salad. Such items not only provided a meaningful glimpse into the character and personality of Melba Maxey, but remind us that, even during the worst of times, people try to maintain a sense of normalcy, a "life goes on" attitude. And some of us are more successful at it than others.

The interviews done with family members and others are cited in the notes. See the introduction for more information on the interviews.

Homer Maxey World War II Scrapbook, collection of the authors.

I. A. Stephens, "Two Special Friends." Transcript of speech, March 1990, collection of the authors.

Letters to members of First United Methodist Church of Lubbock. Reproduced in

First Methodist News, a bulletin of First Methodist Church of Lubbock, date unknown, collection of the authors.

Melba Maxey journal, collection of the authors.

Map

City of Lubbock Archives. "City of Lubbock History of Annexation by Decade."

Legal Documentation Related to the Maxey Case

As previously stated, other than books, most (if not all) of the materials listed here are currently in the possession of the authors, and as the book goes to press, we are organizing them with an eye to making them available to the public in a central archive. This also pertains to our collection of papers on the Maxey case. Such an archive should be of great help to researchers in the future.

Some documents, including appellate court rulings in the Maxey case, are available online from various sources. Appendix 1 consists of a list of all the appeals in the Maxey case. Appendix 2 consists of a summary of the most significant appellate rulings in the case.

INDEX

113, 128, 139, 148, 151, 152–56,
161, 172, 181, 200, 219–20, 238,
241, 253, 264; relationship with J.
B Maxey, 90–91; reorganization, 87;
reputation, 96, 116–17, 201, 227,
252, 263–69
Citizens National Bank Center, 91
Citizens National Bank Co., 108, 169
Citizens National Bank Corp., 108, 183
Citizens National Bank Tower, 91, 92,
94
Citizens United v. Federal Election Commission, 6
Civil War, 22
Clark, William, 20–21, 274
Cobb, DeEtte Maxey (niece), 29, 73,
75–76
Cobb, Tom, 93
Cobb's department stores, 60, 93
Code of Judicial Conduct, 212
codes of ethics, 4, 10, 103, 110, 112–13,
163, 165, 166–67, 222, 226, 250. *See
also* gentleman's agreement; Maxey
case, allegations of misconduct
Coleman, B. C., 118
collateral estoppel, 211, 213, 215, 261
conflict of interest, 18–19, 90–91,
102–3, 110, 125, 142, 143, 163–64,
212, 220, 224, 229, 243
Connelly's Pontiac Showroom, 72
Conoco. *See* Continental Oil Company,
Construction Battalions, 45
Continental Bank of Chicago, 209
Continental Oil Company, 42–43, *43*,
119, 120
Coronado, Francisco Vásquez de, 20
corporate personhood, 6
corporate responsibility, 6, 211, 221, 247
Cox, Jackie, 69
Cox, Paris, 23
Crenshaw, Dupree & Milam, 69

D

Daily Journal, 41
Daniel, Price, 214–15
Davis, Dan, 105, 107
Davis, Mac, 72
Davis, Perry, 229, 250, 253–54
Day, Bobby, 112, 270–72
Dean, Bill, 90, 160
Dean, Jennie, 160
Denton, Elinor, 160, 299n53
Denton, James, 160, 299n53
Denton, James Gray, 4, 6, 210, 214–15,
247, 299n53
Denton, Tommy, 214
Denton family, 76, 299n53
Dodson, Carlton, 116, 158, 260
double jeopardy, 211
Drumwright, Dorothy, 131, 132, 159,
173, 179, 237–38
Drumwright, William Ed, 110, 131–33,
138, 159, 162, 171–76, 178–81, 198,
229–31, 234–38, 254, 266, 268
Duggan, Tom, 137, 138
Dunlap's (department store), 69, 106

E

Eisenberg, W. F., 106, 107
Eisenhower, Dwight, 100
Elliott, Carla Maxey (daughter), 12, *15*,
30, 39–40, 44, 48, *49*, 72–76, 77,
79, 82, 83, 94, 95, 98, 104, 109, 113,
122, 127, 132, 136, 147, 158–60,
182, 200, 203–4, *205*, 207, 209, 225,
240, 269, 272
Elliott, Tommy, 73, *74*, 77, 78, 80,
83–85, 94, 97, 101, 104, 109, 113,
122, 126–27, 129, 132, 136, 141–43,
160, 203–4, 207, 209, 225, 258
Ellwood, Isaac L., 26, 82
Ellwood family, 106, 140
Ely, Joe, 72

Index

Maxey, James Barney (J. B.; "Big Daddy"; father), 7, 19, 27–36, *27, 30, 34, 36,* 41, 44, 50, 87, 90–91, 113, 119, 226

Maxey, James Barney (brother), 28

Maxey, James Joseph (paternal grandfather), 29

Maxey, Melba Mae Tatom (wife), 7, *15, 18, 37,* 41–42, *49,* 50, 65, 75, 76, 78, 81, 86, 94, 98, 113, 127, 136, 143, 145, *146,* 147, 158–60, *159,* 171, 182, 183, *198,* 199, 200, 202–3, *205,* 207, 225–27, 240, 268–72, *270, 273,* 274–75, *280*

Maxey, Nannie Elizabeth Goodnight (paternal grandmother), 29

Maxey, Robert (brother), 7, *27,* 28, 34, 35, 45, *45,* 50, *55,* 57, 59, 75, 113–14, 143, 275

Maxey case, 83: allegations of conspiracy, 3, 9, 16, 17, 18, 91, *92,* 96, 115, 123–24, 133, 162, 183–84, 220, 230, 238, 255, 264; allegations of fraud, 3, 9, 16, 102, 113, 133, 238; allegations of misconduct, 4, 6, 16, 112–13, 212, 214, 215, 222, 248 (*see also* codes of ethics); chronology of litigations, 289–90; Citizen National Bank's claims, 145–96; defendants, 15–16, 17, 94–95, 104–8; duration, 3, 4, 16; exemplary damages, 200; filing of suit, 94–95; impact on community, 3, 6, 8, 9, 16, 103–4, 116–17, 160, 224, 227, 232, 234, 246, 263; jury, 112, 118–21, 136, 151, 158, 182–83, 199–200, 209–10, 256–57; Maxey's claims, 112–44; media coverage, 12, 106, 117, 125, 145, 148, 150, 151, 157–58, 161, 171, 180, 185, 200–201, 203, 225–26, 228, 230–31, 233–34, 242, 245, 247–48, 266–69,

312n13; monetary damages awarded, 3, 4, 258–59; monetary damages sought, 3, 8, 9, 15; new trial, 217–21, 222–59, 261, 312n13; pretrial hearings, 106–9; toll on family, 19; verdict and appeals, 4, 197–216, 259, 291–92

Maxey Lumber Company, 43, 45, 48, 54, 56, 60, 68, 83, 95, 109, 120, 121, 123, 128, 139, 200, 210, 218, 224, 251, 253–55, 258, 261

Maxey Park (Lubbock), 35

Maxey Place Addition, 44, 120

Maxey v. TCB. See Maxey case, new trial

May, Kenneth, 125, 150, 151, 157–58, 161, 171, 185, 200–201

McClain, Meredith, 68–69

McDade, Thomas, 265

McDonald & Shafer, 114

McDougal, Delbert, 80, *280,* 281

McKinney property, 150

McMillan, W. G., Jr., 17–18

Medlock, W. E., 191–92, 196

Melba Addition, 44, 120

Merriman, Edwin, 105, 180

Middleton, Roy, 63

Midway, 46

Milam, James, 69, 130, 134, 225

Miller, Claude, 154

Mobil Oil Company, 114

Modern Manor apartments, 58, 85

Monterey High School, 73

Monterey Lubbock Corporation, 94, 139, 152, 164–65, 169, 183, 188, 200, 241

Montford, John T., 275

Moody, Bobby, 95, 147, 172

Moore, Melvin, 190

Moore, Patricia S., 12, 107, 108, 115–116, 123–124, 129, 132–36, 138, 141, 145, 148, 154, 165–68, 171–74,

W

Wakefield, Jack, 132, 171, 173, 231, 234

Walters, G. C., 248–49, 254

Waples-Platter Grocery Company, 41, 119

Warnicke, Mr., 137

Wayne, John, 72

Western Land and Live Stock Company, 23

West Texas Oxygen Company, 105

Wheelock, Frank E., 23–26, *25*

Wheelock, Stillman, 23

Whiteside, Clarence, 63

Wiggins, D. M., 105, 107

Wilburton ranch, 81, 190

Wilcox, Herbert, 106, 107

Williams, E. W., Jr., 4, 8, 12, 17–18, 76, 86–89, 91, 103–7, 109, 113, 116, 117, 122–23, 126–31, 133–34, 137–40, 142, 148, 152–54, 156, 162–63, 170–72, 179–80, 183, 184, 186–89, 197–98, 209, 211, 217–19, 224, 227–28, 238, 242–43, 247–51, 254, 262–63, 266–69

Wilson, Jimmy, 78

Wofford, Jane Livermore, 99–100, 158, 161, 208

Wolfforth, George, *25*

Women's League, 65

Woodruff, Charles, 118

World War II, 7, 13, *14*, 44–55, 56, 101, 120–21

Y

Yee, E. Y., *25*

Young, Miss, 65

Z

Zachry Co. v. Thibodeaux, 212

Zink, John, 150